Akka in Action

RAYMOND ROESTENBURG
ROB BAKKER
ROB WILLIAMS

MANNING
SHELTER ISLAND

Manning Publications Co.   Development editor: Jeff Bleiel
20 Baldwin Road   Review editor: Olivia Booth
PO Box 761   Copyeditors: Benjamin Berg, Andy Carroll
Shelter Island, NY 11964   Technical proofreader: Doug Warren
                                       Project editor: Kevin Sullivan
                                          Proofreader: Katie Tennant
                                           Typesetter: Dottie Marsico
                                       Cover designer: Marija Tudor

ISBN 9781617291012
Printed in the United States of America
1 2 3 4 5 6 7 8 9 10 – EBM – 21 20 19 18 17 16

brief contents

contents

preface

Writing good, concurrent, and distributed applications is hard. Having just finished a project that demanded a lot of low-level concurrency programming in Java, I was on the lookout for simpler tools for the next project, which promised to be even more challenging.

In March 2010 I noticed a tweet by Dean Wampler that made me look into Akka:

W00t! RT @jboner: #akka 0.7 is released: http://bit.ly/9yRGSB

After some investigation into the source code and building a prototype, we decided to use Akka. It was immediately apparent that this new programming model would really simplify the problems we experienced in the previous project.

I convinced Rob Bakker to join me in a bleeding-edge technology adventure, and together we took the leap to build our first project with Scala and Akka. We reached out early to Jonas Bonér (creator of Akka) for help, and later found out that we were among the first-known production users of Akka. We completed the project, and many others followed; the benefits of using Akka were obvious every time.

In those days, there wasn't a lot of information available online, so I decided to start blogging about it as well as contribute to the Akka project.

I was completely surprised when I was asked to write this book. I asked Rob Bakker if he wanted to write the book together. Later, we realized we needed more help, and Rob Williams joined us. He had been building projects with Java and Akka.

We're happy that we could finally finish this book and write about a version of Akka (2.4.9) that really provides a comprehensive set of tools for building distributed and concurrent applications. We're grateful that so many MEAP readers gave us feedback over time. The tremendous support from Manning Publications was invaluable for us as first-time authors.

One thing that we all agreed on and had experienced before using Akka is that writing distributed and concurrent applications on the JVM needed better, simpler tools. We hope that we will convince you that Akka provides just that.

RAYMOND ROESTENBURG

acknowledgments

It took a lot of time to write this book. During that time, many people have helped us out and we thank them for the time they contributed. To all the readers who bought the MEAP edition of the book, thank you for all the feedback that greatly improved this book and for your ongoing patience over the years. We hope you will enjoy the final result and that you learned a lot during the MEAP process.

Special thanks go out to members of the Akka core team, specifically Jonas Bonér, Viktor Klang, Roland Kuhn, Patrik Nordwall, Björn Antonsson, Endre Varga, and Konrad Malawski, who all provided inspiration and invaluable input.

We also want to thank Edwin Roestenburg and CSC Traffic Management in the Netherlands, who trusted us enough to start using Akka for mission-critical projects and provided an incredible opportunity for us to gain our initial experience with Akka. We also want to thank Xebia for the work hours Ray could spend on the book and for providing an incredible workplace for furthering experience with Akka.

We thank Manning Publications for placing their trust in us. This is our first book, so we know this was a high-risk venture for them. We want to thank the following staff at Manning for their excellent work: Mike Stephens, Jeff Bleiel, Ben Berg, Andy Carroll, Kevin Sullivan, Katie Tennant, and Dottie Marsico.

Our thanks to Doug Warren, who gave all chapters a thorough technical proof-read. Many other reviewers provided us with helpful feedback during the writing and development process: Andy Hicks, David Griffith, Dušan Kysel, Iain Starks, Jeremy Pierre, Kevin Esler, Mark Janssen, Michael Schleichardt, Richard Jepps, Robin Percy, Ron Di Frango, and William E. Wheeler.

Last but not least, we want to thank the significant people in our lives who supported us as we worked on the book. Ray thanks his wife Chanelle, and Rob Williams thanks his mom, Gail, and Laurie.

about this book

This book introduces the Akka toolkit and explains its most important modules. We focus on the actor programming model and the modules that support actors for building concurrent and distributed applications. Throughout the book, we take time to show how code can be tested, which is an important aspect of day-to-day software development. We use the Scala programming language in all our examples.

After the basics of coding and testing actors, we look at all the important aspects that you will encounter when building a real-world application with Akka.

Intended audience

This book is intended for anyone who wants to learn how to build applications with Akka. The examples are in Scala, so it's expected that you already know some Scala or are interested in learning some Scala as you go along. You're expected to be familiar with Java, as Scala runs on top of the JVM.

Roadmap

The book includes seventeen chapters.

Chapter 1 introduces Akka actors. You'll learn how the actor programming model solves a couple of key issues that traditionally make scaling applications very hard.

Chapter 2 dives directly into an example HTTP service built with Akka to show how quickly you can get a service up and running in the cloud. It gives a sneak peek into what you'll learn in chapters to come.

Chapter 3 is about unit testing actors using ScalaTest and the akka-testkit module.

Chapter 4 explains how supervision and monitoring make it possible to build reliable, fault-tolerant systems out of actors.

Chapter 5 introduces futures, extremely useful and simple tools for combining function results asynchronously. You'll also learn how to combine futures and actors.

Chapter 6 is about the akka-remote module, which makes it possible to distribute actors across a network. You'll also learn how you can unit test distributed actor systems.

Chapter 7 explains how the Typesafe Config Library is used to configure Akka. It also details how you can use this library to configure your own application components.

Chapter 8 details structural patterns for actor-based applications. You'll learn how to implement a couple of classic enterprise integration patterns.

Chapter 9 explains how to use routers. Routers can be used for switching, broadcasting, and load balancing messages between actors.

Chapter 10 introduces the message channels that can be used to send messages from one actor to another. You'll learn about point-to-point and publish-subscribe message channels for actors. You'll also learn about dead-letter and guaranteed-delivery channels.

Chapter 11 discusses how to build finite state machine actors with the FSM module and also introduces agents that can be used to share state asynchronously.

Chapter 12 explains how to integrate with other systems. In this chapter, you'll learn how to integrate with various protocols using Apache Camel and how to build an HTTP service with the akka-http module.

Chapter 13 introduces the akka-stream module. You'll learn how to build streaming applications with Akka. This chapter details how to build a streaming HTTP service that processes log events.

Chapter 14 explains how to use the akka-cluster module. You'll learn how to dynamically scale actors in a network cluster.

Chapter 15 introduces the akka-persistence module. In this chapter, you'll learn how to record and recover durable state with persistent actors and how to use the cluster singleton and cluster sharding extensions to build a clustered shopping cart application.

Chapter 16 discusses key parameters of performance in actor systems and provides tips on how to analyze performance issues.

Chapter 17 looks ahead to two upcoming features that we think will become very important: the akka-typed module that makes it possible to check actor messages at compile time, and the akka-distributed-data module, which provides distributed in-memory state in a cluster.

Code conventions and downloads

All source code in listings or in text is in a `fixed-width font like this` to separate it from ordinary text. Code annotations accompany many of the listings, highlighting important concepts. The code for the examples in this book is available for download from the publisher's website at www.manning.com/books/akka-in-action and from GitHub at https://github.com/RayRoestenburg/akka-in-action.

Software requirements

Scala is used in all examples, and all code is tested with Scala 2.11.8. You can find Scala here: http://www.scala-lang.org/download/.

Be sure to install the latest version of sbt (0.13.12 as of this writing); if you have an older version of sbt installed, you might run into issues. You can find sbt here: http://www.scala-sbt.org/download.html.

Java 8 is required by Akka 2.4.9, so you'll need to have it installed as well. It can be found here: http://www.oracle.com/technetwork/java/javase/downloads/jdk8-downloads-2133151.html.

Author Online

Purchase of *Akka in Action* includes free access to a private web forum run by Manning Publications, where you can make comments about the book, ask technical questions, and receive help from the authors and from other users. To access the forum and subscribe to it, point your web browser to https://www.manning.com/books/akka-in-action. This page provides information on how to get on the forum after you're registered, what kind of help is available, and the rules of conduct on the forum.

Manning's commitment to our readers is to provide a venue where a meaningful dialogue between individual readers and between readers and the authors can take place. It isn't a commitment to any specific amount of participation on the part of the authors, whose contribution to the AO forum remains voluntary (and unpaid). We suggest you try asking the authors some challenging questions, lest their interest stray! The AO forum and the archives of previous discussions will be accessible from the publisher's website as long as the book is in print.

About the authors

RAYMOND ROESTENBURG is an experienced software craftsman, polyglot programmer, and software architect. He is an active member of the Scala community and an Akka committer, and he contributed to the Akka-Camel module.

ROB BAKKER is an experienced software developer focused on concurrent backend systems and system integration. He has used Scala and Akka in production from version 0.7.

ROB WILLIAMS is the founder of ontometrics, a practice focused on Java solutions that include machine learning. He first used actor-based programming a decade ago and has used it for several projects since.

About the cover illustration

The illustration of a Chinese emperor on the cover of *Akka in Action* is taken from Thomas Jefferys' *A Collection of the Dresses of Different Nations, Ancient and Modern* (four volumes), London, published between 1757 and 1772. The title page states that these are hand-colored copperplate engravings, heightened with gum arabic. Thomas Jefferys (1719–1771) was called "Geographer to King George III." He was an English cartographer who was the leading map supplier of his day. He engraved and printed maps for government and other official bodies and produced a wide range of commercial maps and atlases, especially of North America. His work as a mapmaker sparked an interest in local dress customs of the lands he surveyed and mapped, an interest that is brilliantly displayed in this four-volume collection.

Fascination with faraway lands and travel for pleasure were relatively new phenomena in the late-eighteenth century, and collections such as this one were popular, introducing both the tourist as well as the armchair traveler to the inhabitants of other countries. The diversity of the drawings in Jefferys' volumes speaks vividly of the uniqueness and individuality of the world's nations some 200 years ago. Dress codes have changed since then, and the diversity by region and country, so rich at the time, has faded away. It is now often hard to tell the inhabitant of one continent from another. Perhaps, trying to view it optimistically, we have traded a cultural and visual diversity for a more varied personal life, or a more varied and interesting intellectual and technical life.

At a time when it is hard to tell one computer book from another, Manning celebrates the inventiveness and initiative of the computer business with book covers based on the rich diversity of regional life of two centuries ago, brought back to life by Jefferys' pictures.

Introducing Akka

Up until the middle of the '90s, just before the internet revolution, it was completely normal to build applications that would only ever run on a single computer, a single CPU. If an application wasn't fast enough, the standard response would be to wait for a while for CPUs to get faster; no need to change any code. Problem solved. Programmers around the world were having a free lunch, and life was good.

In 2005 Herb Sutter wrote in *Dr. Dobb's Journal* about the need for a fundamental change (link: http://www.gotw.ca/publications/concurrency-ddj.htm). In short: a limit to increasing CPU clock speeds has been reached, and the free lunch is over.

If applications need to perform faster, or if they need to support more users, they will have to be *concurrent*. (We'll get to a strict definition later; for now let's

1

simply define this as *not single-threaded*. That's not really correct, but it's good enough for the moment.)

Scalability is the measure to which a system can adapt to a change in demand for resources, without negatively impacting performance. *Concurrency* is a means to achieve scalability: the premise is that, if needed, more CPUs can be added to servers, which the application then automatically starts making use of. It's the next best thing to a free lunch.

Around the year 2005 when Herb Sutter wrote his excellent article, you'd find companies running applications on clustered multiprocessor servers (often no more than two to three, just in case one of them crashed). Support for concurrency in programming languages was available but limited and considered black magic by many mere mortal programmers. Herb Sutter predicted in his article that "programming languages ... will increasingly be forced to deal well with concurrency."

Let's see what changed in the decade since! Fast-forward to today, and you find applications running on large numbers of servers in the cloud, integrating many systems across many data centers. The ever-increasing demands of end users push the requirements of performance and stability of the systems that you build.

So where are those new concurrency features? Support for concurrency in most programming languages, especially on the JVM, has hardly changed. Although the implementation details of concurrency APIs have definitely improved, you still have to work with low-level constructs like threads and locks, which are notoriously difficult to work with.

Next to scaling up (increasing resources; for example, CPUs on existing servers), *scaling out* refers to dynamically adding more servers to a cluster. Since the '90s, nothing much has changed in how programming languages support networking, either. Many technologies still essentially use RPC (remote procedure calls) to communicate over the network.

In the meantime, advances in cloud computing services and multicore CPU architecture have made computing resources ever more abundant.

PaaS (Platform as a Service) offerings have simplified provisioning and deployment of very large distributed applications, once the domain of only the largest players in the IT industry. Cloud services like AWS EC2 (Amazon Web Services Elastic Compute Cloud) and Google Compute Engine give you the ability to literally spin up thousands of servers in minutes, while tools like Docker, Puppet, Ansible, and many others make it easier to manage and package applications on virtual servers.

The number of CPU cores in devices is also ever-increasing: even mobile phones and tablets have multiple CPU cores today.

But that doesn't mean that you can afford to throw any number of resources at any problem. In the end, everything is about cost and efficiency. So it's all about effectively scaling applications, or in other words, getting bang for your buck. Just as you'd never use a sorting algorithm with exponential time complexity, it makes sense to think about the cost of scaling.

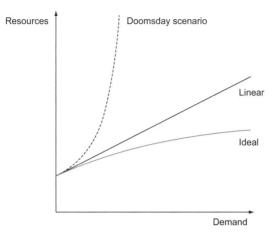

Figure 1.1 Demand against resources

You should have two expectations when scaling your application:

- The ability to handle any increase of demand with finite resources is unrealistic, so ideally you'd want the required increase of resources to be growing slowly when demand grows, linear or better. Figure 1.1 shows the relationship between demand and number of required resources.
- If resources have to be increased, ideally you'd like the complexity of the application to stay the same or increase slowly. (Remember the good ol' free lunch when no added complexity was required for a faster application!) Figure 1.2 shows the relationship between number of resources and complexity.

Both the number and complexity of resources contribute to the total cost of scaling.

We're leaving a lot of factors out of this back-of-the-envelope calculation, but it's easy to see that both of these rates have a big impact on the total cost of scaling.

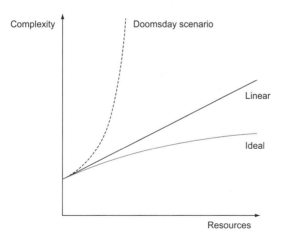

Figure 1.2 Complexity against resources

One doomsday scenario is where you'd need to pay increasingly more for more underutilized resources. Another nightmare scenario is where the complexity of the application shoots through the roof when more resources are added.

This leads to two goals: complexity has to stay as low as possible, and resources must be used efficiently while you scale the application.

Can you use the common tools of today (threads and RPC) to satisfy these two goals? Scaling out with RPC and scaling up with low-level threading aren't good ideas. RPC pretends that a call over the network is no different from a local method call. Every RPC call needs to block the current thread and wait for a response from the network for the local method call abstraction to work, which can be costly. This impedes the goal of using resources efficiently.

Another problem with this approach is that you need to know exactly where you scale up or scale out. Multithreaded programming and RPC-based network programming are like apples and pears: they run in different contexts, using different semantics and running on different levels of abstraction. You end up hardcoding which parts of your application are using threads for scaling up and which parts are using RPC for scaling out.

Complexity increases significantly the moment you hardcode methods that work on different levels of abstraction. Quick—what's simpler, coding with two entangled programming constructs (RPC and threads), or using just one programming construct? This multipronged approach to scaling applications is more complicated than necessary to flexibly adapt to changes in demand.

Spinning up thousands of servers is simple today, but as you'll see in this first chapter, the same can't be said for programming them.

1.1   *What is Akka?*

In this book we'll show how the Akka toolkit, an open source project built by Lightbend, provides a simpler, single programming model—one way of coding for concurrent and distributed applications—the *actor programming model.* Actors are (fitting for our industry) nothing new at all, in and of themselves. It's the way that actors are provided in Akka to scale applications both up and out on the JVM that's unique. As you'll see, Akka uses resources efficiently and makes it possible to keep the complexity relatively low while an application scales.

Akka's primary goal is to make it simpler to build applications that are deployed in the cloud or run on devices with many cores and that efficiently leverage the full capacity of the computing power available. It's a toolkit that provides an actor programming model, runtime, and required supporting tools for building scalable applications.

1.2   *Actors: a quick overview*

First off, Akka is centered on actors. Most of the components in Akka provide support in some way for using actors, be it for configuring actors, connecting actors to the network, scheduling actors, or building a cluster out of actors. What makes Akka unique is how effortlessly it provides support and additional tooling for building actor-based applications, so that you can focus on thinking and programming in actors.

Briefly, actors are a lot like message queues without the configuration and message broker installation overhead. They're like programmable message queues shrunk to microsize—you can easily create thousands, even millions of them. They don't "do" anything unless they're sent a message.

Messages are simple data structures that can't be changed after they've been created, or in a single word, they're *immutable*.

Actors can receive messages one at a time and execute some behavior whenever a message is received. Unlike queues, they can also send messages (to other actors).

Everything an actor does is executed asynchronously. Simply put, you can send a message to an actor without waiting for a response. Actors aren't like threads, but messages sent to them are pushed through on a thread at some point in time. How actors are connected to threads is configurable, as you'll see later; for now it's good to know that this is not a hardwired relationship.

We'll get a lot deeper into exactly what an actor is. For now the most important aspect of actors is that you build applications by sending and receiving messages. A message could be processed locally on some available thread, or remotely on another server. Exactly where the message is processed and where the actor lives are things you can decide later, which is very different compared to hardcoding threads and RPC-style networking. Actors make it easy to build your application out of small parts that resemble networked services, only shrunk to microsize in footprint and administrative overhead.

The Reactive Manifesto

The Reactive Manifesto (http://www.reactivemanifesto.org/) is an initiative to push for the design of systems that are more robust, more resilient, more flexible, and better positioned to meet modern demands. The Akka team has been involved in writing the Reactive Manifesto from the beginning, and Akka is a product of the ideas that are expressed in this manifesto.

In short, efficient resource usage and an opportunity for applications to automatically scale (also called *elasticity*) is the driver for a big part of the manifesto:

- Blocking I/O limits opportunities for parallelism, so nonblocking I/O is preferred.
- Synchronous interaction limits opportunities for parallelism, so asynchronous interaction is preferred.
- Polling reduces opportunity to use fewer resources, so an event-driven style is preferred.
- If one node can bring down all other nodes, that's a waste of resources. So you need isolation of errors (resilience) to avoid losing all your work.

> **(continued)**
>   - Systems need to be elastic: If there's less demand, you want to use fewer resources. If there's more demand, use more resources, but never more than required.
>
> Complexity is a big part of cost, so if you can't easily test it, change it, or program it, you've got a big problem.

1.3   *Two approaches to scaling: setting up our example*

In the rest of this chapter, we'll look at a business chat application and the challenges faced when it has to scale to a large number of servers (and handle millions of simultaneous events). We'll look at what we'll call the *traditional approach*, a method that you're probably familiar with for building such an application (using threads and locks, RPC, and the like) and compare it to Akka's approach.

The traditional approach starts with a simple in-memory application, which turns into an application that relies completely on a database for both concurrency and mutating state. Once the application needs to be more interactive, we'll have no choice but to poll this database. When more network services are added, we'll show that the combination of working with the database and the RPC-based network increases complexity significantly. We'll also show that isolating failure in this application becomes very hard as we go along. We think that you'll recognize a lot of this.

We'll then look at how the actor programming model simplifies the application, and how Akka makes it possible to write the application once and scale it to any demand (thereby handling concurrency issues on any scale needed). Table 1.1 highlights the differences between the two approaches. Some of the items will become clear in the next sections, but it's good to keep this overview in mind.

Table 1.1   Differences between approaches

Objective	Traditional method	Akka method
Scaling	Use a mix of threads, shared mutable state in a database (Create, Insert, Update, Delete), and web service RPC calls for scaling.	Actors send and receive messages. No shared mutable state. Immutable log of events.
Providing interactive information	Poll for current information.	Event-driven: push when the event occurs.
Scaling out on the network	Synchronous RPC, blocking I/O.	Asynchronous messaging, nonblocking I/O.
Handling failures	Handle all exceptions; only continue if everything works.	Let it crash. Isolate failure, and continue without failing parts.

Imagine that we have plans to conquer the world with a state-of-the art chat application that will revolutionize the online collaboration space. It's focused on business users where teams can easily find each other and work together. We have tons of ideas on how this interactive application can connect to project management tools and integrate with existing communication services.

In good Lean Startup spirit, we start with an MVP (minimal viable product) of the chat application to learn as much as possible from our prospective users about what they need. If this ever takes off, we could potentially have millions of users (who doesn't chat, or work together in teams?). And we know that there are two forces that can slow our progress to a grinding halt:

- *Complexity*—The application becomes too complex to add any new features. Even the simplest change takes a huge amount of effort, and it becomes harder and harder to test properly; what will fail this time?
- *Inflexibility*—The application isn't adaptive; with every big jump in number of users, it has to be rewritten from scratch. This rewrite takes a long time and is complex. While we have more users than we can handle, we're split between keeping the existing application running and rewriting it to support more users.

We've been building applications for a while and choose to build it the way we have in the past, taking the traditional approach, using low-level threads and locks, RPC, blocking I/O, and, first on the menu in the next section, mutating state in a database.

1.4 Traditional scaling

We start on one server. We set out to build the first version of the chat application, and come up with a data model design, shown in figure 1.3. For now we'll just keep these objects in memory.

A Team is a group of Users, and many Users can be part of some Conversation. Conversations are collections of messages. So far, so good.

We flesh out the behavior of the application and build a web-based user interface. We're at the point where we can show the application to prospective users and give demos. The code is simple and easy to manage. But so far this application only runs in

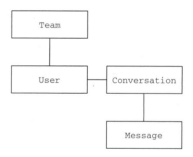

Figure 1.3   Data model design

memory, so whenever it's restarted, all Conversations are lost. It can also only run on one server at this point. Our web app UI built with [insert shiny new JavaScript library] is so impressive that stakeholders want to immediately go live with it, even though we repeatedly warn that it's just for demo purposes! Time to move to more servers and set up a production environment.

1.4.1 Traditional scaling and durability: move everything to the database

We decide to add a database to the equation. We have plans to run the web application on two front-end web servers for availability, with a load balancer in front of it. Figure 1.4 shows the new setup.

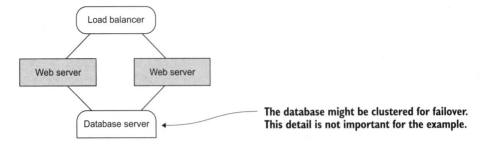

Figure 1.4   Load balancer/failover

The code is becoming more complex because now we can't just work with in-memory objects anymore; how would we keep the objects consistent on the two servers? Someone on our team shouts *"We need to go stateless!"* and we remove all feature-rich objects and replace them with database code.

The state of the objects doesn't simply reside in memory on the web servers anymore, which means the methods on the objects can't work on the state directly; essentially, all important logic moves to database statements. The change is shown in figure 1.5.

This move to statelessness leads to the decision to replace the objects with some database access abstraction. For the purpose of this example, it's irrelevant which one;

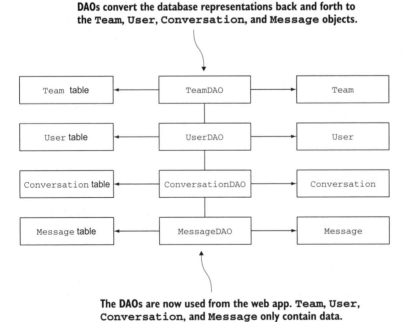

Figure 1.5   Data access objects

in this case, we're feeling a bit retro and use DAOs (data access objects, which execute database statements).

A lot of things change:

- We don't have the same guarantees anymore that we had before when we, for instance, called a method on the `Conversation` to add a `Message`. Before, we were guaranteed that `addMessage` would never fail, since it was a simple operation on an in-memory list (barring the exceptional case that the JVM runs out of memory). Now, the database might return an error at any `addMessage` call. The insert might fail, or the database might not be available at that exact moment because the database server crashes or because there's a problem with the network.

- The in-memory version had a sprinkling of locks to make sure that the data wouldn't get corrupted by concurrent users. Now that we're using "Database X," we'll have to find out how to handle that problem, and make sure that we don't end up with duplicate records or other inconsistent data. We have to find out how to do exactly that with the Database X library. Every simple method call to an object effectively becomes a database operation, of which some have to work in concert. Starting a `Conversation`, for instance, at least needs both an insert of a row in the `Conversation` and the message table.

- The in-memory version was easy to test, and unit tests ran fast. Now, we run Database X locally for the tests, and we add some database test utilities to isolate tests. Unit tests run a lot slower now. But we tell ourselves, "At least we're testing those Database X operations too," which were not as intuitive as we expected—very different from the previous databases we worked with.

We probably run into performance problems when we're porting the in-memory code directly to database calls, since every call now has network overhead. So we design specific database structures to optimize query performance, which are specific to our choice of database (SQL or NoSQL, it doesn't matter). The objects are now a sad anemic shadow of their former selves, merely holding data; all the interesting code has moved to the DAOs and the components of our web application. The saddest part of this is that we can hardly reuse any of the code that we had before; the structure of the code has completely changed.

The "controllers" in our web application combine DAO methods to achieve the changes in the data (`findConversation`, `insertMessage`, and so on). This combination of methods results in an interaction with the database that we can't easily predict; the controllers are free to combine the database operations in any way, as in figure 1.6.

The figure shows one of the possible flows through the code, for adding a `Message` to a `Conversation`. You can imagine that there are numerous variations of database access flows through the use of the DAOs. Allowing any party to mutate or query records at any point in time can lead to performance problems that we can't predict, like deadlocks and other issues. It's exactly the kind of complexity we want to avoid.

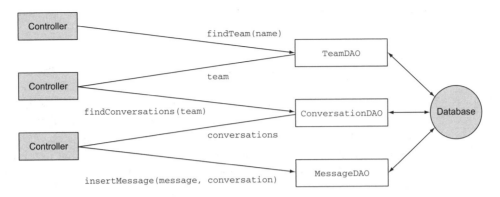

Figure 1.6   DAO interaction

The database calls are essentially RPC, and almost all standard database drivers (say, JDBC) use blocking I/O. So we're already in the state that we described before, using threads and RPC together. The memory locks that are used to synchronize threads and the database locks to protect mutation of table records are really not the same thing, and we'll have to take great care to combine them. We went from one to two interwoven programming models.

We just did our first rewrite of the application, and it took a lot longer than expected.

> **THIS IS A DRAMATIZATION**   The traditional approach to build the team chat app goes sour in a catastrophic way. Although exaggerated, you've probably seen projects run into at least some of these problems (we definitely have seen similar cases first-hand). To quote Dean Wampler from his presentation "Reactive Design, Languages, and Paradigms" (https://deanwampler.github .io/polyglotprogramming/papers/):
>
> > *In reality, good people can make almost any approach work, even if the approach is suboptimal.*

So is this example project impossible to complete with the traditional approach? No, but it's definitely suboptimal. It will be very hard to keep complexity low and flexibility high while the application scales.

1.4.2   *Traditional scaling and interactive use: polling*

We run in this configuration for a while and the users are increasing. The web application servers aren't using a lot of resources; most are spent in (de-)serialization of requests and responses. Most of the processing time is spent in the database. The code on the web server is mostly waiting for a response from the database driver.

We want to build more interactive features now that we have the basics covered. Users are used to Facebook and Twitter and want to be notified whenever their name is mentioned in a team conversation, so they can chime in.

We want to build a `Mentions` component that parses every message that's written and adds the mentioned contacts to a notification table, which is polled from the web application to notify mentioned users.

The web application now also polls other information more often to more quickly reflect changes to users, because we want to give them a true interactive experience.

We don't want to slow down the conversations by adding database code directly to the application, so we add a message queue. Every message written is sent to it asynchronously, and a separate process receives messages from the queue, looks up the users, and writes a record in a notifications table.

The database is really getting hammered at this point. We find out that the automated polling of the database together with the `Mentions` component are causing performance problems with the database. We separate out the `Mentions` component as a service and give it its own database, which contains the notifications table and a copy of the users table, kept up to date with a database synchronization job, as shown in figure 1.7.

Not only has the complexity increased again, it's becoming more difficult to add new interactive features. Polling the database wasn't such a great idea for this kind of application, but there are no other real options, because all the logic is right there in the DAOs, and Database X can't "push" anything into the web server.

We've also added more complexity to the application by adding a message queue, which will have to be installed and configured, and code will have to get deployed. The message queue has its own semantics and context to work in; it's not the same as the database RPC calls, or as the in-memory threading code. Fusing all this code together responsibly will be, once again, more complex.

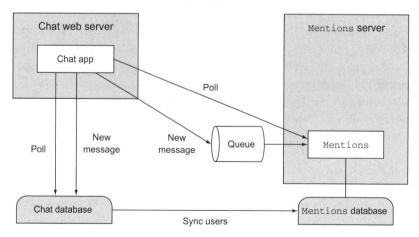

Figure 1.7 Service component

1.4.3   *Traditional scaling and interactive use: polling*

Users start to give feedback that they would love a way to find contacts with *typeahead* (the application gives suggestions while the user types part of a contact's name) and automatically receive suggestions for teams and current conversations based on their recent email conversations. We build a `TeamFinder` object that calls out to several web services like Google Contacts API and Microsoft Outlook.com API. We build web service clients for these, and incorporate the finding of contacts, as in figure 1.8.

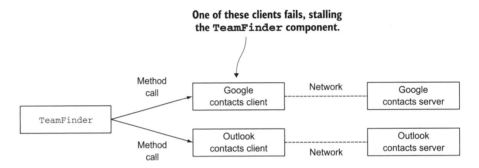

Figure 1.8   Team finder

We find out that one of the services fails often and in the worst possible way—we get long timeouts, or traffic has slowed down to only a few bytes per minute. And because the web services are accessed one after the other, waiting for a response, the lookup fails after a long time even though many valid suggestions could have been made to the user from the service that worked just fine.

Even worse, though we collected our database methods in DAOs and the contacts lookup in a `TeamFinder` object, the controllers are calling these methods like any other. This means that sometimes a user lookup ends up right between two database methods, keeping connections open longer than we want, eating up database resources. If the `TeamFinder` fails, everything else that's part of the same flow in the application fails as well. The controller will throw an exception and won't be able to continue. How do we safely separate the `TeamFinder` from the rest of the code?

It's time for another rewrite, and it doesn't look like the complexity is improving. In fact, we're now using four programming models: one for the in-memory threads, one for the database operations, one for the `Mentions` message queue, and one for the contacts web services.

How do we move from 3 servers to, say, 10, and then to 100 servers, if this should be required? It's obvious that this approach doesn't scale well: we need to change direction with every new challenge.

In the next section, you'll find out if there's a design strategy that doesn't require us to change direction with every new challenge.

1.5 Scaling with Akka

Let's see if it's possible to deliver on the promise to use only actors to meet the scaling requirements of the application. Since it's probably still unclear to you what actors are, exactly, we'll use objects and actors interchangeably and focus on the conceptual difference between this approach and the traditional approach.

Table 1.2 shows this difference in approaches.

Table 1.2   Actors compared to the traditional approach

Goal	Traditional approach	Akka approach (actors)
Make conversation data durable, even if the application restarts or crashes.	Rewrite code into DAOs. Use the database as one big shared mutable state, where all parties create, update, insert, and query the data.	Continue to use in-memory state. Changes to the state are sent as messages to a log. This log is only reread if the application restarts.
Provide interactive features (Mentions).	Poll the database. Polling uses a lot of resources even if there's no change in the data.	Push events to interested parties. The objects notify interested parties only when there's a significant event, reducing overhead.
Decoupling of services; the Mentions and chat features shouldn't be interfering with each other.	Add a message queue for asynchronous processing.	No need to add a message queue; actors are asynchronous by definition. No extra complexity; you're familiar with sending and receiving messages.
Prevent failure of the total system when critical services fail or behave outside of specified performance parameters for any given time.	Try to prevent any error from happening by predicting all failure scenarios and catching exceptions for these scenarios.	Messages are sent asynchronously; if a message isn't handled by a crashed component, it has no impact on the stability of the other components.

It would be great if we could write the application code once, and then scale it any way we like. We want to avoid radically changing the application's main objects; for example, how we had to replace all logic in the in-memory objects with DAOs in section 1.4.1.

The first challenge we wanted to solve was to safekeep conversation data. Coding directly to the database moved us away from one simple in-memory model. Methods that were once simple turned into database RPC commands, leaving us with a mixed programming model. We have to find another way to make sure that the conversations aren't lost, while keeping things simple.

1.5.1 Scaling with Akka and durability: sending and receiving messages

Let's first solve the initial problem of just making Conversations durable. The application objects must save Conversations in some way. The Conversations must at least be recovered when the application restarts.

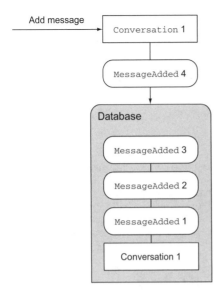

Figure 1.9   Persist conversations

Figure 1.9 shows how a `Conversation` sends a `MessageAdded` to the database log for every message that's added in-memory.

The `Conversation` can be rebuilt from these objects stored in the database whenever the web server (re)-starts, as shown in figure 1.10.

Exactly how this all works is something we'll discuss later. But as you can see, we only use the database to recover the messages in the conversation. We don't use it to express our code in database operations. The `Conversation` actor sends messages to

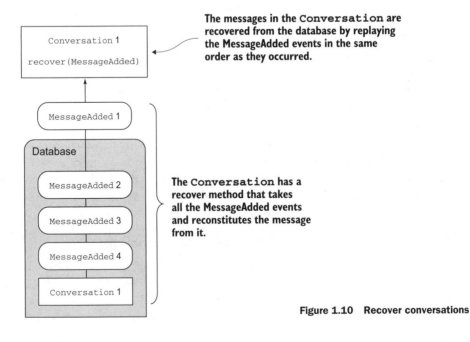

The messages in the `Conversation` are recovered from the database by replaying the MessageAdded events in the same order as they occurred.

The `Conversation` has a recover method that takes all the MessageAdded events and reconstitutes the message from it.

Figure 1.10   Recover conversations

the log, and receives them again on startup. We don't have to learn anything new; it's just sending and receiving messages.

CHANGES KEPT AS A SEQUENCE OF EVENTS

All changes are kept as a sequence of events, in this case `MessageAdded` events. The current state of the `Conversation` can be rebuilt by replaying the events that occurred to the in-memory `Conversation`, so it can continue where it left off. This type of database is often called a *journal*, and the technique is known as *event sourcing*. There's more to event sourcing, but for now this definition will do.

What's important to note here is that the journal has become a uniform service. All it needs to do is store all events in sequence, and make it possible to retrieve the events in the same sequence as they were written to the journal. There are some details that we'll ignore for now, like serialization—if you can't wait, go look at chapter 15 on actor persistence.

SPREADING OUT THE DATA: SHARDING CONVERSATIONS

The next problem is that we're still putting all our eggs in one server. The server restarts, reads all conversations in memory, and continues to operate. The main reason for going stateless in the traditional approach is that it's hard to imagine how we would keep the conversations consistent across many servers. And what would happen if there were too many conversations to fit on one server?

A solution for this is to divide the conversations over the servers in a predictable way or to keep track of where every conversation lives. This is called *sharding* or *partitioning*. Figure 1.11 shows some conversations in shards across two servers.

We can keep using the simple in-memory model of `Conversations` if we have a generic event-sourced journal and a way to indicate how `Conversations` should be partitioned. Many details about these two capabilities will be covered in chapter 15. For now, we'll assume that we can simply use these services.

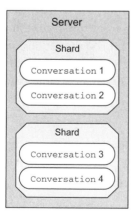 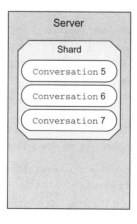

Figure 1.11   Sharding

1.5.2 *Scaling with Akka and interactive use: push messages*

Instead of polling the database for every user of the web application, we could find out if there's a way to notify the user of an important change (an event) by directly sending messages to the user's web browser.

 The application can also send event messages internally as a signal to execute particular tasks. Every object in the application will send an event when something interesting occurs. Other objects in the application can decide if an event is interesting and take action on it, as in figure 1.12.

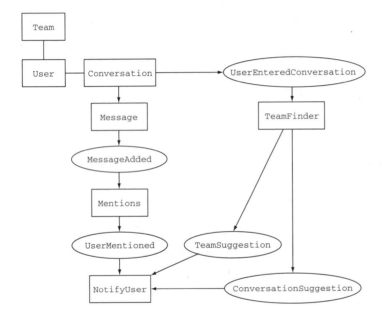

Figure 1.12 Events

The events (depicted as ellipses) decouple the system where there used to be undesired coupling between the components. The Conversation only publishes that it added a Message and continues its work. Events are sent through a publish-subscribe mechanism, instead of the components communicating with each other directly. An event will eventually get to the subscribers, in this case to the Mentions component. It's important to note that, once again, we can model the solution to this problem by simply sending and receiving messages.

1.5.3 *Scaling with Akka and failure: asynchronous decoupling*

It's preferable that users be able to continue to have Conversations even if the Mentions component has crashed. The same goes for the TeamFinder component: existing conversations should be able to continue. Conversations can continue to publish events while subscribers, like the Mentions component and the TeamFinder object, crash and restart.

The `NotifyUser` component could keep track of connected web browsers and send `UserMentioned` messages directly to the browser when they occur, relieving the application from polling.

This event-driven approach has a couple of advantages:

- It minimizes direct dependencies between components. The conversation *doesn't know about the* `Mentions` *object* and *could not care less what happens with the event.* The conversation can continue to operate when the `Mentions` object crashes.
- The components of the application are loosely coupled in time. It doesn't matter if the `Mentions` object gets the events a little later, as long as it gets the events eventually.
- The components are decoupled in terms of location. The `Conversation` and `Mentions` object can reside on different servers; the events are just messages that can be transmitted over the network.

The event-driven approach solves the polling problem with the `Mentions` object, as well as the direct coupling with the `TeamFinder` object. In chapter 5 on futures, we'll look at some better ways to communicate with web services than sequentially waiting for every response. It's important to note that, once again, we can model the solution to this problem by simply sending and receiving messages.

1.5.4 *The Akka approach: sending and receiving messages*

Let's recap what we've changed so far: `Conversations` are now stateful in-memory objects (actors), storing their internal state, recovering from events, partitioned across servers, sending and receiving messages.

You've seen how communicating between objects with messages instead of calling methods directly is a winning design strategy.

A core requirement is that messages are sent and received in order, one at a time to every actor, when one event is dependent on the next, because otherwise we'd get unexpected results. This requires that the `Conversation` keeps its own messages secret from any other component. The order can never be kept if any other component can interact with the messages.

It shouldn't matter if we send a message locally on one server or remotely to another. So we need some service that takes care of sending the messages to actors on other servers if necessary. It will also need to keep track of where actors live and be able to provide references so other servers can communicate with the actors. This is one of the things that Akka does for you, as you'll soon see. Chapter 6 discusses the basics of distributed Akka applications, and chapter 13 discusses clustered Akka applications (in short, groups of distributed actors).

The `Conversation` doesn't care what happens with the `Mentions` component, but on the application level we need to know when the `Mentions` component doesn't work anymore to show users that it's temporarily offline, among other things. So we need some kind of monitoring of actors, and we need to make it possible to reboot these if

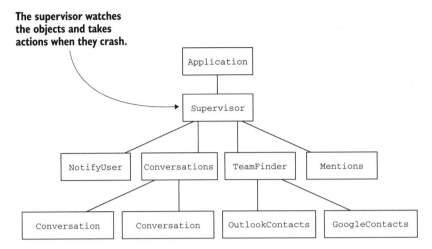

Figure 1.13   **High-level structure**

necessary. This monitoring should work across servers as well as locally on one server, so it will also have to use sending and receiving messages. A possible high-level structure for the application is shown in figure 1.13.

The supervisor watches over the components and takes action when they crash. It can, for example, decide to continue running when the Mentions component or the TeamFinder doesn't work. If both Conversations and NotifyUser stop working completely, the supervisor could decide to restart completely or stop the application, since there's no reason to continue. A component can send a message to the supervisor when it fails, and the supervisor can send a message to a component to stop, or try to restart. As you'll see, this is conceptually how Akka provides error recovery, which is discussed in chapter 4 on fault tolerance.

In the next section, we'll first talk about actors in general, and then talk about Akka actors.

1.6   *Actors: one programming model to rule up and out*

Most general-purpose programming languages are written in sequence (Scala and Java being no exception to the rule). A concurrent programming model is required to bridge the gap between sequential definition and parallel execution.

Whereas parallelization is all about executing processes simultaneously, concurrency concerns itself with defining processes that *can* function simultaneously, or *can* overlap in time, but don't necessarily *need* to run simultaneously. A concurrent system is not by definition a parallel system. Concurrent processes can, for example, be executed on one CPU through the use of time slicing, where every process gets a certain amount of time to run on the CPU, one after another.

The JVM has a standard concurrent programming model (see figure 1.14), where, roughly speaking, processes are expressed in objects and methods, which are executed on threads. Threads might be executed on many CPUs in parallel, or using

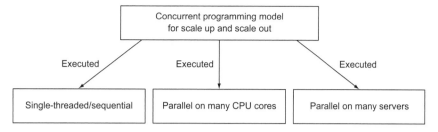

Figure 1.14   Concurrent programming model

some sharing mechanism like time slicing on one CPU. As we discussed earlier, threads can't be applied directly to scaling out, only to scaling up.

The concurrent programming model that we're after should function for one CPU or many, one server or many servers. The actor model chooses the abstraction of sending and receiving messages to decouple from the number of threads or the number of servers that are being used.

1.6.1   An asynchronous model

If we want the application to scale to many servers, there's an important requirement for the programming model: it will have to be *asynchronous*, allowing components to continue working while others haven't responded yet, as in the chat application (see figure 1.15).

The figure shows a possible configuration of the chat application, scaled to five servers. The supervisor has the responsibility to create and monitor the rest of the application. The supervisor now has to communicate over the network, which might fail, and every server could possibly crash as well. If the supervisor used synchronous

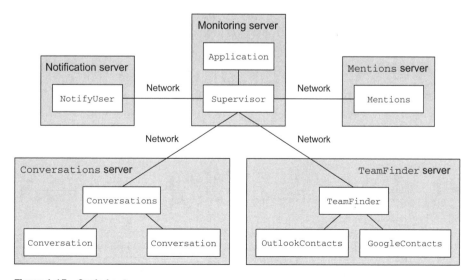

Figure 1.15   Scaled out

communication, waiting for every response of every component, we could get in the problematic situation where one of the components doesn't respond, blocking all other calls from happening. What would happen, for instance, if the conversations server is restarting and not responding to the network interface yet, while the supervisor wants to send out messages to all components?

1.6.2 *Actor operations*

Actors are the primary building blocks in the actor model. All the components in the example application are actors, shown in figure 1.16. An actor is a lightweight process that has only four core operations: create, send, become, and supervise. All of these operations are asynchronous.

> **THE ACTOR MODEL—NOT NEW** The actor model is not new and has actually been around for quite a while; the idea was introduced in 1973 by Carl Hewitt, Peter Bishop, and Richard Steiger. The Erlang language and its OTP middleware libraries, developed by Ericsson around 1986, support the actor model and have been used to build massively scalable systems with requirements for high availability. An example of the success of Erlang is the AXD 301 switch product, which achieves a reliability of 99.9999999%, also known as *nine nines* reliability. The actor model implementation in Akka differs in a couple of details from the Erlang implementation, but has definitely been heavily influenced by Erlang, and shares a lot of its concepts.

SEND

An actor can only communicate with another actor by sending it messages. This takes *encapsulation* to the next level. In objects we can specify which methods can be publicly called and which state is accessible from the outside. Actors don't allow any access to internal state, for example, the list of messages in a conversation. Actors can't share mutable state; they can't, for instance, point to a shared list of conversation messages and change the conversation in parallel at any point in time.

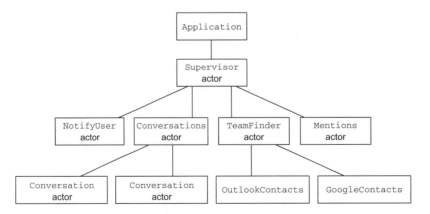

Figure 1.16 Components

The Conversation actor can't simply call a method on any other actor, since that could lead to sharing mutable state. It has to send it a message. Sending messages is always asynchronous, in what is called a *fire and forget* style. If it's important to know that another actor received the message, then the receiving actor should just send back an acknowledgement message of some kind.

The Conversation actor doesn't have to wait and see what happens with a message to the Mentions actor; it can send off a message and continue its work. Asynchronous messaging helps in the chat application to decouple the components; this was one of the reasons why we wanted to use a message queue for the Mentions object, which is now unnecessary.

The messages need to be immutable, meaning that they can't be changed once they're created. This makes it impossible for two actors to change the same message by mistake, which could result in unexpected behavior.

> **WHAT, NO TYPE SAFETY?**　Actors can receive any message, and you can send any message you want to an actor (it just might not process the message). This basically means that type checking of the messages that are sent and received is limited. That might come as a surprise, since Scala is a statically typed language and a high level of type safety has many benefits. This flexibility is both a cost (less is known about actors' type correctness at runtime) and a benefit (how would static types be enforced over a network of remote systems?). The last word hasn't been said on this, and the Akka team is researching how to define a more type-safe version of actors, which we might see details of in a next version of Akka. Stay tuned.

So what do we do when a user wants to edit a message in a Conversation? We could send an EditMessage message to the conversation. The EditMessage contains a modified copy of the message, instead of updating the message in place in a shared messages list. The Conversation actor receives the EditMessage and replaces the existing message with the new copy.

Immutability is an absolute necessity when it comes to concurrency and is another restriction that makes life simpler, because there are fewer moving parts to manage.

The order of sent messages is kept between a sending and receiving actor. An actor receives messages one at a time. Imagine that a user edits a message many times; it would make sense that the user eventually sees the result of the final edit of the message. The order of messages is only guaranteed per sending actor, so if many users edit the same message in a conversation, the final result can vary depending on how the messages are interleaved over time.

CREATE

An actor can create other actors. Figure 1.17 shows how the Supervisor actor creates a Conversations actor. As you can see, this automatically creates a hierarchy of actors. The chat application first creates the Supervisor actor, which in turn creates all

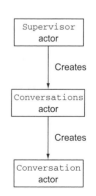

Figure 1.17　Create

other actors in the application. The `Conversations` actor recovers all `Conversations` from the journal. It then creates a `Conversation` actor for every `Conversation`, which in turn recovers itself from the journal.

BECOME

State machines are a great tool for making sure that a system only executes particular actions when it's in a specific state.

Actors receive messages one at a time, which is a convenient property for implementing state machines. An actor can change how it handles incoming messages by swapping out its behavior.

Imagine that users want to be able to close a `Conversation`. The `Conversation` starts out in a started state and becomes closed when a `CloseConversation` is received. Any message that's sent to the closed `Conversation` could be ignored. The `Conversation` swaps its behavior from adding messages to itself to ignoring all messages.

SUPERVISE

An actor needs to supervise the actors that it creates. The supervisor in the chat application can keep track of what's happening to the main components, as shown in figure 1.18.

Figure 1.18   Supervise

The `Supervisor` decides what should happen when components fail in the system. It could, for example, decide that the chat application continues when the `Mentions` component and `Notify` actor have crashed, since they're not critical components. The `Supervisor` gets notified with special messages that indicate which actor has crashed, and for what reason. The `Supervisor` can decide to restart an actor or take the actor out of service.

Any actor can be a supervisor, but only for actors that it creates itself. In figure 1.19 the `TeamFinder` actor supervises the two connectors for looking up contacts. In this case it could decide to take the `OutlookContacts` actor out of service because it failed too often. The `TeamFinder` will then continue looking up contacts from Google only.

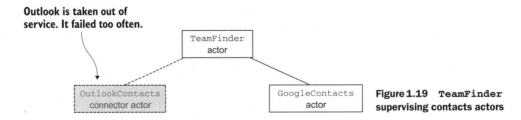

Figure 1.19   TeamFinder supervising contacts actors

Actors: decoupled on three axes

Another way to look at actors is how they're decoupled, on three axes, for the purpose of scaling:

- Space/Location
- Time
- Interface

Decoupling on exactly these three axes is important because this is exactly the flexibility that's required for scaling. Actors might run at the same time if there are enough CPUs, or might run one after the other if not. Actors might be co-located, or far apart, and in a failure scenario actors might receive messages that they can't handle.

- *Space*—An actor gives no guarantee and has no expectation about where another actor is located.
- *Time*—An actor gives no guarantee and has no expectation about when its work will be done.
- *Interface*—An actor has no defined interface. An actor has no expectation about which messages other components can understand. Nothing is shared between actors; actors never point to or use a shared piece of information that changes in place. Information is passed in messages.

Coupling components in location, time, and interface is the biggest impediment to building applications that can recover from failure and scale according to demand. A system built out of components that are coupled on all three axes can only exist on one runtime and will fail completely if one of its components fails.

Now that we've looked at the operations that an actor can perform, let's look at how Akka supports actors and what's required to make them actually process messages.

1.7 Akka actors

So far we've discussed the actor programming model from a conceptual perspective and why you would want to use it. Let's see how Akka implements the actor model and get closer to where the rubber meets the road. We'll look at how everything connects together—which Akka components do what. In the next section, we'll start with the details of actor creation.

1.7.1 ActorSystem

The first thing we'll look at is how actors are created. Actors can create other actors, but who creates the first one? See figure 1.20.

The chat application's first actor is the `Supervisor` actor. All the actors shown in figure 1.20 are part of the same application. How do we make actors part of one bigger whole, one bigger picture? The answer that Akka provides for this is the `Actor-System`. The first thing that every Akka application does is create an `ActorSystem`. The actor system can create so called top-level actors, and it's a common pattern to

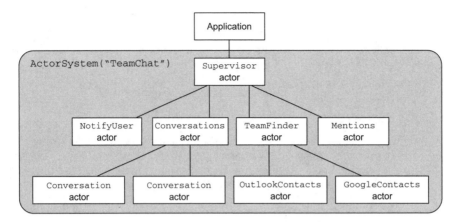

Figure 1.20 `TeamChatActorSystem`

create only one top-level actor for all actors in the application—in our case, the `Supervisor` actor that monitors everything.

We've touched on the fact that we'll need support capabilities for actors, like remoting and a journal for durability. The `ActorSystem` is also the nexus for these support capabilities. Most capabilities are provided as *Akka extensions*, modules that can be configured specifically for the `ActorSystem` in question. A simple example of a support capability is the scheduler, which can send messages to actors periodically.

An `ActorSystem` returns an address to the created top-level actor instead of the actor itself. This address is called an `ActorRef`. The `ActorRef` can be used to send messages to the actor. This makes sense when you think about the fact that the actor could be on another server.

Sometimes you'd like to look up an actor in the actor system. This is where `Actor-Paths` come in. You could compare the hierarchy of actors to a URL path structure. Every actor has a name. This name needs to be unique per level in the hierarchy: two sibling actors can't have the same name (if you don't provide a name, Akka generates one for you, but it's a good idea to name all your actors). All actor references can be located directly by an actor path, absolute or relative.

1.7.2   *ActorRef, mailbox, and actor*

Messages are sent to the actor's `ActorRef`. Every actor has a mailbox—it's a lot like a queue. Messages sent to the `ActorRef` will be temporarily stored in the mailbox to be processed later, one at a time, in the order they arrived. Figure 1.21 shows the relationship between the `ActorRef`, the mailbox, and the actor.

How the actor actually processes the messages is described in the next section.

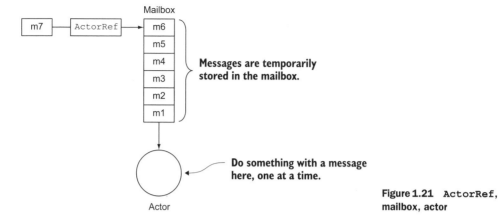

Figure 1.21 `ActorRef`, mailbox, actor

1.7.3   *Dispatchers*

Actors are invoked at some point by a dispatcher. The dispatcher pushes the messages in the mailbox through the actors, so to speak. This is shown in figure 1.22.

The type of dispatcher determines which threading model is used to push the messages through. Many actors can get messages pushed through on several threads, as shown in figure 1.23.

Figure 1.23 shows that messages m1 through m6 are going to be pushed through by the dispatcher on threads 1 and 2, and x4 through x9 on threads 3 and 4. This figure shouldn't make you think that you can or should control exactly which message will be

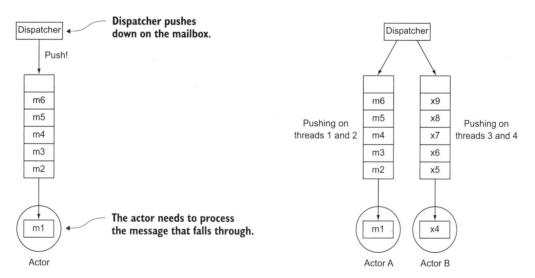

Figure 1.22   Dispatcher pushes messages through mailbox

Figure 1.23   Dispatcher pushing messages through many actors

pushed through on which thread. What's important here is that you can configure the threading model to quite some extent. All kinds of dispatchers can be configured in some way, and you can allocate a dispatcher to an actor, a specific group of actors, or to all actors in the system.

So when you send a message to an actor, all you're really doing is leaving a message behind in its mailbox. Eventually a dispatcher will push it through the actor. The actor, in turn, can leave a message behind for the next actor, which will be pushed through at some point.

Actors are lightweight because they run on top of dispatchers; the actors aren't necessarily directly proportional to the number of threads. Akka actors take a lot less space than threads: around 2.7 million actors can fit in 1 GB of memory. That's a big difference compared to 4096 threads for 1 GB of memory, which means that you can create different types of actors more freely than you would when using threads directly.

There are different types of dispatchers to choose from that can be tuned to specific needs. Being able to configure and tune the dispatchers and the mailboxes that are used throughout the application gives a lot of flexibility when performance tuning. We give a couple of simple tips on performance tuning in chapter 15.

> **CALLBACK HELL**   A lot of frameworks out there provide asynchronous programming through callbacks. If you've used any of these, chances are high you've been to a place that is called *Callback Hell*, where every callback calls another callback, which calls another callback, and so on.
>
> Compare this to how the dispatcher chops up the messages in mailboxes and pushes them through on a given thread. Actors don't need to provide a callback in a callback, all the way down to some sulfur pit, which is good news. Actors simply drop off messages in mailboxes and let the dispatcher sort out the rest.

1.7.4   *Actors and the network*

How do Akka actors communicate with each other across the network? `ActorRefs` are essentially addresses to actors, so all you need to change is how the addresses are linked to actors. If the toolkit takes care of the fact that an address can be local or remote, you can scale the solution just by configuring how the addresses are resolved.

Akka provides a remoting module (which we'll discuss in chapter 6) that enables the transparency you seek. Akka passes messages for a remote actor on to a remote machine where the actor resides, and passes the results back across the network.

The only thing that has to change is how the reference to remote actors is looked up, which can be achieved solely through configuration, as you'll see later. The code stays exactly the same, which means that you can often transition from scaling up to scaling out without having to change a single line of code.

The flexibility of resolving an address is heavily used in Akka, as we'll show throughout this book. Remote actors, clustering, and even the test toolkit use this flexibility.

1.8 Summary

Let's recap what you've learned in this chapter. Scaling is traditionally hard to get right. Both inflexibility and complexity quickly get out of control when scaling is required. Akka actors take advantage of key design decisions that provide more flexibility to scale.

Actors are a programming model for scaling up and out, where everything revolves around sending and receiving messages. Although it's not a silver bullet for every problem, being able to work with one programming model reduces some of the complexity of scaling.

Akka is centered on actors. What makes Akka unique is how effortlessly it provides support and additional tooling for building actor-based applications, so that you can focus on thinking and programming in actors.

At this point you should have an intuition that actors can give you more flexibility at a decent level of complexity, making it far easier to scale. But there's a lot more to be learned and, as always, the devil is in the details.

But first, let's get up and running with actors in the next chapter and build a simple HTTP server and deploy it on a PaaS (platform as a service)!

Up and running 2

Our goal here is to show you how quickly you can make an Akka app that not only does something nontrivial, but is built to do it to scale, even in its easiest, early incarnations. We'll clone a project from github.com that contains our example, and then we'll walk through the essentials that you need to know to start building Akka apps. First we'll look at the dependencies that you need for a minimal app, using Lightbend's *Simple Build Tool (sbt)* to create a single JAR file that can be used to run the app. We'll build a minimal ticket-selling app, and in its first iteration we'll build a minimal set of REST services. We'll keep it as simple as possible to focus on essential Akka features. Finally we'll show you how easy it is to deploy this app to the cloud and get it working on Heroku, a popular cloud provider. What will be most remarkable is how quickly we get to this point!

One of the most exciting things about Akka is how easy it is to get up and running, and how flexible it is, given its small footprint runtime, as you'll soon see. We'll ignore some of the infrastructure details, and chapter 12 will go into more detail on how to use Akka HTTP, but you'll leave this chapter with enough information to build serious REST interfaces of all types. You'll see in the next chapter how we can combine this with *TDD (test-driven development)*.

2.1 Clone, build, and test interface

To make things easier, we've published the source code for the app on github.com, along with all the code for this book. The first thing you have to do is clone the repo to a directory of your choice.

Listing 2.1 Clone the example project

```
git clone https://github.com/RayRoestenburg/akka-in-action.git
```
Clone Git repo with complete, working example code

This will create a directory named *akka-in-action* that contains the directory *chapter-up-and-running*, which contains the example project for this chapter. We expect that you're already familiar with Git and GitHub, among other tools. We'll use sbt, Git, the Heroku toolbelt, and `httpie` (an easy to use command-line HTTP client) in this chapter.

> **NOTE** Please note that Akka 2.4 requires Java 8. If you've installed an earlier version of sbt, please make sure to remove it and upgrade to version 0.13.7 or higher. It's also useful to use sbt-extras from Paul Phillips (https://github.com/paulp/sbt-extras), which automatically figures out which version of sbt and Scala to use.

Let's look at the structure of the project. sbt follows a project structure similar to Maven. The major difference is that sbt allows for the use of Scala in the build files, and it has an interpreter. This makes it considerably more powerful. For more information on sbt, see the Manning Publications title *SBT in Action* (by Joshua Suereth and Matthew Farwell; www.manning.com/suereth2/). Inside the chapter-up-and-running directory, all the code for the server can be found in src/main/scala; configuration files and other resources in src/main/resources; and the tests in src/test/scala. The project should build right out of the box. Run the following command inside the chapter-up-and-running directory and keep your fingers crossed:

```
sbt assembly
```
Compiles and packages the code into a single JAR

You should see sbt booting up, getting all needed dependencies, running all the tests, and finally building one fat JAR into target/scala-2.11/goticks-assembly-1.0.jar. You could run the server by simply running the commands in the followng listing.

Listing 2.2 Running the JAR

```
java -jar target/scala-2.11/goticks-assembly-1.0.jar
RestApi bound to /0:0:0:0:0:0:0:0:5000
```
Runs the app like any other Java code

Output to the console: HTTP server is started and listens on port 5000

Now that we've verified that the project builds correctly, it's time to talk about what it does. In the next section, we'll start with the build file and then look at the resources, and the actual code for the services.

2.1.1   *Build with sbt*

Let's first look at the build file. We're using the simple sbt DSL (domain-specific language) for build files in this chapter because it gives us all we need right now. As we go forward in the book, we'll be back to add more dependencies, but you can see that for your future projects you'll be able to get going quickly, and without the aid of a template, or by cutting and pasting large build files from other projects. If you haven't worked with the sbt settings DSL before, it's important to note that you need to put an empty line between setting lines in the file (which is not required in full configuration mode, in which case you can write Scala code as usual). The build file is located directly under the chapter-up-and-running directory in a file called build.sbt.

Listing 2.3   The sbt build file

```
enablePlugins(JavaServerAppPackaging)    ◁──  Needed for deploying to Heroku
                                               (coming up)
name := "goticks"

version := "1.0"

organization := "com.goticks"

libraryDependencies ++= {
  val akkaVersion       = "2.4.9"
  Seq(
    "com.typesafe.akka" %% "akka-actor"       % akkaVersion,
    "com.typesafe.akka" %% "akka-http-core"   % akkaVersion,
    "com.typesafe.akka" %% "akka-http-experimental"  % akkaVersion,
    "com.typesafe.akka" %% "akka-http-spray-json-experimental"  %
      akkaVersion,
    "io.spray"          %% "spray-json"       % "1.3.1",
    "com.typesafe.akka" %% "akka-slf4j"       % akkaVersion,
    "ch.qos.logback"    %  "logback-classic"  % "1.1.3",
    "com.typesafe.akka" %% "akka-testkit"     % akkaVersion   % "test",
    "org.scalatest"     %% "scalatest"        % "2.2.0"       % "test"
  )
}
```

Info about our app → (points to `name`, `version`, `organization` lines)

The version of Akka we're using → (points to `val akkaVersion = "2.4.9"`)

Tells sbt about remote repositories to get dependencies from (points to `libraryDependencies ++= {`)

The Akka actor module dependency (Lightbend was formerly Typesafe; hence the package names) (points to `"com.typesafe.akka" %% "akka-actor"`)

In case you were wondering where the libraries are downloaded from, sbt uses a set of predefined repositories, including a Lightbend repository that hosts the Akka libraries that we use here. For those with experience in Maven, this looks decidedly more compact. Like Maven, once we have the repository and dependency mapped, we can easily get newer versions by just changing a single value.

Every dependency points to a Maven artifact in the format *organization % module % version* (the %% is for automatically using the right Scala version of the library). The most important dependency here is the *akka-actor* module. Now that we have our build file set up, we can compile the code, run the tests, and build the JAR file. Run the following command in the chapter-up-and-running directory.

```
sbt clean compile test
```
◁────────── **Delete target; then compile and run tests**

If any dependencies still need to be downloaded, sbt will do that automatically. Now that we have the build file in place, let's take a closer look at what we're trying to achieve with this example in the next section.

2.1.2 Fast-forward to the GoTicks.com REST server

Our ticket-selling service will allow customers to buy tickets to all sorts of events, concerts, sports games, and the like. Let's say we're part of a startup called GoTicks.com, and in this first iteration we've been assigned to build the backend REST server for the first version of the service. Right now we want customers to get a numbered ticket to a show. Once all the tickets are sold for an event, the server should respond with a 404 (Not Found) HTTP status code. The first thing we'll implement in the REST API will have to be the addition of a new event (since all other services will require the presence of an event in the system). A new event only contains the name of the event—say "RHCP" for the Red Hot Chili Peppers—and the total number of tickets we can sell for the given venue.

The requirements for the RestApi are shown in table 2.1.

Table 2.1 REST API

Description	HTTP method	URL	Request body	Status code	Response example

Create an event	POST	/events/RHCP	{ "tickets" : 250}	201 Created	{
					    "name": "RHCP",
					    "tickets": 250
					}

Get all events	GET	/events	N/A	200 OK	[{ event : "RHCP", tickets : 249 }, { event : "Radiohead", tickets : 130 }]
Buy tickets	POST	/events/RHCP/tickets	{ "tickets" : 2 }	201 Created	{ "event" : "RHCP", "entries" : [{ "id" : 1 }, { "id" : 2 }] }
Cancel an event	DELETE	/events/RHCP	N/A	200 OK	{ event : "RHCP", tickets : 249 }

Let's build the app and run it inside sbt. Go to the chapter-up-and-running directory and execute the following command.

Listing 2.5   Starting up the app locally with sbt

```
sbt run                          ←——————— Tells the build tool to compile and run our app

[info] Running com.goticks.Main
INFO  [Slf4jLogger]: Slf4jLogger started
RestApi bound to /0:0:0:0:0:0:0:0:5000
```

As are most build tools, sbt is similar to `make`: if the code needs to be compiled, it will be; then packaged, and so on. Unlike a lot of build tools, sbt can also deploy and run the app locally. If you get an error, make sure that you're not already running the server in another console, or that some other process isn't already using port 5000. Let's see if everything works by using `httpie`,[1] a human-readable HTTP command-line tool that makes it simple to send HTTP requests. It has support for JSON and handles the required housekeeping in headers, among other things. First let's see if we can create an event with a number of tickets.

Listing 2.6   Creating an event from the command line

```
http POST localhost:5000/events/RHCP tickets:=10          ←┐ httpie command simply
                                                           │ sends POST request
HTTP/1.1 201 Created                            ←──────────┘ to our running server,
Connection: keep-alive                                       with one parameter
Content-Length: 76
Content-Type: text/plain; charset=UTF-8           Response from the
Date: Mon, 20 Apr 2015 12:13:35 GMT               server (201 Created
Proxy-Connection: keep-alive                      indicates success)
Server: GoTicks.com REST API

{
    "name": "RHCP",
    "tickets": 10
}
```

The parameter is transformed into a JSON body. Notice the parameter uses `:=` instead of `=`. This means that the parameter is a non-string field. The format of our command is translated into { `"tickets"` : 10}. The whole following block is the complete HTTP response dumped by `httpie` to the console. The event is now created. Let's create another one:

```
http POST localhost:5000/events/DjMadlib tickets:=15
```

Now let's try out the GET request. Per the REST conventions, a GET whose URL ends with an entity type should return a list of known instances of that entity.

---

[1] You can get httpie here: https://github.com/jakubroztocil/httpie

Listing 2.7　Requesting a list of all events

```
http GET localhost:5000/events                          ◁──┐  Requests a list of all
...                                                         │  current Event instances
HTTP/1.1 200 OK                                      ◁──────┤
Connection: keep-alive                                      │
Content-Length: 110                                         │
Content-Type: application/json; charset=UTF-8        Completes response
Date: Mon, 20 Apr 2015 12:18:01 GMT                  from our HTTP server
Proxy-Connection: keep-alive                         (200 indicates success)
Server: GoTicks.com REST API

{
    "events": [
        {
            "name": "DjMadlib",
            "tickets": 15
        },
        {
            "name": "RHCP",
            "tickets": 10
        }
    ]
}
```

Notice that we see both events, and all the tickets are still available. Now let's see if we can buy two tickets for the RHCP event.

Listing 2.8　Purchasing two tickets to RHCP

```
http POST localhost:5000/events/RHCP/tickets tickets:=2   ◁──┐  Sends a POST to
                                                             │  request 2 tickets
HTTP/1.1 201 Created                                   ◁─────┤
Connection: keep-alive
Content-Length: 74                                    Server response in the
Content-Type: application/json; charset=UTF-8         console (201 Created
Date: Mon, 20 Apr 2015 12:19:41 GMT                   indicates the tickets
Proxy-Connection: keep-alive                          have been created)
Server: GoTicks.com REST API

{
    "entries": [
        {
            "id": 1                     ◁─────────┐
        },                                        │  The tickets we
        {                                         │  purchased, as JSON
            "id": 2                     ◁─────────┘
        }
    ],
    "event": "RHCP"
}
```

The presumption here is that there are at least two `Tickets` left for this `Event`; otherwise, we'd have gotten a 404.

If you do the GET with path /events again, you should see the following response.

Listing 2.9   GET after two events created

```
HTTP/1.1 200 OK
Content-Length: 91
Content-Type: application/json; charset=UTF-8
Date: Mon, 20 Apr 2015 12:19:42 GMT
Server: GoTicks.com REST API

[
  {
    "event":
    "DjMadlib",
    "nrOfTickets": 15
  },
  {
    "event":
    "RHCP",
    "nrOfTickets": 8
  }
]
```

As expected, there are now only 8 tickets left for RHCP. You should get a 404 after buying all tickets.

Listing 2.10   Results when seats are gone

```
HTTP/1.1 404 Not Found                          ◁──────┐  Server responds with
Content-Length: 83                                      │  404 when we're out of
Content-Type: text/plain                               │  Tickets for an Event
Date: Tue, 16 Apr 2013 12:42:57 GMT
Server: GoTicks.com REST API

The requested resource could not be found
but may be available again in the future.
```

That concludes all the API calls in the REST API. Clearly, at this point, the application supports the basic `Event` CRUD cycle, from creation of the actual `Event` through the sale of all the tickets until they're sold out. This isn't comprehensive; for instance, we're not accounting for events that won't sell out, but whose tickets will need to become unavailable once the actual event has started. Now let's look at the details of how we're going to get to this result in the next section.

2.2   *Explore the actors in the app*

In this section we'll look at how the app is built. You can participate and build the actors yourself, or just follow along from the source code on github.com. As you now know, actors can perform four operations; create, send/receive, become, and supervise. In this example we'll only touch on the first two operations. First, we'll take a look at the overall structure: how operations will be carried out by the various collaborators (actors) to provide the core functionality—creating events, issuing tickets, and finishing events.

2.2.1 Structure of the app

The app consists of two actor classes in total. The first thing we have to do is create an actor system that will contain all the actors. After that the actors can create each other. Figure 2.1 shows the sequence.

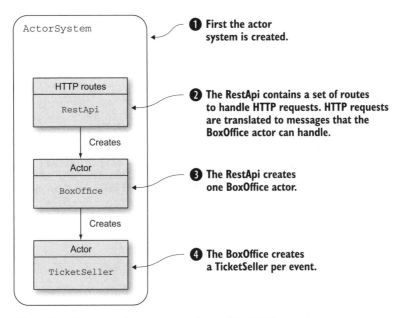

Figure 2.1   Actor creation sequence triggered by REST request

The `RestApi` contains a number of *routes* to handle the HTTP requests. The routes define how HTTP requests should be handled using a convenient DSL, which is provided by the akka-http module. We'll discuss the routes in section 2.2.4. The `RestApi` is basically an adapter for HTTP: it takes care of converting from and to JSON, and provides the required HTTP response. We'll show later how we connect this actor to an HTTP server. Even in this simplest example, you can see how the fulfillment of a request spawns a number of collaborators, each with specific responsibilities. The `TicketSeller` eventually keeps track of the tickets for one particular event and sells the tickets. Figure 2.2 shows how a request for creating an `Event` flows through the actor system (this was the first service we showed in table 2.1).

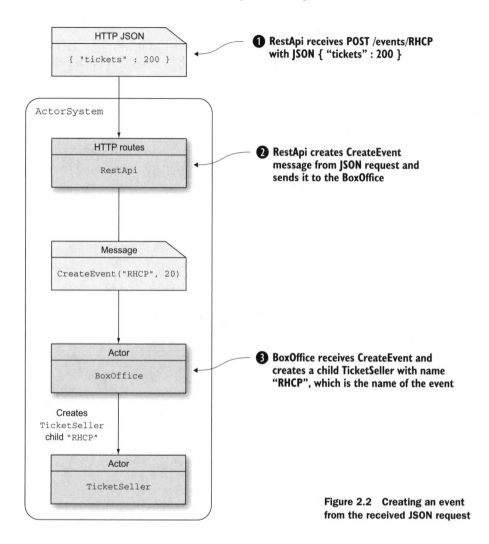

Figure 2.2   Creating an event from the received JSON request

The second service we discussed was the ability for a Customer to purchase a ticket (now that we have an Event). Figure 2.3 shows what should happen when such a ticket purchase request is received (as JSON).

Let's step back and start looking at the code as a whole. First up: the Main class, which starts everything up. The Main object is a simple Scala app that you can run just like any other Scala app. It's similar to a Java class with a main method. Before we get into the complete listing of the Main class, let's look at the most important expressions first, starting with the import statements in listing 2.11.

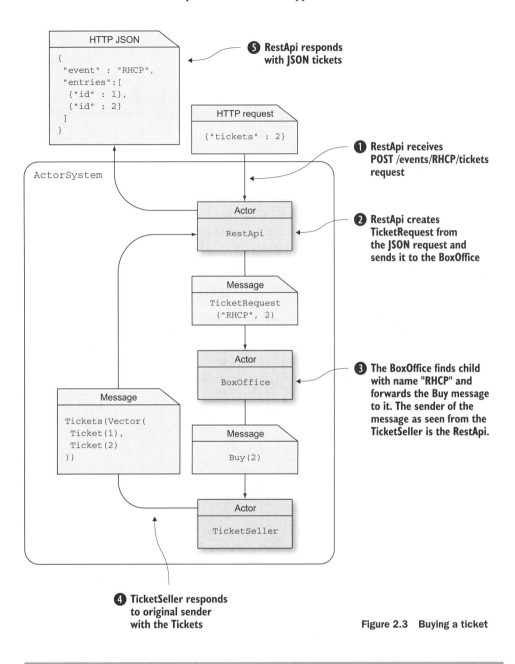

Figure 2.3 Buying a ticket

The diagram shows the following steps:

HTTP JSON
```
{
  "event" : "RHCP",
  "entries":[
    {"id" : 1},
    {"id" : 2}
  ]
}
```
❺ RestApi responds with JSON tickets

HTTP request
```
{"tickets" : 2}
```
❶ RestApi receives POST /events/RHCP/tickets request

ActorSystem

Actor
RestApi
❷ RestApi creates TicketRequest from the JSON request and sends it to the BoxOffice

Message
```
TicketRequest
  ("RHCP", 2)
```

Actor
BoxOffice
❸ The BoxOffice finds child with name "RHCP" and forwards the Buy message to it. The sender of the message as seen from the TicketSeller is the RestApi.

Message
```
Tickets(Vector(
  Ticket(1),
  Ticket(2)
))
```

Message
```
Buy(2)
```

Actor
TicketSeller

❹ TicketSeller responds to original sender with the Tickets

Listing 2.11 Main class import statements

```
import akka.actor.{ ActorSystem , Actor, Props }      Actor-related code is located
import akka.event.Logging                             in akka.actor package
import akka.util.Timeout                              Logging extension
                                                      Asking requires timeout
import akka.http.scaladsl.Http
                                                      HTTP-related code is located
                                                      in akka.http package
```

```
import akka.http.scaladsl.Http.ServerBinding
import akka.http.scaladsl.server.Directives._
import akka.stream.ActorMaterializer

import com.typesafe.config.{ Config, ConfigFactory }
```
Imports typesafe configuration library

The `Main` class needs to create an `ActorSystem` first. It then creates the `RestApi`, gets the HTTP extension, and binds the `RestApi` routes to the HTTP extension. How this is done is shown a little later. Akka uses so-called *extensions* for many supporting tools, as you'll see in the rest of this book; `Http` and `Logging` are the first examples of these.

We don't want to hardcode configuration parameters like the host and port that the server should listen to, so we use the *Typesafe Config Library* to configure this (chapter 7 goes into the details of using this configuration library).

The following listing shows the essential expressions to start the `ActorSystem` and the `HTTP` extension, and get the `RestApi` routes to bind to HTTP, which is the responsibility of the `Main` object.

Listing 2.12   Starting the HTTP server

```
object Main extends App
    with RequestTimeout {
  val config = ConfigFactory.load()
  val host = config.getString("http.host")
  val port = config.getInt("http.port")

  implicit val system = ActorSystem()
  implicit val ec = system.dispatcher

  val api = new RestApi(system, requestTimeout(config)).routes

  implicit val materializer = ActorMaterializer()
  val bindingFuture: Future[ServerBinding] =
    Http().bindAndHandle(api, host, port)
}
```
Gets the host and a port from the configuration

bindAndHandle is asynchronous and requires an implicit ExecutionContext.

RestApi provides the HTTP routes

Starts HTTP server with the RestAPI routes

The `Main` object extends `App` like any Scala application.

The `ActorSystem` is *active* immediately after it has been created, starting any thread pools as required.

`Http()` returns the HTTP extension. `bindAndHandle` binds the routes defined in the `RestApi` to the HTTP server. `bindAndHandle` is an asynchronous method that returns a `Future` before it has completed. We'll gloss over the details of this for now and get back to it later (in chapter 5 on futures). The `Main` app doesn't exit immediately, and the `ActorSystem` creates non-daemon threads and keeps running (until it's terminated).

The `RequestTimeout` trait is shown for completeness sake, which makes it possible for the `RestApi` to use the configured request timeout in akka-http.

Listing 2.13 The `Main` object

```
trait RequestTimeout {                                          Uses the default request
  import scala.concurrent.duration._                            timeout of akka-http
  def requestTimeout(config: Config): Timeout = {       ◁───    server configuration
    val t = config.getString("spray.can.server.request-timeout")
    val d = Duration(t)
    FiniteDuration(d.length, d.unit)
  }
}
```

Getting the request timeout is extracted into a `RequestTimeout` trait (which you can skip for now; don't worry if the code isn't immediately clear).

You really don't need to understand all the details of how the HTTP extension is making all of this possible yet because we'll cover them in detail later.

The actors in the app communicate with each other through messages. The messages that an actor can receive or send back on a request are bundled together in the actors' companion object. The `BoxOffice` messages are shown next.

Listing 2.14 `BoxOffice` messages

```
case class CreateEvent(name: String, tickets: Int)  ◁─── Message to create an event
case class GetEvent(name: String)                   ◁─── Message to get an event
case object GetEvents                               ◁─── Message to request all events
case class GetTickets(event: String, tickets: Int) ◁─── Message to get tickets for an event
case class CancelEvent(name: String)                ◁─── Message to cancel the event

case class Event(name: String, tickets: Int)        ◁─── Message describing the event
case class Events(events: Vector[Event])            ◁─── Message to describe a list of events

sealed trait EventResponse                          ◁─── Message response to CreateEvent
case class EventCreated(event: Event) extends EventResponse    ◁─┐
case object EventExists extends EventResponse                    │
                                                    Message to indicate the
                                                    event was created
     Message to indicate that
     the event already exists
```

The `TicketSeller` sends or receives the messages shown next.

Listing 2.15 `TicketSeller` messages

```
Message to add tickets
to the TicketSeller

  └─▷ case class Add(tickets: Vector[Ticket])
      case class Buy(tickets: Int)             ◁─┘ Message to buy tickets
                                                   from the TicketSeller
A ticket ─▷ case class Ticket(id: Int)
      case class Tickets(event: String,             A list of tickets
                                                     for an event
                  entries: Vector[Ticket] = Vector.empty[Ticket])  ◁─┘
```

```
      case object GetEvent
      case object Cancel
```

A message containing the
remaining tickets for the event

A message to
cancel the event

As is typical of REST apps, we have an interface that revolves around the lifecycles of
the core entities: Events and Tickets. All of these messages are immutable (since they
are case classes or objects). The Actors have to be designed to get all the information
they need, and produce all that is needed if they enlist any collaborators. This lends
itself well to REST. In the next sections, we'll look at the Actors in more detail. We'll
start from the TicketSeller and work our way up.

2.2.2 The actor that handles the sale: TicketSeller

The TicketSeller is created by the BoxOffice and simply keeps a list of tickets. Every
time tickets are requested, it takes the number of requested tickets off the list. The following listing shows the code for the TicketSeller.

Listing 2.16 `TicketSeller` implementation

The list of
tickets

Adds the new tickets to the
existing list of tickets when
Tickets message is received

Returns an
event
containing
the number
of tickets
left when
GetEvent is
received

```
class TicketSeller(event: String) extends Actor {
  import TicketSeller._

  var tickets = Vector.empty[Ticket]

  def receive = {
    case Add(newTickets) => tickets = tickets ++ newTickets
    case Buy(nrOfTickets) =>
      val entries = tickets.take(nrOfTickets).toVector
      if(entries.size >= nrOfTickets) {
        sender() ! Tickets(event, entries)
        tickets = tickets.drop(nrOfTickets)
      } else sender() ! Tickets(event)
    case GetEvent => sender() ! Some(BoxOffice.Event(event, tickets.size))
    case Cancel =>
      sender() ! Some(BoxOffice.Event(event, tickets.size))
      self ! PoisonPill
  }
}
```

Takes a number of tickets off the list and responds with a Tickets
message containing the tickets if there are enough tickets
available; otherwise, responds with an empty Tickets message

The TicketSeller keeps track of the available tickets using an immutable list. A mutable list could have been safe as well because it's only available within the actor and
therefore never accessed from more than one thread at any given moment.

Still, you should prefer immutable lists. You might forget that it is mutable when
you return a part of the list or the entire list to another actor. For instance, look at the
take method that we use to get the first couple of tickets off the list. On a mutable list
(scala.collection.mutable.ListBuffer), take returns a list of the same type
(ListBuffer), which is obviously mutable.

In the next section we'll look at the BoxOffice actor.

2.2.3 The BoxOffice actor

The BoxOffice needs to create a TicketSeller child for every event and delegate the selling to the TicketSeller responsible for the requested event. The following listing shows how the BoxOffice responds to a CreateEvent message.

Listing 2.17 BoxOffice creates TicketSellers

```
def createTicketSeller(name: String) =
  context.actorOf(TicketSeller.props(name), name)       ◁──── Creates a TicketSeller using
                                                              its context, defined in a
                                                              separate method so it's easy
                                                              to override during testing
def receive = {
  case CreateEvent(name, tickets) =>
    def create() = {                                    ◁──── A local method that
      val eventTickets = createTicketSeller(name)             creates the ticket seller,
      val newTickets = (1 to tickets).map { ticketId =>       adds the tickets to the
        TicketSeller.Ticket(ticketId)                         ticket seller, and responds
      }.toVector                                              with EventCreated
      eventTickets ! TicketSeller.Add(newTickets)
      sender() ! EventCreated
    }
    context.child(name).fold(create())(_ => sender() ! EventExists)  ◁──┐

                                      Creates and responds with EventCreated,
                                               or responds with EventExists
```

The BoxOffice creates a TicketSeller for each event that doesn't exist yet. Notice that it uses its *context* instead of the actor system to create the actor; actors created with the context of another actor are its children and subject to the parent actor's supervision (much more about that in subsequent chapters). The BoxOffice builds up a list of numbered tickets for the event and sends these tickets to the TicketSeller. It also responds to the sender of the CreateEvent message that the Event has been created (the RestApi actor is the sender here). The following listing shows how the BoxOffice responds to the GetTickets message.

Listing 2.18 Getting tickets

```
                                      Sends an empty Tickets message if
                                      the ticket seller couldn't be found
case GetTickets(event, tickets) =>
  def notFound() = sender() ! TicketSeller.Tickets(event)   ◁──┘
  def buy(child: ActorRef) =
    child.forward(TicketSeller.Buy(tickets))
                                                              Executes notFound or buys
  context.child(event).fold(notFound())(buy)   ◁──           with the found TicketSeller
```

Buys from the found TicketSeller ⯈

The Buy message is forwarded to a TicketSeller. Forwarding makes it possible for the BoxOffice to send messages as a proxy for the RestApi. The response of the TicketSeller will go directly to the RestApi.

The next message, GetEvents, is more involved and will get you extra credit if you get it the first time. We're going to ask all TicketSellers for the number of tickets they have left and combine all the results into a list of events. This gets interesting because ask is an asynchronous operation, and at the same time we don't want to wait and block the BoxOffice from handling other requests.

The following code uses a concept called *futures*, which will be explained further in chapter 5, so if you feel like skipping it now that's fine. If you're up for a tough challenge though, let's look at the code!

Listing 2.19   Getting tickets

```
case GetEvents =>                                   A local method definition for
  import akka.pattern.ask                           asking all TicketSellers about
  import akka.pattern.pipe                           the events they sell tickets for

  def getEvents = context.children.map { child =>
    self.ask(GetEvent(child.path.name)).mapTo[Option[Event]]
  }
  def convertToEvents(f: Future[Iterable[Option[Event]]]) =
    f.map(_.flatten).map(l=> Events(l.toVector))

  pipe(convertToEvents(Future.sequence(getEvents))) to sender()
```

ask returns a Future, a type that will eventually contain a value. getEvents returns Iterable[Future[Option[Event]]]; sequence can turn this into a Future[Iterable[Option[Event]]]. pipe sends the value inside the Future to an actor the moment it's complete, in this case the sender of the GetEvents message, the RestApi.

We're going to ask all TicketSellers. Asking GetEvent returns an Option[Event], so when mapping over all TicketSellers we'll end up with an Iterable[Option[Event]]. This method flattens the Iterable[Option[Event]] into a Iterable[Event], leaving out all the empty Option results. The Iterable is transformed into an Events message.

Right now we'll skim over this example and just look at the concepts. What's happening here is that an ask method returns immediately with a *future*. A future is a value that's going to be available at some point in the future (hence the name). Instead of waiting for the response value (the event containing the number of tickets left), we get a future reference (which you could read as "use for future reference"). We never read the value directly, but instead we define what should happen once the value becomes available. We can even combine a list of future values into one list of values and describe what should happen with this list once all of the asynchronous operations complete.

The code finally sends an Events message back to the sender once all responses have been handled, by using another pattern, pipe, which makes it easier to eventually send the values inside futures to actors.

Don't worry if this isn't immediately clear; we have a whole chapter devoted to this subject. We're just trying to get you curious about this awesome feature—check out chapter 5 on futures if you can't wait to find out how these nonblocking asynchronous operations work.

That concludes the salient details of the BoxOffice. We have one actor left in the app, which will be handled in the next section: the RestApi.

2.2.4   *RestApi*

The RestApi uses the Akka HTTP routing DSL, which will be covered in detail in chapter 12. Services interfaces, as they grow, need more sophisticated routing of requests. Since we're really just creating an Event and then selling the Tickets to it, our routing requirements are few at this point. The RestApi defines a couple of classes that it uses to convert from and to JSON, shown next.

Listing 2.20   Event messages used in the RestApi

```
case class EventDescription(tickets: Int) {        ◁────  Message containing the initial
  require(tickets > 0)                                     number of tickets for the event
}

case class TicketRequest(tickets: Int) {           ◁────  Message containing the
  require(tickets > 0)                                     required number of tickets
}

case class Error(message: String)          ◁────  Messages containing an error
```

Let's look at the details of doing simple request routing in the following listings. First, the RestApi needs to handle a POST request to create an Event.

Listing 2.21   Event route definition

```
def eventRoute =
  pathPrefix("events" / Segment) { event =>
    pathEndOrSingleSlash {                              Creates event using
      post {                                            createEvent method that
        // POST /events/:event                          calls BoxOffice actor
        entity(as[EventDescription]) { ed =>
          onSuccess(createEvent(event, ed.tickets)) {   ◁
            BoxOffice.EventCreated(event) => complete(Created, event)
            case BoxOffice.EventExists =>
                    val err = Error(s"$event event exists already.")
                    complete(BadRequest, err)          ◁
          }
        }
      } ~
      get {
        // GET /events/:event
        onSuccess(getEvent(event)) {
          _.fold(complete(NotFound))(e => complete(OK, e))
        }
      } ~
      delete {
        // DELETE /events/:event
        onSuccess(cancelEvent(event)) {
          _.fold(complete(NotFound))(e => complete(OK, e))
        }
      }
    }
  }
```

Completes request with 201 Created when result is successful

Completes request with 400 BadRequest if event could not be created

The route uses a BoxOfficeApi trait, which has methods that wrap the interaction with the BoxOffice actor so that the route DSL code stays nice and clean, shown next.

Listing 2.22   BoxOffice API to wrap all interactions with the BoxOffice actor

```
trait BoxOfficeApi {
  import BoxOffice._

  def createBoxOffice(): ActorRef

  implicit def executionContext: ExecutionContext
  implicit def requestTimeout: Timeout

  lazy val boxOffice = createBoxOffice()

  def createEvent(event: String, nrOfTickets: Int) =
    boxOffice.ask(CreateEvent(event, nrOfTickets))
      .mapTo[EventResponse]

  def getEvents() =
    boxOffice.ask(GetEvents).mapTo[Events]

  def getEvent(event: String) =
    boxOffice.ask(GetEvent(event))
      .mapTo[Option[Event]]

  def cancelEvent(event: String) =
    boxOffice.ask(CancelEvent(event))
      .mapTo[Option[Event]]

  def requestTickets(event: String, tickets: Int) =
    boxOffice.ask(GetTickets(event, tickets))
      .mapTo[TicketSeller.Tickets]
}
```

The RestApi implements the createBoxOffice method to create a BoxOffice child actor. The following code shows a snippet of the DSL that's used to sell the tickets.

Listing 2.23   Ticket route definition

```
def ticketsRoute =
  pathPrefix("events" / Segment / "tickets") { event =>        Unmarshalls JSON
    post {                                                      tickets request
      pathEndOrSingleSlash {                                    into TicketRequest
        // POST /events/:event/tickets                          case class
        entity(as[TicketRequest]) { request =>              ◄──
          onSuccess(requestTickets(event, request.tickets)) { tickets =>
            if(tickets.entries.isEmpty) complete(NotFound)   ◄──
            else complete(Created, tickets)               ◄──────      Responds with
          }                                                            404 Not Found
        }                                                              if the tickets
      }                                                                aren't available
    }
  }              Responds with 201 Created,
                 marshalling the tickets to a
                 JSON entity
```

The messages are automatically converted back to JSON. You can find the details of how this is done in chapter 12. That concludes all the actors in the first iteration of the GoTicks.com application. If you followed along or even tried to build this yourself, congratulations! You've just seen how to build your first fully asynchronous Akka actor app with a fully functional REST API. While the app itself is rather trivial, we've already made it so that the processing is fully concurrent, and the actual selling of tickets is both scalable (because it's already concurrent) and fault tolerant (you'll see much more on that). This example also showed how you can do asynchronous processing within the synchronous request/response paradigm of the HTTP world. We hope that you've found that it takes only a few lines of code to build this app. Compare that to a more traditional toolkit or framework and we're sure that you're pleasantly surprised to see how little code was needed. For a little cherry on the top, we'll show you what we need to do to deploy this minimal app to the cloud. We'll get this app running on Heroku.com in the next section.

2.3 Into the cloud

Heroku.com is a popular cloud provider that has support for Scala applications, and free instances that you can play with. In this section we'll show you how easy it is to get the GoTicks.com app up and running on Heroku. We expect that you've already installed the Heroku toolbelt (see https://toolbelt.heroku.com/). If not, please refer to the Heroku website (https://devcenter.heroku.com/articles/heroku-command) for how to install it. You'll also need to sign up for an account on heroku.com. Visit their site—the signup speaks for itself. In the next section, we'll first create an app on heroku.com. After that we'll deploy it and run it.

2.3.1 Create the app on Heroku

First, log in to your Heroku account and create a new Heroku app that will host our GoTicks.com app. Execute the following commands in the chapter-up-and-running directory.

Listing 2.24 Create the app on Heroku

```
heroku login
heroku create

Creating damp-bayou-9575... done,
stack is cedar
http://damp-bayou-9575.herokuapp.com/
|
git@heroku.com:damp-bayou-9575.git
```

You should see something like the response shown in the listing.

We need to add a couple of things to our project so Heroku understands how to build our code. First the project/plugins.sbt file.

Listing 2.25 `BoxOffice` API to wrap all interactions with the `BoxOffice` actor

Uses assembly to create one big JAR file, needed for deployment to Heroku

```
resolvers += Classpaths.typesafeReleases              ←───  Uses the Typesafe
                                                            Releases repository

addSbtPlugin("com.eed3si9n" % "sbt-assembly" % "0.13.0")    Uses the packager to
                                                            create startup scripts
addSbtPlugin("com.typesafe.sbt" % "sbt-native-             for running the app
    packager" % "1.0.0")              ←──────────────       on Heroku
```

This is a pretty minor intrusion to build one fat JAR and build a native script (in the case of Heroku, this is a Bash shell script; Heroku runs on Ubuntu Linux). We also need a *Procfile* right under the chapter-up-and-running directory, which tells Heroku that our app should be run on a *web dyno*—one of the types of processes Heroku runs on its virtual dyno manifold. The Procfile is shown next.

Listing 2.26 Heroku Procfile

```
web: target/universal/stage/bin/goticks
```

It specifies that Heroku should run the Bash script that the `sbt-native-packager` plugin has built. Let's first test to see if everything runs locally:

```
sbt clean compile stage              ←──  Cleans target, then builds our
                                          archive but doesn't deploy
heroku local                                              ←──  Tells Heroku to
23:30:11 web.1 | started with pid 19504                       grab archive
23:30:12 web.1 | INFO  [Slf4jLogger]: Slf4jLogger started    and start up
23:30:12 web.1 | REST interface bound to /0:0:0:0:0:0:0:0:5000  our app locally
23:30:12 web.1 | INFO  [HttpListener]: Bound to /0.0.0.0:5000
```

Heroku manages to load the app; we have a PID.

This is all that's required to prepare an application for deployment on Heroku. It lets us go through the whole cycle locally so that we're working at maximum speed while getting our first deploy done. Once we actually deploy to Heroku, you'll see that all subsequent pushes to the cloud instances are accomplished directly through Git by simply pushing the desired version of the source to our remote instance. The deployment of the app to the Heroku cloud instance is described in the next section.

2.3.2 *Deploy and run on Heroku*

We've just verified that we could locally run the app with `heroku local`. We created a new app on Heroku with `heroku create`. This command also added a `git remote` with the name *heroku* to the Git configuration. All we have to do now is make sure all changes are committed locally to the Git repository. After that, push the code to Heroku with the following command:

```
git subtree push --prefix chapter-up-and-running heroku master ⟵── Pushes to Heroku
                                                                    to deploy
----> Scala app detected                         ⟵─────────┐
-----> Installing OpenJDK 1.6...                            │
.... // resolving downloads, downloading dependencies      Just as before, Heroku
....                                                        now builds app, this
-----> Compiled slug size is 43.1MB                        time on remote instance
-----> Launching... done,
  v1 http://damp-bayou-9575.herokuapp.com deployed to Heroku

To git@heroku.com:damp-bayou-9575.git
* [new branch] master -> master           ⟵──────────┐  Finally, like any other Git push,
                                                         success: master now on remote
```

This assumes that you committed any changes to your master branch and that the
project resides in the root of the Git repo. Heroku hooks into the Git push process
and identifies the code as a Scala app. It downloads all dependencies on the cloud,
compiles the code, and starts the application. Finally, you should see something like
the output shown in the listing.

Using the project akka-in-action from GitHub

Normally, you'd use `git push heroku master` to deploy to Heroku. When you're using
our project akka-in-action from GitHub, this command won't work, because the application
isn't in the root of the Git repo. To make this work, you need to tell Heroku that
it should use a subtree, as follows:

```
git subtree push --prefix chapter-up-and-running heroku master
```

For more info see the README.md file within the chapter-up-and-running directory.

This shows the console on creation of the app; note that Heroku figured out that our
app is a Scala app, so it installed the OpenJDK, and then compiled and launched the
source in the instance. The app is now deployed and started on Heroku. You can now
use `httpie` again to test the app on Heroku.

Listing 2.27 Test Heroku instance with `httpie`

```
http POST damp-bayou-9575.herokuapp.com/events/RHCP tickets:=250
http POST damp-bayou-9575.herokuapp.com/events/RHCP/tickets tickets:=4
```

These commands should result in the same responses we saw before (see listing 2.10).
Congratulations, you just deployed your first Akka app to Heroku! With that, we con-
clude this first iteration of the GoTicks.com app. Now that the app is deployed on
Heroku, you can call it from anywhere.

2.4   *Summary*

In this chapter you've seen how little is necessary to build a fully functional REST service out of actors. All interactions were asynchronous. The service performed as expected when we tested it with the `httpie` command-line tool.

We even deployed our app (via Heroku.com) into the cloud! We hope you got excited about what a quick, out-of-the-box experience Akka offers. The GoTicks.com app isn't ready for production yet. There's no persistent storage for tickets. We've deployed to Heroku, but web dynos can be replaced at any time, so only storing the tickets in memory won't work in real life. The app is scaled up but has not scaled out yet to multiple nodes.

But we promise to look into those topics in later chapters, where we'll gradually get closer to a real-world system. In the next chapter, we'll look at how to test actor systems.

Test-driven development with actors

In this chapter

- Unit testing actors synchronously
- Unit testing actors asynchronously
- Unit testing actor messaging patterns

It's amusing to think back to when TDD first appeared on the scene—the primary objection was that tests took too long, and thus held up development. Though you rarely hear that today, there's a vast difference in the testing load both between different stacks, and through different phases (such as unit versus integration tests). Everyone has a rapid, fluid experience on the unit side, when testing is confined to a single component. Tests that involve collaborators are where ease and speed generally evaporate rapidly. Actors provide an interesting solution to this problem for the following reasons:

- Actors are a more direct match for tests because they embody behavior (and almost all TDD has at least some BDD—behavior-driven development—in it).
- Too often, regular unit tests test only the interface, or have to test the interface and functionality separately.

- Actors are built on messaging, which has huge advantages for testing, because you can easily simulate behaviors by sending messages.

Before we start testing (and coding), we'll take several of the concepts from the previous chapter and show their expression in code, introducing the Actor API for creating actors, and then sending and receiving messages. We'll cover important details about how actors are actually run and some rules you have to follow to prevent problems. After that, we'll move on to the implementation of some common scenarios, taking a test-driven approach to writing actors, immediately verifying that the code does what we expect. At each step along the way, we'll focus first on the goal that we'll try to achieve with the code (one of the main points of TDD). Next, we'll write a test specification for the `Actor`, which will start the development of the code (TDD/test-first style). Then we'll write enough code to make the test pass, and repeat. Rules that need to be followed to prevent accidentally sharing state will be discovered as we go, as well as some of the details of how actors work in Akka that have an impact on test development.

3.1   *Testing actors*

First, we'll work on how to test sending and receiving messages, in fire-and-forget style (one-way) followed by request-response style (two-way) interaction. We'll use the *ScalaTest* unit-testing framework that's also used to test Akka itself. ScalaTest is an xUnit-style testing framework; if you're not familiar with it and would like to know more about it, please visit www.scalatest.org/ for more information. The ScalaTest framework is designed for readability, so it should be easy to read and follow the test without much introduction. On first exposure, testing `Actors` is more difficult than testing normal objects for a couple of reasons:

- *Timing*—Sending messages is asynchronous, so it's difficult to know when to assert expected values in the unit test.
- *Asynchronicity*—Actors are meant to be run in parallel on several threads. Multi-threaded tests are more difficult than single-threaded tests and require concurrency primitives like locks, latches, and barriers to synchronize results from various actors. This is exactly the kind of thing you want to get further away from. Incorrect usage of just one barrier can block a unit test, which in turn halts the execution of a full test suite.
- *Statelessness*—An actor hides its internal state and doesn't allow access to this state. Access should only be possible through the `ActorRef`. Calling a method on an actor and checking its state, which is something you'd like to be able to do when unit testing, is prevented by design.
- *Collaboration/Integration*—If you wanted to do an integration test of a couple of actors, you'd need to eavesdrop on the actors to assert that the messages have the expected values. It's not immediately clear how this can be done.

Luckily, Akka provides the akka-testkit module. This module contains a number of testing tools that makes testing actors a lot easier. The test kit module makes a couple of different types of tests possible:

- *Single-threaded unit testing*—An actor instance is normally not accessible directly. The test kit provides a `TestActorRef` that allows access to the underlying actor instance. This makes it possible to test the actor instance directly by calling the methods that you've defined, or even call the receive function in a single threaded environment, just as you're used to when testing normal objects.
- *Multithreaded unit testing*—The test kit module provides the `TestKit` and `TestProbe` classes, which make it possible to receive replies from actors, inspect messages, and set timing bounds for particular messages to arrive. `TestKit` has methods to assert expected messages. Actors are run using a normal dispatcher in a multithreaded environment.
- *Multiple JVM testing*—Akka also provides tools for testing multiple JVMs, which comes in handy when you want to test remote actor systems. Multi-JVM testing will be discussed in chapter 6.

`TestKit` has `TestActorRef` extending the `LocalActorRef` class and sets the dispatcher to a `CallingThreadDispatcher` that's built for testing only. (It invokes the actors on the calling thread instead of on a separate thread.) This provides one of the key junction points for advancing the previously listed solutions.

Depending on your preference, you might use one of the styles more often. The option that's closest to actually running your code in production is the multithreaded style, testing with the `TestKit` class. We'll focus more on the multithreaded approach to testing, since this can show problems with the code that won't be apparent in a single-threaded environment. (You probably won't be surprised that we also prefer a classical unit testing approach over mocking.)

Before we start, we'll have to do a little preparation so that we don't repeat ourselves unnecessarily. Once an actor system is created, it's started and continues to run until it's stopped. In all our tests, we need to create actor systems and we have to stop them. To make life easier, let's build a small trait we can use for all the tests that makes sure that the system under test is automatically stopped when the unit test ends.

Listing 3.1 Stop the system after all tests are done

```
import org.scalatest.{ Suite, BeforeAndAfterAll }
import akka.testkit.TestKit                               Extends from the
                                                          BeforeAndAfterAll ScalaTest trait
trait StopSystemAfterAll extends BeforeAndAfterAll {  ◁
  this: TestKit with Suite =>                         ◁   This trait can only be used if it's mixed
  override protected def afterAll() {                     in with a test that uses the TestKit.
    super.afterAll()
    system.shutdown()        ◁                           Shuts down the system
  }                                                       provided by the TestKit after
}                                                         all tests have executed
```

We've placed this file in the directory src/test/scala/aia/testdriven, because all the test code should be placed within the src/test/scala directory, which is the root directory of the all the test code. We'll mixin this trait when we write our tests, so that the system is automatically shut down after all tests are executed. The TestKit exposes a system value, which can be accessed in the test to create actors and everything else you would like to do with the system.

In the next sections, we'll use the test kit module to test some common scenarios when working with actors, both in a single-threaded and in a multithreaded environment. There are only a few different ways for the actors to interact with each other. We'll explore the different options that are available and test the specific interaction with the test kit module.

3.2   *One-way messages*

Remember, we've left the land of "invoke a function and wait on the response," so the fact that our examples merely send one-way messages with tell is deliberate. Given this fire-and-forget style, we don't know when the message arrives at the actor, or even if it arrives, so how do we test this? What we'd like to do is send a message to an actor, and after sending the message, check that the actor has done the work it should've done. An actor that responds to messages should do something with a message and take some kind of action, like send a message to another actor, store some internal state, interact with another object, or interact with I/O. If the actor's behavior is completely invisible from the outside, we can only check if it handled the message without any errors, and we could try to look into the state of the actor with the TestActorRef. There are three variations that we'll look at:

- *SilentActor*—An actor's behavior is not directly observable from the outside; it might be an intermediate step that the actor takes to create some internal state. We want to test that the actor at least handled the message and didn't throw any exceptions. We want to be sure that the actor has finished. We want to test the internal state change.
- *SendingActor*—An actor sends a message to another actor (or possibly many actors) after it's done processing the received message. We'll treat the actor as a black box and inspect the message that's sent out in response to the message it received.
- *SideEffectingActor*—An actor receives a message and interacts with a normal object in some kind of way. After we send a message to the actor, we'd like to assert if the object was affected.

We'll write a test for each type of actor in this list that will illustrate the means of verifying results in tests you write.

3.2.1 SilentActor examples

Let's start with the `SilentActor`. Since it's our first test, let's briefly go through the use of `ScalaTest`.

Listing 3.2 First test for the silent actor type

Extends from TestKit and provides an actor system for testing

WordSpecLike provides easy-to-read DSL for testing in BDD style

```
class SilentActor01Test extends TestKit(ActorSystem("testsystem"))
  with WordSpecLike
  with MustMatchers
  with StopSystemAfterAll {

  "A Silent Actor" must {
    "change state when it receives a message, single threaded" in {
      //Write the test, first fail
      fail("not implemented yet")
    }
    "change state when it receives a message, multi-threaded" in {
      //Write the test, first fail
      fail("not implemented yet")
    }
  }
}
```

Makes sure the system is stopped after all tests

MustMatchers provides easy-to-read assertions

Write tests as textual specifications

Every "in" describes a specific test

This code is the basic skeleton that we need to start running a silent actor test. We use the `WordSpec` style of testing, which is BDD, since it makes it possible to write the test as a number of textual specifications, which will also be shown when the test is run (the tests are the behavior specification). In the preceding code, we create a specification for the silent actor type with a test that should, as it says, "change internal state when it receives a message." Right now, it always fails, since it's not implemented yet—as is expected in *red-green-refactor* style, where you first make sure the test fails (red), then implement the code to make it pass (green), after which you might refactor the code to make it nicer. In the following listing we define an `Actor` that does nothing, and will always fail the tests.

Listing 3.3 First failing implementation of the silent actor type

```
class SilentActor extends Actor {
  def receive = {
    case msg =>
  }
}
```

Swallows any message; doesn't keep any internal state

To run all the tests at once, run the command sbt test. But it's also possible to run only one test. To do this, start sbt in the interactive mode and run the testOnly command. In the next example, we run the test aia.testdriven.SilentActor01Test:

```
sbt
...
> testOnly aia.testdriven.SilentActor01Test
```

Now let's first write the test to send the silent actor a message and check that it changes its internal state. The SilentActor actor will have to be written for this test to pass, as well as its *companion* object (an object that has the same name as the actor). The companion object contains the message protocol; that is, all the messages that SilentActor supports, which is a nice way of grouping messages that are related to each other, as you'll see later. The following listing is a first pass at this.

Listing 3.4   Single-threaded test internal state

```
"change internal state when it receives a message, single" in {
  import SilentActor._                                           ◁——— Imports the messages

  val silentActor = TestActorRef[SilentActor]
  silentActor ! SilentMessage("whisper")
  silentActor.underlyingActor.state must (contain("whisper"))    ◁———
}
```
Gets the underlying actor and asserts the state

Creates a TestActorRef for single-threaded testing

This is the simplest version of the typical TDD scenario: trigger something and check for a state change. Now let's write the SilentActor actor. The next listing shows our first version of the actual actor implementation.

Listing 3.5   SilentActor implementation

```
object SilentActor {                              ◁——— A companion object that keeps
  case class SilentMessage(data: String)                related messages together
  case class GetState(receiver: ActorRef)
}
                                                  The message type that the
                                                  SilentActor can process
class SilentActor extends Actor {
  import SilentActor._
  var internalState = Vector[String]()

  def receive = {
    case SilentMessage(data) =>
      internalState = internalState :+ data      ◁——— State is kept in a vector; every
  }                                                    message is added to this vector

  def state = internalState                       ◁———
}
```
State method returns the built-up vector

Since the returned list is immutable, the test can't change the list and cause problems when asserting the expected result. It's completely safe to set/update the `internal-State` var, since the `Actor` is protected from multithreaded access. In general, it's good practice to prefer vars in combination with immutable data structures, instead of vals in combination with mutable data structures. (This prevents accidentally sharing mutable state if you send the internal state in some way to another actor.)

Now let's look at the multithreaded version of this test. As you'll see, we'll have to change the code for the actor a bit as well. Just like in the single-threaded version where we added a state method to make it possible to test the actor, we'll have to add some code to make the multithreaded version testable. The following listing shows how we make this work.

Listing 3.6 Multithreaded test of internal state

A companion object that keeps related messages together

```
    "change internal state when it receives a message, multi" in {
      import SilentActor._

      val silentActor = system.actorOf(Props[SilentActor], "s3")
      silentActor ! SilentMessage("whisper1")
      silentActor ! SilentMessage("whisper2")
      silentActor ! GetState(testActor)
      expectMsg(Vector("whisper1", "whisper2"))
    }
```

Test system is used to create an actor

Message is added to the companion to get state

Used to check what message(s) have been sent to the testActor

The multithreaded test uses the `ActorSystem` that's part of the `TestKit` to create a `SilentActor` actor.

An actor is always created from a `Props` object. The `Props` object describes how the actor should be created. The simplest way to create a `Props` is to create it with the actor type as its type argument, in this case `Props[SilentActor]`. A `Props` created this way will eventually create the actor using its default constructor.

Since we now can't just access the actor instance when using the multithreaded actor system, we'll have to come up with another way to see state change. For this a `GetState` message is added, which takes an `ActorRef`. The `TestKit` has a `testActor`, which you can use to receive messages that you expect. The `GetState` method we added is so we can have our `SilentActor` send its internal state there. That way we can call the `expectMsg` method, which expects one message to be sent to the `testActor` and asserts the message; in this case it's a `Vector` with all the data fields in it.

Timeout settings for the expectMsg* methods

The `TestKit` has several versions of the `expectMsg` and other methods for asserting messages. All of these methods expect a message within a certain amount of time; otherwise, they time out and throw an exception. The timeout has a default value that can be set in the configuration using the `akka.test.single-expect-default` key.

(continued)
A *dilation factor* is used to calculate the actual time that should be used for the time-out (it's normally set to 1, which means the timeout is not dilated). Its purpose is to provide a means of leveling machines that can have vastly different computing capabilities. On a slower machine, we should be prepared to wait a bit longer (it's common for developers to run tests on their fast workstations, and then commit and have slower continuous integration servers fail). Each machine can be configured with the factor needed to achieve a successful test run (check out chapter 7 for more details on configuration). The max timeout can also be set on the method directly, but it's better to just use the configured values, and change the values across tests in the configuration if necessary.

Now all we need is the code for the silent actor that can also process GetState messages.

Listing 3.7 `SilentActor` implementation

```
object SilentActor {
  case class SilentMessage(data: String)
  case class GetState(receiver: ActorRef)          GetState message is added
}                                                   for testing purposes

class SilentActor extends Actor {
  import SilentActor._
  var internalState = Vector[String]()

  def receive = {
    case SilentMessage(data) =>
      internalState = internalState :+ data
    case GetState(receiver) => receiver ! internalState   Internal state is
  }                                                        sent to ActorRef in
}                                                          GetState message
```

The internal state is sent back to the ActorRef in the GetState message, which in this case will be the testActor. Since the internal state is an immutable Vector, this is completely safe. This is it for the SilentActor types: single- and multithreaded variants. Using these approaches, we can construct tests that are familiar to most programmers: state changes can be inspected and asserted upon by leveraging a few tools in the TestKit.

3.2.2 *SendingActor example*

It's common for an actor to take an ActorRef through a props method, which it will use at a later stage to send messages to. In this example we'll build a SendingActor that sorts lists of events and sends the sorted lists to a receiver actor.

Listing 3.8 Sending actor test

```
"A Sending Actor" must {
  "send a message to another actor when it has finished processing" in {
    import SendingActor._
    val props = SendingActor.props(testActor)          ◄──────┐
    val sendingActor = system.actorOf(props, "sendingActor")  │

    val size = 1000                              Receiver is passed to
    val maxInclusive = 100000                    props method that
                                                 creates Props; in the test
    def randomEvents() = (0 until size).map{ _ =>  we pass in a testActor
      Event(Random.nextInt(maxInclusive))
    }.toVector

    val unsorted = randomEvents()        ◄──┐  Randomized
    val sortEvents = SortEvents(unsorted)   │  unsorted list of
    sendingActor ! sortEvents               │  events is created

    expectMsgPF() {
      case SortedEvents(events) =>        ◄──┐  testActor should
        events.size must be(size)           │  receive a sorted
        unsorted.sortBy(_.id) must be(events)│  Vector of Events
    }
  }
}
```

A `SortEvents` message is sent to the `SendingActor`. The `SortEvents` message contains events that must be sorted. The `SendingActor` should sort the events and send a `SortedEvents` message to a receiver actor. In the test we pass in the `testActor` instead of a real actor that would process the sorted events, which is easily done, since the receiver is just an `ActorRef`. Since the `SortEvents` message contains a random vector of events, we can't use an `expectMsg(msg)`; we can't formulate an exact match for it. In this case we use `expectMsgPF`, which takes a partial function just like the receive of the actor. Here we match the message that was sent to the `testActor`, which should be a `SortedEvents` message containing a sorted vector of `Events`. If we run the test now, it will fail because we haven't implemented the message protocol in `SendingActor`. Let's do that now.

Listing 3.9 `SendingActor` implementation

```
                                               receiver is passed through the Props to
                                               the constructor of the SendingActor; in
object SendingActor {                          the test we pass in a testActor.
  def props(receiver: ActorRef) =
    Props(new SendingActor(receiver))   ◄──┘
  case class Event(id: Long)                   The SortedEvent message
  case class SortEvents(unsorted: Vector[Event]) ◄── is sent to the SendingActor.
  case class SortedEvents(sorted: Vector[Event])
}                                                 ◄──┐ The SortedEvent message
                                                     is sent to the receiver
class SendingActor(receiver: ActorRef) extends Actor { after the SendingActor
  import SendingActor._                               has sorted it.
  def receive = {
    case SortEvents(unsorted) =>                       SortEvents and
      receiver ! SortedEvents(unsorted.sortBy(_.id))   SortedEvents both use
                                                       an immutable Vector.
```

We once again create a companion that contains the message protocol. It also contains a props method that creates the Props for the actor. In this case the actor needs to be passed the actor reference of the receiver, so another variation of Props is used.

Calling Props(arg) translates to calling the Props.apply method, which takes a by-name creator parameter. By-name parameters are evaluated when they're referenced for the first time, so new SendingActor(receiver) is only executed once Akka needs to create it. Creating the Props in the companion object has the benefit that you can't refer to an actor's internals, in the case where you would need to create an actor from an actor. Using something internal to the actor from the Props could lead to race conditions, or it could cause serialization issues if the Props itself were used inside a message that needs to be sent across the network. We'll use this recommended practice for creating props as we go along.

The SendingActor sorts the unsorted Vector using the sortBy method, which creates a sorted copy of the vector, which can be safely shared. The SortedEvents is sent along to the receiver. Once again, we take advantage of the immutable property of case classes and of the immutable Vector data structure.

Let's look at some variations of the SendingActor type. Table 3.1 shows some common variations on the theme.

Table 3.1   **SendingActor types**

Actor	Description
MutatingCopyActor	The actor creates a mutated copy and sends the copy to the next actor, which is the case described in this section.
ForwardingActor	The actor forwards the message it receives; it doesn't change it at all.
TransformingActor	The actor creates a different type of message from the message that it receives.
FilteringActor	The actor forwards some messages it receives and discards others.
SequencingActor	The actor creates many messages based on one message it receives and sends the new messages one after the other to another actor.

The MutatingCopyActor, ForwardingActor, and TransformingActor can all be tested in the same way. We can pass in a testActor as the next actor to receive messages and use expectMsg or expectMsgPF to inspect the messages. The FilteringActor is different in that it addresses the question of how we can assert that some messages were *not* passed through. The SequencingActor needs a similar approach. How can we assert that we received the correct number of messages? The next test will show you how.

Let's write a test for the FilteringActor. The FilteringActor that we'll build should filter out duplicate events. It will keep a list of the last messages that it has received, and will check each incoming message against this list to find duplicates. (This is comparable to the typical elements of mocking frameworks that allow you to assert on invocations, counts of invocations, and absence.)

Listing 3.10 `FilteringActor test`

```
"filter out particular messages" in {
  import FilteringActor._
  val props = FilteringActor.props(testActor, 5)
  val filter = system.actorOf(props, "filter-1")
  filter ! Event(1)                                    ◁——  Sends a couple of events,
  filter ! Event(2)                                          including duplicates
  filter ! Event(1)
  filter ! Event(3)
  filter ! Event(1)
  filter ! Event(4)
  filter ! Event(5)
  filter ! Event(5)                                         Receives messages until
  filter ! Event(6)                                         the case statement
  val eventIds = receiveWhile() {              ◁——          doesn't match anymore
    case Event(id) if id <= 5 => id
  }
  eventIds must be(List(1, 2, 3, 4, 5))       ◁——          Asserts that the duplicates
  expectMsg(Event(6))                                       aren't in the result
}
```

The test uses a `receiveWhile` method to collect the messages that the `testActor` receives until the `case` statement doesn't match. In the test, the `Event(6)` doesn't match the pattern in the `case` statement, which defines that all `Event`s with an ID less than or equal to 5 will be matched, popping us out of the `while` loop. The `receiveWhile` method returns the collected items as they're returned in the partial function as a list. Now let's write the `FilteringActor` that will guarantee this part of the specification.

Listing 3.11 `FilteringActor implementation`

```
object FilteringActor {
  def props(nextActor: ActorRef, bufferSize: Int) =
    Props(new FilteringActor(nextActor, bufferSize))
  case class Event(id: Long)
}                                                        Max size for the
                                                         buffer is passed
                                                         into constructor
class FilteringActor(nextActor: ActorRef,
                     bufferSize: Int) extends Actor {  ◁
  import FilteringActor._
  var lastMessages = Vector[Event]()
  def receive = {
    case msg: Event =>
      if (!lastMessages.contains(msg)) {                 Event is sent to
        lastMessages = lastMessages :+ msg               next actor if it's not
        nextActor ! msg                      ◁——         found in the buffer
        if (lastMessages.size > bufferSize) {
          // discard the oldest
          lastMessages = lastMessages.tail   ◁——         Oldest event in the buffer
        }                                                is discarded when max
      }                                                  buffer size is reached
  }
}
```

Vector of last messages is kept ▷

This `FilteringActor` keeps a buffer of the last messages that it received in a `Vector` and adds every received message to that buffer if it doesn't already exist in the list. Only messages that aren't in the buffer are sent to the `nextActor`. The oldest message that was received is discarded when a max `bufferSize` is reached to prevent the `last-Messages` list from growing too large and possibly causing us to run out of space.

The `receiveWhile` method can also be used for testing a `SequencingActor`; you could assert that the sequence of messages that's caused by a particular event is as expected. Two methods for asserting messages that might come in handy when you need to assert a number of messages are `ignoreMsg` and `expectNoMsg`. `ignoreMsg` takes a partial function just like the `expectMsgPF` method, only instead of asserting the message, it ignores any message that matches the pattern. This can come in handy if you're not interested in many messages, but only want to assert that particular messages have been sent to the `testActor`. `expectNoMsg` asserts that no message has been sent to the `testActor` for a certain amount of time, which we could have also used in between the sending of duplicate messages in the `FilteringActor` test. The test in the next listing shows an example of using `expectNoMsg`.

Listing 3.12   `FilteringActor` implementation

```
"filter out particular messages using expectNoMsg" in {
  import FilteringActor._
  val props = FilteringActor.props(testActor, 5)
  val filter = system.actorOf(props, "filter-2")
  filter ! Event(1)
  filter ! Event(2)
  expectMsg(Event(1))
  expectMsg(Event(2))
  filter ! Event(1)
  expectNoMsg
  filter ! Event(3)
  expectMsg(Event(3))
  filter ! Event(1)
  expectNoMsg
  filter ! Event(4)
  filter ! Event(5)
  filter ! Event(5)
  expectMsg(Event(4))
  expectMsg(Event(5))
  expectNoMsg()
}
```

Since `expectNoMsg` has to wait for a timeout to be sure that no message was received, this test will run more slowly.

As you've seen, TestKit provides a `testActor` that can receive messages, which we can assert with `expectMsg` and other methods. A `TestKit` has only one `testActor`, and since `TestKit` is a class that you need to extend, how would you test an actor that sends messages to more than one actor? The answer is the `TestProbe` class. The `TestProbe` class is much like `TestKit`, only you can use this class without having to extend from it. Simply create a `TestProbe` with `TestProbe()` and start using it. `TestProbe` will be used often in the tests that we'll write in this book.

3.2.3 *SideEffectingActor example*

The next listing shows a very simple `Greeter` actor that prints a greeting according to the message it receives. (It's the actor-based version of a "Hello World" example.)

Listing 3.13 The `Greeter` actor

```
import akka.actor.{ActorLogging, Actor}

case class Greeting(message: String)

class Greeter extends Actor with ActorLogging {          Prints the
  def receive = {                                        greeting it
    case Greeting(message) => log.info("Hello {}!", message)   receives
  }
}
```

The `Greeter` does just one thing: it receives a message and outputs it to the console. The `SideEffectingActor` allows us to test scenarios such as these: where the effect of the action isn't directly accessible. Though many cases fit this description, this next listing sufficiently illustrates the final means of testing for an expected result.

Listing 3.14 Testing `HelloWorld`

```
import Greeter01Test._

class Greeter01Test extends TestKit(testSystem)          Uses the testSystem
  with WordSpecLike                                      from the
  with StopSystemAfterAll {                              GreeterOlTest object

  "The Greeter" must {
    "say Hello World! when a Greeting("World") is sent to it" in {
      val dispatcherId = CallingThreadDispatcher.Id
      val props = Props[Greeter].withDispatcher(dispatcherId)
      val greeter = system.actorOf(props)
      EventFilter.info(message = "Hello World!",
        occurrences = 1).intercept {                     Intercepts the log messages
          greeter ! Greeting("World")                    that were logged
        }
    }
  }
}

object Greeter01Test {                                   Creates a system with a
  val testSystem = {                                     configuration that attaches
    val config = ConfigFactory.parseString(              a test event listener
      """
        akka.loggers = [akka.testkit.TestEventListener]
      """)
    ActorSystem("testsystem", config)
  }
}
```

Single-threaded environment (annotation pointing to `val props = Props[Greeter]...` area)

The `Greeter` is tested by inspecting the log messages that it writes using the `Actor-Logging` trait. The test kit module provides a `TestEventListener` that you can configure to handle all events that are logged. The `ConfigFactory` can parse a configuration file from a String; in this case we only override the event handlers list.

The test is run in a single-threaded environment because we want to check that the log event has been recorded by the `TestEventListener` when the `Greeter` is sent the "World" `Greeting`. We use an `EventFilter` object, which can be used to filter log messages. In this case we filter out the expected message, which should only occur once. The filter is applied when the intercept code block is executed, which is when we send the message.

The preceding example of testing a `SideEffectingActor` shows that asserting some interactions can get complex quickly. In many situations, it's easier to adapt the code a bit so that it's easier to test. Clearly, if we pass the listeners to the class under test, we don't have to do any configuration or filtering; we'll simply get each message our `Actor` under test produces. The following listing shows an adapted `Greeter` actor that can be configured to send a message to a *listener* actor whenever a greeting is logged.

Listing 3.15   Simplifying testing of the `Greeter` Actor with a listener

```
object Greeter02 {
  def props(listener: Option[ActorRef] = None) =            Constructor takes an
    Props(new Greeter02(listener))                          optional listener;
}                                                            default set to None
class Greeter02(listener: Option[ActorRef])
  extends Actor with ActorLogging {
  def receive = {
    case Greeting(who) =>
      val message = "Hello " + who + "!"
      log.info(message)                                     Optionally sends
      listener.foreach(_ ! message)                         to the listener
  }
}
```

The `Greeter02` actor is adapted so that it takes an `Option[ActorRef]`, which is by default set to `None` in the `props` method. After it successfully logs a message, it sends a message to the listener if the `Option` is not empty. When the actor is used normally without specifying a listener, it runs as usual. The following listing is the updated test for this `Greeter02` actor.

Listing 3.16   Simpler `Greeter` Actor test

```
class Greeter02Test extends TestKit(ActorSystem("testsystem"))
  with WordSpecLike
  with StopSystemAfterAll {

  "The Greeter" must {
    "say Hello World! when a Greeting("World") is sent to it" in {
      val props = Greeter02.props(Some(testActor))          Sets the listener
                                                            to the testActor
```

```
      val greeter = system.actorOf(props, "greeter02-1")
      greeter ! Greeting("World")
      expectMsg("Hello World!")                         ⟵──────── Asserts the message as usual
    }
    "say something else and see what happens" in {
      val props = Greeter02.props(Some(testActor))
      val greeter = system.actorOf(props, "greeter02-2")
      system.eventStream.subscribe(testActor, classOf[UnhandledMessage])
      greeter ! "World"
      expectMsg(UnhandledMessage("World", system.deadLetters, greeter))
    }
  }
}
```

As you can see, the test has been greatly simplified. We simply pass in a `Some(testActor)` to the `Greeter02` constructor, and assert the message that's sent to the `testActor` as usual.

In the next section we'll look at two-way messages, and how these can be tested.

3.3 *Two-way messages*

You've already seen an example of two-way messages in the multithreaded test for the `SendingActor` style actor, where we used a `GetState` message that contained an `ActorRef`. We simply called the `!` operator on this `ActorRef` to respond to the `GetState` request. As shown before, the `tell` method has an implicit `sender` reference.

In this test we'll use the `ImplicitSender` trait. This trait changes the implicit sender in the test to the actor reference of the test kit. The following listing shows how the trait is mixed in.

Listing 3.17 `ImplicitSender`

```
class EchoActorTest extends TestKit(ActorSystem("testsystem"))
  with WordSpecLike
  with ImplicitSender                  ⟵──────   Sets the implicit sender to
  with StopSystemAfterAll {                       the TestKit its actor reference
```

Two-way messages are easy to test in a black box fashion: a request should result in a response, which you can simply assert. In the following test, we'll test an `EchoActor`, an actor that echoes any request back in a response.

Listing 3.18 Testing echoes

```
    "Reply with the same message it receives without ask" in {
      val echo = system.actorOf(Props[EchoActor], "echo2")
      echo ! "some message"                          ⟵────── Sends a message to the actor
      expectMsg("some message")      ⟵──────
    }                                           Asserts the message as usual
```

We just send the message, and the `EchoActor` will send the response back to the actor reference of the test kit, which was set automatically as the `sender` by the `Implicit-Sender` trait. The `EchoActor` stays exactly the same. It just sends a message back to the sender. The next listing shows this.

Listing 3.19 `EchoActor`

```
class EchoActor extends Actor {
  def receive = {
    case msg =>
      sender() ! msg                    Whatever is received is simply
  }                                      sent back to (implicit) sender
}
```

The `EchoActor` reacts exactly the same way whether the `ask` pattern was used or the `tell` method; the preceding is the preferred way to test two-way messages.

Our journey in this section has taken us through actor-testing idioms that are offered by Akka's `TestKit`. They all serve the same goal: making it easy to write unit tests that need access to results that can be asserted on. The `TestKit` provides methods for both single-threaded and multithreaded testing. We can even "cheat" a little and get at the underlying actor instance during testing. Categorizing actors by how they interact with others gives us a template for how to test the actor, which was shown for the `SilentActor`, `SendingActor`, and `SideEffectingActor` types. In most cases the easiest way to test an actor is to pass a `testActor` reference to it, which can be used to assert expectations on the messages that are sent out by the actor under test. The `testActor` can be used to take the place of a sender in a request-response, or it can just act like the next actor that an actor is sending messages to. Finally, you saw that in many cases it makes sense to prepare an actor for testing, especially if the actor is "silent," in which case it's beneficial to add an optional listener to the actor.

3.4   Summary

Test-driven development is more than a quality control mechanism; it's a way of working. Akka was designed to support TDD. Since the bedrock of regular unit testing is to invoke a method and get a response that can be checked for an expected result, we had to look, in this chapter, for ways to adopt a new mindset to go along with our message-based, asynchronous style.

Actors also bring some new powers to the seasoned TDD programmer:

- Actors embody behavior; tests are fundamentally a means of checking behavior.
- Message-based tests are cleaner: only immutable state goes back and forth, precluding the possibility of tests corrupting the state they're testing.
- With an understanding of the core test actors, you can now write unit tests of actors of all kinds.

This chapter was an introduction to Akka's way of testing, and the tools that Akka provides. The real proof of their value lies in the chapters ahead as we use these to achieve the promise of TDD: rapid development of tested, working code.

In the next chapter we'll look at how actor hierarchies are formed and how supervision strategies and lifecycle monitoring can be used to build fault-tolerant systems.

Fault tolerance

This chapter covers Akka's tools for making applications more resilient. The first section describes the *let-it-crash* principle, including supervision, monitoring, and actor lifecycle features. Of course, we'll look at some examples that show how to apply these to typical failure scenarios.

4.1 What fault tolerance is (and what it isn't)

Let's start with a definition of what we mean when we say a system is *fault tolerant*, and why you'd write code to embrace the notion of failure. In an ideal world, a system is always available and can guarantee that it will be successful with each undertaken action. The only two paths to this ideal are using components that can never fail or accounting for every possible fault by providing a recovery action, which is also assured of success. In most architectures, what you have instead is a catch-all mechanism that will terminate as soon as an uncaught failure arises. Even if an application attempts to provide recovery strategies, testing them is hard, and being sure that the recovery strategies themselves work adds another layer of complexity. In the procedural world, each attempt to do something requires a return code that's checked against a list of possible faults. Exception handling has become a fixture of modern languages, promising a less onerous path to providing the various required means of recovery. But though it has succeeded in yielding code that doesn't need to have fault checks on every line, the propagation of faults to ready handlers hasn't significantly improved.

The idea of a system that's free of faults sounds great in theory, but the sad fact is that building one that's also highly available and distributed is simply not possible for any non-trivial system. The main reason for this is because large parts of any non-trivial system aren't under your control, and these parts can break. Then there's the prevalent problem of responsibility: as collaborators interact, often using shared components, it's not clear who's responsible for which possible faults. A good example of potentially unavailable resources is the network: it can go away at any time or be partly available, and if you want to continue operation, you'll have to find some other way to continue communicating, or maybe disable communication for a while. You might depend on third-party services that can misbehave, fail, or simply be sporadically unavailable. The servers your software runs on can fail or can be unavailable, or even experience total hardware failure. You obviously can't magically make a server reappear out of its ashes or automatically fix a broken disk to guarantee writing to it. This is why *let it crash* was born in the rack-and-stack world of the telcos, where failed machines were common enough to make their availability goals impossible without a plan that accounted for them.

Since you can't prevent all failures from happening, you'll have to be prepared to adopt a strategy, keeping the following in mind:

- Things break. The system needs to be *fault tolerant* so that it can stay available and continue to run. Recoverable faults shouldn't trigger catastrophic failures.
- In some cases, it's acceptable if the most important features of the system stay available as long as possible, while in the meantime failing parts are stopped and cut off from the system so that they can't interfere with the rest of the system, producing unpredictable results.
- In other cases, certain components are so important that they need to have active backups (probably on a different server or using different resources) that can kick in when the main component fails, so that the unavailability is quickly remedied.
- A failure in certain parts of the system shouldn't crash the entire system, so you need a way to isolate particular failures that you can deal with later.

Of course, the Akka toolkit doesn't include a fault tolerance silver bullet. You'll still need to handle specific failures, but will be able to do it in a cleaner, more application-specific way. The Akka features described in table 4.1 will enable you to build the fault tolerant behavior you need.

Table 4.1   Available fault avoidance strategies

Strategy	Description
Fault containment or isolation	A fault should be contained within a part of the system and not escalate to a total crash.
Structure	Isolating a faulty component means that some structure needs to exist to isolate it from the rest of the system; the system will need a defined structure in which active parts can be isolated.
Redundancy	A backup component should be able to take over when a component fails.
Replacement	If a faulty component can be isolated, you can also replace it in the structure. The other parts of the system should be able to communicate with the replaced component just as they did before with the failed component.
Reboot	If a component gets into an incorrect state, you need the ability to get it back to a defined initial state. The incorrect state might be the reason for the fault, and it might not be possible to predict all the incorrect states the component can get into because of dependencies out of your control.
Component lifecycle	A faulty component needs to be isolated, and if it can't recover, it should be terminated and removed from the system or re-initialized with a correct starting state. Some defined lifecycle will need to exist to start, restart, and terminate the component.
Suspend	When a component fails, you'd like all calls to the component to be suspended until the component is fixed or replaced, so that when it is, the new component can continue the work without dropping a beat. The call that was handled at the time of failure should also not disappear—it could be critical to your recovery, and further, it might contain information that's critical to understanding why the component failed. You might want to retry the call when you're sure that there was another reason for the fault.
Separation of concerns	It would be great if the fault-recovery code could be separated from the normal processing code. Fault recovery is a cross-cutting concern in the normal flow. A clear separation between normal flow and recovery flow will simplify the work that needs to be done. Changing the way the application recovers from faults will be simpler if you've achieved this clean separation.

"But wait a minute," you might say, "Why can't we just use plain old objects and exceptions to recover from failures?" Normally exceptions are used to back out of a series of actions to prevent an inconsistent state instead of recovering from a failure in the sense we've discussed so far. But let's see how hard it would be to add fault recovery using exception handling and plain old objects in the next section.

4.1.1   *Plain old objects and exceptions*

Let's look at an example of an application that receives logs from multiple threads, "parses" interesting information out of the files into row objects, and writes these rows into some database. Some file watcher process keeps track of added files and informs many threads in some way to process the new files. Figure 4.1 gives an overview of the application and highlights the part that we'll zoom in on ("in scope").

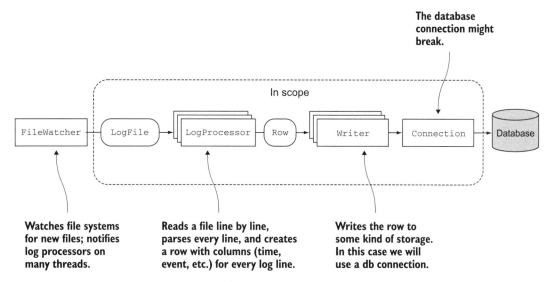

Figure 4.1 Process logs application

If the database connection breaks, we want to be able to create a new connection to another database and continue writing, instead of backing out. If the connection starts to malfunction, we might want to shut it down so that no part of the application uses it anymore. In some cases, we'll want to just reboot the connection, hopefully to get rid of some temporary bad state in it. Pseudo code will be used to illustrate where the potential problem areas are. We'll look at the case where we want to just get a new connection to the same database using standard exception handling.

First, we set up all objects that will be used from the threads. After setup, they'll be used to process the new files that the file watcher finds. We set up a database writer that uses a connection. Figure 4.2 shows how the writer is created.

The dependencies for the writer are passed to the constructor as you'd expect. The database factory settings, including the different URLs, are passed in from the thread that creates the writer. Next we set up some log processors; each gets a reference to a writer to store rows, as shown in figure 4.3.

Figure 4.2 Create a writer

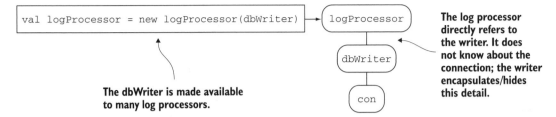

The dbWriter is made available
to many log processors.

The log processor
directly refers to
the writer. It does
not know about the
connection; the writer
encapsulates/hides
this detail.

Figure 4.3   Create log processors

Figure 4.4 shows how the objects call each other in this example application.

The flow shown in figure 4.4. gets called from many threads to simultaneously process files found by the file watcher. Figure 4.5 shows a call stack where a `DbBroken-ConnectionException` is thrown, which indicates that we should switch to another connection. The details of every method are omitted; the diagram only shows where an object eventually calls another object.

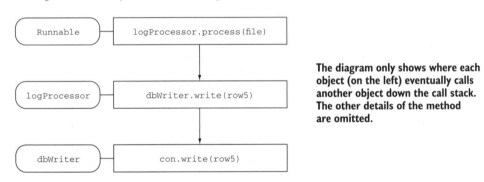

The diagram only shows where each
object (on the left) eventually calls
another object down the call stack.
The other details of the method
are omitted.

Figure 4.4   Call stack diagram

Instead of just throwing the exception up the stack, we'd like to recover from the `DbBrokenConnectionException` and replace the broken connection with a working one. The first problem we face is that it's hard to add the code to recover the connection in a way that doesn't break the design. Also, we don't have enough information to re-create the connection: we don't know which lines in the file have already been processed successfully and which line was being processed when the exception occurred.

Making both the processed lines and the connection information available to all objects would break our simple design and violate some basic best practices like encapsulation, inversion of control, and single responsibility, to name a few. (Good luck at the next code peer review with your clean coding colleagues!) We just want the faulty component replaced. Adding recovery code directly into the exception handling will entangle the functionality of processing log files with database connection recovery logic. Even if we find a spot to re-create the connection, we'd have to be very careful that other threads don't get to use the faulty connection while we're trying to replace it with a new one, because otherwise some rows would be lost.

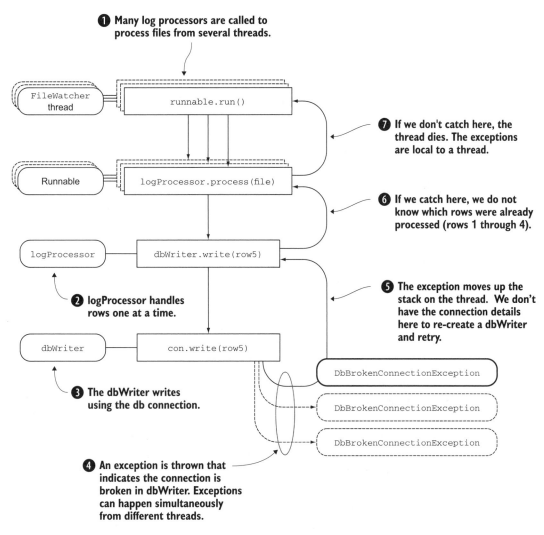

Figure 4.5 Call stack while processing log files

Also, communicating exceptions between threads isn't a standard feature; you'll have to build this yourself, which isn't a trivial thing to do. Let's look at the fault tolerance requirements to see if this approach even stands a chance:

- *Fault isolation*—Isolation is made difficult by the fact that many threads can throw exceptions at the same time. You'll have to add some kind of locking mechanism. It's hard to really remove the faulty connection out of the chain of objects: the application would have to be rewritten to get this to work. There's no standard support for cutting off the use of the connection in the future, so this needs to be built into the objects manually with some level of indirection.

- *Structure*—The structure that exists between objects is simple and direct. Every object possibly refers to other objects forming a graph; it isn't possible to simply replace an object in the graph at runtime. You'll have to create a more involved structure yourself (again, with a level of indirection between the objects).

- *Redundancy*—When an exception is thrown, it goes up the call stack. You might miss the context for making the decision of which redundant component to use, or lose the context of which input data to continue with, as seen in the preceding example.

- *Replacement*—There's no default strategy in place to replace an object in a call stack; you'll have to find a way to do it yourself. There are dependency injection frameworks that provide some features for this, but if any object refers directly to the old instance instead of through the level of indirection, you're in trouble. If you intend to change an object in place, you'd better make sure it works for multithreaded access.

- *Reboot*—Similar to replacement, getting an object back to an initial state is not automatically supported and takes another level of indirection that you'll have to build. All the dependencies of the object will have to be reintroduced as well. If these dependencies also need to be rebooted (let's say the log processor can also throw some recoverable error), things can get quite complicated with regard to ordering.

- *Component lifecycle*—An object only exists after it's been constructed or it's garbage collected and removed from memory. Any other mechanism is something you'll have to build yourself.

- *Suspend*—The input data or some of its context is lost or not available when you catch an exception and throw it up the stack. You'll have to build something yourself to buffer the incoming calls while the error's unresolved. If the code is called from many threads, you'll need to add locks to prevent multiple exceptions from happening at the same time. And you'll need to find a way to store the associated input data to retry again later.

- *Separation of concerns*—The exception-handling code is interwoven with the processing code and can't be defined independently of the processing code.

So that's not looking very promising: getting everything to work correctly is going to be complex and a real pain. It looks like some fundamental features are missing for adding fault tolerance to our application in an easy way:

- Re-creating objects and their dependencies and replacing these in the application structure isn't available as a first-class feature.
- Objects communicate with each other directly, so it's hard to isolate them.
- The fault-recovery code and the functional code are tangled up with each other.

Luckily we have a simpler solution. You've already seen some of the actor features that can help simplify these problems. Actors can be (re-)created from `Props` objects, are part of an actor system, and communicate through actor references instead of direct references. In the next section, we'll look at how actors provide a way to untangle the functional code from the fault-recovery code, and how the actor lifecycle makes it possible to suspend and restart actors (without invoking the wrath of the concurrency gods) in the course of recovering from faults.

4.1.2   *Let it crash*

In the previous section, you learned that building a fault-tolerant application with plain old objects and exception handling is quite a complex task. Let's look at how actors simplify this task. What should happen when an `Actor` processes a message and encounters an exception? We already discussed why we don't want to just graft recovery code into the operational flow, so catching the exception inside an actor where the business logic resides is not an option.

Instead of using one flow to handle both normal code and recovery code, an Akka `Actor` provides two separate flows: one for normal logic and one for fault recovery logic. The normal flow consists of actors that handle normal messages; the recovery flow consists of actors that monitor the actors in the normal flow. Actors that monitor other actors are called *supervisors*. Figure 4.6 shows a supervisor monitoring an actor.

Instead of catching exceptions in an actor, we'll just let the actor crash. The actor code for handling messages only contains normal processing logic and no error handling or fault recovery logic, so it's effectively not part of the recovery process, which keeps things much clearer. The mailbox for a crashed actor is suspended until the supervisor in the recovery flow has decided what to do with the exception. How does an actor become a supervisor? Akka has chosen to enforce *parental supervision*, meaning

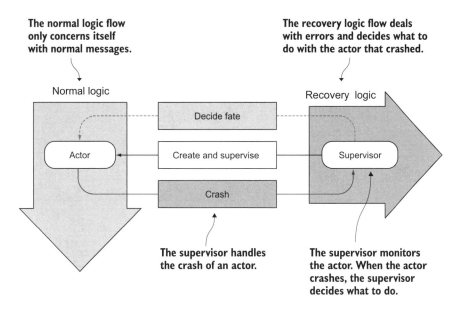

Figure 4.6   Normal and recovery flow

that any actor that creates actors automatically becomes the supervisor of those actors. A supervisor doesn't "catch exceptions;" rather it decides what should happen with the crashed actors that it supervises based on the cause of the crash. The supervisor doesn't try to fix the actor or its state. It simply renders a judgment on how to recover, and then triggers the corresponding strategy. The supervisor has four options when deciding what to do with the actor:

- *Restart*—The actor must be re-created from its `Props`. After it's restarted (or rebooted, if you will), the actor will continue to process messages. Since the rest of the application uses an `ActorRef` to communicate with the actor, the new actor instance will automatically get the next messages.
- *Resume*—The same actor instance should continue to process messages; the crash is ignored.
- *Stop*—The actor must be terminated. It will no longer take part in processing messages.
- *Escalate*—The supervisor doesn't know what to do with it and escalates the problem to its parent, which is also a supervisor.

Figure 4.7 gives an example of the strategy that we could choose when we build the log-processing application with actors. The supervisor is shown to take one of the possible actions when a particular crash occurs.

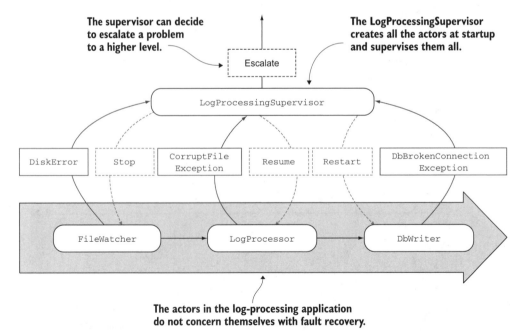

Figure 4.7   Normal and recovery flow in the log-processing application

Figure 4.7 shows a solution for making the log processing fault tolerant, at least for the broken connection problem. When the `DbBrokenConnectionException` occurs, the `dbWriter` actor crashes and is replaced with a re-created `dbWriter` actor.

We'll need to take some special steps to recover the failed message, which we'll discuss in detail later when we talk about how to implement a restart. Suffice it to say that in most cases, you don't want to reprocess a message, because it probably caused the error in the first place. An example of that would be the case of the `logProcessor` encountering a corrupt file: reprocessing corrupt files could end up in what's called a *poisoned mailbox*—no other message will ever get processed because the corrupting message is failing over and over again. For this reason, Akka chooses not to provide the failing message to the mailbox again after a restart, but there's a way to do this yourself if you're absolutely sure that the message didn't cause the error, which we'll discuss later. The good news is that if a job is processing tens of thousands of messages, and one is corrupt, default behavior will result in all the other messages being processed normally; the one corrupt file won't cause a catastrophic failure and erase all the other work done to that point (and prevent the remainder from occurring).

Figure 4.8 shows how a crashed `dbWriter` actor instance is replaced with a fresh instance when the supervisor chooses to restart.

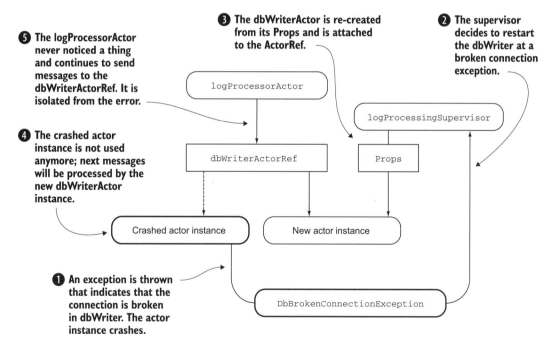

Figure 4.8 Handling the `DbBrokenConnectionException` with a restart

Let's recap the benefits of the let-it-crash approach:

- *Fault isolation*—A supervisor can decide to terminate an actor. The actor is removed from the actor system.
- *Structure*—The actor system hierarchy of actor references makes it possible to replace actor instances without other actors being affected.
- *Redundancy*—An actor can be replaced by another. In the example of the broken database connection, the fresh actor instance could connect to a different database. The supervisor could also decide to stop the faulty actor and create another type instead. Another option would be to route messages in a load-balanced fashion to many actors, which will be discussed in chapter 9.
- *Replacement*—An actor can always be re-created from its `Props`. A supervisor can decide to replace a faulty actor instance with a fresh one, without having to know any of the details for re-creating the actor.
- *Reboot*—This can be done through a restart.
- *Component lifecycle*—An actor is an active component. It can be started, stopped, and restarted. In the next section, we'll go into the details of how the actor goes through its lifecycle.
- *Suspend*—When an actor crashes, its mailbox is suspended until the supervisor decides what should happen with the actor.
- *Separation of concerns*—The normal actor message-processing and supervision fault recovery flows are orthogonal, and can be defined and evolve completely independently of each other.

In the next sections, we'll get into the coding details of the actor lifecycle and supervision strategies.

4.2   *Actor lifecycle*

You've seen that an actor can restart to recover from a failure. But how can you correct the actor state when the actor is restarting? To answer that question, we need to take a closer look at the actor lifecycle. An actor is automatically started by Akka when it's created. The actor will stay in the `Started` state until it's stopped, at which point the actor is in the `Terminated` state. When the actor is terminated, it can't process messages anymore and will be eventually garbage collected. When the actor is in a `Started` state, it can be restarted to reset the internal state of the actor. As we discussed in the previous section, the actor instance is replaced by a fresh actor instance. The restart can happen as many times as necessary. During the lifecycle of an actor, there are three types of events:

- The actor is created and started—for simplicity we'll refer to this as the *start* event.
- The actor is restarted on the *restart* event.
- The actor is stopped by the *stop* event.

There are several hooks in place in the `Actor` trait, which are called when the events happen to indicate a lifecycle change. You can add some custom code in these hooks that can be used to re-create a specific state in the fresh actor instance, for example, to process the message that failed before the restart, or to clean up some resources. In the next sections, we'll look at the three events and how the hooks can be used to run custom code. The order in which the hooks occur is guaranteed, although they're called asynchronously by Akka.

4.2.1 Start event

An actor is created and automatically started with the `actorOf` method. Top-level actors are created with the `actorOf` method on the `ActorSystem`. A parent actor creates a child actor using the `actorOf` on its `ActorContext`. Figure 4.9 shows the process.

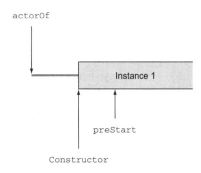

   After the instance is created, the actor will be started by Akka. The `preStart` hook is called just before the actor is started. To use this trigger, you have to override the `preStart` method.

Figure 4.9   Starting an actor

Listing 4.1   `preStart` lifecycle hook

```
override def preStart() {
  println("preStart")        ⟵——— Do some work
}
```

This hook can be used to set the initial state of the actor. You can also initialize the actor through its constructor.

4.2.2 Stop event

The next lifecycle event that we'll discuss is the stop event. We'll get back to the restart event later, because its hooks have dependencies on the start and stop hooks. The stop event indicates the end of the actor lifecycle and occurs once, when an actor is stopped. An actor can be stopped using the `stop` method on the `ActorSystem` and `ActorContext` objects, or by sending a `PoisonPill` message to an actor. Figure 4.10 shows the process.

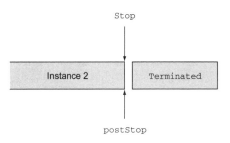

Figure 4.10   Stopping an actor

The `postStop` hook is called just before the actor is terminated. When the actor is in the `Terminated` state, the actor doesn't get any new messages to handle. The `postStop` method is the counterpart of the `preStart` hook.

Listing 4.2   `postStop` lifecycle hook

```
override def postStop(): Unit = {
  println("postStop")          ⟵─── Do some work
}
```

Normally this hook implements the opposite function of `preStart`, and releases resources created in the `preStart` method and possibly stores the last state of the actor somewhere outside of the actor in the case that the next actor instance needs it. A stopped actor is disconnected from its `ActorRef`. After the actor is stopped, the `ActorRef` is redirected to the `deadLettersActorRef` of the actor system, which is a special `ActorRef` that receives all messages that are sent to dead actors.

4.2.3   *Restart event*

During the lifecycle of an actor, it's possible that its supervisor will decide that the actor has to be restarted. This can happen more than once, depending on the number of errors that occur. This event is more complex than the start or stop events, because the instance of an actor is replaced. Figure 4.11 shows the process.

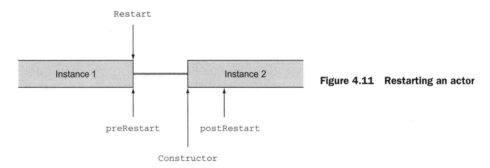

Figure 4.11   Restarting an actor

When a restart occurs, the `preRestart` method of the crashed actor instance is called. In this hook, the crashed actor instance is able to store its current state, just before it's replaced by the new actor instance.

Listing 4.3   `preRestart` lifecycle hook

```
override def preRestart(reason: Throwable, message:     ⟵─── Exception thrown by the actor
Option[Any]): Unit = {                           ⟵─┐
  println("preRestart")
  super.preRestart(reason, message)     ⟵─┐        When error occurred within
}                                                  the receive function, this is
                                                   the message the actor was
          Warning: call the super implementation   trying to process
```

Be careful when overriding this hook. The default implementation of the `preRestart` method stops all the child actors of the actor and then calls the `postStop` hook. If you forget to call `super.preRestart`, this default behavior won't occur. Remember that actors are (re-)created from a `Props` object. The `Props` object eventually calls the constructor of the actor. The actor can create child actors inside its constructor. If the children of the crashed actor aren't stopped, you could end up with increasingly more child actors when the parent actor is restarted.

It's important to note that a restart doesn't stop the crashed actor in the same way as the stop methods (described earlier when discussing the `stop` event). As you'll see later, it's possible to monitor the death of an actor. A crashed actor instance in a restart doesn't cause a `Terminated` message to be sent for the crashed actor. The fresh actor instance, during restart, is connected to the same `ActorRef` the crashed actor was using before the fault. A stopped actor is disconnected from its `ActorRef` and redirected to the `deadLettersActorRef` as described by the `stop` event. What both the stopped actor and the crashed actor have in common is that by default, the `post-Stop` is called after they've been cut off from the actor system.

The `preRestart` method can take two arguments: the reason for the restart and, optionally, the message that was being processed when the actor crashed. The supervisor can decide what should (or can) be stored to enable state restoration as part of restarting. This can't be done using local variables, because after restarting, a fresh actor instance will take over processing. One solution for keeping state beyond the death of the crashed actor is for the supervisor to send a message to the actor—the message will go in its mailbox. (This is done by the actor sending a message to its own `ActorRef`, which is available on the actor instance through the `self` value.) Other options include writing to something outside of the actor, like a database or the file system. This all depends completely on your system and the behavior of the actor.

Which brings us back to the log-processing example, where we didn't want to lose the `Row` message in the case of a `dbWriter` crash. The solution in that case could be to send the failed `Row` message to the `self` `ActorRef` so it would be processed by the fresh actor instance. One issue to note with this approach is that by sending a message back onto the mailbox, the order of the messages on the mailbox is changed. The failed message is pushed off the top of the mailbox and will be processed later than other messages that have been waiting in the mailbox. In the case of the `dbWriter`, this isn't an issue, but keep this in mind when using this technique.

After the `preStart` hook is called, a new instance of the actor class is created and therefore the constructor of the actor is executed, through the `Props` object. After that, the `postRestart` hook is called on this fresh actor instance.

Listing 4.4 `postRestart` lifecycle hook

```
override def postRestart(reason: Throwable): Unit = {     ◁─┐ Exception that was
  println("postRestart")                                        thrown by the actor
  super.postRestart(reason)          ◁─┐ Warning: call the
}                                        super implementation
```

Here too, we start with a warning. The super implementation of postRestart is called because this will trigger the preStart function by default. The super.postRestart can be omitted if you're certain that you don't want preStart to be called when restarting; in most cases, though, this isn't going to be the case. preStart and post-Stop are called by default during a restart, and they're called during the start and stop events in the lifecycle, so it makes sense to add code there for initialization and cleanup, respectively, killing two birds with one stone.

The argument reason is the same as received in the preRestart method. In the overridden hook, the actor is free to restore itself to some last known correct state, for example, by using information stored by the preRestart function.

4.2.4   *Putting the lifecycle pieces together*

When you put all the different events together, you get the full lifecycle of an actor, as shown in figure 4.12. In this case only one restart is shown.

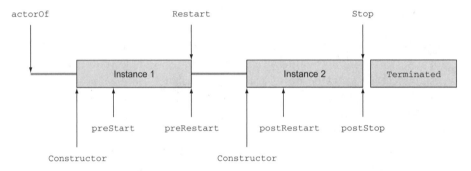

Figure 4.12   Full lifecycle of an actor

Putting all the lifecycle hooks together in one Actor, you can see the different events occurring.

Listing 4.5   Example lifecycle hooks

```
class LifeCycleHooks extends Actor
                  with ActorLogging{
  System.out.println("Constructor")

  override def preStart(): Unit = {
    println("preStart")
  }
  override def postStop(): Unit = {
    println("postStop")
  }
  override def preRestart(reason: Throwable, message: Option[Any]): Unit = {
    println("preRestart")
    super.preRestart (reason, message)
  }
  override def postRestart(reason: Throwable): Unit = {
```

```
      println("postRestart")
      super.postRestart(reason)
    }
  def receive = {
    case "restart" =>
      throw new IllegalStateException("force restart")
    case msg: AnyRef =>
      println("Receive")
      sender() ! msg
  }
}
```

In the following test, we trigger all three lifecycle events. The sleep just before the stop makes sure that we can see the postStop happening.

Listing 4.6   Testing lifecycle triggers

```
val testActorRef = system.actorOf(            ◁─── Start actor
  Props[LifeCycleHooks], "LifeCycleHooks")
testActorRef ! "restart"                       ◁─── Restart actor
testActorRef.tell("msg", testActor)
expectMsg("msg")
system.stop(testActorRef)                       ◁─── Stop actor
Thread.sleep(1000)
```

The result of the test is the following.

Listing 4.7   Output test lifecycle hooks

```
Constructor                      │  Starts event
preStart                         │
preRestart force restart         │
postStop                         │
Constructor                         Restarts event
postRestart force restart        │
preStart                         │
Receive                          │
postStop            ◁─── Stops event
```

Every actor goes through this lifecycle; it's started and possibly restarted several times until the actor is stopped and terminated. The preStart, preRestart, postRestart, and postStop hooks enable an actor to initialize and clean up state and control and restore its state after a crash.

4.2.5   *Monitoring the lifecycle*

The lifecycle of an actor can be monitored. The lifecycle ends when the actor is terminated. An actor is terminated if the supervisor decides to stop the actor, if the stop method is used to stop the actor, or if a PoisonPill message is sent to the actor, which indirectly causes the stop method to be called. Since the default implementation of the preRestart method stops all the actor's children with the stop methods, these children are also terminated in the case of a restart. The crashed actor instance in a restart isn't terminated in this sense. It's removed from the actor system, but not by using the `stop` method, directly or indirectly. This is because the `ActorRef` will continue to live on after the restart; the actor instance hasn't been terminated, but replaced by a new one. The `ActorContext` provides a `watch` method to monitor the death of an actor and an `unwatch` to de-register as monitor. Once an actor calls the `watch` method on an actor reference, it becomes the monitor of that actor reference. A `Terminated` message is sent to the monitor actor when the monitored actor is terminated. The `Terminated` message only contains the `ActorRef` of the actor that died. The fact that the crashed actor instance in a restart isn't terminated in the same way as when an actor is stopped now makes sense, because otherwise you'd receive many terminated messages whenever an actor restarts, which would make it impossible to differentiate the final death of an actor from a temporary restart. The following example shows a `DbWatcher` actor that watches the lifecycle of a `dbWriterActorRef`.

Listing 4.8   Watching the lifecycle of a `dbWriter`

Watches the lifecycle of the dbWriter

```
class DbWatcher(dbWriter: ActorRef) extends Actor with ActorLogging {
  context.watch(dbWriter)
  def receive = {                                        actorRef of terminated actor is
    case Terminated(actorRef) =>                         passed in Terminated message
      log.warning("Actor {} terminated", actorRef)    ◁⎯⎯ Watcher logs the fact that
  }                                                          dbWriter was terminated
}
```

As opposed to supervision, which is only possible from parent to child actors, monitoring can be done by any actor. As long as the actor has access to the `ActorRef` of the actor that needs to be monitored, it can simply call `context.watch(actorRef)`, after which it will receive a `Terminated` message when the actor is terminated. Monitoring and supervision can be combined as well, and can be powerful, as you'll see in the next section.

We haven't discussed yet how a supervisor actually decides the fate of an actor—whether the child should be terminated, restarted, or stopped. This will be the main topic of the next section, where we'll get into the details of supervision. In the next section, we'll first look at how the supervisor hierarchy is built up, followed by the strategies that a supervisor can use.

4.3   *Supervision*

In this section we'll look at the details of supervision. We'll take the log-processing example application and show you different types of supervision strategies. We'll focus on the supervisor hierarchy under the */user* actor path, which will also be referred to as the *user space*. This is where all application actors live. First we'll discuss various ways to define a hierarchy of supervisors for an application and what the benefits and drawbacks are of each. Then we'll look at how supervisor strategies can be customized per supervisor.

4.3.1 *Supervisor hierarchy*

The supervisor hierarchy is simply a function of the act of actors creating each other: every actor that creates another is the supervisor of the created child actor.

The supervision hierarchy is fixed for the lifetime of a child actor. Once the child is created by the parent, it will fall under the supervision of that parent as long as it lives; there's no such thing as adoption in Akka. The only way for the supervisor parent to cease its responsibilities is by terminating the child actor. So it's important to choose the right supervision hierarchy from the start in your application, especially if you don't plan to terminate parts of the hierarchy to replace them with completely different subtrees of actors.

The most dangerous actors (actors that are most likely to crash) should be as low down the hierarchy as possible. Faults that occur far down the hierarchy can be handled or escalated by more supervisors than a fault that occurs high up in the hierarchy. When a fault occurs in the top level of the actor system, it could restart all the top-level actors or even shut down the actor system.

Let's look at the supervisor hierarchy of the log-processing application as we intended in the previous section, illustrated in figure 4.7, in section 4.1.2.

In this setup, the LogProcessingSupervisor creates all the actors in the application. We connect the actors directly to each other using ActorRefs. Every actor knows the ActorRef of the next actor it sends messages to. The ActorRefs need to stay alive and always need to refer to a next actor instance. If an actor instance were to be stopped, the ActorRef would refer to the system's deadLetters, which would break the application. A restart will need to be used in all cases in the supervisor because of this, so that the same ActorRef can be reused at all times, because it stays valid.

The benefit of this approach is that the actors talk to each other directly and the LogProcessingSupervisor only supervises and creates instances. The drawback is that we can only use restart, because otherwise messages will be sent to the dead-Letters and get lost. Also, stopping the FileWatcher on a DiskError doesn't cause the LogProcessor or DbWriter to be stopped, since they aren't children in the hierarchy of the FileWatcher. For instance, we would need to stop the DbWriter and create a new one in the case that we would want to change the database URL, for example, if we know that the database node has completely failed due to a DbNodeDownException. The original Props are used on Restart to create the DbWriter, which will always refer to the same database URL. So in that case we need a different solution.

Figure 4.13 shows a different approach. The LogProcessingSupervisor doesn't create all the actors; the FileWatcher creates a LogProcessor, and the LogProcessor in turn creates a DbWriter.

The normal and recovery flows are still defined separately in a supervision strategy and a receive method, even though the FileWatcher and LogProcessor now create and supervise actors as well as handle the normal message flow.

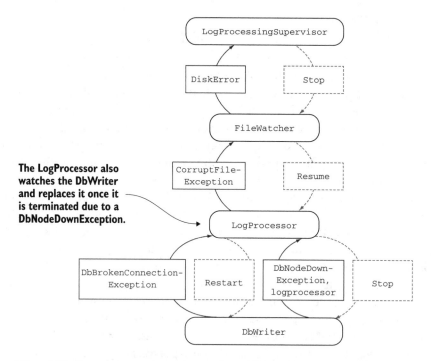

Figure 4.13 Every actor creates and supervises child actors.

The benefit of this approach is that the LogProcessor can now watch the DbWriter, decide to stop it when it throws a DbNodeException, and re-create a fresh DbWriter with an alternative URL to a completely different database node, once it receives the Terminated message.

The LogProcessingSupervisor now also does not have to do the supervision for the entire application, it just supervises and monitors the FileWatchers. If the Log-ProcessingSupervisor would monitor both FileWatchers and DbWriters, you would have to differentiate between a terminated FileWatcher and a DbWriter, leading to less isolated code for dealing with issues of subcomponents. The source code on GitHub has a few more examples of different supervision styles. The following example shows how the hierarchy shown in figure 4.13 is built up in an application. In the next section, we'll look at the supervisors and the strategies they use in detail.

Listing 4.9 Building the supervisor hierarchy

```
object LogProcessingApp extends App {
  val sources = Vector("file:///source1/", "file:///source2/")
  val system = ActorSystem("logprocessing")
  val databaseUrls = Vector(
    "http://mydatabase1",
    "http://mydatabase2",
```

```
      "http://mydatabase3"
  )

  system.actorOf(
    LogProcessingSupervisor.props(sources, databaseUrls),
    LogProcessingSupervisor.name
  )
}
```

The first url is the initial url; the rest are alternatives if a DbNodeDownException is received.

The preceding code shows how the log-processing application is built up. Only one top-level actor, the `LogProcessingSupervisor`, is created using `system.actorOf`—all other actors are created further down the line. In the next section, we'll revisit each actor and you'll see how they exactly create their children.

Now that you know a bit more about how to structure the supervision hierarchy of an application, let's look in the next section at the different supervisor strategies that are available.

4.3.2 Predefined strategies

The top-level actors in an application are created under the `/user` path and supervised by the *user guardian*. The default supervision strategy for the user guardian is to restart its children on any `Exception`, except when it receives internal exceptions that indicate that the actor was killed or failed during initialization, at which point it will stop the actor in question. This strategy is known as the *default strategy*. Every actor has a default supervisor strategy, which can be overridden by implementing the `supervisorStrategy` method. There are two predefined strategies available in the `SupervisorStrategy` object: the `defaultStrategy` and the `stoppingStrategy`. As the name implies, the default strategy is default for all actors; if you don't override the strategy, an actor will always use the default. The default strategy is defined as follows in the `SupervisorStrategy` object.

Listing 4.10 Default supervisor strategy

```
final val defaultStrategy: SupervisorStrategy = {
  def defaultDecider: Decider = {
    case _: ActorInitializationException => Stop
    case _: ActorKilledException => Stop
    case _: Exception => Restart
  }
  OneForOneStrategy()(defaultDecider)
}
```

Decider chooses a Directive by pattern matching on the exceptions

Stop, Restart, Resume, and Escalate: directives

OneForOneStrategy that uses the defaultDecider is returned

The preceding code uses the `OneForOneStrategy`, which we haven't discussed yet. Akka allows you to make a decision about the fate of the child actors in two ways: all children share the same fate and the same recovery is applied to the lot, or a decision is rendered and the remedy is applied only to the crashed actor. In some cases you might want to stop only the child actor that failed. In other cases you might want to stop all child actors if one of them fails, maybe because they all depend on a particular resource. If an exception is thrown that indicates that the shared resource has failed completely, it might be better to immediately stop all child actors together instead of waiting for this to happen individually for every child. The OneForOneStrategy determines that child actors won't share the same fate: only the crashed child will be decided upon by the Decider. The other option is to use an AllForOneStrategy, which uses the same decision for all child actors even if only one crashed. The next section will describe the OneForOneStrategy and AllForOneStrategy in more detail. The following example shows the definition of the stoppingStrategy, which is defined in the SupervisorStrategy object.

Listing 4.11   Stopping supervisor strategy

```
final val stoppingStrategy: SupervisorStrategy = {
  def stoppingDecider: Decider = {
    case _: Exception => Stop          <─── Decides to stop on any Exception
  }
  OneForOneStrategy()(stoppingDecider)
}
```

The stopping strategy will stop any child that crashes on any Exception. These built-in strategies are nothing out of the ordinary. They're defined in the same way you could define a supervisor strategy yourself. So what happens if an Error is thrown, like a ThreadDeath or an OutOfMemoryError, by an actor that's supervised using the preceding stoppingStrategy? Any Throwable that isn't handled by the supervisor strategy will be escalated to the parent of the supervisor. If a fatal error reaches all the way up to the user guardian, the user guardian won't handle it, since the user guardian uses the default strategy. In that case, an uncaught exception handler in the actor system causes the actor system to shut down. In most cases it's good practice not to handle fatal errors in supervisors, but instead gracefully shut down the actor system, since a fatal error can't be recovered from.

4.3.3   Custom strategies

Each application will have to craft strategies for each case that requires fault tolerance. As you've seen in the previous sections, there are four different types of actions a supervisor can take to resolve a crashed actor. These are the building blocks we'll use. In this section, we'll return to the log processing and build the specific strategies it requires from these elements:

- *Resume* the child, ignore errors, and keep processing with the same actor instance.
- *Restart* the child, remove the crashed actor instance, and replace it with a fresh actor instance.
- *Stop* the child and terminate the child permanently.
- *Escalate* the failure and let the parent actor decide what action needs to be taken.

First we'll look at the exceptions that can occur in the log-processing application. To simplify the example, a couple of custom exceptions are defined.

Listing 4.12 Exceptions in the log-processing application

```
@SerialVersionUID(1L)
class DiskError(msg: String)
  extends Error(msg) with Serializable
```
Unrecoverable Error occurs when disk for the source has crashed

```
@SerialVersionUID(1L)
class CorruptedFileException(msg: String, val file: File)
  extends Exception(msg) with Serializable
```
Exception occurs when log file is corrupt and can't be processed

```
@SerialVersionUID(1L)
class DbNodeDownException(msg: String)
  extends Exception(msg) with Serializable
```
Exception occurs when database node has fatally crashed.

The messages that the actors send to each other in the log-processing application are kept together in the companion object of the respective actor.

Listing 4.13 `LogProcessor` companion object

```
object LogProcessor {
  def props(databaseUrls: Vector[String]) =
    Props(new LogProcessor(databaseUrls))
  def name = s"log_processor_${UUID.randomUUID.toString}"
  // represents a new log file
  case class LogFile(file: File)
}
```
props to create the LogProcessor

Every LogProcessor gets a unique name.

The log file that is received from the FileWatcher. The LogProcessor will process these.

First let's start at the bottom of the hierarchy and look at the database writer that can crash on a DbBrokenConnectionException. When this exception happens, the dbWriter should be restarted.

Listing 4.14 `DbWriter` actor

```
object DbWriter  {
  def props(databaseUrl: String) =
    Props(new DbWriter(databaseUrl))
  def name(databaseUrl: String) =
    s"""db-writer-${databaseUrl.split("/").last}"""

  case class Line(time: Long, message: String, messageType: String)
}
class DbWriter(databaseUrl: String) extends Actor {
  val connection = new DbCon(databaseUrl)

  import DbWriter._
  def receive = {
```
Creates a human-readable name

A line in the log file parsed by the LogProcessor Actor

```
      case Line(time, message, messageType) =>
        connection.write(Map('time -> time,
          'message -> message,
          'messageType -> messageType))
    }

    override def postStop(): Unit = {
      connection.close()
    }
  }
```

> **Writing to the connection could crash the actor.**

> **Close the connection if the actor crashes or stops.**

The DbWriter is supervised by the LogProcessor.

Listing 4.15   LogProcessor supervises and monitors DbWriter

```
class LogProcessor(databaseUrls: Vector[String])
    extends Actor with ActorLogging with LogParsing {
  require(databaseUrls.nonEmpty)

  val initialDatabaseUrl = databaseUrls.head
  var alternateDatabases = databaseUrls.tail

  override def supervisorStrategy = OneForOneStrategy() {
    case _: DbBrokenConnectionException => Restart
    case _: DbNodeDownException => Stop
  }

  var dbWriter = context.actorOf(
    DbWriter.props(initialDatabaseUrl),
    DbWriter.name(initialDatabaseUrl)
  )
  context.watch(dbWriter)

  import LogProcessor._

  def receive = {
    case LogFile(file) =>
      val lines: Vector[DbWriter.Line] = parse(file)
      lines.foreach(dbWriter ! _)
    case Terminated(_) =>
      if(alternateDatabases.nonEmpty) {
        val newDatabaseUrl = alternateDatabases.head
        alternateDatabases = alternateDatabases.tail
        dbWriter = context.actorOf(
          DbWriter.props(newDatabaseUrl),
          DbWriter.name(newDatabaseUrl)
        )
        context.watch(dbWriter)
      } else {
        log.error("All Db nodes broken, stopping.")
        self ! PoisonPill
      }
  }
}
```

> **Restart when retrying a connection might work.**

> **Stop when re-connecting will always fail.**

> **Create the dbWriter child actor and watch it.**

> **Send lines to the dbWriter**

> **If the dbWriter is terminated, create a new dbWriter from the next alternative URL, and watch it.**

> **All alternatives failed; stop the LogProcessor.**

If the database connection is broken, the database writer will be re-created from the `Props` object. The `DbWriter` creates a new connection in its constructor from a `databaseUrl`.

The `dbWriter` is replaced if the `DbNodeDownException` is detected. The `LogProcessor` stops itself through a `PoisonPill` if all alternatives have been exhausted. The line that was being processed when the `DbBrokenConnectionException` crashed the actor is lost. We'll look at a solution for this later in this section. The next actor up the hierarchy in the logs application is the `LogProcessor`.

The `LogProcessor` crashes when a corrupt file is detected. In that case we don't want to process the file any further; thus, we ignore it. The `FileWatcher` resumes the crashed actor.

Listing 4.16 FileWatcher supervises LogProcessor

```scala
class FileWatcher(source: String,
                  databaseUrls: Vector[String])
  extends Actor with ActorLogging with FileWatchingAbilities {
  register(source)                                          ⟵  Registers on a source URI in file-watching API

  override def supervisorStrategy = OneForOneStrategy() {
    case _: CorruptedFileException => Resume              ⟵  Resume if a corrupt file is detected
  }
  val logProcessor = context.actorOf(
    LogProcessor.props(databaseUrls),
    LogProcessor.name
  )
  context.watch(logProcessor)                              ⟵  Create and watch LogProcessor

  import FileWatcher._

  def receive = {
    case NewFile(file, _) =>                               ⟵  Sent by file-watching API when new file is encountered
      logProcessor ! LogProcessor.LogFile(file)
    case SourceAbandoned(uri) if uri == source =>
      log.info(s"$uri abandoned, stopping file watcher.")
      self ! PoisonPill                                    ⟵
    case Terminated(`logProcessor`) =>
      log.info(s"Log processor terminated, stopping file watcher.")
      self ! PoisonPill
  }
}
```

FileWatcher kills itself when source has been abandoned, indicating to file-watching API not to expect more new files from source

FileWatcher should stop when LogProcessor stops because database alternatives have been exhausted in DbWriter

We'll not get into the details of the file-watching API; it's hypothetically provided in a `FileWatchingAbilities` trait. The `FileWatcher` doesn't take any dangerous actions and will continue to run until the file-watching API notifies the `FileWatcher` that the source of files is abandoned. The `LogProcessingSupervisor` monitors the `File-`

Watchers for termination, and it also handles the DiskError that could've happened at any point lower in the supervisor hierarchy. Since the DiskError isn't defined lower down the hierarchy, it will automatically be escalated. This is an unrecoverable error, so the FileWatchingSupervisor decides to stop all the actors in the hierarchy when this occurs. An AllForOneStrategy is used so that if any of the file watchers crashes with a DiskError, all file watchers are stopped.

Listing 4.17 LogProcessingSupervisor

```
object LogProcessingSupervisor {
  def props(sources: Vector[String], databaseUrls: Vector[String]) =
    Props(new LogProcessingSupervisor(sources, databaseUrls))
  def name = "file-watcher-supervisor"
}

class LogProcessingSupervisor(
  sources: Vector[String],
  databaseUrls: Vector[String]
) extends Actor with ActorLogging {

  var fileWatchers: Vector[ActorRef] = sources.map { source =>
    val fileWatcher = context.actorOf(
      Props(new FileWatcher(source, databaseUrls))
    )
    context.watch(fileWatcher)          ◁────── Watch every FileWatcher
    fileWatcher
  }

  override def supervisorStrategy = AllForOneStrategy() {
    case _: DiskError => Stop          ◁────── Stop a FileWatcher on DiskError. The LogProcessor and DbWriter created further down the hierarchy are also automatically stopped.
  }

  def receive = {
    case Terminated(fileWatcher) =>          ◁────── Terminated message is received for a file watcher.
      fileWatchers = fileWatchers.filterNot(_ == fileWatcher)
      if (fileWatchers.isEmpty) {
        log.info("Shutting down, all file watchers have failed.")
        context.system.terminate()          ◁────── When all file watchers are terminated, terminate the actor system so that the application terminates.
      }
  }
}
```

The OneForOneStrategy and AllForOneStrategy will continue indefinitely by default. Both strategies have default values for the constructor arguments maxNrOf-Retries and withinTimeRange. In some cases you might like the strategy to stop after a number of retries or when a certain amount of time has passed. Simply set these arguments to the desired values. Once configured with the constraints, the fault is escalated if the crash is not solved within the time range specified or within a maximum number of retries. The following code gives an example of an impatient database supervisor strategy.

Listing 4.18 Impatient database supervisor strategy

```
override def supervisorStrategy = OneForOneStrategy(
  maxNrOfRetries = 5,
  withinTimeRange = 60 seconds) {
    case _: DbBrokenConnectionException => Restart
  }
```

◁ — **Escalates the issue if the problem hasn't been resolved within 60 seconds or it has failed to be solved within five restarts**

NOTE It's important to note that there's no delay between restarts; the actor will be restarted as fast as possible. If you require some form of delay between restarts, Akka provides a special `BackOffSupervisor` actor that you can pass the `Props` of your own actor to. This `BackOfSupervisor` creates the actor from the `Props` and supervises it, and does use a delay mechanism to prevent fast restarts.

This mechanism can be used to prevent an actor from continuously restarting without any effect. When you use this functionality, you would probably combine this with the watch functionality to implement a strategy when the supervised actor has terminated; for example, try to create the actor again after a while.

4.4   Summary

Fault tolerance is one of the most exciting aspects of Akka, and it's a critical component in the toolkit's approach to concurrency. The philosophy of "let it crash" is not a doctrine of ignoring the possible malfunctions that might occur, or the toolkit swooping in and healing any faults. It's somewhat the opposite: the programmer needs to anticipate recovery requirements, but the tools to deliver them without meeting a catastrophic end (or having to write a ton of code) are unparalleled. In the course of making our example log processor fault tolerant, you saw that

- Supervision means you have a clean separation of recovery code.
- The fact that the actor model is built on messages means that even when an actor goes away, you can still continue to function.
- You can resume, abandon, restart; the choice is yours, given the requirements in each case.
- You can even escalate through the hierarchy of supervisors.

Again, Akka's philosophy shines through here: pull the actual operational needs of the application up into the code, but do it in a structured way, with support from the toolkit. The result is that sophisticated fault tolerance that would be difficult to achieve can be built and tested while the code is being written, without a tremendous amount of extra effort.

Now that you know how Akka can help you implement functionality in a concurrent system by using actors and how to deal with errors within these actors, you can start building an application. In the next section we'll build several different types of actor-based applications, and will look at how to provide services like configuration, logging, and deployment.

5
Futures

In this chapter we'll introduce *futures*. In short, futures are extremely useful and simple tools for combining functions asynchronously. The Akka toolkit initially provided its own future implementation. At the same time, several other libraries also had a future type, like the *Twitter Finagle* and *scalaz* libraries. Having proven its usefulness, the *scala.concurrent* package was redesigned through the Scala Improvement Process (SIP-14) to include Future as a common foundation in the standard Scala library. The Future type has been included in the standard library since Scala 2.10.

Like actors, futures are important asynchronous building blocks that create an opportunity for parallel execution. Both actors and futures are great tools best used for different use cases. It's a question of the right tool for the right job. We'll start with describing the type of use case that futures are best suited for, and work through some examples in section 5.1, "Use cases for futures." Whereas actors provide a mechanism to build a system out of concurrent *objects*, futures provide a mechanism to build a system out of asynchronous *functions*.

A future makes it possible to process the result of a function without ever waiting in the current thread for the result. Exactly how you can achieve this will become clear in section 5.2. We'll focus on showing you examples of how to best use futures instead of diving into the abstraction details that make the Future[T] type possible. Futures are *composable* with other futures, which in short means that they can be freely combined in many ways. You'll learn how to compose flows of asynchronous web service calls in section 5.4 and how to handle errors in section 5.3.

You don't have to choose between futures or actors; they can be used together. Akka provides common actor and future patterns that make it easy to work with both, which is detailed in section 5.5.

5.1   Use cases for futures

In the chapters so far, you've learned a lot about actors.

To contrast the best use cases for futures, we'll briefly think about use cases that *can* be implemented with actors, but not without unwanted complexity. Futures will make these use cases a lot simpler to implement. Actors are great for processing many messages, capturing state, and reacting with different behavior based on the state they're in and the messages they receive. They're resilient *objects* that can live on for a long time even when problems occur, using monitoring and supervision.

Futures are the tool to use when you would rather use *functions* and don't want or need to keep any state to do the job.

A *future* is a placeholder for a function result (a success or failure) that will be available at some point in the future. It's effectively an asynchronous result handle. It gives you a way to point at a result that will eventually become available. Figure 5.1 shows the concept.

A future is a read-only placeholder. It can't be changed from the outside. A future will contain a successful result or a failure once the function is completed. After completion, the result inside the future can't change and can be read many times; it will

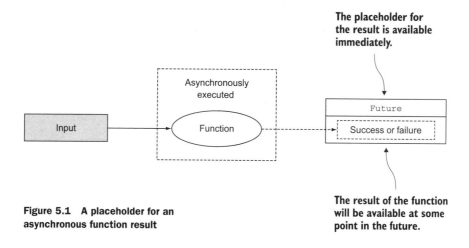

Figure 5.1   A placeholder for an asynchronous function result

always give the same result. Having a placeholder for the result makes it easier to combine many functions that are executed asynchronously. You can simply say what should be done with it once it's there, as you'll see in the next sections. For example, it gives you a way to call a web service without blocking the current thread.

> **THIS IS NOT POJF (PLAIN OLD JAVA FUTURE)**   To prevent any confusion, if you're familiar with the `java.util.concurrent.Future` class in Java 7, you might think that the `scala.concurrent.Future` discussed in this chapter is just a Scala wrapper around this Java class. This is not the case. The `java.util` `.concurrent.Future` class requires polling and only provides a way to get to the result with a blocking `get` method, whereas the Scala future makes it possible to combine function results without blocking or polling, as you'll learn in this chapter. The `CompletableFuture<T>` introduced in Java 8 (after `Future[T]` was already available in Scala) is more comparable.

To understand this better, we'll look at another use case for the ticket system. We'd like to create a web page with extra information about the event and the venue. The ticket would simply link to this web page so that customers can access it from their mobile device, for instance. We might want to show a weather forecast for the venue when it's an open-air event, route planning to the event around the time of the event (should I take public transport or drive by car?), where to park, or suggestions for similar future events that the customer might be interested in.

Futures are especially handy for *pipelining*, where one function provides the input for a next function, fanning out to many functions in parallel, later to combine the results of these functions. The `TicketInfo` service will find related information for an event based on the ticket number. Any service that provides a part of the information might be down, and we don't want to block on every service request while aggregating the information. Rest assured that we'll start off with simple examples. Figure 5.2 shows the goal we'll work towards in this chapter.

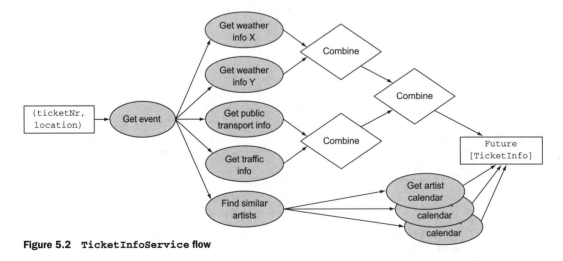

Figure 5.2 `TicketInfoService` flow

Figure 5.3 Chain asynchronous functions

If services don't respond in time or fail, their information should not be shown. To be able to show the route to the event, we'll first need to find the event using the ticket number, which is shown in figure 5.3.

In this case `getEvent` and `getTraffic` are both functions that do asynchronous web service calls, executed one after the other. The `getTrafficInfo` web service call takes an `Event` argument. `getTrafficInfo` is called the moment the event becomes available in the `Future[Event]` result. This is very different from calling the `getEvent` method and polling and waiting for the event on the current thread. We simply define a flow, and the `getTrafficInfo` function will be called *eventually*, without polling or waiting on a thread. The functions execute as soon as they can. The current thread doesn't have to wait for the execution of the web service calls. Limiting waiting threads is obviously *a good thing* because they should instead be doing something useful.

Figure 5.4 shows a simple example where calling services asynchronously is ideal. It shows a mobile device calling the `TicketInfo` service, which aggregates information from a weather and traffic service.

Not having to wait for the weather service before calling the traffic service decreases the latency of the mobile device request. The more services need to be called, the more dramatic the effect on latency will be since the responses can be processed in parallel. Figure 5.5 shows another use case. In this case we'd like the fastest result of two competing weather services.

Maybe weather service X is malfunctioning and times out on the request. In that case you wouldn't want to wait for this timeout, but rather use the fast response of weather service Y, which is working as expected.

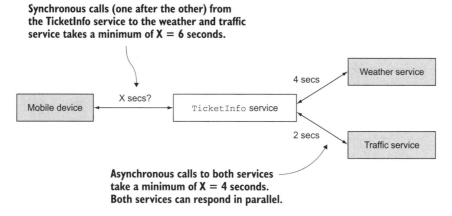

Figure 5.4 Aggregating results, sync versus async

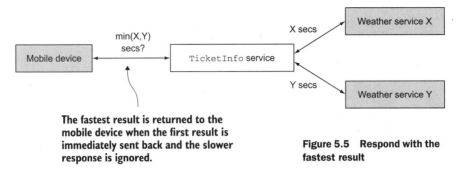

The fastest result is returned to the
mobile device when the first result is
immediately sent back and the slower
response is ignored.

**Figure 5.5   Respond with the
fastest result**

It's not as if these scenarios are impossible to execute with actors. It's just that we'd
have to do a lot of work for such a simple use case. Take the example of aggregating
weather and traffic information. Actors have to be created, messages defined, and
receive functions implemented as part of an ActorSystem. We'd have to think about
how to handle timeouts, when to stop the actors, and how to create new actors for
every web page request and combine the responses. Figure 5.6 shows how actors could
be used to do this.

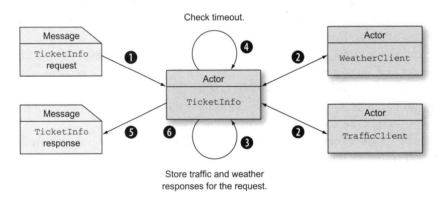

❶ Create TicketInfo actor and send request.

❷ Create child actors and send request; correlate
request with responses.

❸ Store the responses of the child actors.

❹ Send scheduled timeout message to TicketInfo actor
in case one of the child actors does not respond.

❺ Send back aggregated information response at timeout
or when both responses have been received.

❻ Stop TicketInfo actor and child actors after
sending; only do this once per request.

**Figure 5.6   Combine web
service requests with actors**

We need two separate actors for the weather and traffic web service calls so that they can be called in parallel. How the web service calls are combined will need to be coded in the `TicketInfoActor` for every specific case. That's a lot of work for just calling two web services and combining the results. Note however that actors are a better choice when fine-grained control over state is required, or when actions need to be monitored or possibly retried.

So although actors are a great tool, they're not the "be all and end all" on our quest to never block again. In this case a tool specifically made for combining function results would be a lot simpler.

There are some variations on the preceding use case where futures are the best tool for the job. In general the use cases have one or more of the following characteristics:

- You don't want to block (wait on the current thread) to handle the result of a function.
- Calling a function once-off and handling the result at some point in the future.
- Combining many once-off functions and combining the results.
- Calling many competing functions and only using some of the results, for instance only the fastest response.
- Calling a function and returning a default result when the function throws an exception so the flow can continue.
- Pipelining these kind of functions, where one function depends on one or more results of other functions.

In the next sections we're going to look at the details of implementing the `Ticket-Info` service with futures. We'll start with just calling one web service asynchronously.

5.2　*In the future nobody blocks*

It's time to build the `TicketInfoService` and we're not explicitly going to sit on any thread waiting idly by. We're going to start with the `TicketInfo` service and try to execute the two steps in figure 5.7 so that we can provide traffic information about the route to the event.

The first step is to get the event for the ticket number. The big difference between calling a function synchronously and calling it asynchronously is the flow in which you define your program. Listing 5.1 shows an example of a *synchronous* web service call to get the event for the ticket number.

Figure 5.7　Get traffic information about the event

Listing 5.1   Synchronous call

```
val request = EventRequest(ticketNr)
val response: EventResponse = callEventService(request)
val event: Event = response.event
```

Creates the request

Reads the event value

Blocks main thread until the response is completed

Listing 5.1 shows three lines of code executed on some thread. The flow is simple: a function is called and its return value is immediately accessible on the same thread. The program obviously can't continue on the same thread before the value is accessible. Scala expressions are strict (evaluated immediately), so every line in the code has to "produce a complete value."

Let's see what we need to do to change this synchronous web service call into an asynchronous one. In the preceding case, the callEventService is a blocking call to a web service; it needs to wait on a thread for the response. We'll first wrap the callEventService into a code block and execute it on a separate thread. The following listing shows the change in the code.

Listing 5.2   Asynchronous call

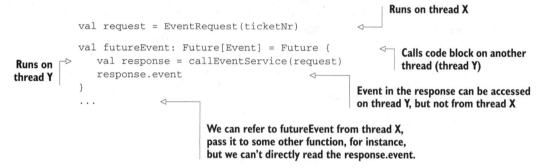

```
val request = EventRequest(ticketNr)

val futureEvent: Future[Event] = Future {
    val response = callEventService(request)
    response.event
}
...
```

Runs on thread X

Calls code block on another thread (thread Y)

Runs on thread Y

Event in the response can be accessed on thread Y, but not from thread X

We can refer to futureEvent from thread X, pass it to some other function, for instance, but we can't directly read the response.event.

Future { ... } is shorthand for a call to the apply method on the Future object with the code block as its only argument, Future.apply(codeblock). It's a helper function to (immediately) execute the "code block" on another thread. (This is possible because the code block argument is *passed by name*, more on that later) The code block that returns an Event is only evaluated once.

In case you're new to Scala, the last expression in a block is automatically the return value. The Future.apply method returns a Future of whatever type the code block evaluates to, in this case a Future[Event].

The type of the futureEvent value is explicitly type annotated for this example but can be omitted because of type inference in Scala. Throughout this chapter we'll add type annotations so it's easier to follow along.

FUTURE APPLY FUNCTION ARGUMENTS The code block provided to the Future.apply method is *passed by name*. A pass-by-name argument only gets evaluated the first time it's referenced *inside* the function. In the case of the Future, it's evaluated on another thread. The code block in listing 5.2 refers to the request value from the other thread (we called it thread X in the example). Referring to a value like this is called *closing over* a value, in this case closing over the request, which is how we bridge between the main thread and the other thread and pass the request to the web service call.

Great, the web service is now called on a separate thread, and we could handle the response right there. Let's see how we can chain the call to callTrafficService to get the traffic information for the event in listing 5.3. As a first step we'll print the route to the event to the console.

Listing 5.3 Handling the event result

```
futureEvent.foreach { event =>                              ◁── Asynchronously processes
  val trafficRequest = TrafficRequest(                          the event result when it
    destination = event.location,                               becomes available
    arrivalTime = event.time
  )
  val trafficResponse = callTrafficService(trafficRequest)   ◁──
  println(trafficResponse.route)                                Calls the traffic service synchronously
}                                                               with a request based on the event,
                                                                returning a TrafficResponse
```
Prints the route to the console → `println(trafficResponse.route)`

The preceding listing uses the foreach method on Future, which calls the code block with the event result when it becomes available. The code block is only called when the callEventService is successful.

In this case we expect to use the Route later on as well, so it would be better if we could return a Future[Route]. The foreach method returns Unit, so we'll have to use something else. The next listing shows how this is done with the map method.

Listing 5.4 Chaining the event result

Handles the event and returns a Future[Route]

```
val futureRoute: Future[Route] = futureEvent.map { event =>  ◁──
  val trafficRequest = TrafficRequest(
    destination = event.location,
    arrivalTime = event.time
  )                                                           Still calling the
  val trafficResponse = callTrafficService(trafficRequest)  ◁── callTrafficService
  trafficResponse.route      ◁──                              synchronously,
}                                                             which directly
         Returns the value to the map function,               returns a
         which turns it into a Future[Route]                  response
```

Both foreach and map should be familiar to you from using the scala.collections library and standard types like Option and List. Conceptually the Future.map method is similar to, for example, `Option.map`. Where the `Option.map` method calls a code block if it contains some value and returns a new `Option[T]` value, the `Future.map` method eventually calls a code block when it contains a successful result and returns a new `Future[T]` value—in this case, a `Future[Route]` because the last line in the code block returns a `Route` value. Once again the type of `futureRoute` is explicitly defined, which can be omitted. The following code shows how you can chain both web service calls directly.

Listing 5.5 `getRoute` method with `Future[Route]` result

```
val request = EventRequest(ticketNr)

val futureRoute: Future[Route] = Future {
  callEventService(request).event
}.map { event =>                               <———— Chains on the Future[Event]
  val trafficRequest = TrafficRequest(
    destination = event.location,
    arrivalTime = event.time
  )
  callTrafficService(trafficRequest).route     <———— Returns the route
}
```

If we refactor into a `getEvent` method that takes a `ticketNr` and a `getRoute` method that takes an event argument, the code in the following listing would chain the two calls. The methods `getEvent` and `getRoute` respectively return a `Future[Event]` and `Future[Route]`.

Listing 5.6 Refactored version

```
val futureRoute: Future[route] = getEvent(ticketNr).flatMap { event =>   <┐
  getRoute(event)                                                          │
}              We need to use flatMap; otherwise, futureRoute              │
                        would be a Future[Future[Route]].                  │
```

The preceding listing shows that we now use `flatMap` to compose `getEvent` and `getRoute`. If we used `map` we would end up with `Future[Future[Route]]`. With `flatMap` you need to return a `Future[T]`, which is returned as the result. (This is once again similar to `Option.flatMap`, for instance.)

The `callEventService` and `callTrafficService` methods in the previous examples were blocking calls to show the transition from a synchronous to an asynchronous call. To really benefit from the asynchronous style, the preceding `getEvent` and `getRoute` should be implemented with a nonblocking I/O API and return futures directly to minimize the amount of blocking threads. The akka-http module provides an asynchronous HTTP client. In the next sections, you can assume that the web service calls are implemented with akka-http.

A detail that has been omitted so far is that you need to provide an *implicit* `ExecutionContext` to use futures. If you don't provide this, your code won't compile. The following code shows how you can import an implicit value for the global execution context.

```
import scala.concurrent.Implicits.global    ⟵── Uses the global ExecutionContext
```

The `ExecutionContext` is an abstraction for executing tasks on some thread pool implementation. If you're familiar with the `java.util.concurrent` package, it can be compared to a `java.util.concurrent.Executor` interface with extras.

The import shown in listing 5.7 puts the *global execution context* in implicit scope so that the future can use it to execute the code block on some thread.

In section 5.5, "Combining futures with actors," you'll see that the dispatcher of an actor system can be used as an `ExecutionContext` as well, which is a better choice than the global execution context since you can't know what other processes might use the global execution context.

The next section will explain the `Promise[T]` type. If you can simply use APIs that return `Future`, then you probably won't run into `Promise[T]` very often. This means you can come back to this short section once you do and skip some of the details, moving right along to the next section if you prefer, which will show how you can recover from error results.

5.2.1   *Promises are promises*

If a future is only for reading, what's doing the writing? You guessed it, it's the `Promise[T]`. If you look closely at the source code of `Future[T]` and its default implementation, you'll see that internally it's made up of two sides, the read-only future side and the write-only *promise* side. They're like two sides of the same coin.

There's a lot of tricky indirection in the source code of `Promise` and `Future`, which is left as an exercise to the reader who really wants to know the low-level details.

It's easiest to see how a promise works by looking at an example. You can use `Promise[T]` to wrap an existing multithreaded callback-style API into an API that returns `Future[T]`. In this case we'll look at a small block of code for sending records to *Apache Kafka*. Without getting into too much detail, a Kafka cluster makes it possible to write records to an append-only log. A log is partitioned and replicated across a number of servers called *brokers* for scalability and failover reasons. Most importantly for this example, a `KafkaProducer` can send records asynchronously to the Kafka brokers. The `KafkaProducer` has a `send` method that takes a callback argument. The callback will be called once the record has been successfully sent to the cluster. The following listing shows how you can use a promise to wrap this callback-style method and return a future instead.

> Creates a Promise of the expected
> result type, RecordMetadata

```
def sendToKafka(record: ProducerRecord): Future[RecordMetadata] = {
  val promise: Promise[[RecordMetadata] = Promise[RecordMetadata]()   ⟵──┘
```

```
                 val future: Future[RecordMetadata] = promise.future    ◄──────────────────────┐
Writes a failure                                                                                │
   to the promise   val callback = new Callback() {                      ◄────────────────────┐ │
   if there's an      def onCompletion(metadata: RecordMetadata, e: Exception): Unit = {      │ │
        error.  └┐      if (e != null) promise.failure(e)                                      │ │
                └►      else promise.success(metadata)            This is the Kafka callback   │ │
   Writes a   ┌►     }                                            that's used to indicate that │ │
   success to │    }                                              sending has completed. It's  │ │
   the promise │    producer.send(record, callback)     ◄─┐      called once after sending the │ │
   otherwise  │    future  ◄─┐                            │      record has completed on       │ │
             │  }            │                            │              another thread.       │ │
                             │                            │                                    │ │
                    Returns the future to        Does the actual                               │ │
                    the user of the              sending, passing      Gets a reference to the │ │
                    sendToKafka method           in the callback       Future[RecordMetadata]  │ │
                                                                       that we can pass on ─────┘ │
```

The code is type annotated again for clarity. A promise can only be completed once. `promise.success(metadata)` and `promise.failure(e)` are shorthand for `promise.complete(Success(metadata))` and `promise.complete(Failure(e))`, respectively. An `IllegalStateException` is thrown if the promise has already been completed and you try to complete it again.

In this simple example we didn't have to do much, other than getting a reference to the future and completing the promise. In more complex usage scenarios, you'll need to make sure that every other data structure you need can be safely used in a multithreaded context. The source code for `Promise` and `Future` is a great source of inspiration for this.

Now that you know how a promise can be used to wrap a callback API, we'll go a little deeper down the rabbit hole for those who are interested in how the promise and future work internally. It's not essential to know this, so feel free to skip ahead to the next section. Figure 5.8 shows how the `Future.apply` method creates a promise and returns a future on thread X.

We're leaving out some details here, but the figure shows in broad lines how `Future.apply` creates a `Runnable` subclass. The `Runnable` holds on to a promise so that it can use it once it's run on another thread. The same promise is returned *as a future* from `Future.apply`. Again, we're leaving out some indirection, but essentially `DefaultPromise[T]` extends both `Future[T]` and `Promise[T]`, so it can "act like both types."

What is essential here is that both the `Runnable` and the client of the `Future.apply` get a reference to the same value, `DefaultPromise`. `DefaultPromise` is built to be used from several threads at the same time, so this is safe. Figure 5.9 shows what happens when `PromiseCompletingRunnable` is run on another thread, which we'll call thread Y.

The `PromiseCompletingRunnable` completes the promise just like we did in the Kafka example, which causes all registered callbacks to be called with the end result of the body. Once again a lot of detail is left out here. Callbacks are only called once, callbacks are run themselves on an executor, and the implementation of `Future` and `Promise` makes sure that all of this happens correctly using low-level concurrent programming techniques. Looking further into these details is left as an exercise to the reader.

As promised, the next section will show you how you can recover from error results.

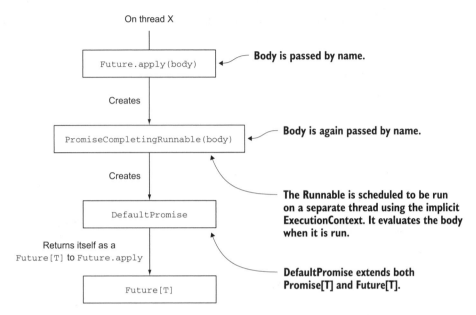

Figure 5.8   Creating the promise and future

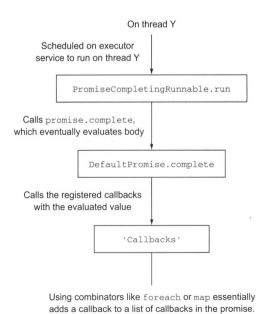

Figure 5.9   Completing the promise

5.3   *Futuristic errors*

The future results in the previous section were expected to always succeed. Let's look at what happens if an `Exception` is thrown in the code block. To illustrate, we're going to immediately throw an `Exception`. We'll `foreach` on the future and print the result. Start up a Scala REPL session on the command line and follow along with the next listing.

Listing 5.9   Throwing an exception from the future

```
scala> :paste
// Entering paste mode (ctrl-D to finish)

import scala.concurrent._
import ExecutionContext.Implicits.global

val futureFail = Future { throw new Exception("error!")}
futureFail.foreach(value => println(value))

// Exiting paste mode, now interpreting.

futureFail: scala.concurrent.Future[Nothing] =
   scala.concurrent.impl.Promise$DefaultPromise@193cd8e1

scala>
```

Tries to print the value once the future has completed

Nothing gets printed since exception occurred

The `Exception` is thrown in some thread. The first thing you notice is that you don't see a stack trace in the console, which you would've seen if the exception were thrown in the main REPL thread. The `foreach` block didn't get executed. This is because the future isn't completed with a successful value. One of the ways to get to the exception is to use the `onComplete` method. This method also takes a code block like `foreach` and `map`, but in this case it provides a `scala.util.Try` argument. The `Try` can be a `Success` or a `Failure`. The following REPL session shows how it can be used to print the exception.

Listing 5.10   Using `onComplete` to handle success and failure

```
scala> :paste
// Entering paste mode (ctrl-D to finish)

import scala.util._
import scala.concurrent._
import ExecutionContext.Implicits.global

val futureFail = Future { throw new Exception("error!")}
futureFail.onComplete {
  case Success(value) => println(value)
  case Failure(e) => println(e)
}

// Exiting paste mode, now interpreting.

java.lang.Exception: error!
```

Imports statement for Try, Success, and Failure

The block is given a try value. Try supports pattern matching, so we can just give onComplete a partial function that matches on Success or Failure.

Prints the successful value

Prints the non-fatal exception

Exception is printed

The onComplete method makes it possible to handle the success or failure result. Take note in this example that the onComplete callback is executed even if the future has already finished, which is quite possible in this case since an exception is directly thrown in the future block. This is true for all functions that are registered on a future.

> **FATAL AND NON-FATAL EXCEPTIONS** Fatal exceptions are never handled by a future. If you would create a Future { new OutOfMemoryError("arghh") }, you would find out that the future isn't created at all; the OOME (OutOfMemory-Error) is thrown straight through. There's a scala.util.control.NonFatal extractor that gets applied inside the future logic, which is there for a good reason. It would be a terrible idea to be able to ignore important fatal errors or render them invisible. Fatal exceptions are VirtualMachineError, Thread-Death, InterruptedException, LinkageError, and ControlThrowable (currently, just look in the source code of scala.util.control.NonFatal). Most of these should be familiar; ControlThrowable is a marker for exceptions that shouldn't normally be caught.

The onComplete method returns Unit, so we can't chain to a next function. Similarly there's an onFailure method that makes it possible to match exceptions. onFailure also returns Unit, so we can't use it for further chaining. The following listing shows the use of onFailure.

Listing 5.11 Using `onFailure` to match on all non-fatal exceptions

```
futureFail.onFailure {            ◁─── Called when the function has failed
  case e => println(e)            ◁─── Matches on all non-fatal exception types
}
```

We'll need to be able to continue accumulating information in the TicketInfo service when exceptions occur. The TicketInfo service aggregates information about the event and should be able to leave out parts of the information if the required service throws an exception. Figure 5.10 shows how the information around the event will be accumulated in a TicketInfo class for a part of the flow of the TicketInfo service.

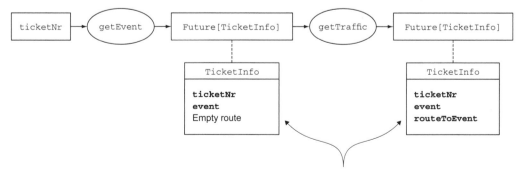

Figure 5.10 Accumulate information about the event in `TicketInfo`

Every step adds information to the TicketInfo contained in the Future. The route is initially empty. (Bold means the element has been added to the TicketInfo value.)

The getEvent and getTraffic methods are modified to return Future[TicketInfo], which will be used to accumulate information further down the chain. The Ticket-Info class is a simple case class that contains optional values for the service results. The following listing shows the TicketInfo case class. In the next sections we'll add more information to this class, like a weather forecast and suggestions for other events.

Listing 5.12   `TicketInfo` case class

```
case class TicketInfo(ticketNr:String,
                      event:Option[Event]=None,
                      route:Option[Route]=None)
```
All extra information about the ticketNr is optional and empty by default

It's important to note that you should always use immutable data structures when working with futures. Otherwise, it would be possible to share mutable state between futures that possibly use the same objects. We're safe here since we're using case classes and Options, which are immutable. When a service call fails, the chain should continue with the TicketInfo that it had accumulated so far. Figure 5.11 shows how a failed GetTraffic call should be handled.

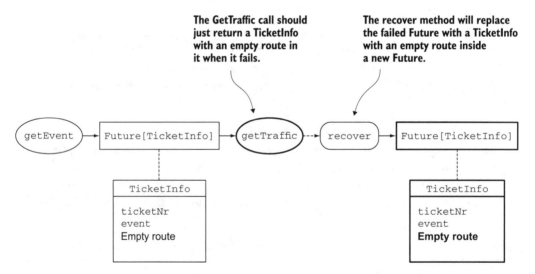

The GetTraffic call should just return a TicketInfo with an empty route in it when it fails.

The recover method will replace the failed Future with a TicketInfo with an empty route inside a new Future.

Figure 5.11   Ignore failed service response

The recover method can be used to achieve this. This method makes it possible to define what result must be returned when exceptions occur. The following listing shows how it can be used to return the input TicketInfo when a TrafficService-Exception is thrown.

Listing 5.13   Using `recover` to continue with an alternative future result

Gets event; returns a Future[TicketInfo]

```
val futureStep1: Future[TicketInfo] = getEvent(ticketNr)

val futureStep2: Future[TicketInfo] = futureStep1.flatMap { ticketInfo =>
  getTraffic(ticketInfo).recover {
    case _: TrafficServiceException => ticketInfo
  }
}
```

getTraffic returns a Future[TicketInfo]

recover with a Future containing the initial TicketInfo value

flatMap is used so we can directly return a Future[TicketInfo] instead of a TicketInfo value from code block

The `recover` method defines that it must return the original `ticketInfo` as the future result when a `TrafficServiceException` occurs. The `getTraffic` method normally creates a copy of the `TicketInfo` value with the route added to it. In this example we use `flatMap` instead of `map` on the future returned by `getEvent`. In the code block passed to `map`, you need to return a `TicketInfo` value, which will be wrapped in a new `Future`. With `flatMap` you need to return a `Future[TicketInfo]` directly. Since `getTraffic` already returns a `Future[TicketInfo]`, it's better to use `flatMap`.

Similarly there's a `recoverWith` method where the code block must return a `Future[TicketInfo]` instead of a `TicketInfo`. Be aware that the code block passed to the `recover` method call is executed *synchronously* after the error has been returned, so it's best to keep the `recover` block simple.

In the preceding code there's still a problem left. What will happen if the first `getEvent` call fails? The code block in the `flatMap` call won't be called because `futureStep1` has failed, so there's no value to chain the next call on. `futureStep2` will equal `futureStep1`, a failed future result. If we want to return an empty `TicketInfo` containing only the `ticketNr`, we must recover for the first step as well, which is shown in the following listing.

Listing 5.14   Using `recover` to return an empty `TicketInfo` if `getEvent` failed

```
val futureStep1: Future[TicketInfo] = getEvent(ticketNr)

val futureStep2: Future[TicketInfo] = futureStep1.flatMap { ticketInfo =>
  getTraffic(ticketInfo).recover {
    case _:TrafficServiceException => ticketInfo
  }
}.recover {
  case e => TicketInfo(ticketNr)
}
```

Returns an empty TicketInfo which only contains the ticketNr in case getEvent failed

The code block in the `flatMap` call won't be executed when `futureStep1` fails. The `flatMap` will simply return a failed future result. The last `recover` call in the preceding listing turns this failed `Future` into a `Future[TicketInfo]`. Now that you've learned how you can recover from errors in a chain of futures, we'll look at more ways to combine futures for the `TicketInfo` service.

5.4   *Combining futures*

In the previous sections, you were introduced to map and flatMap to chain asynchronous functions with futures. In this section we'll look at more ways to combine asynchronous functions with futures. Both the Future[T] trait and the Future object
provide *combinator methods* like flatMap and map to combine futures. These combinator
methods are similar to flatMap, map, and others found in the *Scala Collections API*. They
make it possible to create pipelines of transformations from one immutable collection
to the next, solving a problem step by step. In this section we'll only scratch the surface
of the possibilities of combining futures in a functional style. If you'd like to know
more about functional programming in Scala, we recommend *Functional Programming
in Scala* by Paul Chiusano and Rúnar Bjarnason (Manning Publications, 2014).

The TicketInfo service needs to combine several web service calls to provide the
additional information. We'll use the combinator methods to add information to the
TicketInfo step by step, using functions that take a TicketInfo and return a
Future[TicketInfo]. At every step, a copy of the TicketInfo case class is made,
which is passed on to the next function, eventually building a complete TicketInfo
value. The TicketInfo case class, as well as the other case classes that are used in the
service, has been updated and is shown in the following listing.

Listing 5.15   Improved `TicketInfo` class

```
case class TicketInfo(ticketNr:String,
                      userLocation:Location,
                      event:Option[Event]=None,
                      travelAdvice:Option[TravelAdvice]=None,
                      weather:Option[Weather]=None,
                      suggestions:Seq[Event]=Seq())          ◁──  TicketInfo case class
                                                                  collects travel advice,
case class Event(name:String,location:Location,                   weather, and event
                 time:DateTime)                                   suggestions

case class Weather(temperature:Int, precipitation:Boolean)

case class RouteByCar(route:String,
                      timeToLeave:DateTime,
                      origin:Location,
                      destination:Location,
                      estimatedDuration:Duration,              To keep example simple,
                      trafficJamTime:Duration)      ◁──────    the route is just a string

case class TravelAdvice(routeByCar:Option[RouteByCar]=None,
  publicTransportAdvice: Option[PublicTransportAdvice]=None)

case class PublicTransportAdvice(advice:String,
  timeToLeave:DateTime,                              To keep example
  origin:Location, destination:Location,            simple, the advice
  estimatedDuration:Duration)         ◁─────────    is just a string

case class Location(lat:Double, lon:Double)

case class Artist(name:String, calendarUri:String)
```

All items are optional except the ticket number and the location of the user. Every step in the flow will add some information by copying the argument TicketInfo and modifying properties in the new TicketInfo value, passing it to the next function. The associated information will be left empty if a service call can't be completed, as we've shown in the section on futuristic errors. Figure 5.12 shows the flow of asynchronous web service calls and the combinators that we'll use in this example.

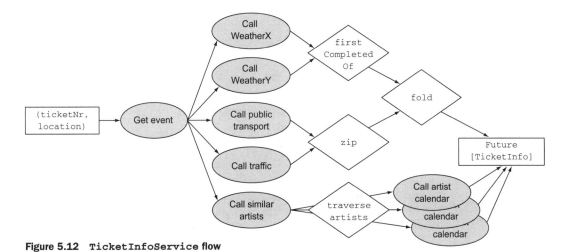

Figure 5.12 `TicketInfoService` **flow**

The combinators are shown as diamonds in the figure. We'll look at every combinator in more detail. The flow starts with a ticketNr and a GPS location of the user of the TicketInfo service and eventually completes a TicketInfo future result. The fastest response from the weather services is used. Public transport and car route information are combined in a TravelAdvice. At the same time, similar artists are retrieved and the calendar for each Artist is requested. This results in suggestions for similar events. All futures are eventually combined into a Future[TicketInfo]. Eventually this final Future[TicketInfo] will have an onComplete callback that completes the HTTP request with a response back to the client, which we'll omit in these examples.

We'll start with combining the weather services. The TicketInfo service needs to call out to many weather services in parallel and use the quickest response. Figure 5.13 shows the combinators used in the flow.

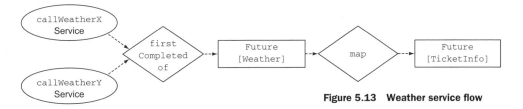

Figure 5.13   Weather service flow

Both weather services return a `Future[Weather]`, which needs to be turned into a `Future[TicketInfo]` for the next step. If one of the weather services is unresponsive, we can still inform the client about the weather with the response of the other service. The following listing shows how the `Future.firstCompletedOf` method is used in the `TicketInfoService` flow to respond to the first completed service.

Listing 5.16 Using `firstCompletedOf` to get the fastest response

```
def getWeather(ticketInfo: TicketInfo): Future[TicketInfo] = {

  val futureWeatherX: Future[Option[Weather]] =
    callWeatherXService(ticketInfo).recover(withNone)

  val futureWeatherY: Future[Option[Weather]] =
    callWeatherYService(ticketInfo).recover(withNone)

  val futures: List[Future[Option[Weather]]] =
    List(futureWeatherX, futureWeatherY)

  val fastestResponse: Future[Option[Weather]] =
    Future.firstCompletedOf(futures)

  fastestResponse.map { weatherResponse =>
    ticketInfo.copy(weather = weatherResponse)
  }
}
```

Error recovery is extracted out into a withNone function (omitted here). It simply recovers with a None value.

First completed Future[Weather].

Copy weather response into a new ticketInfo. Return the copy as the result of the map code block.

Map code block transforms the completed Weather value into TicketInfo, resulting in a Future[TicketInfo].

The first two futures are created for the weather service requests. The `Future.first-CompletedOf` function creates a new `Future` out of the two provided weather service future results. It's important to note that `firstCompletedOf` returns the first *completed* future. A future is completed with a successful value or a failure. With the preceding code, the `ticketInfo` service won't be able to add weather information when, for example, the WeatherX service fails faster than the WeatherY service can return a correct result. For now, this will do since we'll assume that an unresponsive service or a poorly performing service will respond slower than a correctly functioning service. Instead of `firstCompletedOf`, we could use `find`. `find` takes some futures and a predicate function to find a matching future and returns a `Future[Option[T]]`. The next listing shows how `find` can be used to get the first *successful* future result.

Listing 5.17 Using `find` to get the first successful result

```
val futures: List[Future[Option[Weather]]] =
  List(futureWeatherX, futureWeatherY)

val fastestSuccessfulResponse: Future[Option[Weather]] =
  Future.find(futures)(maybeWeather => !maybeWeather.isEmpty)
      .map(_.flatten)
```

First non-empty result is a match.

Result needs to be flattened, since find takes a TraversableOnce[Future[T]] and returns Future[Option[T]], and in this case T is actually Option[T]. (The futures value is List[Future[Option[Weather]]], not List[Future[Weather]].)

The public transport and car route service need to be processed in parallel and combined into a `TravelAdvice` when both results are available. Figure 5.14 shows the combinators used in the flow to add the travel advice.

Figure 5.14 Travel advice flow

`getTraffic` and `getPublicTransport` return two different types inside a future, `RouteByCar` and `PublicTransportAdvice`, respectively. These two values are first put together in a tuple value. The tuple is then mapped into a `TravelAdvice` value. The `TravelAdvice` class is shown in the following listing.

Listing 5.18 `TravelAdvice` class

```
case class TravelAdvice(
  routeByCar:Option[RouteByCar] = None,
  publicTransportAdvice: Option[PublicTransportAdvice] = None
)
```

Based on this information, the user can decide to travel by car or by public transport. The following listing shows how the `zip` combinator can be used for this.

Listing 5.19 Using `zip` and `map` to combine route and public transport advice

```
def getTravelAdvice(info:TicketInfo,
                    event:Event): Future[TicketInfo] = {

  val futureR: Future[Option[RouteByCar]] = callTraffic(
    info.userLocation,
    event.location,
    event.time
  ).recover(withNone)

  val futureP: Future[Option[PublicTransporAdvice]] =
    callPublicTransport(info.userLocation,
      event.location,
      event.time
    ).recover(withNone)

  futureR.zip(futureP)                               ⟵   Zip Future[RouteByCar] and
    .map {                                          ⟵    Future[PublicTransportAdvice]
      case(routeByCar, publicTransportAdvice) =>          into Future[(RouteByCar,
        val travelAdvice = TravelAdvice                    PublicTransportAdvice)].
                        (routeByCar,
                         publicTransportAdvice)       Transform the future
        info.copy(travelAdvice = Some(travelAdvice))  route and public
    }                                                 transport advice into a
}                                                     Future[TicketInfo].
```

The preceding code first zips the future public transport and route by car together into a new `Future` that contains both results inside a tuple value. It then maps over the combined future and turns the result into a `Future[TicketInfo]`, so it can be chained further down the line. You can use a *for comprehension* instead of using the `map` method. This can sometimes lead to more-readable code. The following listing shows how it can be used; it does exactly the same thing as `zip` and `map` in the previous listing.

Listing 5.20   Using a for-comprehension to combine route and public transport advice

**Future created by the zip method evaluates at some point
into a routeByCar and publicTransportAdvice tuple**

```
for(
  (route, advice) <- futureRoute.zip(futurePublicTransport);
  travelAdvice = TravelAdvice(route, advice)
) yield info.copy(travelAdvice = Some(travelAdvice))
```

**for-comprehension yields a TicketInfo, which is returned
as a Future[TicketInfo] from the for-comprehension,
similar to how the map method does this**

If you're not familiar with for comprehensions, you could think of them as iterating over a collection. In the case of a future, we "iterate" over a collection that eventually contains one value or nothing (in the case of an exception).

The next part of the flow we'll look at is the suggestion of similar events. Two web services are used, including a similar artist service that returns information about artists similar to the one performing at the event. The artist information is used to call a specific calendar service per artist to request the next planned event close to the event location, which will be suggested to the user. The following listing shows how the suggestions are built up.

Listing 5.21   Using for-comprehension and `traverse` to map

```
def getSuggestions(event: Event): Future[Seq[Event]] = {

  val futureArtists: Future[Seq[Artists]] = callSimilarArtistsService(event)

  for(
    artists <- futureArtists
    events <- getPlannedEvents(event, artists)
  ) yield events
}
```

Returns a Future[Seq[Artist]], a Future to similar artists.

Returns a Future[Seq[Events]], a future list of planned events for every artist.

"artists" evaluates at some point to a Seq[Artist].

"events" evaluates at some point to a Seq[Events], a planned event for every called artist.

for-comprehension returns the Seq[Event] as a Future[Seq[Event]].

The preceding example is more involved. The code is split up over a couple of methods for clarity, although this can obviously be inlined. The `getPlannedEvents` is only executed once the artists are available. The `getPlannedEvents` uses the `Future.sequence` method to build a `Future[Seq[Event]]` out of a `Seq[Future[Event]]`. In other words, it combines many futures into one single future that contains a list of the results. The code for getPlannedEvents is shown in the following listing.

Listing 5.22 Combining future arrays using `sequence`

```
def getPlannedEvents(event: Event,
                     artists: Seq[Artist]): Future[Seq[Event]] = {
  val events: Seq[Future[Event]] = artists.map { artist=>
    callArtistCalendarService(artist, event.location)
  }
  Future.sequence(events)
}
```

Returns a Future[Seq[Event]], a list of planned events, one for every similar artist.

Maps over the Seq[Artists]. For every artist, calls the calendar service. "events" value is a Seq[Future[Event]].

Turns the Seq[Future[Event]] into a Future[Seq[Event]]. Eventually returns a list of events when the results of all asynchronous callArtistCalendarService calls are completed.

The sequence method is a simpler version of the traverse method. The following example shows how getPlannedEvent looks when we use traverse instead.

Listing 5.23 Combining again, this time with `traverse`

```
def getPlannedEventsWithTraverse(
  event: Event,
  artists: Seq[Artist]
): Future[Seq[Event]] = {
  Future.traverse(artists) { artist =>
    callArtistCalendarService(artist, event.location)
  }
}
```

traverse takes a code block, which is required to return a Future. It allows you to traverse a collection and at the same time create the future results.

Using sequence, we first had to create a Seq[Future[Event]] so we could transform it into a Future[Seq[Event]]. With traverse, we can do the same but without the intermediate step of first creating a Seq[Future[Event]].

It's time for the last step in the TicketInfoService flow. The TicketInfo value that contains the Weather information needs to be combined with the TicketInfo containing the TravelAdvice. We'll use the fold method to combine two TicketInfo values into one. The following listing shows how it's used.

Listing 5.24 Combining one more time, with `fold`

```
val ticketInfos = Seq(infoWithTravelAdvice, infoWithWeather)
val infoWithTravelAndWeather: Future[TicketInfo] =
  Future.fold(ticketInfos)(info) {
    (acc, elem) =>
```

fold returns result of previously executed code block in the accumulator (acc) value. It passes every element to the code block, in this case every TicketInfo value.

fold is called with the list and the accumulator is initialized with the ticketInfo that only contains event information.

Creates a list of the TicketInfo containing travel advice and the TicketInfo containing weather

```
val (travelAdvice, weather) = (elem.travelAdvice, elem.weather)    ◁──────┐
    acc.copy(
       travelAdvice = travelAdvice.orElse(acc.travelAdvice),
  ┌─▷   weather = weather.orElse(acc.weather)
  │    )
```

**Extracts optional travelAdvice and
weather properties out of ticketInfo**

**Copies the travelAdvice or the weather into
the accumulated TicketInfo, whichever is
filled. Copy is returned as next value of acc
for the next invocation of the code block.**

The `fold` method works just like `fold` on data structures like `Seq[T]` and `List[T]`, which you're probably familiar with. It's often used instead of traditional `for` loops to build up some data structure through iterating over a collection. `fold` takes a collection, an initial value, and a code block. The code block is fired for every element in the collection. The block takes two arguments: a value to accumulate state in and the element in the collection that is next. In the preceding case, the initial `TicketInfo` value is used as the initial value. At every iteration of the code block, a copy of the `TicketInfo` is returned that contains more information, based on the elements in the ticketInfo's list.

The complete flow is shown in the following listing.

Listing 5.25 Complete `TicketInfoService` flow

```
def getTicketInfo(ticketNr:String,
                  location:Location):Future[TicketInfo] = {
  val emptyTicketInfo = TicketInfo(ticketNr, location)
  val eventInfo = getEvent(ticketNr, location)
                  .recover(withPrevious(emptyTicketInfo))

  eventInfo.flatMap { info =>

    val infoWithWeather = getWeather(info)

    val infoWithTravelAdvice = info.event.map { event =>
      getTravelAdvice(info, event)
    }.getOrElse(eventInfo)

    val suggestedEvents = info.event.map { event =>
      getSuggestions(event)
    }.getOrElse(Future.successful(Seq()))

    val ticketInfos = Seq(infoWithTravelAdvice, infoWithWeather)

    val infoWithTravelAndWeather = Future.fold(ticketInfos)(info) { (acc, elem) =>
      val (travelAdvice, weather) = (elem.travelAdvice, elem.weather)

      acc.copy(travelAdvice = travelAdvice.orElse (acc.travelAdvice),
           weather = weather.orElse(acc.weather))
    }
    for(info <- infoWithTravelAndWeather;
      suggestions <- suggestedEvents
    ) yield info.copy(suggestions = suggestions)
```

**Calls getEvent,
which returns a
Future[TicketInfo]**

**Creates a TicketInfo
with Weather
information**

**Creates a TicketInfo
with TravelAdvice
information**

**Gets a future
list of
suggested
events.**

**Combines weather
and travel into one
TicketInfo**

**Eventually adds the
suggestions as well**

```
  }
}

// error recovery functions to minimize copy/paste
type Recovery[T] = PartialFunction[Throwable,T]

// recover with None
def withNone[T]:Recovery[Option[T]] = {
  case e => None
}

// recover with empty sequence
def withEmptySeq[T]:Recovery[Seq[T]] = {
  case e => Seq()
}

// recover with the ticketInfo that was built in the previous step
def withPrevious(previous:TicketInfo):Recovery[TicketInfo] = {
  case e => previous
}
```

> Error recovery methods used in the TicketInfoService flow

That concludes the `TicketInfoService` example using futures. As you've seen, futures can be combined in many ways, and the combinator methods make it easy to transform and sequence asynchronous function results. The entire `TicketInfo-Service` flow doesn't make one blocking call. If the calls to the hypothetical web services would be implemented with an asynchronous HTTP client like the *spray-client* library, the amount of blocking threads would be kept to a minimum for I/O as well. At the time of writing this book, an increasing number of asynchronous client libraries in Scala for I/O, but also for database access, have been written that provide future results.

In the next section we'll look at how futures can be combined with actors.

5.5 Combining futures with actors

In chapter 2 we used akka-http for our first REST service. That chapter already showed that the `ask` method returns a future. The following example was given.

Listing 5.26 Collecting event information

```
class BoxOffice(implicit timeout: Timeout) extends Actor {

  // ... skipping code


  case GetEvent(event) =>
    def notFound() = sender() ! None
    def getEvent(child: ActorRef) = child forward TicketSeller.GetEvent
    context.child(event).fold(notFound())(getEvent)


  case GetEvents =>
    import akka.pattern.ask
    import akka.pattern.pipe
```

> Timeout needs to be defined for ask. If ask doesn't complete within the timeout, the future will contain a timeout exception.

> Import ask pattern, which adds the ask method to ActorRef

> Import pipe pattern, which adds the pipe method to ActorRef

```
def getEvents: Iterable[Future[Option[Event]]] = context.children.map {
  child =>
  self.ask(GetEvent(child.path.name)).mapTo[Option[Event]]
}
def convertToEvents(f: Future[Iterable[Option[Event]]]): Future[Events] =
  f.map(_.flatten).map(l=> Events(l.toVector))

pipe(
  convertToEvents(Future.sequence(getEvents))
) to sender()
```

Iterate over all child actors; ask GetEvent on every child.

This local definition flattens an iterable collection of options into a list with only results in it (the None cases are discarded). It then transforms the Iterable[Event] into an Events value.

Future is piped to the sender. No need to close over the future callback.

Local method definition for asking GetEvent on self, meaning the BoxOffice. The ask method returns a Future result. Because Actors can send back any message, the returned Future is not typed. We use the mapTo method to convert the Future[Any] to a Future[Option[Event]]. The mapTo will complete with a failed Future if the actor responds with a different message than an Option[Event].

Going from the inside out, getEvents is turned from Iterable [Future[Option[Event]]] into Future[Iterable[Option[Event]]] by Future.sequence. Future[Iterable[Option[Event]]] is turned into Future[Events] by convertToEvents.

There's a lot going on here, but this example should be a lot clearer now than it was in chapter 2. To reiterate, the example shows how the BoxOffice actor can collect the number of tickets that every ticket seller has left.

This example shows a couple of important details. First of all, we *pipe* the result to the sender. This is a smart thing to do because the sender is part of the actor context, which can differ at every message the actor receives. The future callback can *close over* the values it needs to use. The sender could have a completely different value at the time the callback is invoked. Piping to the sender removes the need to refer to the sender() from inside the future callback.

Be aware when using futures from actors that the ActorContext provides a current view of the Actor. And since actors are stateful, it's important to make sure that the values that you close over aren't mutable from another thread. The easiest way to prevent this problem is to use immutable data structures and pipe the future to an actor, as shown in the example. Another is to "capture" the current value of sender() in a value.

5.6   *Summary*

This chapter gave an introduction to futures. You've learned how to use futures to create a flow out of asynchronous functions. The goal has been to minimize explicitly blocking and waiting on threads, maximize resource usage, and minimize unnecessary latency.

A future is a placeholder for a function result that will eventually be available. It's a great tool for combining functions into asynchronous flows. Futures make it possible to define transformations from one result to the next. Since futures are all about function results, it's no surprise that a functional approach needs to be taken to combine these results.

The combinator methods for futures provide a "transformational style" similar to the combinators found in the Scala collections library. Functions are executed in parallel and, where needed, in sequence, eventually providing a meaningful result. A future can contain a successful value or a failure. Luckily, failures can be recovered with a replacement value to continue the flow.

The value contained in a future should be immutable to ensure that no accidental mutable state is shared. Futures can be used from actors, but you need to avoid referencing mutable actor state from a future. The sender reference of an actor needs to be captured into a value before it can be safely used, for instance. Futures are used in the Actor API as the response of an `ask` method. Future results can also be provided to an actor with the `pipe` pattern.

Now that you know about futures, we'll go back to actors in the next chapter. This time we'll scale the GoTicks.com app with remote actors.

Your first distributed
Akka app

In this chapter

- Introducing scaling out
- Distributing the GoTicks.com app
- Distributing actors with the remote module
- Testing distributed actor systems

So far we've only looked at building an Akka actor system on one node. This chapter will serve as an introduction to scaling out Akka applications. You'll build your first distributed Akka app right here. We'll take the GoTicks.com app from chapter 2 and scale it out.

We'll start off with some common terminology and a quick look at the different approaches Akka takes to scale out. You'll be introduced to the akka-remote module and how it provides an elegant solution for communicating between actors across the network. We'll scale the GoTicks.com app out to two nodes: a frontend and a backend server. You'll find out how you can unit test the app using the multi-JVM test kit.

118

This chapter will just get you acquainted with scaling out your apps; later chapters will round out your knowledge. For example, in chapter 9 we'll use routers to distribute the load over several actors that can be remote actors, and chapter 13 will introduce you to clustering. Chapter 13 will dive into the details of scaling out once you're more familiar with how to build a real-world Akka application.

6.1 Scaling out

You might have hoped that this was going to be a chapter about a silver bullet to make any application scale out to thousands of machines, but here's the truth: distributed computing is hard. Notoriously hard. Don't stop reading! Akka will at least give you some really nice tools that make your life in distributed computing a little easier. Once again, Akka doesn't promise a free lunch, but just as actors simplify concurrent programming, you'll see that they also simplify the move to truly distributed computing. We'll bring back our GoTicks.com project and make it distributed.

Most network technologies use a blocking remote procedure call (RPC)–style of interaction for communicating with objects across the network, which tries to mask the difference between calling an object locally or remotely. The idea is that a local programming model is simplest, so let the programmer just work in that way, and then transparently make it possible to remote some of the calls when and where required. This style of communication works for point-to-point connections between servers, but it isn't a good solution for large-scale networks, as you'll see in the next section. Akka takes a different approach when it comes to scaling out applications across the network. It gives us the best of both approaches: we have relative transparency of remoting collaborators, but we don't have to change our actor code—you'll see the top layer looks the same.

Before we dive in, we'll look at examples of network topologies and some common terminology in the following section, just in case you're not too familiar with these. If you're already an expert in the field, you might want to skip right to section 6.2.

6.1.1 Common network terminology

When we refer to a *node* in this chapter, we mean a running application that communicates across the network. It's a connection point in a network topology. It's part of a distributed system. Many nodes can run on one server, or they can run on separate servers. Figure 6.1 shows some common network topologies.

A node has a specific *role* in the distributed system. It has a specific responsibility to execute particular tasks. A node could, for example, take part in a distributed database, or it could be one of many web servers that fulfill frontend web requests.

A node uses a specific network *transport protocol* to communicate with other nodes. Examples of transport protocols are TCP/IP and UDP. Messages between the nodes are sent over the transport protocol and need to be encoded and decoded into network-specific *protocol data units*. The protocol data units contain a stored representation of the messages as byte arrays. Messages need to be translated to and from bytes, respec-

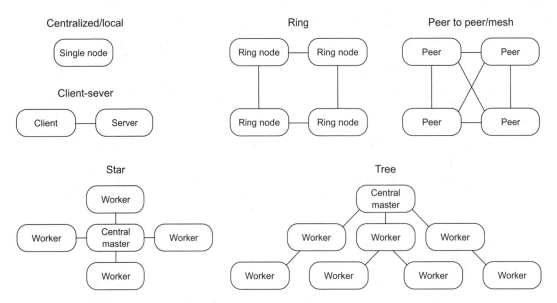

Figure 6.1   Common network topologies

tively known as *serialization* and *deserialization*. Akka provides a serialization module for this purpose, which we'll briefly touch on in this chapter.

When nodes are part of the same distributed system, they share a *group membership*. This membership can be *static* or *dynamic* (or even a mix of both). In a static membership, the number of nodes and the role of every node are fixed and can't change during the lifetime of the network. A dynamic membership allows for nodes to take on different roles and for nodes to join and leave the network.

The static membership is obviously the simplest of the two. All servers hold a reference to the other nodes' network addresses at startup. But it's also less resilient; a node can't simply be replaced by another node running on a different network address.

The dynamic membership is more flexible and makes it possible for a group of nodes to grow and shrink as required. It enables dealing with failed nodes in the network, possibly automatically replacing them. It's also far more complex than the static membership. When a dynamic membership is properly implemented, it needs to provide a mechanism to dynamically join and leave the group, detect and deal with network failures, identify unreachable/failed nodes in the network, and provide some kind of *discovery* mechanism through which new nodes can find an existing group on the network, since the network addresses aren't statically defined.

Now that we've briefly looked at network topologies and common terminology, the next section will look at why Akka uses a distributed programming model for building both local and distributed systems.

6.1.2 *Reasons for a distributed programming model*

Our ultimate goal is to scale to many nodes, and often the starting point is a local app on one node: your laptop. What changes when we want to make the step to one of the distributed topologies discussed in the previous section? Can't we abstract away the fact that all these nodes run on one "virtual node" and let some clever tool work out all the details so we don't have to change the code running on the laptop at all? The short answer is no.[1] We can't simply abstract the differences between a local and distributed environment. Luckily, you don't have to take our word for it. According to the paper *A Note on Distributed Computing*,[2] there are four important areas in which local programming differs from distributed programming that can't be ignored. The four areas are latency, memory access, partial failure, and concurrency. The following list briefly summarizes the differences in the four areas:

- *Latency*—Having the network in between collaborators means far more time for each message—an approximate time for an L1 cache reference is 0.5 nanoseconds, a fetch from main memory takes 100 nanoseconds, and sending a packet from the Netherlands to California takes around 150 milliseconds—as well as delays due to traffic, re-sent packets, intermittent connections, and so on.
- *Partial failure*—Knowing if all parts of a distributed system are still functioning is a hard problem to solve when parts of the system are not always visible, disappear, and even reappear.
- *Memory access*—Getting a reference to an object in memory in a local system can't intermittently fail, which can be the case for getting a reference to an object in a distributed setting.
- *Concurrency*—There's no one "owner" of everything, and the preceding factors mean the plan to interleave operations can go awry.

Using a local programming model in a distributed environment fails at scale because of these differences. Akka provides the *exact opposite*: a distributed programming model for both a distributed and a local environment. The previously mentioned paper refers to this choice and states that distributed programming would be simpler this way, but also states that it could make local programming unnecessarily hard—as hard as distributed programming.

But times have changed. Almost two decades later, we have to deal with many CPU cores. And increasingly more tasks simply need to be distributed in the cloud. Enforcing a distributed programming model for local systems has the advantage that it simplifies concurrent programming, as you've seen in the previous chapters. We've already gotten used to asynchronous interactions, expect partial failures (even embrace it), and we use a shared-nothing approach to concurrency, which both simplifies programming for many CPU cores and prepares us for a distributed environment.

---

[1] Software suppliers that still sell you this idea will obviously disagree!
[2] Jim Waldo, Geoff Wyant, Ann Wollrath, and Sam Kendall, Sun Microsystems, Inc., 1994.

We'll show you that this choice provides a solid foundation for building both local and distributed applications that are fit for the challenges of today. Akka provides a simple API for asynchronous programming as well as the tools you need to test your applications locally and remotely. Now that you understand the reasoning behind a distributed programming model for both local and distributed systems, in the following sections we'll look at how we can scale out the GoTicks.com App that we built in chapter 2.

6.2   *Scaling out with remoting*

Since this is an introduction to scaling out, we'll use the relatively simple example GoTicks.com app from chapter 2. In the next sections, we'll change the app so it runs on more than one node. Although the GoTicks.com app is an oversimplified example, it will give you a feel for the changes you need to make to an app that hasn't made any accommodations for scaling.

We'll define a static membership between two nodes using a client-server network topology, since it's the easiest path from local to distributed. The roles for the two nodes in this setup are frontend and backend. The REST interface will run on a frontend node. The BoxOffice and all TicketSellers will run on a backend node. Both nodes have a static reference to each other's network addresses. Figure 6.2 shows the change that we'll make.

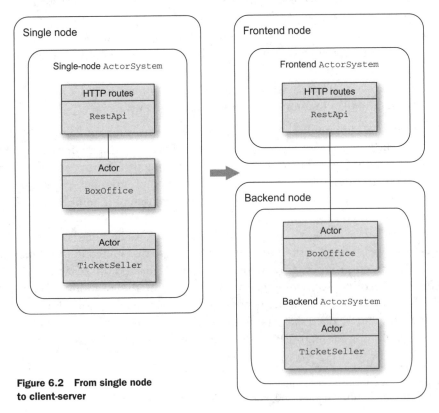

Figure 6.2   From single node to client-server

We'll use the akka-remote module to make this change. The `BoxOffice` actor creates `TicketSeller` actors when new `Events` are created in the local version of the app. In the client-server topology, this will have to be done as well. As you'll see, the akka-remote module makes it possible to create and deploy actors remotely. The frontend will look up the `BoxOffice` actor on a backend node on its known address, which creates the `TicketSeller` actors. We'll also look at a variation of this where the frontend remotely deploys a `BoxOffice` actor on the backend node.

In the next section, we'll get our hands dirty with remoting. We'll start with looking at the changes that need to be made to the sbt build file, and then look at the changes we have to make to the rest of the code.

6.2.1 Making the GoTicks.com app distributed

The chapter-remoting folder in the akka-in-action directory contains a modified version of the example from chapter 2. You can follow along by making the changes on top of the chapter 2 sample as described here. The first thing we need to do is add the dependencies for akka-remote and the `akka-multinode-testkit` in the sbt build file.

Listing 6.1   Build file changes for distributed GoTicks

Dependency on akka-remote module

```
"com.typesafe.akka" %% "akka-remote"             % akkaVersion,        ◁─┘
"com.typesafe.akka" %% "akka-multi-node-testkit" % akkaVersion % "test", ◁─┐
```

Dependency on multi-node test kit for testing distributed actor systems

---

These dependencies are pulled in automatically when you start sbt, or you can run sbt `update` to explicitly pull in the dependencies. Now that you have the dependencies updated and ready to go, let's look at the changes that we need to make for connecting frontend and backend. The actors on the frontend and backend will need to get a reference to their collaborator, which is the topic of the next section.

6.2.2 Remote REPL action

Akka provides two ways to get a reference to an actor on a remote node. One is to look up the actor by its path; the other is to create the actor, get its reference, and deploy it remotely. We'll start with the former option.

The REPL console is a great interactive tool for quickly exploring new Scala classes. Let's get two actor systems up in two REPL sessions using the sbt console. The first session contains the backend actor system, and the second session the frontend actor system. To create the backend session, start a terminal in the chapter-remoting folder using sbt `console`. We need to enable remoting, so the first thing we need to do is provide some configuration. Normally an *application.conf* configuration file in your src/main/resources folder would contain this information, but in the case of a REPL

session, we can just load it from a `String`. Listing 6.2 contains the REPL commands to
execute using the `:paste` command.

Listing 6.2 REPL commands for loading up remoting

```
scala> :paste
// Entering paste mode (ctrl-D to finish)

val conf = """
akka {
  actor {
    provider = "akka.remote.RemoteActorRefProvider"
  }
  remote {
    enabled-transports = ["akka.remote.netty.tcp"]
    netty.tcp {
      hostname = "0.0.0.0"
      port = 2551
    }
  }
}
"""

// Exiting paste mode, now interpreting.
...

scala>
```

Selects the remote
ActorRef provider to
bootstrap remoting

Configuration section
for remoting

Enables the
TCP
transport

Settings for the TCP
transport, host, and
port to listen on

To end paste command,
enter Ctrl-D.

We'll load this configuration string into an `ActorSystem`. Most notably it defines a specific `ActorRefProvider` for remoting, which bootstraps the akka-remote module. As
the name suggests, it also takes care of providing your code with `ActorRefs` to remote
actors. The following listing first imports the required config and actor packages, and
then loads the config into an actor system.

Listing 6.3 Remoting config

```
scala> import com.typesafe.config._
import com.typesafe.config._

scala> import akka.actor._
import akka.actor._

scala> val config = ConfigFactory.parseString(conf)
config: com.typesafe.config.Config = ....

scala> val backend = ActorSystem("backend", config)
[Remoting] Starting remoting
.....
[Remoting] Remoting now listens on addresses:
[akka.tcp://backend@0.0.0.0:2551]
backend: akka.actor.ActorSystem = akka://backend
```

Parses the String into
a Config object

Creates the ActorSystem
with the parsed Config
object

If you've been typing along, you just started your first remote-enabled `ActorSystem`
from a REPL; it's that simple! Depending on your perspective, that's five lines of code
to bootstrap and start a server.

The backend `ActorSystem` is created with the config object, which enables remoting. If you forget to pass the config to the `ActorSystem`, you'll end up with an `ActorSystem` that runs, but isn't enabled for remoting because the default application.conf that's packaged with Akka doesn't bootstrap remoting. The `Remoting` module now listens on all interfaces (0.0.0.0) on port 2551 for the backend actor system. Let's add a simple actor that just prints whatever it receives to the console so we can see that everything works.

Listing 6.4 Create and start a backend `Actor` that prints incoming messages

```scala
scala> :paste
// Entering paste mode (ctrl-D to finish)

class Simple extends Actor {
  def receive = {
    case m => println(s"received $m!")
  }
}

// Exiting paste mode, now interpreting.

defined class Simple

scala> backend.actorOf(Props[Simple], "simple")
res0: akka.actor.ActorRef = Actor[akka://backend/user/simple#485913869]
```

> **Creates the Simple actor in the backend actor system with the name "simple"**

The `Simple` actor is now running in the backend actor system. It's important to note that the `Simple` actor is created with the name `"simple"`. This will make it possible to find it by name when we connect to the actor system over the network. Time to start up another terminal: fire up `sbt console`, and create another remoting-enabled actor system, the frontend. We'll use the same commands as before, except for the fact that we want to make sure that the frontend actor system runs on a different TCP port.

Listing 6.5 Creating the frontend actor system

```scala
scala> :paste
// Entering paste mode (ctrl-D to finish)

val conf = """
akka {
  actor {
    provider = "akka.remote.RemoteActorRefProvider"
  }
  remote {
    enabled-transports = ["akka.remote.netty.tcp"]
    netty.tcp {
      hostname = "0.0.0.0"
      port = 2552
    }
  }
}
"""
```

> **Runs the frontend on a different port than the backend so they can both run on the same machine**

```
import com.typesafe.config._

import akka.actor._

val config = ConfigFactory.parseString(conf)

val frontend= ActorSystem("frontend", config)
// Exiting paste mode, now interpreting.

...
[INFO] ... Remoting now listens on addresses:
    [akka.tcp://frontend@0.0.0.0:2552]
...
frontend: akka.actor.ActorSystem = akka://frontend

scala>
```

The configuration is loaded into the frontend actor system. The frontend actor system is now also running, and remoting has started. Let's get a reference to the Simple actor on the backend actor system from the frontend side. First we'll construct an actor path. Figure 6.3 shows how the path is built up.

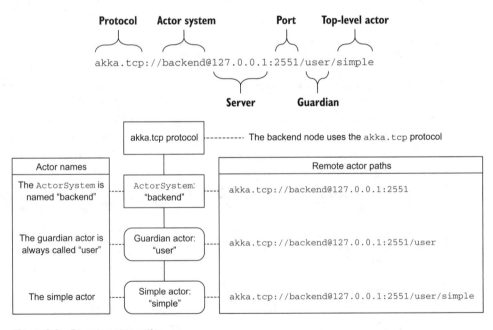

Figure 6.3 Remote actor paths

We can construct the path as a String and use the `actorSelection` method on the frontend actor system to find it.

Listing 6.6 Using `actorSelection`

```
scala> :paste
// Entering paste mode (ctrl-D to finish)
val path = "akka.tcp://backend@0.0.0.0:2551/user/simple"      ⟵  Path to remote
val simple = frontend.actorSelection(path)                    ⟵  Simple Actor
// Exiting paste mode, now interpreting.                          Selects actor
path: String = akka.tcp://backend@0.0.0.0:2551/user/simple        with an
simple: akka.actor.ActorSelection = ActorSelection[              ActorSelection
  Anchor(akka.tcp://backend@0.0.0.0:2551/), Path(/user/simple)]
```

Think of the `actorSelection` method as a query in the actor hierarchy. In this case the query is an exact path to a remote actor. The `ActorSelection` is an object that represents all the actors that have been found in the actor system with the `actorSelection` method. The `ActorSelection` can be used to send a message to all actors that match the query. We don't need the exact `ActorRef` of the `Simple` actor for now; we only want to try and send a message to it, so the `ActorSelection` will do. Since the backend actor system is already running in the other console, you should be able to do the following:

```
scala> simple ! "Hello Remote World!"
scala>
```

When you switch to the terminal where you started the backend actor system, you should see the following printed message:

```
scala> received Hello Remote World!!
```

The REPL console shows you that the message was sent from the frontend to the backend. Being able to interactively explore remoting systems using a REPL console is pure gold in our opinion, so you can expect more of it in other chapters.

Under the covers, the "Hello Remote World!" message was serialized, sent to a TCP socket, received by the remoting module, deserialized, and forwarded to the `Simple` actor running on the backend.

> **NOTE** Although Java serialization is easy to use in the REPL example here, it should never be used in any real distributed application. Java serialization doesn't support schema evolution; a minor code change can stop systems from communicating. It's slow compared to other options, and various security problems have been identified if objects are deserialized from an untrusted source. Akka will log a warning if you do choose to use it.

You probably noticed that we didn't write any special code for serialization, so why did it work? It's because we sent a simple `String` (`"Hello Remote World!"`). Akka uses Java serialization by default for any message that needs to be sent across the wire.

Other serializers are also available, and you can write your own custom serializer as well, which is a topic we'll deal with in part 3. The Akka *remote message protocol* has a field that contains the name of the serializer that was used for the message so that the receiving remote module can deserialize the payload bytes. The class that's used to represent a message needs to be `Serializable`, and it needs to be available on the classpath on both sides. Luckily "standard" case classes and case objects are serializable[3] by default, and are used as messages in the GoTicks.com app.

Now that you've seen how you can look up a remote actor and send a message to it in the REPL, let's look at how we can apply it in the GoTicks.com app in the next section.

6.2.3   Remote lookup

Instead of directly creating a `BoxOffice` actor in the `RestApi` actor, we'll look it up on the backend node. Figure 6.4 shows what we're going to try to achieve.

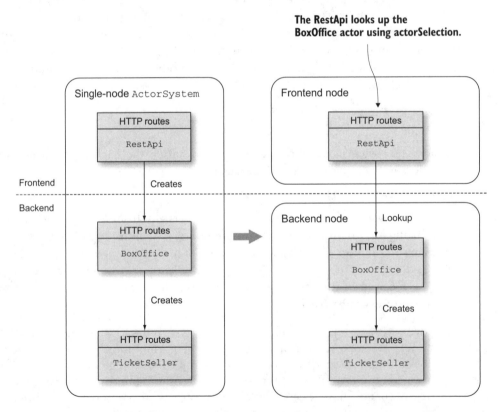

Figure 6.4   Remote lookup of the `BoxOffice` actor

---

[3]   `Serializable` is a marker interface and guarantees nothing. You need to verify that it works if you use non-standard constructs.

In the previous version of the code, the RestApi directly created a child BoxOffice actor:

```
val boxOffice = context.actorOf(Props[BoxOffice], "boxOffice")
```

This call made the boxOffice a direct child of the RestApi. To make the app a bit more flexible, and to make it possible to run it both in a single node and in a client server, we'll add specific Main objects to run the app in a couple of different modes, which will be shown in this chapter. Every Main class creates or references the Box-Office in a slightly different way. The code from chapter 2 has been refactored a little to make running the different scenarios easier. This trait is shown in the next listing, as well as the change we need to make to the RestApi code.

A SingleNodeMain, a FrontendMain, and a BackendMain are created to start the app in single-node mode or to start a frontend and backend separately. The next listing shows the interesting code (as snippets) of the three main classes.

Listing 6.7   Highlights from the core actors

Snippet from SingleNodeMain

Startup of HTTP server; binding routes has been moved to a Startup trait.

.. code omitted reading config and creating actor system

```
object SingleNodeMain extends App
    with Startup {

  val api = new RestApi() {

    def createBoxOffice: ActorRef = system.actorOf(BoxOffice.props,
      BoxOffice.name)
  }

  startup(api.routes)
}
```

.. code omitted

Creates BoxOffice as before

Creating an anonymous class from the RestApi trait, setting up how the BoxOffice must be created

```
object FrontendMain extends App
    with Startup {

  val api = new RestApi() {

    def createPath(): String =

    def createBoxOffice: ActorRef = {
      val path = createPath()
      system.actorOf(Props(new RemoteLookupProxy(path)), "lookupBoxOffice")
    }
  }

  startup(api.routes)
}
```

Snippet from FrontendMain

.. code omitted reading config and creating actor system

.. code omitted reading config and creating actor system

.. code omitted creating path to the remote actor

Lookup the BoxOffice on the remote node

Creating an anonymous class from the RestApi trait, setting up how the BoxOffice must be created

Startup of HTTP server; binding routes has been moved to a Startup trait.

```
object BackendMain extends App with RequestTimeout {    ← Snippet fromBackendMain

  system.actorOf(BoxOffice.props, BoxOffice.name)    ←┐ Creates a top-level boxoffice
}                                                         actor on backend
```

.. code omitted reading config and creating actor system

All main classes load their configuration from a specific configuration file; the
SingleNodeMain, FrontendMain, and BackendMain load from the files singlenode
.conf, frontend.conf, and backend.conf, respectively. The singlenode.conf file is a
copy of the application.conf from chapter 2. The backend.conf file needs the remote
configuration just like our REPL example and logging configuration. The following
listing shows the content of backend.conf.

Listing 6.8 backend.conf containing the backend configuration

```
akka {
  loglevel = DEBUG
   stdout-loglevel = WARNING
   event-handlers = ["akka.event.slf4j.Slf4jLogger"]

  actor {
    provider = "akka.remote.RemoteActorRefProvider"
  }
  remote {
    enabled-transports = ["akka.remote.netty.tcp"]
    netty.tcp {
      hostname = "0.0.0.0"
      port = 2551
    }
  }
}
```

More details about the logging configuration can be found in chapter 7, "Configuration, logging, and deployment."

The frontend.conf file will be a mix of singlenode.conf, backend.conf, and
an extra config section for looking up the box office actor. The RemoteBoxOffice-
Creator loads these extra configuration properties.

Listing 6.9 frontend.conf containing the frontend configuration

```
akka {
  loglevel = DEBUG
  stdout-loglevel = DEBUG
  loggers = ["akka.event.slf4j.Slf4jLogger"]

  actor {
    provider = "akka.remote.RemoteActorRefProvider"
  }

  remote {
    enabled-transports = ["akka.remote.netty.tcp"]
    netty.tcp {
```

```
      hostname = "0.0.0.0"
      port = 2552
    }
  }
  http {
    server {
      server-header = "GoTicks.com REST API"
    }
  }
}
http {
  host = "0.0.0.0"
  host = ${?HOST}
  port = 5000
  port = ${?PORT}
}
backend {
  host = "0.0.0.0"
  port = 2551
  protocol = "akka.tcp"
  system = "backend"
  actor = "user/boxOffice"
}
```

The frontend needs the new the backend configuration to be able to connect to the remote BoxOffice. Getting an ActorSelection to the remote actor was fine in the REPL console, just to try out sending a message, when we were certain that the backend was present. In this case we'd like to work with an ActorRef instead, since the single-node version used one. We create a new actor RemoteLookupProxy, which is responsible for the lookup of the remote BoxOffice and forwarding the messages. The FrontendMain object creates the RemoteLookupProxy actor to look up the BoxOffice actor.

Listing 6.10 Looking up the remote `BoxOffice`

Creates path to BoxOffice

```
def createPath(): String = {
  val config = ConfigFactory.load("frontend").getConfig("backend")
  val host = config.getString("host")
  val port = config.getInt("port")
  val protocol = config.getString("protocol")
  val systemName = config.getString("system")
  val actorName = config.getString("actor")
  s"$protocol://$systemName@$host:$port/$actorName"
}

def createBoxOffice: ActorRef = {
  val path = createPath()
  system.actorOf(Props(new RemoteLookupProxy(path)), "lookupBoxOffice")
}
```

Loads frontend.conf configuration and gets backend config section properties to build the path

Returns an Actor that looks up box office actor. The Actor is constructed with one argument: the path to the remote BoxOffice.

The `FrontendMain` object creates a separate `RemoteLookupProxy` actor to look up the `boxOffice`. In previous versions of Akka, you could use the `actorFor` method to directly get an `ActorRef` to the remote actor. This method has been deprecated, because the returned `ActorRef` didn't behave exactly the same way as a local `ActorRef` in the case that the related actor died. An `ActorRef` returned by `actorFor` could point to a newly spawned remote actor instance, while this was never the case in a local context. At the time, remote actors couldn't be watched for termination like local actors, which was another reason to deprecate this method.

This brings us to the reason for the `RemoteLookupProxy` actor:

- The backend actor system might not have started up yet, or it could have crashed, or it could have been restarted.
- The `boxOffice` actor itself could also have crashed and restarted.
- Ideally, we would start the backend node before the frontend, so the frontend could do the lookup once at startup.

The `RemoteLookupProxy` actor will take care of these scenarios. Figure 6.5 shows how the `RemoteLookupProxy` sits between the `RestApi` and the `BoxOffice`. It transparently forwards messages for the `RestApi`.

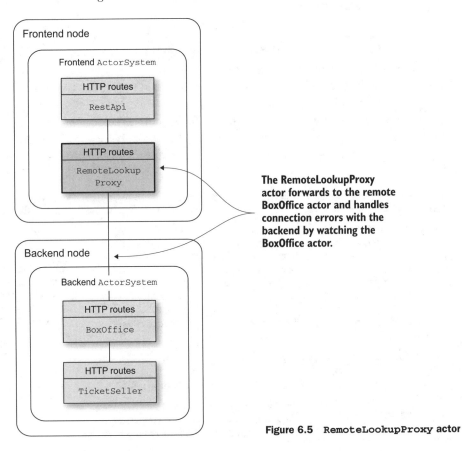

The RemoteLookupProxy actor forwards to the remote BoxOffice actor and handles connection errors with the backend by watching the BoxOffice actor.

Figure 6.5   `RemoteLookupProxy` actor

The `RemoteLookupProxy` actor is a state machine that can only be in one of two states we've defined: identify or active (see listing 6.12). It uses the `become` method to switch its receive method to identify or active. The `RemoteLookupProxy` tries to get a valid `ActorRef` to the `BoxOffice` when it doesn't have one yet in the identify state, or it forwards all messages sent to a valid `ActorRef` to the `BoxOffice` in the active state. If the `RemoteLookupProxy` detects that the `BoxOffice` has been terminated, it tries to get a valid `ActorRef` again when it receives no messages for a while. We'll use remote `DeathWatch` for this. It sounds like something new, but from the perspective of API usage it's exactly the same thing as normal actor monitoring/watching.

Listing 6.11 Remote lookup

Sends a ReceiveTimeout message if no message has been received for 3 seconds

```
import scala.concurrent.duration._

class RemoteLookupProxy(path:String) extends Actor with ActorLogging {
  context.setReceiveTimeout(3 seconds)
  sendIdentifyRequest()
```
Immediately starts to request identity of the actor

Selects actor by path
```
  def sendIdentifyRequest(): Unit = {
    val selection = context.actorSelection(path)
    selection ! Identify(path)
  }
```
Sends an Identify message to the actorSelection

Actor is initially in identify receive state
```
  def receive = identify
```

Changes to active receive state
```
  def identify: Receive = {
    case ActorIdentity(`path`, Some(actor)) =>
      context.setReceiveTimeout(Duration.Undefined)
      log.info("switching to active state")
      context.become(active(actor))
      context.watch(actor)
```
Actor has been identified, and an ActorRef to it is returned

No longer sends a ReceiveTimeout if actor gets no messages, since it is now active

Watches remote actor for termination
```
    case ActorIdentity(`path`, None) =>
      log.error(s"Remote actor with path $path is not available.")
```
Actor is not (yet) available; backend is unreachable or not started

```
    case ReceiveTimeout =>
      sendIdentifyRequest()
```
Keeps trying to identify remote actor if no message is received

```
    case msg:Any =>
      log.error(s"Ignoring message $msg, not ready yet.")
  }
```
No messages are sent in identify receive state

Active receive state
```
  def active(actor: ActorRef): Receive = {
    case Terminated(actorRef) =>
      log.info("Actor $actorRef terminated.")
      context.become(identify)
      log.info("switching to identify state")
```
If remote actor is terminated, RemoteLookupProxy actor should change its behavior to the identify receive state

```
        context.setReceiveTimeout(3 seconds)
        sendIdentifyRequest()

   case msg: Any => actor forward msg
 }
```

Forwards all other messages when remote actor is active

As you can see, the monitoring API, which was described in chapter 4, is exactly the same for local and remote actors. Simply watching an `ActorRef` will ensure that the actor gets notified of termination of an actor, regardless of whether it's remote or local. Akka uses a sophisticated protocol to statistically detect that a node is unreachable. We'll look at this protocol in more detail in chapter 14. The `ActorRef` to the `BoxOffice` is retrieved using a special `Identify` message that's sent to the `ActorSelection`. The remote module of the backend `ActorSystem` responds with an `ActorIdentity` message that contains a `correlationId` and an optional `ActorRef` to the remote actor. In the pattern match of the `ActorIdentity`, we use backticks around the variable `path`. This means that the `correlationId` of the `ActorIdentify` must be equal to the value of `path`. When we forget those backticks, we define a new variable `path`, which contains the value of the `correlationId` of the message.

That concludes the changes we had to make to the GoTicks.com app to move from a single node to a frontend and backend node. Apart from being able to communicate remotely, the frontend and backend can boot separately, and the frontend will look up the `BoxOffice` and can communicate with it when it's available, and can take action when it's not.

The last thing you could do is actually run the `FrontendMain` and `BackendMain` classes. We'll start up two terminals and use `sbt run` to run a `Main` class in the project. You should get the following output in the terminals:

```
[info] ...
[info] ... (sbt messages)
[info] ...

Multiple main classes detected, select one to run:

[1] com.goticks.SingleNodeMain
[2] com.goticks.FrontendMain
[3] com.goticks.BackendMain

Enter number:
```

Select `FrontendMain` in one terminal and `BackendMain` in another. See what happens if you kill the `sbt` process that runs the `BackendMain` and restart it again. You can test if the app works with the same `httpie` commands as before; for example, `http PUT localhost:5000/events event=RHCP nrOfTickets:=10` to create an event with 10 tickets, and `http GET localhost:5000/ticket/RHCP` to get a ticket to the event. If you try to kill the backend process and start it up again, you'll see in the console that the `RemoteLookupProxy` class switches from active to identify and back. You'll also notice that Akka reports errors about the remote connection to the other node. If you're not interested in logging these remote lifecycle events, you can switch the logging off by adding the following to the remote config section:

```
remote {
  log-remote-lifecycle-events = off
}
```

The remote lifecycle events are logged by default. This makes it easier to find problems when you start out with the remote module and, for example, make a minor mistake in the actor path syntax. You can subscribe to the remote lifecycle events using the actor system's `eventStream`, which is described in chapter 10 on channels. Since remote actors can be watched like any local actor, there's no need to act on these events individually for the sake of connection management.

Let's review the changes:

- A `FrontendMain` object was added to look up the `BoxOffice` on the backend.
- The `FrontendMain` object adds a `RemoteLookupProxy` actor in between the `RestApi` and the `BoxOffice`. It forwards all messages it receives to the `BoxOffice`. It identifies the `ActorRef` to the `BoxOffice` and remotely monitors it.

As said in the beginning of this section, Akka provides two ways to get an `ActorRef` to a remote actor. In the next section, we'll look at the second option, namely, remote deployment.

6.2.4 Remote deployment

Remote deployment can be done programmatically or through configuration. We'll start with the preferred approach: configuration. Of course, this is preferred because changes to the cluster settings can be made without rebuilding the app. The standard `SingleNodeMain` object creates the `boxOffice` as a top-level actor:

```
val boxOffice = system.actorOf(Props[BoxOffice],"boxOffice")
```

The local path to this actor would be /boxOffice, omitting the user guardian actor. When we use configured remote deployment, all we have to do is tell the frontend actor system that when an actor is created with the path /boxOffice, the actor shouldn't be created locally, but remotely. This is done with the piece of configuration in the next listing.

Listing 6.12 Configuration of the `RemoteActorRefProvider`

```
actor {
  provider = "akka.remote.RemoteActorRefProvider"

  deployment {                                       Actor with this path will
    /boxOffice {                                     be deployed remotely
      remote = "akka.tcp://backend@0.0.0.0:2552"
    }
  }
}
```

Remote address where the actor should be deployed. The IP address or host name has to match exactly with the interface the remote backend actor system is listening on.

Remote deployment can also be done programmatically, which is shown for completeness' sake. In most cases it's better to configure the remote deployment of actors through the configuration system (using properties), but in some cases, for example, if you're referencing different nodes by CNAMES (which are themselves configurable), you might do the configuration in code. Fully dynamic remote deployment makes more sense when using the akka-cluster module because it's built specifically to support dynamic membership. An example of programmatic remote deployment is shown in the following listing.

Listing 6.13 Programmatic remote deploy configuration

```
val uri = "akka.tcp://backend@0.0.0.0:2552"
val backendAddress = AddressFromURIString(uri)        ◁──┐  Creates an address to the
                                                            backend from the URI
val props = Props[BoxOffice].withDeploy(
  Deploy(scope = RemoteScope(backendAddress))    ◁──┐  Creates a Props with a
)                                                      remote deployment scope
context.actorOf(props, "boxOffice")
```

The preceding code creates and deploys the BoxOffice remotely to the backend as well. The Props configuration object specifies a remote scope for deployment.

It's important to note that remote deployment doesn't require that Akka automatically deploy the actual class file(s) for the BoxOffice actor into the remote actor system in some way; the code for the BoxOffice needs to already be present on the remote actor system for this to work, and the remote actor system needs to be running. If the remote backend actor system crashes and restarts, the ActorRef won't automatically point to the new remote actor instance. Since the actor is going to be deployed remotely, it can't already be started by the backend actor system as we did in the BackendMain. Because of this a couple of changes have to be made. We start with new Main classes for starting the backend (BackendRemoteDeployMain) and the frontend (FrontendRemoteDeployMain).

Listing 6.14 Main objects for starting the backend and the frontend

```
// the main class to start the backend node.
object BackendRemoteDeployMain extends App {
  val config = ConfigFactory.load("backend")          ┐  Not creating the boxOffice
  val system = ActorSystem("backend", config)    ◁──┘  actor anymore
}
                                                  ┐  The main class to start
object FrontendRemoteDeployMain extends App   ◁──┘  the frontend node.
    with Startup {
  val config = ConfigFactory.load("frontend-remote-deploy")
  implicit val system = ActorSystem("frontend", config)

  val api = new RestApi() {
    implicit val requestTimeout = configuredRequestTimeout(config)
    implicit def executionContext = system.dispatcher
```

```
def createBoxOffice: ActorRef =          ⟵──┐  Creating the boxOffice,
  system.actorOf(                             │  automatically uses the
    BoxOffice.props,                          │  configuration
    BoxOffice.name
  )
}

startup(api.routes)
}
```

When you run these `Main` classes with two terminals like before and create some
events with `httpie`, you'll see something similar to the following message in the console of the frontend actor system:

```
// very long message, formatted in a couple of lines to fit.
INFO  [frontend-remote]: Received new event Event(RHCP,10), sending to
Actor[akka.tcp://backend@0.0.0.0:2552/remote/akka.tcp/
      frontend@0.0.0.0:2551/user/boxOffice#-1230704641]
```

This shows that the frontend actor system is actually sending a message to the remote
deployed `boxOffice`. The actor path is different than you'd expect. It keeps track of
where the actor was deployed from. The remote daemon that listens for the backend
actor system uses this information to communicate back to the frontend actor system.

What we've worked up so far works, but there's one problem with this approach. If
the backend actor system isn't started when the frontend tries to deploy the remote
actor, the deployment obviously fails, but what is maybe not so obvious is that the
`ActorRef` is still created. Even if the backend actor system is started later, the created
`ActorRef` doesn't work. This is the correct behavior, since it's not the same actor
instance—as distinguished from the prior failure cases we saw, where only the actor
itself is restarted, in which case the ref will still point to the recreated actor.

If we want to do something when the remote backend crashes or the remote `box-`
`Office` actor crashes, we'll have to make some more changes. We'll have to watch the
`boxOfficeActorRef` like we did before and take actions when this happens. Since the
`RestApi` has a val reference to the `boxOffice`, we'll need to once again put an actor in
between the way we did with the `RemoteLookupProxy` actor. This in-between actor will
be called `RemoteBoxOfficeForwarder`.

The configuration needs to be changed slightly because the `boxOffice` now has
the path `/forwarder/boxOffice` because of the `RemoteBoxOfficeForwarder` in
between. Instead of the `/boxOffice` path in the deployment section, it should now
read as `/forwarder/boxOffice`.

The following listing shows the `RemoteBoxOfficeForwarder` that will watch the
remote deployed actor.

Listing 6.15   Watch mechanisms for remote actors

```
object RemoteBoxOfficeForwarder {
  def props(implicit timeout: Timeout) = {
    Props(new RemoteBoxOfficeForwarder)
  }
```

```
    def name = "forwarder"
}

class RemoteBoxOfficeForwarder(implicit timeout: Timeout)
    extends Actor with ActorLogging {
  context.setReceiveTimeout(3 seconds)                     Remotely deploys and
                                                           watches the BoxOffice
  deployAndWatch()

  def deployAndWatch(): Unit = {
    val actor = context.actorOf(BoxOffice.props, BoxOffice.name)
    context.watch(actor)
    log.info("switching to maybe active state")
    context.become(maybeActive(actor))                    Switches to "maybe
    context.setReceiveTimeout(Duration.Undefined)         active" once the actor is
  }                                                        deployed. We can't be
                                                           sure without using lookup
  def receive = deploying                                 if the actor is deployed.

  def deploying: Receive = {
    case ReceiveTimeout =>
      deployAndWatch()

    case msg: Any =>
      log.error(s"Ignoring message $msg, remote actor is not ready yet.")
  }

  def maybeActive(actor: ActorRef): Receive = {
    case Terminated(actorRef) =>                           Deployed BoxOffice is
      log.info("Actor $actorRef terminated.")              terminated so it's certain that
      log.info("switching to deploying state")             a retry deployment is needed
      context.become(deploying)
      context.setReceiveTimeout(3 seconds)
      deployAndWatch()

    case msg: Any => actor forward msg
  }
}
```

The preceding RemoteBoxOfficeForwarder looks very similar to the RemoteLookup-
Proxy class in the previous section, in that it's also a state machine. In this case it's in
one of two states: deploying or maybeActive. Without doing an actor selection
lookup, we can't be sure that the remote actor is actually deployed. The exercise to
add remote lookup with actorSelection to the RemoteBoxOfficeForwarder is left to
the reader; for now the maybeActive state will do.

The Main class for the frontend needs to be adapted to create the RemoteBox-
OfficeForwarder:

```
object FrontendRemoteDeployWatchMain extends App
    with Startup {
  val config = ConfigFactory.load("frontend-remote-deploy")
  implicit val system = ActorSystem("frontend", config)

  val api = new RestApi() {
    val log = Logging(system.eventStream, "frontend-remote-watch")
    implicit val requestTimeout = configuredRequestTimeout(config)
    implicit def executionContext = system.dispatcher
```

```
    def createBoxOffice: ActorRef = {
      system.actorOf(
        RemoteBoxOfficeForwarder.props,
        RemoteBoxOfficeForwarder.name
      )
    }
  }

  startup(api.routes)
}
```

⊲ ⌐ **Creates a forwarder that watches
and deploys the remote BoxOffice**

We have created a new `Main` class `FrontendRemoteDeployWatchMain` that contains these changes.

Running the `FrontendRemoteDeployWatchMain` and the `BackendRemoteDeploy-Main` on two `sbt console` terminals shows how the remote deployed actor is watched and how it's redeployed when the backend process is killed and restarted again, or when the frontend is started before the backend.

In case you just read over the previous paragraph and though "meh," read that paragraph again. The app is automatically redeploying an actor when the node it runs on reappears and continues to function. This is cool stuff and we've only scratched the surface!

That concludes this section on remote deployment. We've looked at both remote lookup and remote deployment, and what's required to do this in a resilient way. Even in the situation where you only have two servers, it's a major benefit to have resilience built in from the start. In both lookup and deployment examples, the nodes are free to start up in any order. The remote deployment example could have been done purely by changing the deployment configuration, but we would've ended up with a too-naive solution that didn't take node or actor crashes into consideration and would have required a specific startup order.

In the next section, we'll look at the multi-JVM `sbt` plugin and the `akka-multi-node-testkit`, which makes it possible to test the frontend and backend nodes in the GoTicks app.

6.2.5 *Multi-JVM testing*

Testing actors using remote actors will be more complex, now that we're making the application distributed, because the actors depend on other actors running on different nodes. Ideally we want to make a test that's able to start different nodes and run the test using these different nodes. Figure 6.6 shows an example of testing our REST frontend.

As you see, we need two different JVMs: one for the frontend and the test code, and a server site where the `BoxOffice` is deployed. And maybe more important: this test needs coordination between the two JVMs. Deploying the frontend needs a remote reference to the `BoxOffice` and can only start when the `BoxOffice` is started. The `sbt` multi-JVM plugin will take care of both.

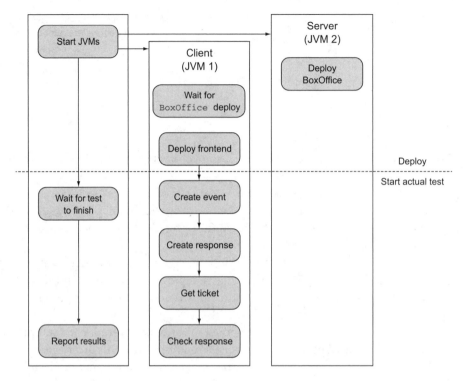

Figure 6.6   Testing example using remote actors

The sbt multi-JVM plugin makes it possible to run tests across multiple JVMs. The plugin needs to be registered with sbt in the project/plugins.sbt file:

```
resolvers += Classpaths.typesafeResolver

addSbtPlugin("com.eed3si9n" % "sbt-assembly" % "0.13.0")

addSbtPlugin("com.typesafe.sbt" % "sbt-start-script" % "0.10.0")

addSbtPlugin("com.typesafe.sbt" % "sbt-multi-jvm" % "0.3.11")
```

We also have to add another sbt build file to use it. The multi-JVM plugin only supports the scala DSL version of sbt project files, so we need to add a GoTicksBuild.scala file in the chapter-remoting/project folder. sbt merges the build.sbt file and the following file automatically, which means that the dependencies don't have to be duplicated in the following listing.

Listing 6.16   Multi-JVM configuration

```
import sbt._
import Keys._
import com.typesafe.sbt.SbtMultiJvm
import com.typesafe.sbt.SbtMultiJvm.MultiJvmKeys.{ MultiJvm }

object GoTicksBuild extends Build {
```

```
lazy val buildSettings = Defaults.defaultSettings ++
                         multiJvmSettings ++
                         Seq(
                         crossPaths    := false
                         )

lazy val goticks = Project(
  id = "goticks",
  base = file("."),
  settings = buildSettings ++ Project.defaultSettings
) configs(MultiJvm)

lazy val multiJvmSettings = SbtMultiJvm.multiJvmSettings ++
  Seq(
    compile in MultiJvm <<=
        (compile in MultiJvm) triggeredBy (compile in Test),
    parallelExecution in Test := false,
    executeTests in Test <<=
    ((executeTests in Test), (executeTests in MultiJvm)) map {
      case ((_, testResults), (_, multiJvmResults))  =>
      val results = testResults ++ multiJvmResults
      (Tests.overall(results.values), results)
    }
  )
}
```

Makes sure our tests are part of the default test compilation

Turns off parallel execution

Makes sure that multi-JVM tests are executed as part of default test target

If you're not an sbt expert, don't worry about the details of this build file. The preceding basically configures the multi-JVM plugin and makes sure that multi-JVM tests are executed along with the normal unit tests. *SBT in Action* (www.manning.com/suereth2/) does a great job at explaining the details of sbt, if you'd like to know more about it.

All the test code for multi-JVM tests need to be added to the src/multi-jvm/scala folder by default. Now that our project is set up correctly for multi-JVM tests, we can start with a unit test for the frontend and backend of the GoTicks.com app. First, a MultiNodeConfig needs to be defined that describes the roles of the nodes that are tested. We create the object class ClientServerConfig, which defines the multi-node config for the client server (frontend and backend) configuration. The following listing shows this new object class.

Listing 6.17 Describing the roles of the nodes tested

```
object ClientServerConfig extends MultiNodeConfig {
  val frontend = role("frontend")              ⟵———— Frontend role
  val backend = role("backend")                ⟵———— Backend role
}
```

Two roles have been defined, the frontend and the backend, as you would expect. The roles will be used to identify the node for unit testing and to run specific code on each node for testing purposes. Before we start to write a test, we need to write some infrastructure code to hook up the test into scalatest.

Listing 6.18   `STMultiNodeSpec` hooks up into `scalatest`

Gets the
rest of the
test traits
we need ⟶

```
import akka.remote.testkit.MultiNodeSpecCallbacks
import org.scalatest.{BeforeAndAfterAll, WordSpec}          Gets callbacks by
import org.scalatest.matchers.MustMatchers                  extending TestKit's
                                                            class methods
trait STMultiNodeSpec extends MultiNodeSpecCallbacks     ⟵
  with WordSpec with MustMatchers with BeforeAndAfterAll {

  override def beforeAll() = multiNodeSpecBeforeAll()     ⟵
                                                            Makes all our tests use
  override def afterAll() = multiNodeSpecAfterAll()        our before and after
}
```

This trait is used to start up and shut down the multi-node test, and you can reuse it for
all your multi-node tests. It's mixed into the unit test specification, which defines the
actual test. In our example we create a test called `ClientServerSpec`, which is shown
next. It's quite a bit of code, so let's break it down. The first thing we need to do is create a `MultiNodeSpec` that mixes in the `STMultiNodeSpec` we just defined. Two versions
of the `ClientServerSpec` will need to run on two separate JVMs. The code in the following listing shows how two `ClientServerSpec` classes are defined for this purpose.

Listing 6.19   Spec classes for multi-node tests

Spec that
will run
on the
backend JVM ⟶

```
                                                         Spec that will run on
                                                         the frontend JVM
class ClientServerSpecMultiJvmFrontend extends ClientServerSpec   ⟵
class ClientServerSpecMultiJvmBackend extends ClientServerSpec

class ClientServerSpec extends MultiNodeSpec(ClientServerConfig)  ⟵  Spec that
with STMultiNodeSpec with ImplicitSender {                           describes
                                                                    what both
  def initialParticipants = roles.size     ⟵                        nodes
                                                                    should do.
                                        Number of nodes that
                                        participate in the test.
```

The `ClientServerSpec` uses the `STMultiNodeSpec` and also an `ImplicitSender` trait.
The `ImplicitSender` trait sets the `testActor` as the default sender for all messages,
which makes it possible to just call `expectMsg` and other assertion functions without
having to set the `testActor` as the sender of messages every time. The code in the
next listing shows how we get the address of the backend node.

Listing 6.20   Getting the address of the backend node

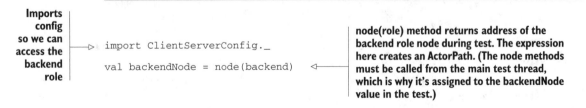

Imports
config
so we can
access the
backend
role ⟶

```
import ClientServerConfig._

val backendNode = node(backend)     ⟵
```

node(role) method returns address of the
backend role node during test. The expression
here creates an ActorPath. (The node methods
must be called from the main test thread,
which is why it's assigned to the backendNode
value in the test.)

The backend and frontend role nodes run on a random port by default. The Test-RemoteBoxOfficeCreator replaces the RemoteBoxOfficeCreator in the test, since it creates a path from a configured host, port, and actor name in the frontend.conf file. Instead, we want to use the address of the backend role node during testing and look up a reference to the boxOffice actor on that node. The preceding listing achieves this. The following listing shows tests of our distributed architecture.

Listing 6.21   Testing the distributed architecture

```
"A Client Server configured app" must {

  "wait for all nodes to enter a barrier" in {
    enterBarrier("startup")
  }

  "be able to create an event and sell a ticket" in {
    runOn(backend) {
      system.actorOf(BoxOffice.props(Timeout(1 second)), "boxOffice")
      enterBarrier("deployed")
    }

    runOn(frontend) {
      enterBarrier("deployed")

      val path = node(backend) / "user" / "boxOffice"
      val actorSelection = system.actorSelection(path)

      actorSelection.tell(Identify(path), testActor)

      val actorRef = expectMsgPF() {
        case ActorIdentity(`path`, Some(ref)) => ref
      }

      import BoxOffice._

      actorRef ! CreateEvent("RHCP", 20000)

      expectMsg(EventCreated(Event("RHCP", 20000)))

      actorRef ! GetTickets("RHCP", 1)

      expectMsg(Tickets("RHCP", Vector(Ticket(1))))
    }

    enterBarrier("finished")
  }
}
```

Annotations (left side):
- **Lets all nodes start up** → enterBarrier("startup")
- **Signals that backend is deployed** → enterBarrier("deployed")
- **Waits for backend node to deploy** → enterBarrier("deployed")
- **Sends an Identify message to the actor selection** → actorSelection.tell(Identify(path), testActor)
- **Expects messages as usual with the TestKit** → expectMsg(...)

Annotations (right side):
- **Tests scenario for frontend and backend node**
- **Runs code in this block on the backend JVM**
- **Creates boxOffice with name boxOffice so the Remote-LookupProxy class can find it**
- **Runs code in this block on the frontend JVM**
- **Gets an actor selection to the remote box office**
- **Waits for boxOffice to report that it's available. The RemoteLookupProxy class will go through the process of getting an ActorRef to the boxOffice.**
- **Indicates that test has completed**

There's quite a lot going on here. The unit test can be broken into three pieces. First, it waits for all nodes to start by using the enterBarrier("startup") call, which executes on both nodes. Second, the unit test continues to specify what code should be run on the frontend node and the backend node. The frontend node waits for the backend node to signal that it is deployed and executes a test. Finally, the unit test waits for all nodes to finish by using the `enterBarrier("finished")`

The backend node only starts the `boxOffice`, so it can be used from the frontend node. Since we would have to add HTTP client requests if we used the real `RestApi`, we'll just go to the `BoxOffice` directly.

After that we can finally test the interactions between the frontend and the backend node. We can use the same methods that we used in chapter 3 for expecting messages. This multi-JVM test can be run by executing the `multi-jvm:test` command in sbt; give it a try.

Figure 6.7 shows how the test actually flows. Note that the coordination of the various collaborators, and their runtimes, is made pretty much automatic by the multi-JVM test kit. Doing this with your own hand-hewn code would be a lot of work.

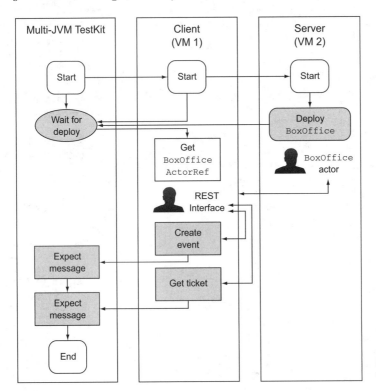

Figure 6.7   Multi-JVM test flow

The chapter-remoting project also has a unit test for a single-node version of the app, and apart from some of the infrastructure setup, the test is basically the same. The example multi-JVM test here just shows how an app that was initially built for a single node can be adapted to run on two nodes. The big difference between the single-node and the client server setup is how the actor reference to the remote system is found; is it looked up or deployed remotely? Having a remote lookup in between the `RestApi` and the `boxOffice` gave us some flexibility and the ability to survive crashes. It gave an interesting problem to solve in the example unit test: how do we wait for the remote `ActorRef` to the `boxOffice` to become available? The `actorSelection` and identity message mechanism were the answer for this.

This concludes our first look at the `multi-node-testkit` module. You'll see more of it in the chapters to come. The preceding test shows an example of how the GoTicks.com app can be unit tested in a distributed environment. In this case it runs on two JVMs on a single machine. As you'll see later in chapter 13, `multi-node-testkit` can also be used to run unit tests on several servers.

6.3 Summary

Do you remember the reason we gave at the beginning of the chapter for why we couldn't just flip a switch and have our app work in a distributed fashion (using remoting)? It was because we have circumstances that we need to account for in the network world that our local-only app is able to completely ignore. As you would expect, much of what we ended up having to actually do in this chapter boiled down to just accounting for those new circumstances, and as predicted, Akka made it easy.

Despite the fact that we had to make some changes, we also found a lot of constancy:

- We benefited from the fact that an `ActorRef` behaves the same whether the actor is local or remote.
- The monitoring API for death watch of distributed systems is exactly the same as for local systems.
- Despite the fact that collaborators were now separated by the network, by simply using forwarding (in the `RemoteLookupProxy` and `RemoteBoxOffice-Forwarder`), we transparently allowed the `RestApi` and `BoxOffice` to communicate with each other.

This is important because taking our app to the next level doesn't require that we either unlearn what we've learned or learn a whole new load of stuff; the basic operations remain largely the same, which is the hallmark of a well-designed toolkit.

You also learned some new things:

- REPL provides an easy, interactive means of getting your stuff going in the distributed topology of your choice.
- The `multi-node-testkit` module makes it incredibly easy to test distributed actor systems, no matter if they're built with akka-remote, akka-cluster, or even both. (Akka is rather unique in providing proper unit testing tools for a distributed environment.)

We've intentionally not dealt with the fact that messages will get lost in the `Remote-LookupProxy` and `RemoteBoxOfficeForwarder` when the backend node isn't available. In upcoming chapters, you'll see

- How a reliable proxy can be used for messaging between peer nodes (chapter 10, "Message channels")
- How to fix GoTicks.com to deal with the fact that the state of the Ticket-Sellers is lost when a backend node crashes (chapter 14, "Actor Persistence")
- How state can be replicated across a cluster (chapter 14, "Actor Persistence")

But these solutions aren't needed for the basic understanding of Akka and will be covered in the later chapters of the book. Before you get simple applications running, you need some utility functions to create an actual application like the configuration, logging, and deployment of an application. This will be covered in the next chapter.

Configuration, logging, and deployment

In this chapter

- Using the configuration library
- Logging application-level events and debug messages
- Packaging and deployment of Akka-based applications

Thus far, we've focused on creating actors and working with the actor system. To create an application that can actually be run, we'll need several other things to be bundled with it before it's ready for deployment. First, we'll dive into how Akka supports configuration, and then we'll look at logging, including how you can use your own logging framework. Last, we'll go through a deployment example.

7.1 Configuration

Akka uses the Typesafe Config Library, which sports a state-of-the-art set of capabilities. The typical features are there: the ability to define properties in different ways and then reference them in the code (job one of configuration is to grant runtime flexibility by making it possible to use variables outside the code). There's also a sophisticated means of merging multiple configuration files based on simple conventions that determine how overrides will occur. One of the most important requirements of a configuration system is providing a means of targeting multiple environments (such as development, testing, production), without having to explode the bundle. You'll see how that's done, as well.

7.1.1 *Trying out Akka configuration*

Like other Akka libraries, the Typesafe Config Library takes pains to minimize the dependencies that are needed; it has no dependencies on other libraries. We'll start with a quick tour of how to use the configuration library.

The library uses a hierarchy of properties. Figure 7.1 shows a possible configuration of an application defining four properties using a self-defined hierarchy. We've grouped all our properties within the MyAppl node and also grouped the database properties.

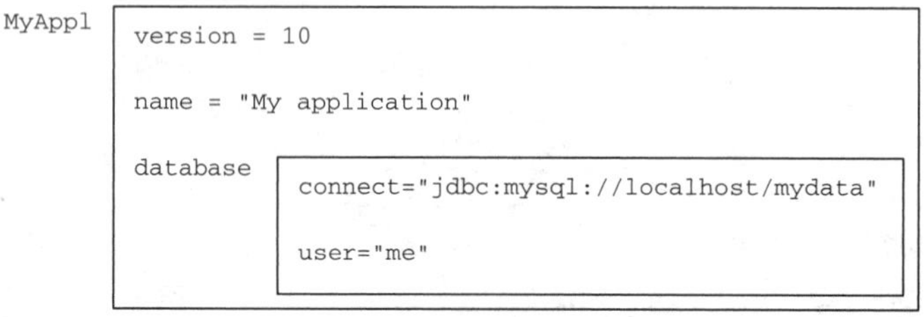

```
MyAppl
        version = 10

        name = "My application"

        database
                  connect="jdbc:mysql://localhost/mydata"

                  user="me"
```

Figure 7.1   Configuration example

The `ConfigFactory` is used to get the configuration. This is often called within the `Main` class of your application. The library also supports the ability to specify which configuration file is used, and in the next sections, we'll look at the configuration files in more detail, but for now we'll start by using the default one.

Listing 7.1   Getting configuration

```
val config = ConfigFactory.load()
```

When using the default, the library will try to find the configuration file. Since the library supports a number of different configuration formats, it looks for different files, in the following order:

- *application.properties*—This file should contain the configuration properties in the Java property file format.
- *application.json*—This file should contain the configuration properties in the JSON style.
- *application.conf*—This file should contain the configuration properties in the HOCON format. This is a format based on JSON but is easier to read. More details on HOCON or the Typesafe Config Library can be found at https://github.com/typesafehub/config.

It's possible to use all the different files at the same time. We use application.conf in the following listing.

Listing 7.2   application.conf

```
MyAppl {
  version = 10
  description = "My application"
  database {                                          Nesting is done by simply
    connect="jdbc:mysql://localhost/mydata"           grouping with {}.
    user="me"
  }
}
```

For simple applications, this file will often suffice. The format looks somewhat like JSON. The primary advantages are that it's more readable and it's easy to see how properties are being grouped. JDBC is a perfect example of properties most apps will need that are better grouped together. In the dependency injection world, you would group items like this by controlling the injection of the properties into objects (such as `DataSource`). This is a simpler approach. Let's look at how we can make use of these properties, now that we've defined them.

There are several methods to get the values as different types, and the period (.) is used as the separator in the path of the property. Not only are the basic types supported, but it's also possible to get lists of these types.

Listing 7.3   Getting properties

```
val applicationVersion = config.getInt("MyAppl.version")
val databaseConnectString = config.getString("MyAppl.database.connect")
```
We can use connect string from inside database braces {} from prior listing

Sometimes, an object doesn't need much configuration. What if you have a class `DBaseConnection` that's creating the database connection? This class needs only the connect string and the user property. When you pass the full configuration to the `DBaseConnection` class, it needs to know the full path of the property. But when you want to reuse `DBaseConnection` within another application, a problem arises. The start of the path is *MyAppl*; another application probably has a different configuration root. Therefore, the path to the property has changed. This can be solved by using the functionality of getting a subtree as your configuration.

Listing 7.4   Getting a configuration subtree

First get subtree by name, which is used in application-specific code

```
val databaseCfg = configuration.getConfig("MyAppl.database")
```

```
val databaseConnectString = databaseCfg.getString("connect")
```

Then reference property as relative to subtree root, which will be used within DBaseConnection

Using this approach, instead of configuration, you give the `databaseCfg` to `DBase-Connection`, and now `DBaseConnection` doesn't need the full path of the property, only the last part—the name of the property. This means `DBaseConnection` can be reused without introducing path problems.

It's also possible to perform substitutions when you have a property that's used multiple times in your configuration, for example, the host name of the database connect string.

```
hostname="localhost"
MyApp1 {
    version = 10
    description = "My application"
    database {
        connect="jdbc:mysql://${hostname}/mydata"
        user="me"
    }
}
```

Simple variable definition, no types needed (note quotes though)

Familiar ${} substitution syntax

Config file variables are often used for things like the application name, or for version numbers, since repeating them in many places in the file could potentially be dangerous. It's also possible to use system properties or environment variables in the substitutions as well.

```
hostname=${?HOST_NAME}
MyApp1 {
  version = 10
  description = "My application"
  database {
    connect="jdbc:mysql://${hostname}/mydata"
    user="me"
  }
}
```

Question mark ? signifies getting the value from an environment variable

But the problem with these properties is that you never know for sure that these properties exit. To account for this, you can make use of the possibility that redefinition of a property overrules the previous definition. And the substitution of a system property or environment variable definition simply vanishes if there's no value for the specified property `HOST_NAME`. The following listing shows how to do this.

Listing 7.7 System property or environment variable substitution with default

```
hostname="localhost"                          ◁─── Define usual simple way first
hostname=${?HOST_NAME}                        ◁─┐
MyApp1 {                                         │ If there's an env var,
  version = 10                                   │ override; otherwise, leave it
  description = "My application"                 │ with value you just assigned
  database {
    connect="jdbc:mysql://${hostname}/mydata"
    user="me"
}
}
```

It's pretty easy to see what's going on here. Defaults are important in configuration because you want to force the user to do as little configuration as possible. Furthermore, it's often the case that apps should run with no configuration until they really need to be pushed into a production environment; development usage can often be done with nothing but defaults.

7.1.2 Using defaults

Let's continue with our simple JDBC configuration. It's generally safe to assume that developers will be connecting to a database instance on their own machine, referenced as `localhost`. As soon as someone wants to see a demo, we'll be scrambling to get the app working on an instance somewhere that will no doubt have different names, and the database will likely be on another machine. The laziest thing we could do is just make a copy of the whole config file and give it a different name, and then have some logic in the app that says "use this file in this environment, and this one in another." The problem with this is that now we have all our configuration in two places. It makes more sense to just override the two or three values that are going to be different in the new target environment. The defaulting mechanism will allow us to do that easily. The configuration library contains a fallback mechanism; the defaults are placed into a configuration object, which is then handed over to the configurator as the fallback configuration source. Figure 7.2 shows a simple example of this.

Preventing null properties

The defaulting mechanism prevents cases where the values are different depending on where they're being used. In view of this principle, when a configuration property is read, the value should always be set. If the framework were to allow the property to be empty, again the code would behave differently based on how (and where) configuration was done. Therefore, if you try to get a config value from the configuration that isn't set, an exception is thrown.

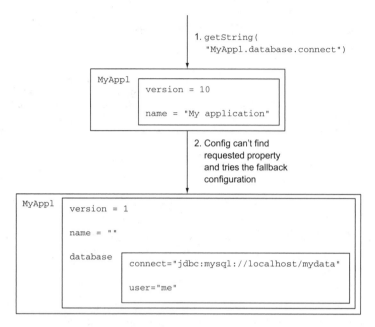

Figure 7.2 Configuration fallback

This fallback structure grants us a lot of flexibility. But for it to provide the defaults we need, we have to know how to configure them. They're configured in the file reference .conf and placed in the root of the JAR file; the idea is that every library contains its own defaults. The configuration library will find all the reference.conf files and integrate these settings into the configuration fallback structure. This way all the needed prop-erties of a library will always have a default and the princi-ple of always getting some value back will be preserved. (Later, you'll see that you can explicitly stipulate defaults programmatically, as well.)

We already mentioned that the configuration library supports multiple formats. There's nothing stopping you from using multiple formats in a single application. Each file can be used as the fallback of another file. And to sup-port the possibility of overruling properties with system properties, the higher-ranking configuration contains these. The structure is always the same, so the relation-ships between defaults and overrides is likewise always the same. Figure 7.3 shows the files the config library uses to build the complete tree, in priority order.

Most applications will use only one of these applica-tion file types. But if you want to provide a set of applica-tion defaults and then override some of them, as we want

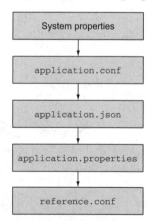

Figure 7.3 Priority of the configuration fallback structure. Highest priority at the top, which overrides definitions in lower files.

to do with our JDBC settings, you can do that. When following this guide, realize that the upper configurations shown in figure 7.3 will overrule the values defined in the lower configurations.

By default, the file application.{conf,json,properties} is used to read the configuration. There are two ways to change the name of the configuration file. The first option is to use an overloaded load function on the `ConfigFactory`. When loading the configuration, the name of the base should be supplied.

Listing 7.8 Changing configuration file

```
val config = ConfigFactory.load("myapp")    <--- Simply ask factory to load new name
```

This way it doesn't try to load application.{conf,json,properties}, but rather myapp.{conf,json,properties}. (This is required if you need to have multiple configurations in a single JVM.)

Another option is to use Java system properties. Sometimes, this is the easiest thing because you can just create a Bash script and set a property, and the app will pick it up and start using it (better than exploding JARs or WARs to monkey with the files inside). The following list explains the three system properties that can be used to control which configuration file should be read:

- `config.resource` specifies a resource name—not a base name; for example, application.conf, not `application`.
- `config.file` specifies a file system path; again, it should include the extension.
- `config.url` specifies a URL.

System properties can be used for the name of the configuration file, when you're using the load method without arguments. Setting system properties is as easy as adding the `-D` option; for example -Dconfig.file="config/myapp.conf" when using the configuration file config/myapp.conf. When using one of these properties, the default behavior of searching for the different `.conf`, `.json`, and `.properties` is skipped.

7.1.3 *Akka configuration*

Okay, you've seen how we can use the configuration library for our application's properties, but what do you need to do when you want to change some of Akka's configuration options? How is Akka using this library? It's possible to have multiple `ActorSystems` that have their own configuration. When no configuration is present at creation, the actor system will create the configuration using the defaults, as shown in the next listing.

Listing 7.9 Default configuration

```
val system = ActorSystem("mySystem")    <--- ConfigFactory.load() is used internally
                                             to create a default config for the config
                                             argument that is omitted here.
```

But it's also possible (and useful) to supply the configuration while creating an Actor-System. The following listing shows a simple way of accomplishing this.

Listing 7.10   Using specified configuration

```
val configuration = ConfigFactory.load("myapp")        ◁──┐
val systemA = ActorSystem("mysystem",configuration)       ◁──┐
```

First load configuration, providing name

Then pass it to ActorSystem constructor

The configuration is within your application; it can be found in the settings of the ActorSystem. This can be accessed within every actor. In the next listing we get the property MyAppl.name.

Listing 7.11   Access to the configuration from the running app

```
val mySystem = ActorSystem("myAppl")
val config = mySystem.settings.config        ◁──┐
val applicationDescription = config.getString("MyAppl.name")     ◁──┐
```

Once ActorSystem is constructed, we can get config just by referencing it using this path.

Then we just get a property as we would ordinarily.

By this point, you've seen how you can use the configuration system for your own properties, and how to use the same system to configure the ActorSystem that's the backbone of Akka. The presumption in these first two sections has been that you have but one Akka app on a given system that's hosting you. In the next section, we'll discuss configuring systems that share a single instance.

7.1.4   Multiple systems

Depending on your requirements, it may be necessary to have different configurations, say, for multiple subsystems, on a single instance (or machine). Akka supports this in several ways. Let's start by looking at cases where you're using several JVMs, but they run in the same environment using the same files. We already described the first option: the use of system properties. When starting a new process, a different configuration file is used. But usually a lot of the configuration is the same for all the subsystems, and only a small part differs. This problem can be solved by using the include option.

   Let's look at an example. Let's say we have a baseConfig file like the one in the next listing.

Listing 7.12   baseConfig.conf

```
MyAppl {
  version = 10
  description = "My application"
}
```

For this example, we start with this simple configuration root, which would most likely have one shared and one differing property; the version number is likely to be the same across subsystems, but we'll probably want different names and descriptions for each subsystem.

Listing 7.13   subAppl.conf

**Simply name config file we want
to include (no extension)**

```
include "baseConfig"              ◁─┘
MyAppl {
  description = "Sub Application"      ◁──── Then provide new description
}
```

Because the include is before the rest of the configuration, the value of `description` in the configuration is overridden just as it was in a single file. This way, you can have one basic configuration and only the differences required in the specific configuration files for each subsystem.

But what if the subsystems are running in the same JVM? Then you can't use the system properties to read other configuration files. How should you do the configuration then? We've already discussed what's needed for this case: you can use an application name when loading the configuration. You can also use the `include` method to group all the configuration that's the same. The only drawback is the possible number of configuration files. If that's a concern, there's another solution that leverages the ability to merge configuration trees using the fallback mechanism.

We start by combining the two configurations into one.

Listing 7.14   combined.conf

```
MyAppl {
  version = 10
  description = "My application"
}

subApplA {                           By lifting this, we get shared
  MyAppl {                           property (version) and
    description = "Sub application"   ◁──── override description
  }
}
```

The trick we're using is that we take a subtree within `subApplA` of the configuration and put that in front of the configuration chain. This is called *lifting a configuration*, because the configuration path is shortened. Figure 7.4 shows how this is done.

When we request the property `MyAppl.description` using `config.getString ("MyAppl.description")`, we get the result `"Sub application"` because the description configuration value was set in the configuration at the highest level (at `subApplA.MyAppl.description`). And when we ask for `MyAppl.version`, we get the value 10

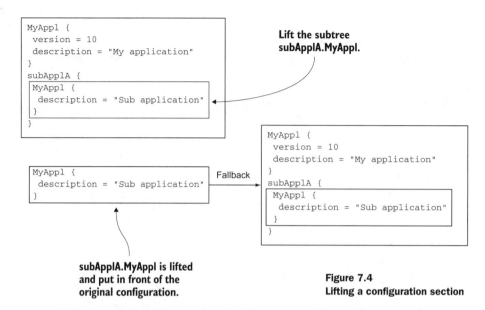

**Figure 7.4
Lifting a configuration section**

because the version configuration value wasn't defined in the higher configuration (inside `subApplA.MyAppl`), so the normal fallback mechanism is used to provide the configuration value. Listing 7.15 shows how we load the configuration to have both the lift and the fallback. Note that the fallback is chained programmatically here (not relying on the file conventions we covered earlier).

Listing 7.15   Lift example with fallback

```
val configuration = ConfigFactory.load("combined")           Select subtree
val subApplACfg = configuration.getConfig("subApplA")        subApplA

val config = subApplACfg.withFallback(configuration)         Add configuration
                                                             as fallback
```

Configuration is a crucial part of delivering applications; though it starts out with meager requirements that are usually easily met, invariably demands appear that can complicate matters, and often the configuration layer of an application becomes very tangled and complex. The Typesafe Config Library provides a number of powerful tools to prevent this from happening:

- Easy defaulting based on convention (with overrides)
- Sophisticated defaulting that allows you to require the least amount of configuration necessary
- Several syntax options: traditional, Java, JSON, and HOCON

We haven't come near to exhausting this topic, but we've shown you enough that you can deal with a pretty broad range of typical requirements that will come up as you start to deploy Akka solutions. In the next section, we tackle logging, which is critical, but developers tend to have strong opinions and they tend to want to use what they're comfortable with. We'll address how Akka allows this, through configuration.

7.2 Logging

Another function each application needs is to be able to write messages to a log file. Because everyone has their own preferences regarding which logging library to use, the Akka toolkit has a logging adapter that supports all kinds of logging frameworks and also minimizes the dependencies on other libraries. As was the case with configuration, there are two sides to logging: how you use the log for your application-level logging needs, and how you can control what Akka puts into the logs (which is a critical part of debugging). We'll cut the same path, starting with how logging with Akka works.

7.2.1 Logging in an Akka application

Just as you would in normal Java or Scala code, you'll have to create a logger instance inside any actor that needs to put messages into the log.

Listing 7.16   Creating a logging adapter

```
class MyActor extends Actor {
  val log = Logging(context.system, this)
  ...
}
```

The first thing that's notable is that the `ActorSystem` is needed. This is done so there's a separation of the logging from the framework. The logging adapter uses the system `eventStream` to send the log messages to the `eventHandler`. The `eventStream` is the publish-subscribe mechanism of Akka (described later). The `eventHandler` receives these message and uses the preferred logging framework to log the message. This way all the actors can log and only one actor has a dependency on the specific logging framework implementation. Which `eventHandler` is used can be configured. Another advantage is that logging means I/O, and I/O is always slow, and in a concurrent environment, this can be even worse because you have to wait until another thread is done writing its log messages. So in a high-performance application, you don't want to wait until the logging is done. Using the Akka logging, the actors don't have to wait to do logging. The following listing shows the configuration required for the default logger to be created.

Listing 7.17   Configuring `eventHandler`

```
akka {
  # Event handlers to register at boot time
  # (Logging$DefaultLogger logs to STDOUT)
  loggers  = ["akka.event.Logging$DefaultLogger"]
  # Options: ERROR, WARNING, INFO, DEBUG
  loglevel = "DEBUG"
}
```

This eventHandler doesn't use a log framework, but logs all the received messages to STDOUT. The Akka toolkit has two implementations of this logging eventHandler. The first—the default logger to STDOUT—has already been mentioned. The second implementation is using SLF4J. This can be found in akka-slf4j.jar. To use this handler, add the following configuration to your application.conf.

Listing 7.18   Using SLF4J `eventHandler`

```
akka {
  loggers = ["akka.event.slf4j.Slf4jLogger"]
  # Options: ERROR, WARNING, INFO, DEBUG
  loglevel = "DEBUG"
}
```

But when STDOUT and SLF4J aren't sufficient, you can create your own eventHandler. You need to create an actor that handles several messages. Here's an example of such a handler.

Listing 7.19   My `eventHandler`

```
import akka.event.Logging.InitializeLogger
import akka.event.Logging.LoggerInitialized
import akka.event.Logging.Error
import akka.event.Logging.Warning
import akka.event.Logging.Info
import akka.event.Logging.Debug

class MyEventListener extends Actor{
  def receive = {
    case InitializeLogger(_) =>
      sender ! LoggerInitialized
    case Error(cause, logSource, logClass, message) =>
      println( "ERROR " + message)
    case Warning(logSource, logClass, message) =>
      println( "WARN " + message)
    case Info(logSource, logClass, message) =>
      println( "INFO " + message)
    case Debug(logSource, logClass, message) =>
      println( "DEBUG " + message)
  }
}
```

Upon receipt of this message, initialization of your handler can be done, and when complete, a LoggerInitialized should be sent to the sender.

An error message is received; log this message or not. Here you can add some logic for filtering log records when your log framework doesn't support this.

A warning message is received.

An information message is received.

A debug message is received.

This is a very simple example and is only showing the message protocol. In real life, this actor will be more complex.

7.2.2 Using logging

Let's revisit the creation of the Akka logger instance that we first showed in listing 7.16. We discussed the first part of the creation process (the `ActorSystem`). If you recall, there was a second parameter; here it is again.

Listing 7.20 Revisiting the creation of the logger

```
class MyActor extends Actor {
  val log = Logging(context.system, this)
  ...
}
```

The second parameter of `Logging` is used as the source of this logging channel, in this case, the class instance. The source object is translated to a `String` to indicate the source of the log messages. The translation to a `String` is done according to the following rules:

- If it's an `Actor` or `ActorRef`, its path is used.
- In case of a `String`, the string is used.
- In case of a class, an approximation of its `simpleName` is used.

For convenience you can also use the `ActorLogging` trait to mixin the log member to actors. This is provided because most of the time you want to use the logging as shown next.

Listing 7.21 Creating logging adapter

```
class MyActor extends Actor with ActorLogging {
  ...
}
```

The adapter also supports using placeholders in the message. Placeholders prevent you from having to check logging levels. If you construct messages with concatenation, the work will be done each time, even if the level precludes the insertion of the message in the log! Using placeholders, you don't have to check the level (for example `if (logger .isDebugEnabled())`), and the message will only be created if it would be included in the log given the current level. The placeholder is the string `{}` in the message.

Listing 7.22 Using placeholders

```
log.debug("two parameters: {}, {}", "one","two")
```

Nothing too disorienting here; most people who've been doing logging in Java or a VM language will find this fairly familiar.

One of the other common logging challenges that can cause developers headaches is learning how to get control of the logging of the various toolkits or frameworks your app is using. In the next section, we'll show how this is done with Akka.

7.2.3 Controlling Akka's logging

While developing an application, you sometimes need a very low level of debug logging. Akka is able to log records when certain internal events happen or the log has processed certain messages. These log messages are intended for developers and aren't meant for operations. Thankfully, given the architecture that we've discussed already, you don't have to worry about the possibility that your chosen logging framework and the one Akka uses aren't the same, or worse, conflict with each other. Akka provides a simple configuration layer that allows you to exert some control over what it outputs to the log, and once you change these settings, you'll see the results in whatever your chosen appenders are (console, file, and so on). The following listing shows the settings you can manipulate to elicit more or less information from Akka in the logs.

Listing 7.23 Akka's logging configuration file

```
akka {
  # logging must be set to DEBUG to use any of the options below
  loglevel =     DEBUG
  # Log level for the very basic logger activated during ActorSystem startup.
  # This logger prints the log messages to stdout (System.out).
  # Options: OFF, ERROR, WARNING, INFO, DEBUG
  stdout-loglevel = "WARNING"
  # Log the complete configuration at INFO level when the actor
  # system is started. This is useful when you are uncertain of
  # what configuration is used.
  log-config-on-start = on
  debug {
    # logging of all user-level messages that are processed by
    # Actors that use akka.event.LoggingReceive enable function of
    # LoggingReceive, which is to log any received message at
    # DEBUG level
    receive = on
    # enable DEBUG logging of all AutoReceiveMessages
    # (Kill, PoisonPill and the like)
    autoreceive = on
    # enable DEBUG logging of actor lifecycle changes
    # (restarts, deaths etc)
    lifecycle = on
    # enable DEBUG logging of all LoggingFSMs for events,
    # transitions and timers
    fsm = on
    # enable DEBUG logging of subscription (subscribe/unsubscribe)
    # changes on the eventStream
    event-stream = on
  }
  remote {
```

> Logs messages received by your Actors; requires the use of akka.event .LoggingReceive when processing messages — points to `receive = on`

```
    # If this is "on", Akka will log all outbound messages at
    # DEBUG level, if off then they are not logged
    log-sent-messages = on
    # If this is "on," Akka will log all inbound messages at
    # DEBUG level, if off then they are not logged
    log-received-messages = on
  }
}
```

The comments explain most of these options (see the annotation for the `receive` property and its additional requirement). Note also that you're shielded from one of the major annoyances of having to tweak the configuration of a framework or toolkit: knowing which packages to change levels on. This is another inherent advantage of message-based systems (the notion that they're pretty self-explanatory, by just watching the message traffic flow between the collaborators). The following listing shows how to use `LoggingReceive` in an actor to log all user-level messages that the actor receives.

Listing 7.24   Using `LoggingReceive`

```
class MyActor extends Actor with ActorLogging {      ◁──┐ Adds LoggingReceive trait
  def receive = LoggingReceive {                         │ so you can see actor
    case ... => ...                                      │ messages as log traces
  }
}
```

Now when you set the property `akka.debug.receive` to `on`, the messages received by your actor will be logged.

Again, we haven't exhausted the topic of logging, but we've shown you enough to really get going, and to ease your understandable anxiety about whether you'll be expected to use some other approach, or have to wrangle with two different loggers (yours and Akka's). Logging is a critical tool that you could argue is even more useful in message-passing systems, where the process of just stepping along a single line of executing code in a debugger is often not possible. In the next section, we'll discuss the last requirement of application delivery: deployment.

7.3   *Deploying actor-based applications*

You've already seen how you can use the `ActorSystem` and actors to do the configuration and logging. But it takes more to create an application. Everything has to come together: the system should be started and a deployment has to be created. In this section we'll show a way to create a distribution for an application. This simple example will give you an idea of how easy it is to create a distribution.

To create a standalone application, we'll use the `sbt-native-packager` plugin to create a distribution. We'll start with the `HelloWorld` actor. This is a simple actor that receives a message and replies with a hello message.

Listing 7.25   `HelloWorld` actor

```
class HelloWorld extends Actor with ActorLogging {          ◁──  Using ActorLogging
  def receive = {                                                 trait to be able to log
    case msg: String  =>                                          messages
      val hello = "Hello %s".format(msg)
      sender() ! hello
      log.info("Sent response {}",hello)
  }
}
```

Next we need an `Actor` that calls the `HelloWorld` actor. Let's call this the `Hello-WorldCaller`.

Listing 7.26   `HelloWorldCaller`

```
class HelloWorldCaller(timer: FiniteDuration, actor: ActorRef)
    extends Actor with ActorLogging {

  case class TimerTick(msg: String)                           Using Akka
                                                              scheduler to send
  override def preStart() {                                   messages to yourself
    super.preStart()
    implicit val ec = context.dispatcher
    context.system.scheduler.schedule(      ◁──
      timer,
      timer,                                 ◁────────  Duration between scheduled triggers
      self,
      new TimerTick("everybody"))            ◁──
  }                                                            Message that's sent
  def receive = {
    case msg: String  => log.info("received {}",msg)
    case tick: TimerTick => actor ! tick.msg
  }
}
```

Duration before schedule is triggered for the first time ──▷ `timer,`

ActorRef where messages are to be ──▷ `self,`

This actor is using the built-in scheduler to generate messages regularly. The scheduler is used to repeatedly send the created `TimerTick`. A message is sent to the actor reference passed to the constructor every time the `TimerTick` is received (the `HelloWorld` actor, in this case). Any `String` message that the `HelloWorld` actor receives is logged.

To create our application, we need to build the actor system at startup.

Listing 7.27   `BootHello`

```
import akka.actor.{ Props, ActorSystem }
import scala.concurrent.duration._                           Extends App trait to be able
                                                             to be called when starting
object BootHello extends App {         ◁──                   the application

  val system = ActorSystem("hellokernel")   ◁───  Creating ActorSystem
```

```
val actor = system.actorOf(Props[HelloWorld])    ◁——— Creates HelloWorld Actor
val config = system.settings.config              ◁——
val timer = config.getInt("helloWorld.timer")         Gets timer duration
system.actorOf(Props(                                  from our configuration
    new HelloWorldCaller(
        timer millis,                  ◁——— Creates a Duration from an Integer. This works
        actor)))    ◁———                     because we've imported scala.concurrent.duration._
}
                      Passes reference of HelloWorld
                      actor to our caller
```

Creates Caller Actor

So now we've built our system and need some resources to make our application work properly. We'll use configuration to define the default value for our timer.

Listing 7.28   reference.conf

```
helloWorld {
  timer = 5000
}
```

Our default is 5000 milliseconds. Be sure that this reference.conf is placed inside your JAR file by placing it in the main/resources directory. Next we have to set up the logger, and this is done in the application.conf.

Listing 7.29   application.conf

```
akka {
  loggers = ["akka.event.slf4j.Slf4jLogger"]
  # Options: ERROR,WARNING,INFO, DEBUG
  loglevel = "DEBUG"
}
```

At this point, we have all our code and resources and need to create a distribution. In this example we use the sbt-native-packager plugin to create the complete distribution. Because we use the sbt-native-packager and we want to include the configuration in the distribution, we have to place the application.conf and the logback.xml in the directory <project home>/src/universal/conf.

The next step is to include the sbt-native-packager in the plugins.sbt file in the <project home>/project directory.

Listing 7.30   project/plugins.sbt

```
addSbtPlugin("com.typesafe.sbt" % "sbt-native-packager" % "1.0.0")
```

The last part we need before we're done is the sbt build file for our project.

Listing 7.31 build.sbt

```
name := "deploy"

version := "0.1-SNAPSHOT"

organization := "manning"

scalaVersion := "2.11.8"

enablePlugins(JavaAppPackaging)

scriptClasspath +="../conf"

libraryDependencies ++= {
  val akkaVersion       = "2.4.9"
  Seq(
    "com.typesafe.akka" %% "akka-actor"     % akkaVersion,
    "com.typesafe.akka" %% "akka-slf4j"     % akkaVersion,
    "ch.qos.logback"    %  "logback-classic" % "1.0.13",
    "com.typesafe.akka" %% "akka-testkit"   % akkaVersion % "test",
    "org.scalatest"     %% "scalatest"      % "2.2.6"     % "test"
  )
}
```

Defines that we have a standalone application → enablePlugins(JavaAppPackaging)

Adds conf directory to the class path. Otherwise, both files (application .conf and logback.xml) can't be found. → scriptClasspath +="../conf"

Defines the application dependencies → libraryDependencies ++= {

Simple build tool: more information

At some point, you'll no doubt want more details on sbt and all it can do. You can read the documentation; the project is hosted on GitHub (https://github.com /sbt/sbt). Manning Publications also has a recently released book, *SBT in Action*, that goes into great detail, working through not only what you can do, but what makes sbt a next-generation build tool.

Now we've defined our project in sbt and are ready to create our distribution. The next listing shows how we can start sbt and run the dist command.

Listing 7.32 Creating distribution

```
sbt
[info] Loading global plugins from home\.sbt\0.13\plugins
[info] Loading project definition from
       \github\akka-in-action\chapter-conf-deploy\project
[info] Set current project to deploy (in build
       file:/github/akka-in-action/chapter-conf-deploy/)
> stage
```

Once sbt is done loading, type stage and press Return. → > stage

sbt creates a distribution in the directory target/universal.stage. This directory contains three subdirectories:

- *bin*—Contains the start scripts: one for Windows and one for Unix
- *lib*—Contains all the JAR files our application depends on
- *conf*—Contains all the configuration files of our application

Now we have a distribution, and all that's left is to run our application. Because we called our application `deploy`, the stage command has created two start files; one can be used for Window platforms and the other for Unix-like systems.

Listing 7.33   Run application

```
deploy.bat
```

```
./deploy
```

And when we look in the log file, we see that every five seconds, the `helloWorld` actor is receiving messages, and the caller receives its messages. Of course, this application has no real utility. But it shows that when you use these simple conventions, it's easy to create a complete distribution for your application.

7.4   Summary

Like so much in development, deployment looks like it's going to be a piece of cake as you approach. Yet in practice, it often turns into a vortex of each component configuring itself from its own resources, with no rhyme or reason behind the overall system approach. As is the case in all things design-wise, Akka's approach is to provide state-of-the-art tools, but with the emphasis on simple conventions that are easy to implement. These tools made making our first app ready to run rather easy. But more importantly, you've seen that you can carry this simplicity forward into much-more-complex realms:

- File conventions for simple overriding of configuration
- Intelligent defaulting: apps can supply most of what's needed
- Granular control over injecting config
- State-of-the-art logging through an adapter and a single dependency point
- Lightweight application bundling
- Using a build tool that also bundles and runs your app

The age of the release engineer being the hardest-working member of the team may be ending. As we go forward with more complex examples in the book, you won't see the deployment layer blow up on us. This is a huge part of the Akka story: it delivers not only a power-packed runtime with messaging and concurrency built in, but the means to get solutions running more rapidly than in the less-powerful application environments most of us are accustomed to.

Structural patterns
for actors

8

One of the immediate concerns with actor-based programming is how you model code that requires collaborators to work together when each unit of work is done in parallel. Collaboration implies some notion of process, and although there can be parallel processes, there will also be cases where it's essential that certain steps happen after required prior steps have been completed. By implementing a few of the classic *enterprise integration patterns* (EIPs), we'll show how Akka allows you to employ these design approaches while still making use of its inherent concurrency.

We'll focus primarily on the most relevant EIPs to show different ways of connecting actors to solve problems. The architectural EIPs will get the most attention in this chapter, since we're considering application structure.

166

We start with the simple pipes and filters pattern. This is the default pattern for most message-passing systems and is straightforward. The classical version is sequential; we'll adapt it to work in our concurrent, message-based architecture. Next will be the scatter-gather pattern, which does provide a means of parallelizing tasks. Actor implementations of these patterns are not only remarkably compact and efficient, but they're free of a lot of the implementation details that quickly seep into messaging patterns (as most of these do).

Finally, we'll look at a less-common routing pattern. The routing slip pattern is a dynamic pipes and filters pattern that's used when the route between several tasks can be established at the beginning of message processing.

8.1 Pipes and filters

The concept of *piping* refers to the ability for one process or thread to pump its results to another processor for additional processing. Most people know about piping from some exposure to Unix, where it originated. The set of piped components is often referred to as a *pipeline*, and most people's experience of it is of each step occurring in sequence with no parallelism. Yet, you'll see that there are often good reasons to want to see independent aspects of a process occur in parallel. That's what we'll show here: first, a description of this pattern's applicability and its form, and then a look at how you can implement it using Akka.

8.1.1 Enterprise integration pattern: pipes and filters

In many systems, a single event will trigger a sequence of tasks. Take, for example, the functionality of a camera to catch speeding motorists. It makes a photo and measures speed. But before the event is sent to central processing, a number of checks are done. If no license plate is found in the photo, the system is unable to process the message any further, and it will be discarded. In this example we also discard the message when the speed is below the maximum legal speed. This means that only messages that contain the license plate of a speeding vehicle end up getting to the central processor. You can probably already see how we'll apply the pipes and filters pattern here: the constraints are filters, and the interconnects are the pipes in this case (see figure 8.1).

Pipes and filters pattern

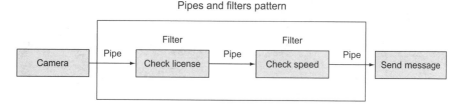

Figure 8.1　Example of pipes and filters

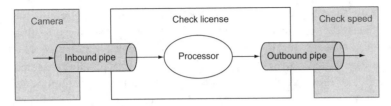

Figure 8.2   Three parts of a filter

Each filter consists of three parts: the inbound pipe where the message is received, the processor of the message, and the outbound pipe where the result of the processing is published (see figure 8.2).

The two pipes are drawn partly outside the filter because the outbound pipe of the check-license filter is also the inbound pipe of the check-speed filter. An important restriction is that each filter must accept and send the same messages, because the outbound pipe of a filter can be the inbound pipe of any other filter in the pattern. This means that all the filters need to have the same interface. This includes the inbound and the outbound pipes. This way it's easy to add new processes, change the order of processes, or remove them. Because the filters have the same interface and are independent, nothing has to be changed, other than potentially adding additional pipes.

8.1.2   *Pipes and filters in Akka*

The filters are the processing units of the message system, so when you apply the pipes and filters pattern to Akka, you use actors to implement your filters. Thanks to the fact that the messaging is supplied behind the scenes, you can just connect a number of actors, and the pipes are already there. It would seem to be simple to implement this pattern with Akka. Are we done here? Not quite. There are two requirements crucial for implementing the pipes and filters pattern: the interface is the same for all the filters, and all of the actors are independent. This means that all the messages received by the different actors should be the same, because the messages are part of the interface of the filter, as shown in figure 8.3. If you were to use different messages, the interface of the next actor would differ and the uniformity requirement would be violated, preventing you from being able to indiscriminately apply filters.

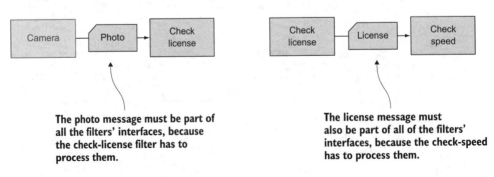

Figure 8.3   Messages sent by different actors

Given the requirement that the input and output to the pipe need be the same, both actors must accept and send the same messages.

Let's create a small example with a Photo message and two filters: the License-Filter and SpeedFilter.

Listing 8.1 A pipe with two filters

```
case class Photo(license: String, speed: Int)                    ◁─────  Message
                                                                          that will
class SpeedFilter(minSpeed: Int, pipe: ActorRef) extends Actor {          be filtered
  def receive = {
    case msg: Photo =>
      if (msg.speed > minSpeed)             ◁──┐  Filters all Photos that
        pipe ! msg                             │  have a speed less
  }                                            │  than the speed limit
}

class LicenseFilter(pipe: ActorRef) extends Actor {
  def receive = {
    case msg: Photo =>
      if (!msg.license.isEmpty)             ◁──┐  Filters all Photos
        pipe ! msg                             │  that have an
  }                                            │  empty License
}
```

There's nothing special about these actor filters. We used actors with one-way messages in section 2.1.2 and in other examples. But because the two actors process and send the same message type, we can construct a pipeline from them, which allows for either one to feed the other its results, meaning the order in which we apply the filters doesn't matter. In the next example, we'll show how this gives us flexibility that comes in handy when we find that the order will have a marked influence on the execution time. Let's see how this works.

Listing 8.2 Pipes and filters test

```
val endProbe = TestProbe()
val speedFilterRef = system.actorOf(              ◁─── Constructs pipeline
  Props(new SpeedFilter(50, endProbe.ref)))
val licenseFilterRef = system.actorOf(
  Props(new LicenseFilter(speedFilterRef)))
val msg = new Photo("123xyz", 60)             ◁──┐  Tests a message
licenseFilterRef ! msg                           │  that should be
endProbe.expectMsg(msg)                          │  passed through

licenseFilterRef ! new Photo("", 60)          ◁──┐  Tests a message
endProbe.expectNoMsg(1 second)                   │  without a license

licenseFilterRef ! new Photo("123xyz", 49)    ◁──┐  Tests a message
endProbe.expectNoMsg(1 second)                   │  with a low speed
```

The check-license filter uses a lot of resources. It has to locate the letters and numbers on the plate, which is CPU-intensive. When we put the camera on a busy road, we find that the filter chain can't keep up with the pace of new photos arriving. Our investigations reveal that 90% of the messages are approved by the license filter, and 50% of the messages are approved by the speed filter.

In this example (shown in figure 8.4) the check-license filter has to process 20 messages each second. To improve performance, it would be better to reorder the filters. Since most of the messages are filtered by the check-speed filter, the load on the check-license filter will be decreased significantly.

As you can see in figure 8.5, when we switch the order of filters, the check-license filter is asked to evaluate 10 licenses per second; reordering halved the load of the filter. And because the interfaces are the same and the processes are independent, we can easily change the order of the actors without changing the functionality or the code. Without the pipes and filters pattern, we had to change both components to get this to work. Using this pattern, the only change is when building the chain of actors at startup time, which can easily be made configurable.

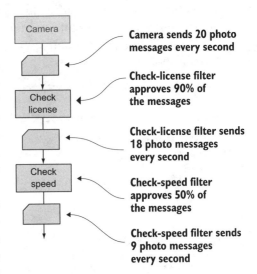

Figure 8.4   Number of processed messages for each filter for initial configuration

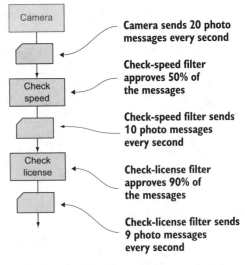

Figure 8.5   Number of processed messages for each filter for altered configuration

Listing 8.3   Changed order of filters

```
val endProbe = TestProbe()
val licenseFilterRef = system.actorOf(
  Props(new LicenseFilter(endProbe.ref)))
val speedFilterRef = system.actorOf(
  Props(new SpeedFilter(50, licenseFilterRef)))
```

Reorders pipeline construction

```
val msg = new Photo("123xyz", 60)
speedFilterRef ! msg
endProbe.expectMsg(msg)

speedFilterRef ! new Photo("", 60)
endProbe.expectNoMsg(1 second)

speedFilterRef ! new Photo("123xyz", 49)
endProbe.expectNoMsg(1 second)
```

You see that it doesn't matter which order we use; the pipeline gives us the same functionality. This flexibility is the strength of this pattern. In our example we used actual filters, but this pattern can be extended; the processing pipeline isn't limited to filters. As long as the process accepts and produces the same types of messages, and is independent of the other processes, this pattern applies. In the next section, you'll see a pattern that enables a divide-and-conquer approach, which requires concurrency, and Akka again makes it easy. We'll scatter units of work among a number of processing actors and then gather their results into a single set, allowing the consumer of the work product to just make a request and get a single response.

8.2 Enterprise integration pattern: scatter-gather

In the previous section, we created a pipeline of tasks that were executed sequentially. The ability to execute tasks in parallel is often preferable. We'll look at the scatter-gather pattern next and see how we can accomplish this. Akka's inherent ability to dispatch work to actors asynchronously provides most of what we need to make this pattern work. The processing tasks (filters in the previous example) are the gather parts; the recipient list is the scatter component. We'll use the `Aggregator` for the gather part (provided by Akka).

8.2.1 Applicability

The pattern can be applied in two different scenarios. The first case is when the tasks are functionally the same, but only one is passed through to the gather component as the chosen result. The second scenario is when work is divided for parallel processing and each processor submits its results, which are then combined into a result set by the aggregator. You'll see the benefits of the pattern clearly in both of our Akka implementations in the following section.

COMPETING TASKS

Let's start with the following problem. A client buys a product, let's say a book at a web shop, but the shop doesn't have the requested book in stock, so it has to buy the book from a supplier. But the shop is doing business with three different suppliers and wants to pay the lowest price. Our system needs to check if the product is available, and at what price. This has to be done for each supplier, and only the supplier with the lowest price will be used. In figure 8.6 we show how the scatter-gather pattern can help here.

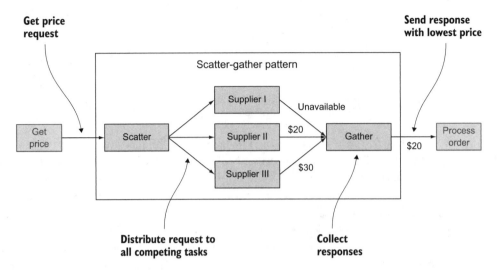

Figure 8.6 Scatter-gather pattern with competing tasks

The message of the client is distributed over three processes, and each process checks the availability and price of the product. The gather process will collect all the results and only pass the messages with the lowest price (in this example, $20). The processing tasks are all focused on one thing—getting the price of the product—but they may be doing it in different ways, because there are multiple suppliers. In pattern parlance, this is the *competing tasks* aspect, as only the best result will be used. For our example, it's the lowest price, but the selection criteria could be different in other cases. Selection in the gather component isn't always based on the content of the message. It's also possible that you only need one solution, in which case the competition is merely determining which is the quickest response. For example, the time it takes to sort a list depends greatly on the algorithm used and the initial unsorted list. When performance is critical, you sort the list in parallel using different sorting algorithms. If you did such a thing with Akka, you'd have one actor doing a bubble sort, one a quicksort, maybe one doing a heap sort. All tasks will result in the same sorted list, but depending on the unsorted list, one of them will be the fastest. In this case the gather will select the first received message and tell the other actors to stop. This is also an example of using the scatter-gather pattern for competing tasks.

PARALLEL COOPERATIVE PROCESSING

Another case where the scatter-gather pattern can be used is when the tasks are performing a subtask. Let's go back to our camera example. While processing a Photo, different information has to be retrieved from the photo and added to the Photo messages, for example, the time the photo was created and the speed of the vehicle. Both actions are independent of each other and can be performed in parallel. When both tasks are ready, the results must be joined together into a single message containing the time and the speed. Figure 8.7 shows the use of scatter-gather for this problem.

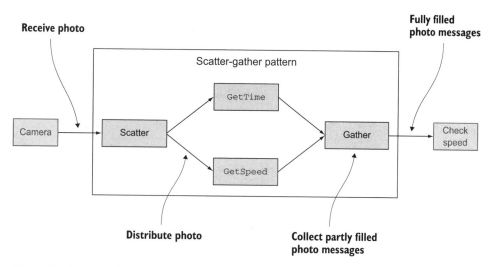

Figure 8.7 Scatter-gather pattern for task parallelization

This pattern starts with scattering a message to multiple tasks: GetTime and GetSpeed. The results of both tasks should be combined into a single message that can be used by other tasks.

8.2.2 *Parallel tasks with Akka*

Let's see how we can implement the scatter-gather pattern in the second scenario with Akka actors. We'll use the photo example. Each component in this pattern is implemented by one actor. In this example we use one type of message, which is used for all tasks. Each task can add the data to the same type message when processing has completed. The requirement that all tasks should be independent can't always be met. This only means that the order of both tasks can't be switched. But all the other benefits of adding, removing, or moving the tasks apply.

We start by defining the message that will be used. This message is received and sent by all components in this example:

```
case class PhotoMessage(id: String,
                        photo: String,
                        creationTime: Option[Date] = None,
                        speed: Option[Int] = None)
```

For our example message, we mock the traffic cameras and image recognition tools by just providing the image. Note that the message has an ID, which can be used by the Aggregator to associate the messages with their respective flows. The other attributes are the creation time and speed; they start empty and are provided by the GetSpeed and GetTime tasks. The next step is to implement the two processing tasks, GetTime and GetSpeed, as in figure 8.8.

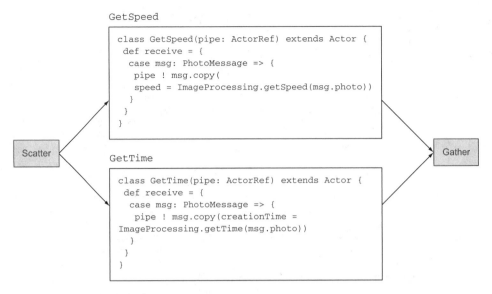

Figure 8.8 Two processing tasks: `GetTime` and `GetSpeed`

The two actors have the same structure, the difference being which attribute is extracted from the image. These actors are doing the actual work, but we need an actor that implements the scatter functionality that will dispatch the images for processing. In the next section, we'll use the recipient list to scatter the tasks; then the results are combined with the aggregator pattern.

8.2.3 *Implementing the scatter component using the recipient list pattern*

When a `PhotoMessage` enters the scatter-gather pattern, the scatter component has to send the message to the processors (the `GetTime` and `GetSpeed` actors from the prior section). We use the simplest implementation of the scatter component, and that's the EIP recipient list. (The scattering of messages can be implemented in a number of ways; any approach that creates multiple messages from one message and distributes it will do.)

The recipient list is a simple pattern because it is one component; its function is to send the received message to multiple other components. Figure 8.9 shows that the received messages are sent to the `GetTime` and `GetSpeed` tasks.

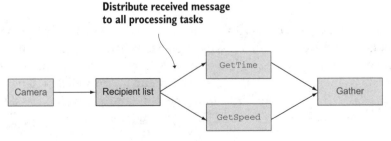

Figure 8.9 Recipient list pattern

Given that we have to perform the same two extractions on every message, the RecipientList is static and the message is always sent to the GetTime and GetSpeed tasks. Other implementations might call for a dynamic recipient list where the receivers are determined based on the message content or the state of the list.

Figure 8.10 shows the simplest implementation of a recipient list; when a message is received, it's sent to members. Let's put our RecipientList to work. We'll start by creating it with Akka testProbes (you first saw these in chapter 3).

Listing 8.4   Recipient list test

```
val endProbe1 = TestProbe()
val endProbe2 = TestProbe()
val endProbe3 = TestProbe()
val list = Seq(endProbe1.ref, endProbe2.ref, endProbe3.ref)      ← Creates
val actorRef = system.actorOf(                                      recipient
  Props(new RecipientList(list)))                                   list
val msg = "message"
actorRef ! msg                                                   ← Sends
endProbe1.expectMsg(msg)                                            message
endProbe2.expectMsg(msg)
endProbe3.expectMsg(msg)                                          All recipients have to
                                                                 receive message
```

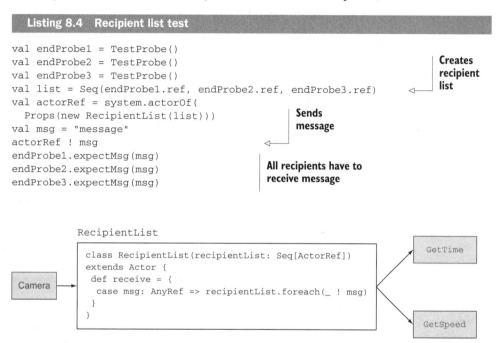

Figure 8.10   RecipientList

When we send a message to the RecipientList actor, the message is received by all probes.

This pattern isn't mind-blowing, but used in the scatter-gather pattern, it is quite useful.

8.2.4   Implementing the gather component with the aggregator pattern

The recipient list is scattering one message into two message flows to GetSpeed and GetTime. Both flows are doing part of the total processing. When both the time and speed have been retrieved, the messages need to be joined into a single result. This is done in the gather component. Figure 8.11 shows the aggregator pattern, which is used as the gather component, just as RecipientList is used as a scatter component.

The aggregator pattern is used to combine multiple messages into one. This can be a selection process when the processing tasks are competing with each other, or

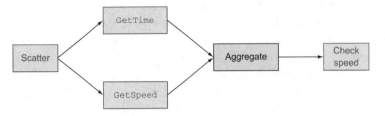

Figure 8.11   Aggregator pattern as gather component

merely combining several messages into one as we do here. One of the characteristics of the aggregator is that the messages have to be stored somehow, and when all messages have been received, the aggregator can process them. To keep it simple we'll implement an `Aggregator` that combines two `PhotoMessages` into one.

Listing 8.5   Aggregator

```
class Aggregator(timeout:Duration, pipe:ActorRef) extends Actor {
  val messages = new ListBuffer[PhotoMessage]          ←── Buffer to store
  def receive = {                                              messages that can't
    case rcvMsg: PhotoMessage => {                             be processed yet
      messages.find(_.id == rcvMsg.id) match {
        case Some(alreadyRcvMsg) => {             ←── This is second (of two)
          val newCombinedMsg = new PhotoMessage(       messages, so we can
            rcvMsg.id,                                 start combining them
            rcvMsg.photo,
            rcvMsg.creationTime.orElse(alreadyRcvMsg.creationTime),
            rcvMsg.speed.orElse(alreadyRcvMsg.speed) )
          pipe ! newCombinedMsg
          //cleanup message                       Removes processed
          messages -= alreadyRcvMsg          ←── message from the list
        }
        case None => messages += rcvMsg       ←── Received the first
      }                                              message, so stores it
    }                                                for processing later
  }
}
```

When a message is received, we check if it's the first message or the second. When it's the first, the message is stored in the `messages` buffer. When it's the second, we can process the messages. Processing in this aggregator combines the messages into one and sends the result to the next process.

Listing 8.6   Aggregator test

```
val endProbe = TestProbe()
val actorRef = system.actorOf(
  Props(new Aggregator(1 second, endProbe.ref)))
val photoStr = ImageProcessing.createPhotoString(new Date(), 60)
val msg1 = PhotoMessage("id1",
```

```
    photoStr,
    Some(new Date()),
    None)
  actorRef ! msg1                        ⊲─── Sends the first message

  val msg2 = PhotoMessage("id1",
    photoStr,
    None,
    Some(60))
  actorRef ! msg2                        ⊲─── Sends the second

  val combinedMsg = PhotoMessage("id1",
    photoStr,
    msg1.creationTime,
    msg2.speed)

  endProbe.expectMsg(combinedMsg)        ⊲─── Expects the combined message
```

The `Aggregator` works as expected. Two messages are sent to it, whenever they're ready, and one combined message is then created and sent on. But because we have state in our actor, we need to ensure that the state is always consistent. What happens when one task fails? When this happens, the first message is stored forever in the buffer, and no one would ever know what happened to this message. As occurrences pile up, our buffer size increases, and eventually it might consume too much memory, which can cause a catastrophic fault. There are many way to solve this; in this example we'll use a timeout. We expect that both processing tasks need about the same amount of time to execute; therefore, both messages should be received around the same time. This time can differ because of the availability of resources needed to process the message. When the second message isn't received within the stipulated timeout, it is presumed lost. The next decision we have to make is how the aggregator should react to the loss of a message. In our example the loss of a message isn't catastrophic, so we want to continue with a message that isn't complete. So, in our implementation, the aggregator will always send a message, even if it didn't receive one of the messages.

To implement the timeout, we'll use the scheduler. Upon receipt of the first message, we schedule a `TimeoutMessage` (providing `self` as the recipient). The messages buffer is checked when the `TimeoutMessage` is received to see if the message is still in the buffer, which is only the case if the second message wasn't received in time. In that case only one message is sent through. If the message isn't in the buffer, then that means that the combined message has already been sent through.

Listing 8.7   Implementing the timeout

```
case class TimeoutMessage(msg:PhotoMessage)

def receive = {
  case rcvMsg: PhotoMessage => {
    messages.find(_.id == rcvMsg.id) match {
      case Some(alreadyRcvMsg) => {
        val newCombinedMsg = new PhotoMessage(
          rcvMsg.id,
```

```
        rcvMsg.photo,
        rcvMsg.creationTime.orElse(alreadyRcvMsg.creationTime),
        rcvMsg.speed.orElse(alreadyRcvMsg.speed) )
      pipe ! newCombinedMsg
      //cleanup message
      messages -= alreadyRcvMsg
    }
    case None => {
      messages += rcvMsg
      context.system.scheduler.scheduleOnce(        ◁─── Schedules timeout
        timeout,
        self,
        new TimeoutMessage(rcvMsg))
    }
  }
}
case TimeoutMessage(rcvMsg) => {                     ◁─── Timeout has expired
  messages.find(_.id == rcvMsg.id) match {
    case Some(alreadyRcvMsg) => {
      pipe ! alreadyRcvMsg                           ◁─┐ Sends first message when
      messages -= alreadyRcvMsg                        │ the second isn't received
    }
    case None => //message is already processed     ◁─┐ Both messages are
  }                                                    │ already processed,
}                                                      │ so does nothing
}
```

We've implemented the timeout; now let's see if it's received when the Aggregator
fails to receive two message in the allowable time:

```
val endProbe = TestProbe()
val actorRef = system.actorOf(
  Props(new Aggregator(1 second, endProbe.ref)))
val photoStr = ImageProcessing.createPhotoString(     ◁─┐ Creates
  new Date(), 60)                                        │ message
val msg1 = PhotoMessage("id1",
  photoStr,
  Some(new Date()),
  None)                                          ┌─ Sends only
actorRef ! msg1                                  ◁─ one message
                                                            ┌─ Waits for timeout and
endProbe.expectMsg(msg1)                                 ◁─┘ receives message
```

As you can see, when we send only one message, the timeout is triggered; we detect a
missing message and send the first message as the combined message.

But this isn't the only problem that can occur. In section 4.2, which described the
lifecycle of an actor, you saw that we have to be careful when using state due to the possible restarts. When the Aggregator fails somehow, we lose all the messages that are
already received, because the Aggregator is restarted. How can we solve this problem?
Before the actor is restarted, the preRestart method is called. This method can be
used to preserve our state. For this Aggregator we can use the simplest solution: have
it resend the messages to itself before restarting. Because we don't depend on the order

of the received messages, this should be fine even when failures occur. We resend the messages from our buffer, and the messages are stored again when the new instance of our actor is started. The complete `Aggregator` is shown in the following listing.

Listing 8.8 Aggregator

```scala
class Aggregator(timeout: FiniteDuration, pipe: ActorRef)
  extends Actor {

  val messages = new ListBuffer[PhotoMessage]
  implicit val ec = context.system.dispatcher
  override def preRestart(reason: Throwable, message: Option[Any]) {
    super.preRestart(reason, message)
    messages.foreach(self ! _)                          Sends all received
    messages.clear()                                    messages to our
  }                                                     own mailbox

  def receive = {
    case rcvMsg: PhotoMessage => {
      messages.find(_.id == rcvMsg.id) match {
        case Some(alreadyRcvMsg) => {
          val newCombinedMsg = new PhotoMessage(
            rcvMsg.id,
            rcvMsg.photo,
            rcvMsg.creationTime.orElse(alreadyRcvMsg.creationTime),
            rcvMsg.speed.orElse(alreadyRcvMsg.speed))
          pipe ! newCombinedMsg
          //cleanup message
          messages -= alreadyRcvMsg
        }
        case None => {
          messages += rcvMsg
          context.system.scheduler.scheduleOnce(
            timeout,
            self,
            new TimeoutMessage(rcvMsg))
        }
      }
    }
    case TimeoutMessage(rcvMsg) => {
      messages.find(_.id == rcvMsg.id) match {
        case Some(alreadyRcvMsg) => {
          pipe ! alreadyRcvMsg
          messages -= alreadyRcvMsg
        }
        case None => //message is already processed
      }
    }                                                   Added for
    case ex: Exception => throw ex                      testing purposes
  }
}
```

We added the ability to throw an exception to trigger a restart for testing purposes. But when we receive the same message type twice, how will our timeout mechanism work? Because we do nothing when the messages are processed, it isn't a problem when we get the timeout twice. And because it is a timeout, we don't want the timer to be reset. In this example only the first timeout will take action when this is necessary, so this simple mechanism will work.

Does our change solve the problem? Let's test it by sending the first message, and make the `Aggregator` restart before sending the second message. We trigger a restart by sending an `IllegalStateException`, which will be thrown by the `Aggregator`. Is the `Aggregator` still able to combine the two messages despite the restart?

Listing 8.9   Aggregator missing a message

```
val endProbe = TestProbe()
val actorRef = system.actorOf(
  Props(new Aggregator(1 second, endProbe.ref)))
val photoStr = ImageProcessing.createPhotoString(new Date(), 60)

val msg1 = PhotoMessage("id1",
  photoStr,
  Some(new Date()),
  None)
actorRef ! msg1                                      ◁── Sends first message

actorRef ! new IllegalStateException("restart")      ◁── Restarts Aggregator

val msg2 = PhotoMessage("id1",
  photoStr,
  None,
  Some(60))
actorRef ! msg2                          ◁── Sends second message
val combinedMsg = PhotoMessage("id1",
  photoStr,
  msg1.creationTime,
  msg2.speed)

endProbe.expectMsg(combinedMsg)
```

The test passes, showing that the `Aggregator` was able to combine the message even after a restart. In messaging, durability refers to the ability to maintain messages in the midst of service disruptions. We implemented the `Aggregator` simply by having the actor resend to itself any messages it might be holding, and we verified that it works with a unit test (so if some aspect of the durable implementation is changed, our test will let us know before we suffer a runtime failure). There's an `Aggregator` in the akka-contrib module (http://doc.akka.io/docs/akka/2.4.2/contrib/aggregator .html), which won't be discussed here.

8.2.5   *Combining the components into the scatter-gather pattern*

With each component tested and ready, we can now make a complete implementation of the pattern. Note that by developing each piece in isolation with unit tests, we enter this final assembly phase confident that each collaborator will do its job successfully.

Listing 8.10 Scatter-gather implementation

```
val endProbe = TestProbe()
val aggregateRef = system.actorOf(
  Props(new Aggregator(1 second, endProbe.ref)))      ◁─── Creates Aggregator
val speedRef = system.actorOf(
  Props(new GetSpeed(aggregateRef)))                  ◁───┐
val timeRef = system.actorOf(                              │ Creates GetSpeed actor
  Props(new GetTime(aggregateRef)))                        │ and pipes it to Aggregator
val actorRef = system.actorOf(
  Props(new RecipientList(Seq(speedRef, timeRef))))   ◁───┐
                                                          │ Creates recipient
val photoDate = new Date()                                │ list of GetTime and
val photoSpeed = 60                                       │ GetSpeed actors
val msg = PhotoMessage("id1",
  ImageProcessing.createPhotoString(photoDate, photoSpeed))

actorRef ! msg                                        ◁───┐ Sends message to
                                                          │ recipient list.
val combinedMsg = PhotoMessage(msg.id,
  msg.photo,
  Some(photoDate),
  Some(photoSpeed))

endProbe.expectMsg(combinedMsg)                       ◁─── Receives combined message
```

Creates GetTime actor and pipes it to Aggregator.

In this example we send one message to the first actor; the `RecipientList`. This actor creates two message flows that can be processed in parallel. Both results are sent to the `Aggregator`, and when both messages are received, a single message is sent to the next step: our probe. This is how the scatter-gather pattern works. In our example we have two tasks, but this pattern doesn't restrict the number of tasks.

The scatter-gather pattern can also be combined with the pipes and filters pattern. This can be done in two ways. The first is to have the complete scatter-gather pattern as part of a pipeline. This means that the complete scatter-gather pattern is implementing one filter. The scatter component accepts the same messages as the other filter components in the filter pipeline, and the gather component sends only those interface messages.

In figure 8.12 you see the filter pipeline, and one of the filters is implemented using the scatter-gather pattern. This results in a flexible solution where we can change the order of filters and add or remove filters without disrupting the rest of the processing logic.

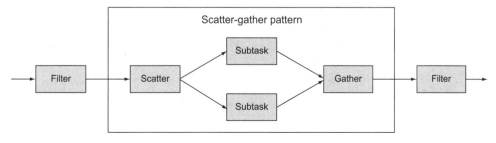

Figure 8.12 Using scatter-gather pattern as filter

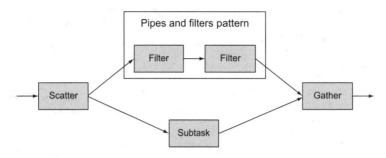

Figure 8.13   Using pipes and filters pattern in a scatter-gather pattern

Another possibility is that the pipeline is part of the scattered flow. This means that the messages are sent through the pipeline before they're gathered.

In figure 8.13 you can see that the scatter-gather pattern results in the message being scattered into two streams. One of the streams is a pipeline, whereas the other is just a single processing task (per the prior example). Combining the patterns can be handy as systems grow larger; it keeps the parts flexible and reusable.

8.3   *Enterprise integration pattern: routing slip*

Another enterprise integration pattern is the routing slip, which can be seen as a dynamic version of the pipes and filters pattern. To explain the benefits of this pattern, we'll use a slightly more complex example. Suppose we have a car factory and we have a default black car. When ordering a new car, the client can choose different options, such as navigation, parking sensors, or gray paint—every car can be customized for each client. When a default car is ordered, the car only needs to be painted black, and all the other steps can be skipped. But when a client wants all the options, the black paint should be skipped, and all the other steps should still be taken. To solve this problem, the routing slip pattern can be used. This routing slip is a roadmap of tasks that have to be executed that's added to the message. The routeSlip is included inside every message. Each task can find the next task to pass the message to when it's finished processing through the routeSlip. The usual metaphor used to explain this concept is the idea of an envelope with an embedded routing slip: it might have a list of people who have to sign off on a document. As the envelope is taken from one person to the next, each person performs the needed inspection, and then marks the envelope with the time when they released the document to the next person.

In figure 8.14 we show two possible customer requests. One example is a customer who orders a default car, and the other example is a customer who wants all the possible options. The SlipRouter needs to determine which steps should be taken and send the message to the first step.

In the default-car example of figure 8.14, the SlipRouter determines that only the step PaintBlack should be executed and creates the routing slip with only this step and the final destination. When the PaintBlack task is finished, it sends the message

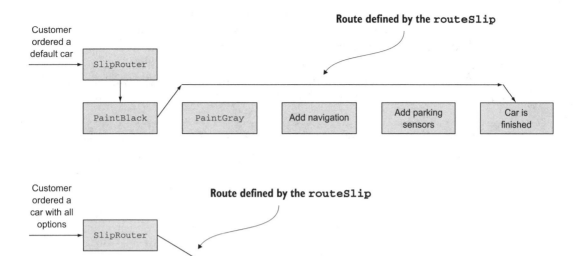

Figure 8.14 Routing slip pattern

to the next step, in this case the final destination, skipping all the other steps. In the second example, since all the options were chosen, the routing slip contains all the steps except the `PaintBlack` step. Every time a task finishes, it sends the message and routing slip to the next step in the list. To make this work, each processing task needs to implement the same interface, because the route is dynamically determined. It is possible to skip tasks or change the order of tasks, and because we use different types of messages, it's possible for a task to receive a message it doesn't know how to process. You saw this requirement also with the pipes and filters pattern. The only difference is that the pipes and filters pattern is a static pipeline: it's fixed for all the messages. The routing slip pattern is dynamic and can create for each message another pipeline; you can look at this pattern as a dynamic pipes and filters pattern. For each message the `SlipRouter` creates a pipeline specific for this message.

When this pattern is used, it's important that the interfaces of the steps are the same and that the tasks are independent, just like the filters in the pipes and filters pattern. Let's start to implement this example by creating the interface messages for each of our tasks:

```
object CarOptions extends Enumeration {
  val CAR_COLOR_GRAY, NAVIGATION, PARKING_SENSORS = Value
}

case class Order(options: Seq[CarOptions.Value])
case class Car(color: String = "",
               hasNavigation: Boolean = false,
               hasParkingSensors: Boolean = false)
```

We need an order with possible options, which is the message the router is using to create a `routeSlip`, and the `Car`, which is the message routed by the `SlipRouter`. Now we need the function for each task to route the message to the next step using the routing slip. As usual, we need a message class, but we'll also make a trait that will add the ability to send the message to the next recipient (based on the routing slip that it contains).

Listing 8.11   Routing messages

```
case class RouteSlipMessage(routeSlip: Seq[ActorRef],          ◄─┐ Actual message
                            message: AnyRef)                      │ that's sent
                                                                  │ between the tasks
trait RouteSlip {

  def sendMessageToNextTask(routeSlip: Seq[ActorRef],
                            message: AnyRef): Unit = {
    val nextTask = routeSlip.head                ◄── Gets next step
    val newSlip = routeSlip.tail
    if (newSlip.isEmpty) {                   ◄─┐ Sends actual message without
      nextTask ! message                        │ the routing slip at last step
    } else {

      nextTask ! RouteSlipMessage(           ◄─┐ Sends message to next step
        routeSlip = newSlip,                      │ and updates routing slip
        message = message)
    }
  }
}
```

We need this function for every task. When the task is finished and has a new `Car` message, the method `sendMessageToNextTask` must be used to find the next task. Now we can implement our tasks.

Listing 8.12   Example tasks

```
class PaintCar(color: String) extends Actor with RouteSlip {      ◄─┐ Our
  def receive = {                                                    │ paint
    case RouteSlipMessage(routeSlip, car: Car) => {                  │ task
      sendMessageToNextTask(routeSlip,
        car.copy(color = color))
    }
  }
}

class AddNavigation() extends Actor with RouteSlip {              ◄─┐ The add
  def receive = {                                                    │ navigation
    case RouteSlipMessage(routeSlip, car: Car) => {                  │ task
      sendMessageToNextTask(routeSlip,
        car.copy(hasNavigation = true))
    }
  }
}
```

```
class AddParkingSensors() extends Actor with RouteSlip {
  def receive = {                                          ◄─┐  The add
    case RouteSlipMessage(routeSlip, car: Car) => {           │  parking
      sendMessageToNextTask(routeSlip,                        │  sensors task
        car.copy(hasParkingSensors = true))
    }
  }
}
```

These tasks update one field of our `Car`, and when done using the `sendMessageTo-NextTask`, send the `Car` to the next step. All we need now is the actual `SlipRouter`, which is also a normal actor that receives an order and creates the routing slip using the options in the order.

Listing 8.13　SlipRouter

```
class SlipRouter(endStep: ActorRef) extends Actor with RouteSlip {
  val paintBlack = context.actorOf(
    Props(new PaintCar("black")), "paintBlack")
  val paintGray = context.actorOf(                            Creates
    Props(new PaintCar("gray")), "paintGray")                 processing
  val addNavigation = context.actorOf(                        tasks
    Props[AddNavigation], "navigation")
  val addParkingSensor = context.actorOf(
    Props[AddParkingSensors], "parkingSensors")

  def receive = {
    case order: Order => {
      val routeSlip = createRouteSlip(order.options)    ◄─── Creates route slip

      sendMessageToNextTask(routeSlip, new Car)         ◄─┐  Sends message and
    }                                                      │  routeSlip to first task
  }

  private def createRouteSlip(options: Seq[CarOptions.Value]):
      Seq[ActorRef] = {
    val routeSlip = new ListBuffer[ActorRef]                  Adds a task
    //car needs a color                                       ActorRef to the
    if (!options.contains(CarOptions.CAR_COLOR_GRAY)) {       routeSlip for every
      routeSlip += paintBlack                                 option that needs
    }                                                         to be processed
    options.foreach {                                    ◄─┘
      case CarOptions.CAR_COLOR_GRAY  => routeSlip += paintGray
      case CarOptions.NAVIGATION      => routeSlip += addNavigation
      case CarOptions.PARKING_SENSORS => routeSlip += addParkingSensor
      case other                      => //do nothing
    }
    routeSlip += endStep
    routeSlip
  }
}
```

The routing slip contains the actor references of the tasks that have to be executed. When a gray color isn't requested, the car is painted black. The last reference is the end step, which is specified when creating the router. Let's see if it works. We start with a default car.

Listing 8.14 Creating default car

```
val probe = TestProbe()                                    Creates routeSlip and
val router = system.actorOf(                               all process steps
  Props(new SlipRouter(probe.ref)), "SlipRouter")

val minimalOrder = new Order(Seq())
router ! minimalOrder                                       Sends request
val defaultCar = new Car(                                   for a default car
  color = "black",
  hasNavigation = false,
  hasParkingSensors = false)
probe.expectMsg(defaultCar)              ◁── Receives default car
```

When we send an order without any options, the router creates the route slip with an `ActorRef` to the `PaintCar` actor with `black` as an argument and a reference to our probe. The `RouteSlipMessage`, which contains both the car and the `RouteSlip`, is sent to the first step, the `PaintCar` step. When this step is finished, the message is sent to the probe. When using all options, the car is sent to all tasks, and when it's received at the end, it contains all the options.

Listing 8.15 Creating car with all options

```
val fullOrder = new Order(Seq(
  CarOptions.CAR_COLOR_GRAY,
  CarOptions.NAVIGATION,
  CarOptions.PARKING_SENSORS))
router ! fullOrder                          ◁── Sends order with all options
val carWithAllOptions = new Car(
  color = "gray",
  hasNavigation = true,
  hasParkingSensors = true)
probe.expectMsg(carWithAllOptions)          ◁── Receives car with all options
```

The routing slip pattern enables you to dynamically create pipelines with all the benefits of the pipes and filters pattern, yet still retain the flexibility to processes messages differently.

8.4   *Summary*

In this chapter we tackled the design of flexible collaborative solutions in Akka using some common enterprise integration patterns. By combining the patterns, you're able to create complex systems. Here are some of the takeaways:

- Scaling processing requires that you distribute work among concurrent collaborators.
- Patterns give you a starting point on standard ways of scaling.
- The actor programming model allows you to focus on the design of your code, not messaging and scheduling implementation details.
- Patterns are building blocks that can be combined to build bigger system parts.

Through all of these implementations, Akka has made it easy to adapt to more-complex requirements without having to change the fundamental approach to constructing our components. Those messages are part of a sequential process. It's possible to process some parts concurrently, but the flow is static and the same for all messages. In the next chapter we'll focus on routing messages to different actors to create a dynamic task structure.

Routing messages

9

In this chapter

- Using the enterprise integration router pattern
- Scaling with Akka routers
- Building a state-based router with become/ unbecome

In the previous chapter we looked at enterprise integration patterns as a way to connect actors to solve a wide range of problems. Yet all those approaches involved processing incoming messages in the same way. But often, you need to handle messages differently.

Routers are essential when you want to scale up or out. For example, when you want to scale up, you need multiple instances of the same task, and routers will decide which instance will process the received message. We'll start this chapter by describing the enterprise router pattern and examine the three reasons for using routing to control message flow:

- Performance
- Message content
- State

We'll then show you how to create routing processes for each of these patterns.

If performance or scaling is why you need to turn to a routing solution, you should use Akka's built-in routers, because they're optimized. Concerns with a message's content or state, on the other hand, will point you to using normal actors.

9.1 *The enterprise integration router pattern*

First, we'll introduce you to the pattern generally—when it applies and how—before we get down to the matter of each specific router implementation. When we move on to implementation, we'll start with the commonly known pattern for routing different messages through a needed set of steps. Let's take a look at the speeding ticket example we introduced earlier. This time, we'll send the messages to the cleanup task or to the next step, depending on the speed of the vehicle in question. When the speed is lower than the maximum allowed speed, the message has to be sent to the cleaning step (instead of just discarding it). But when the speed is higher than the speed limit, it's a violation, and the message should be processed normally. To solve this problem, the router pattern is used. As figure 9.1 shows, the router is able to send messages to different flows.

There are many different reasons to construct logic that makes a decision about where to route a message. As we mentioned in the introduction, there are three reasons for controlling message flow in your applications:

- *Performance*—A task takes a lot of time to process, but the messages can be processed in parallel. So the messages should be divided among different instances. In the speeding ticket example, the evaluation of individual drivers can occur in parallel, because all processing logic resides solely within each captured case.
- *Content of the received message*—The message has an attribute (License, in our example) and depending on the value it has, the message should go to a different task.
- *State of the router*—For example, when the camera is in standby, all the messages have to go to the cleanup task; otherwise, they should be processed normally.

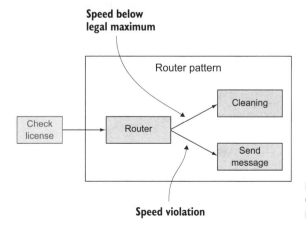

Figure 9.1 Routing logic sending different messages to different process flows

In all cases (no matter what the reason is or the specific logic used), the logic needs to decide which task it should send a message to. The possible tasks a router can choose from are called the *routees* in Akka.

In this chapter we'll show different approaches to routing messages. This will introduce several more Akka mechanisms that are helpful not only when implementing routers, but also in the implementation of your own processes, such as when you want to process messages differently depending on the state of an actor. In section 9.2 we'll start our overview of using routers with an example of a router that makes its decisions based on performance. Scaling is one of the main reasons to use the router functionality of Akka, which is a central component of the overall scaling strategy. In section 9.3 we'll explore routing using normal actors, when message content and state are the key concerns, and we'll show other approaches that use normal actors.

9.2   *Balance load using Akka routers*

One of the reasons to use a router is to balance the load over different actors, to improve the performance of the system when processing a lot of messages. This can be local actors (scale up) or even actors on remote servers (scale out). Part of the core Akka argument for using scaling is easy routing.

In our camera example, the recognize step takes a relatively long time to process. To be able to parallelize this task, we use a router.

In figure 9.2 you see that the router is able to send the message to one of the GetLicense instances. When a message is received by the router, the router picks one of the available processes and sends the message only to that process. When the next message is received, the router picks another process to handle it.

To implement this router, we'll use the built-in router functionality of Akka. In Akka a separation is made between the router, which contains the routing logic, and the actor that represents the router. The router logic decides which routee is selected and can be used within an actor to make a selection. The router actor is a self-contained actor that

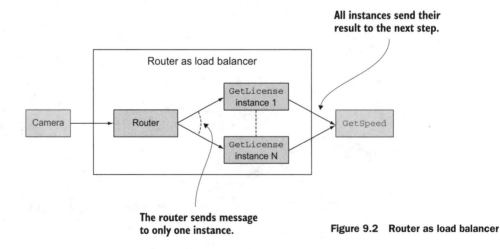

Figure 9.2   Router as load balancer

loads the routing logic and other settings from configuration and is able to manage the routees itself.

The built-in routers come in two varieties:

- *Pool*—These routers manage the routees. They're responsible for creating the routees and removing them from the list if they terminate. A pool can be used when all the routees are created and distributed the same way and there isn't a need for special recovery of the routees.
- *Group*—The group routers don't manage the routees. The routees have to be created by the system and the group router will use the actor selection to find the routees. Group routers also don't watch routees. All the routee management has to be implemented somewhere else within the system. A group can be used when you need to control the routees' lifecycles in a special way or want to have more control over where the routees are instantiated (on which instances).

The most pronounced difference in routers is that the pool router is simplest, as it provides management (throughout the routee lifecycle), but it comes at the cost of having no capacity to customize those behaviors by making routees contain the needed logic.

In figure 9.3 we show the actor hierarchy of the routees and see the difference between using a pool and the group router. The routees are children of the router, and when using the group, the routees can be a child of any other actor (in this example, the `RouteeCreator`). The routees don't need to have the same parent. They just need to be up and running.

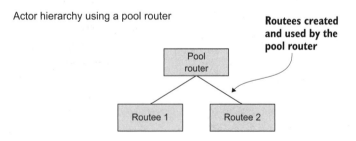

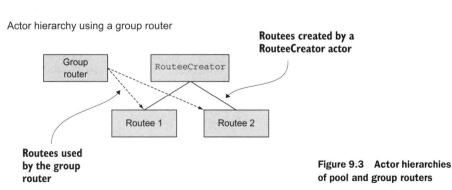

Figure 9.3   Actor hierarchies of pool and group routers

Akka has several built-in routers, summarized in table 9.1. This table shows the router logic and the associated pool and group that use the logic.

Table 9.1   List of available routers within Akka

Logic	Pool	Group	Description
RoundRobinRouting-Logic	RoundRobinPool	RoundRobinGroup	This logic sends the first received message to the first routee, the next message to the second routee, and so on. When all routees have gotten one message, the first routee gets the next, and so forth.
RandomRouting-Logic	RandomPool	RandomGroup	This logic sends every received message to a randomly chosen routee.
SmallestMailbox-RoutingLogic	SmallestMail-boxPool	Not available	This router checks the mailboxes of the routees and chooses the routee with the smallest mailbox. The group version isn't available because it uses the select actor functionality internally, and the mailbox size isn't available using these references.
Not available	BalancingPool	Not available	This router distributes the messages to the idle routees. It does this internally differently than the other routers. It uses one mailbox for all the routees. The router is able to do this by using a special dispatcher for the routees. This is also the reason that only the pool version is available.
BroadcastRouting-Logic	BroadcastPool	BroadcastGroup	Sends the received messages to all the routees. This is not a router as defined in the enterprise integration pattern, but it implements the recipient list.
ScatterGather-FirstCompleted RoutingLogic	ScatterGather-FirstCompleted-Pool	ScatterGather-FirstCompleted-Group	This router sends the message to all the routees and sends the first response to the original sender. Technically, this is a scatter-gather pattern using competing tasks that select the best result, in this case the fastest response.
ConsistentHashing-RoutingLogic	Consistent-HashingPool	Consistent-HashingGroup	This router uses consistent hashing of the message to select a routee. This can be used when you need different messages to be routed to the same routee, but it doesn't matter which routee.

In section 9.2.1 we show a number of different ways to use these routers. The same logical requirements can be fulfilled using either type (the differences, as discussed earlier, are implementation-specific). We'll use the most common router logic—

round-robin, balancing, and consistent hashing—in the next sections. First, we'll start in section 9.2.1 with a pool router, specifically a `BalancingPool` router, because it has some special behavior. In section 9.2.2 you'll learn about the use of a group router; we'll use the `RoundRobinGroup` router for that. We'll end with an example that uses the `ConsistentHashingPool` in section 9.2.3 to explain when and how this router can be used.

9.2.1 Akka pool router

You've seen that several routers are available, and they come in three flavors: the logic to be used in your own actor, a group actor, or a pool actor. We'll start by showing how to use a pool router. When using the pool actor, you don't have to create or manage the routees; that's done by the pool router. A pool can be used when all the routees are created and distributed the same way and there isn't a need for special recovery of the routees. So for "simple" routees, a pool is a good choice.

CREATING A POOL ROUTER

Using a pool router is simple, and is the same for all the different pool routers. There are two different ways to use the pool: using the configuration, or configuring it within the code. We'll start with the configuration, because using it allows you to change the logic used by the router, which isn't possible when configuring the router in code. Let's use a `BalancingPool` for our `GetLicense` actor.

We have to create the router in the code. The router is also an `ActorRef`, which we can use to send our messages.

Listing 9.1 Creating a router using the configuration file

```
val router = system.actorOf(              ⟵———————— Defines router using configuration
    FromConfig.props(Props(new GetLicense(endProbe.ref))),   ⟵┐
    "poolRouter"              ⟵┐                               │ How router should
)                             │ Name of router                 │ create routees
```

This is all you have to do in your code to create a configuration-specified router. But we're not completely done. We have to configure our router.

Listing 9.2 Configuring the router

```
akka.actor.deployment {
  /poolRouter {                          ⟵—— Full name of router
    router = balancing-pool              ⟵—— Logic used by router
    nr-of-instances = 5                  ⟵—— Number of routees in pool
  }
}
```

Those three lines are enough to configure the router. The first line is the name of the router, and it has to be equal to the name used in the code. In our example we've created the router using `system.actorOf` and have created our router at the top level of the actor path; therefore, the name is /poolRouter. If we create the router within another actor, for example, with the name `getLicenseBalancer`, the name of the router within the configuration would be /getLicenseBalancer/poolRouter. This is important; otherwise, the configuration wouldn't be found by the Akka framework.

The next line in the configuration defines the logic which that has to be used, in this case, the balancing pool actor. The last line defines how many routees (5) will be created within the pool.

This is all we have to do when we want to use a pool of `GetLicense` actors instead of only one `GetLicense` actor. The only difference in our code using a pool of actors is to insert `FromConfig.props()`. The rest is just the same. Sending messages to one of the `GetLicense` routees is accomplished simply by sending a message to the returned `ActorRef` of the created router:

```
router !  Photo("123xyz", 60)
```

The router decides which routee gets the message to process. We started this section by mentioning that there are two ways to define a router. The second way is less flexible, but we'll show it for completeness. It's also possible to define the same pool router within the code, as shown next.

Listing 9.3   Creating a `BalancingPool` in code

```
val router = system.actorOf(
  BalancingPool(5).props(Props(new GetLicense(endProbe.ref))),     ⟵─┐
  "poolRouter"                                                Creates a BalancingPool
)                                                                 with 5 routees ⌋
```

The only difference is that we replaced `FromConfig` with `BalancingPool(5)` and have defined the pool and number of routees in the code directly. This is exactly the same as our prior defined configuration.

When you send messages to the router, the message is normally sent to the routees. But there are some messages that are processed by the router itself. Throughout this section we'll cover most of these messages. But we'll start with the `Kill` and `Poison-Pill` messages. These messages aren't sent to the routees, but will be processed by the router. The router will terminate, and when using a pool actor, all the routees will also terminate, due to the parent-child relation.

You've seen that when you send a message to the router, only one routee receives the message, at least for most routers. But it's possible to send one message to all the routees of the router. For this you can use another special message: the `Broadcast` message. When you send this message to the router, the router will send the content of the message to all the routees. `Broadcast` messages work on pool and group routers.

NOTE The only router where the `Broadcast` message doesn't work is the `BalancingPool`. The problem is that all the routees have one and the same mailbox. Let's look at an example of a `BalancingPool` with five instances.

When the router wants to broadcast a message, it tries to send the message to all five routees. Due to the fact that there's only one mailbox, all five messages are placed in the same mailbox. Depending on the load of the different routees, the messages are distributed to the routees, which make the first five requests getting the next message. This will work when the load is equally distributed. But if one routee has a message that takes longer to process than the broadcast message, another routee will process multiple broadcast messages before the busy routee has finished. It's even possible that one routee could get all the broadcast messages and the other four routees none of them. So don't use `Broadcast` in combination with the `BalancingPool`.

REMOTE ROUTEES

In the previous section, the created routees were all local actors, but we mentioned before that it's possible to use routers between multiple servers. Instantiating routees on a remote server isn't hard. You have to wrap your router configuration with the `RemoteRouterConfig` and supply the remote addresses.

Listing 9.4 Wrap configuration in a `RemoteRouterConfig`

```
val addresses = Seq(
  Address("akka.tcp", "GetLicenseSystem", "192.1.1.20", 1234),
  AddressFromURIString("akka.tcp://GetLicenseSystem@192.1.1.21:1234"))

val routerRemote1 = system.actorOf(
  RemoteRouterConfig(FromConfig(), addresses).props(
    Props(new GetLicense(endProbe.ref))), "poolRouter-config")

val routerRemote2 = system.actorOf(
  RemoteRouterConfig(RoundRobinPool(5), addresses).props(
    Props(new GetLicense(endProbe.ref))), "poolRouter-code")
```

Here we show the two examples of constructing an address: using the `Address` class directly or constructing an `Address` from a URI. We also show the two versions of creating a `RouterConfig`. The created pool router will create its routees on the different remote servers. The routees will be deployed in round-robin fashion between the given remote addresses. This way the routees are evenly distributed over the remote servers.

As you can see, it's easy to scale out using routers. All you have to do is use the `RemoteRouterConfig`. There's a similar wrapper that's also able to create routees on several remote servers: `ClusterRouterPool`. This wrapper can be used when you have a cluster (and is described in chapter 14, which is devoted completely to the topic of clustering).

Until now, we've used routers with a static number of routees, but when the load of messages changes a lot, you need to change the number of routees, to get a balanced system. For this you can use a resizer on the pool.

DYNAMICALLY RESIZABLE POOL

When the load changes a lot, you'll want to change the number of routees; when you have too few routees, you'll suffer delays because messages have to wait until a routee is finished. But when you have too many routees, you can waste a lot of resources. In these cases, it would be nice if you could change the pool size dynamically (depending on the load). This can be done with the resize functionality of the pool.

You can configure the resizer to your needs. You can set upper and lower bounds on the number of routees. When you need to increase or decrease the pool, Akka will do so. All this can be configured when defining the pool.

Listing 9.5   Resizer configuration

```
akka.actor.deployment {
  /poolRouter {
    router = round-robin-pool
    resizer {
      enabled = on

      lower-bound = 1
      upper-bound = 10

      pressure-threshold = 1

      rampup-rate = 0.25

      backoff-threshold = 0.3

      backoff-rate = 0.1

      messages-per-resize = 10
    }
  }
}
```

Turns resizer functionality on

Fewest number of routees the router should ever have

Maximum number of routees the router should ever have.

Defines when a routees is under pressure

How fast you're adding routees

When number of routees should decrease

How fast you're removing routees

How fast you're able to change the size again

The first step is to turn the functionality on. Next you can define the upper and lower bounds (on routees). This is done using the attributes lower-bound and upper-bound.

The next attributes are used to define when the pool should expand, and by what number of routees.

We'll start with the increasing part. When the router pool is under pressure (load), you need to increase the number of routees. But when is the pool under pressure? The answer is when all the current routees are under pressure, and when a routee is under pressure is defined using the pressure-threshold attribute. The value of the attribute defines how many messages should be in the mailbox of the routee before it's considered to be under pressure. For example, when the value is set to 1, a routee is under pressure when it has at least one message in its mailbox, and when it's set to 3, the routee needs to have at least three messages in its mailbox. A special case is the value 0. This means that when the routee is processing a message, it's under pressure. Now that you know when a routee is under pressure, we'll look at how the mechanism of adding routees works.

Let's consider the example of a router pool with five instances and whose pressure threshold is set to 0. When this router gets messages, it forwards them to the first four routees. At this moment, four routees are busy and one is idle. The first situation shown in figure 9.4 is that upon receiving the fifth message, nothing happens, because the check is done before assigning the message to a routee. And at this point one routee is still idle, which means the pool isn't under pressure yet.

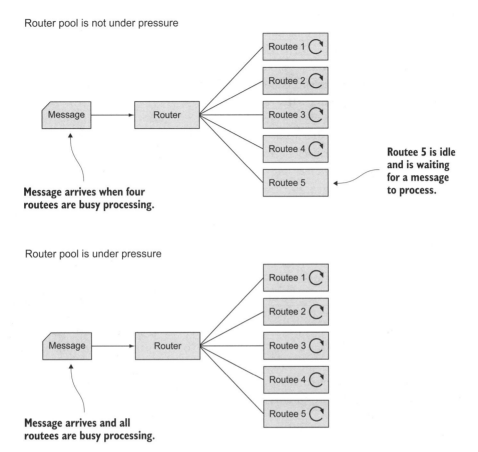

Figure 9.4   A router pool coming under pressure

But when the router receives another message, all the routees are busy processing messages (the second situation in figure 9.4). This means the pool is under pressure at this point, and new routees are added. This resizing isn't done synchronously, because creating a new routee isn't always faster than just waiting for the routee to finish the previous message. In a balanced system, the previous message is probably almost finished. This means that the sixth message isn't routed to the newly created routees, but to one of the already existing routees. But probably the next message can use the newly added routees.

When the pool is under pressure, it adds new routees. The `rampup-rate` defines how many routees are added. The value is a percentage of the total. For example, when you have five routees and the `rampup-rate` is 0.25, the pool will be increased by 25% (rounded up to whole numbers) so the pool will be increased by two routees (5 × 0.25 = 1.25, which is rounded up to 2), resulting in seven routees.

Now that you know how you can increase the pool size, you can also decrease the size. The `backoff-threshold` is the attribute that defines when the router pool will decrease. The back-off won't be triggered until the percentage of routees that are busy is below the `backoff-threshold`. When you have 10 routees, the back-off is triggered when the percentage of busy routees is below 30%. This means that when only two routees (or fewer) are busy, the number of routees in the pool will decrease.

The number of routees removed is defined by the `backoff-rate` and works just like the `rampup-rate`. In this example with 10 routees and a `backoff-rate` of 0.1, it will decrease by one routee ($10 \times 0.1 = 1$).

The last attribute, `messages-per-resize`, will define the number of messages a router has to receive before it's able to do another resize. This is to prevent a situation where the router is continually increasing or decreasing with every message. This can happen when the load is just between two sizes: the load is too big for one pool size, but when it increases the load is too small, which causes the pool to be adjusted every time. Or when the messages come in batches, this attribute can be used to delay the resize action until the next batch of messages arrives.

SUPERVISION

Another function of the router that should be addressed is supervision. Because the router is creating the routees, it's also the supervisor of the actors. When using the default router, it will always escalate to its own supervisor. This can lead to unexpected results. When one routee fails, the router will escalate to its supervisor. This supervisor probably wants the actor to be restarted, but instead of restarting the routee, the supervisor restarts the router. And the behavior of restarting a router will cause all the routees to be restarted, not only the failing one. The effect is that it looks like the router uses an `AllForOneStrategy`. To solve this issue, we can give the router its own strategy when creating the router.

To set this up, all we need to do is create the strategy and associate it with the router:

```
val myStrategy = SupervisorStrategy.defaultStrategy        ◁── Creates supervisor strategy
val router = system.actorOf(
  RoundRobinPool(5,supervisorStrategy = myStrategy).props(Props[TestSuper]),
    "roundrobinRouter"
)
```

Uses supervisor strategy — (label pointing to the RoundRobinPool line)

When one routee is failing, only the failing routee is restarted, and the other routees will proceed without any problem. You can use the default supervisor like in our example, but it's also possible to create a new strategy for the router, or use the strategy of the parent actor of the router. This way all the routees of the given router will behave the same as if they are children of the router's parent.

It's possible to stop the child when there's a failure, but a pool won't spawn a new routee when a routee terminates; it only removes the routee from the pool. When all the routees are terminated, the router will terminate too. Only when you use a resizer will the router not terminate and keep the specified minimum number of routers.

In this section you've seen that router pools are flexible, especially when instantiating the router using the configuration. You're able to change the number of routees and even the router logic. And when you have multiple servers, you can also instantiate routees on different servers, without any complex or difficult constructions.

But sometime the pools are too restricted, and you want more flexibility and control over the creation and management of the routees. These needs can be met by implementing groups.

9.2.2 *Akka group router*

The pools in the previous section were managing the routees for you. Using the group routers, you have to instantiate the routees yourself. This can be necessary when you want to take control of when and where the routees are created. We'll start with creating our group router. Next, we'll show how we can dynamically change the routees using another set of router messages.

CREATING GROUPS

Creating a group is almost the same as creating a pool. The only difference is that a pool needs the number of routee instances, and a group needs a list of routee paths. Let's start with creating the routees. You don't need to do anything special, but in our example we want one parent `Actor` for all our `GetLicense` actors. We'll introduce a `GetLicenseCreator`, which is responsible for creating the `GetLicense` actors. This actor will be used later to create new routees when one terminates.

Listing 9.6 `GetLicenseCreator` creating our routees

```
class GetLicenseCreator(nrActors: Int) extends Actor {

  override def preStart() {
    super.preStart()
    (0 until nrActors).map { nr =>
      context.actorOf(Props[GetLicense], "GetLicense"+nr)       Creates
      system.actorOf(Props( new GetLicenseCreator(2)),"Creator")  routees
    }
  }
  ...
}                                                               Creates
                                                               routee
system.actorOf(Props( new GetLicenseCreator(2)),"Creator")     creator
```

Just as with a pool, there are two ways to create a router group using the configuration and within the code. We'll start with the configuration example.

Listing 9.7 Configuration of the router using a group

```
akka.actor.deployment {
  /groupRouter {                         Full name of router
    router = round-robin-group
    routees.paths = [                     Actor paths of used routees
      "/user/Creator/GetLicense0",
      "/user/Creator/GetLicense1"]
  }
}                                                              Creates
                                                              a group
val router = system.actorOf(FromConfig.props(), "groupRouter")  router
```

Group used by router

As you can see, the configuration barely differs from the pool configuration; nr-of-instances is replaced by routees.paths. Creating a group is even easier than creating a pool, because you don't need to specify how the routees are to be created. And because a group uses actor paths, adding remote actors doesn't need any changes. Just add the full path of the remote actor:

```
akka.actor.deployment {
  /groupRouter {
    router = round-robin-group

    routees.paths = [
      "akka.tcp://AkkaSystemName@10.0.0.1:2552/user/Creator/GetLicense0",
      "akka.tcp://AkkaSystemName@10.0.0.2:2552/user/Creator/GetLicense0"]
  }
}
```

Configuring a group with the code is again easy; you only have to supply a list of the routee paths.

Listing 9.8   Creating a group router with code

```
val paths = List("/user/Creator/GetLicense0",
  "/user/Creator/GetLicense1")

val router = system.actorOf(
  RoundRobinGroup(paths).props(), "groupRouter")
```

At this point we can use our router just as we used a router pool. There's one difference: when a routee terminates. When a routee terminates within a pool, the router detects this and removes the routee from the pool. A group router doesn't support this. When a routee terminates, the group router will still send messages to the routee. This is done because the router doesn't manage the routees and it's possible that the actor will be available at some point.

Let's enhance our GetLicenseCreator to create a new actor when one child terminates. We'll use the watch functionality described in chapter 4.

Listing 9.9   Creating new actors when routee terminates

```
class GetLicenseCreator(nrActors: Int) extends Actor {
  override def preStart() {
    super.preStart()
    (0 until  nrActors).map(nr => {
      val child = context.actorOf(
        Props(new GetLicense(nextStep)), "GetLicense"+nr)
      context.watch(child)
    })
  }

  def receive = {
    case Terminated(child) => {
      val newChild = context.actorOf(
```

Uses a watch on created routees ⟶ (points to `context.watch(child)`)

Re-creates a routee when one terminates ⟶ (points to `case Terminated(child) => {`)

```
            Props(new GetLicense(nextStep)), child.path.name)
        context.watch(newChild)
      }
    }
}
```

When we use this new GetLicenseCreator, the router group can always use the references to the actor without any modification or actions. Let's see this in action. We'll start by creating the routees and then the group, but before we do anything we'll send a PoisonPill to all the routees.

Listing 9.10   Testing the `GetLicenseCreator` that manages the routees

```
val endProbe = TestProbe()

val creator = system.actorOf(                                    ⟵ Creates
  Props(new GetLicenseCreator2(2, endProbe.ref)),"Creator")            routees
val paths = List(
  "/user/Creator/GetLicense0",
  "/user/Creator/GetLicense1")
val router = system.actorOf(                                     ⟵ Creates
  RoundRobinGroup(paths).props(), "groupRouter")                      router

router ! Broadcast(PoisonPill)           ⟵ If message is received by router before
Thread.sleep(100)                            routees are recreated, it will be lost

val msg = PerformanceRoutingMessage(
        ImageProcessing.createPhotoString(new Date(), 60, "123xyz"),
        None,
        None)

//test if the routees respond
router ! msg                                          Tests if new routees
endProbe.expectMsgType[PerformanceRoutingMessage](1 second)   will process requests
```

Kills all routees (annotation pointing to `router ! Broadcast(PoisonPill)`)

As you can see, after the routees are killed, the newly created routees will take over and process the incoming messages. Thread.sleep is the laziest way to make sure that the GetLicenseCreator has re-created the routees. It would be better to publish an event on the event stream once all routees are re-created and subscribe to this event in the test; or add some messages to the GetLicenseCreator to inspect the number of re-created routees; or use the GetRoutees message described in the next section. This is left as an exercise for the reader.

In this example we created new actors with the same path, but it's also possible to remove or add routees to the group using router messages.

DYNAMICALLY RESIZE THE ROUTER GROUP

We talked already about messages that are processed by the router. Now we'll talk about three other messages for managing the group routees, which enables you to get the routees of a given router and add or remove them:

- *GetRoutees*—To get all the current routees, you can send this message to a router, which will reply with a Routees message containing the routees.

- *AddRoutee(routee: Routee)*—Sending this message will add the routee to the router. This message takes a `RouteeTrait` containing the new routee.
- *RemoveRoutee(routee: Routee)*—Sending this message will remove the routee from the router.

But using these messages has some pitfalls. These messages and the replies use the `Routee` trait, which contains only one `send` method. This method enables you to send a message directly to a routee. Other functionality isn't supported without converting the `Routee` to an implementation class.

Using the `GetRoutees` message gives you less information than expected, without casting the `Routee` to the actual implementation. The only actual use is to get the number of routees or when you want to bypass the router. This can be handy when you want to send specific messages to specific routees. The last use for this message is to be sure that a router management message is processed, by sending a `GetRoutees` message right after a router message. Subsequently receiving a `Routees` response means that the router message sent before the `GetRoutees` message has been processed. When you receive the reply (`Routees` message), you know that the previous message was also processed.

The add and remove messages need a `Routee`. When you want to add an actor to the router, you need to convert an `ActorRef` or path to a `Routee`.

There are three implementations of the `Routee` trait available within Akka:

- `ActorRefRoutee(ref: ActorRef)`
- `ActorSelectionRoutee(selection: ActorSelection)`
- `SeveralRoutees(routees: immutable.IndexedSeq[Routee])`

Choosing between the three options, we dispense with the last one, `SeveralRoutees`, because it creates a `Routee` from a list of `Routees`. If we add a routee with the first option, `ActorRefRoutee`, the router will create a watch on the new routee. This sounds like it shouldn't be a problem, but when a router receives a `Terminated` message and it isn't the supervisor of the `Routee`, it will throw an `akka.actor.DeathPact-Exception`, which will terminate the router. This is probably not something you want; you should use the second option, the `ActorSelectionRoutee` implementation, to be able to recover from a termination of a routee.

When removing a routee, you have to use the same `Routee` instance type as you used to add the `Routee`. Otherwise, the routee won't be removed. This is why you also need to use the `ActorSelectionRoutee` when removing a routee.

Let's assume we still need the functionality of resizing a group; we'll probably end up with a solution close to listing 9.11. We'll create a `DynamicRouteeSizer`, which will manage the routees and the number used within the group router. We can change the size by sending a `PreferredSize` message.

Listing 9.11   Example of a routee sizer for a group

```
class DynamicRouteeSizer(nrActors: Int,
                         props: Props,
                         router: ActorRef) extends Actor {
  var nrChildren = nrActors
  var childInstanceNr = 0

  //restart children
  override def preStart() {                          ◁───┐  When starting, creates
    super.preStart()                                      │  number of initial
    (0 until  nrChildren).map(nr => createRoutee())       │  requested routees
  }

  def createRoutee() {
    childInstanceNr += 1
    val child = context.actorOf(props, "routee" + childInstanceNr)
    val selection = context.actorSelection(child.path)
    router ! AddRoutee(ActorSelectionRoutee(selection))   ◁──┐  After creating a new
    context.watch(child)                                      │  child and adding it to
  }                                                           │  the router using the
                                                              │  ActorSelectionRoutee
  def receive = {
    case PreferredSize(size) => {
      if (size < nrChildren) {
        //remove
        context.children.take(nrChildren - size).foreach(ref => {
          val selection = context.actorSelection(ref.path)
          router ! RemoveRoutee(ActorSelectionRoutee(selection))  ◁──┐
        })                                                             │
        router ! GetRoutees                             Removes too many
      } else {                                          routees from the router
        (nrChildren until size).map(nr => createRoutee())
      }
      nrChildren = size                          Checks if we can terminate
    }                                            children or need to re-create
    case routees: Routees => {          ◁────┘   them after a termination
      //translate Routees into a actorPath
      import collection.JavaConversions._
      var active = routees.getRoutees.map{
        case x: ActorRefRoutee => x.ref.path.toString
        case x: ActorSelectionRoutee => x.selection.pathString
      }
      //process the routee list
      for(routee <- context.children) {
        val index = active.indexOf(routee.path.toStringWithoutAddress)
        if (index >= 0) {
          active.remove(index)
        } else {                                     Child is removed from router;
          //Child isn't used anymore by router        now we can terminate the child
          routee ! PoisonPill               ◁────┘
        }
      }                                              Restarting accidentally
      //active contains the terminated routees       terminates children
      for (terminated <- active) {        ◁────┘
        val name = terminated.substring(terminated.lastIndexOf("/")+1)
        val child = context.actorOf(props, name)
```

Changes number of routees ──▷

Creates new routees ──▷

Translates routee list into a list of actor paths ──▷

```
        context.watch(child)
      }
    }
    case Terminated(child) => router ! GetRoutees
  }
}
```

Child has terminated; checks if it was a planned termination by requesting the routees of the router

There's a lot going on here. We start with receiving the `PreferredSize`. There are two options when receiving this message: we have too few or too many routees. When there are too few, we can easily correct this by creating more child actors and adding them to the router. When we have too many, we need to remove them from the router and terminate them. We need to do this in order to prevent the router from sending messages to a killed child actor. This means that we're losing messages. Therefore, we send the `RemoveRoutee` message followed by the `GetRoutees` message. When we get the reply routees, we know that the router won't send any messages to the removed routees, and we can terminate the child actors. We use the `PoisonPill` because we want all previous messages sent to the routee to be processed before stopping it.

Next, we describe the action when a child is terminated. Again there are two possible situations when we get a terminated message. The first one is that we're busy with the downsizing; in this situation we don't have to do anything. In the second situation, an active routee is terminated accidentally. In this case we need to re-create the routee. We want to re-create the child using the same name instead of removing the child from the router and creating a new one, because it's possible that removing a terminated child will cause the router to terminate when that child was the last active routee. To decide what needs to be done, we send a `GetRoutees` message and choose which action needs to be taken when we get the reply.

The last part we need to discuss is what happens if we get the `Routees` reply. We use this message to determine if we can safely terminate a child and if we need to restart a child. To be able to do this, we need the actor paths of the routees, which aren't available in the `Routee` interface. To solve this problem, we use the implementation classes `ActorSelectionRoutee` and `ActorRefRoutee`. The latter class is probably not used within the router, but is added just to be sure. Now that we have a list of actor paths, we can check if we need to stop children or restart them.

To use this sizer, we simply create the router and the sizer actor:

```
val router = system.actorOf(RoundRobinGroup(List()).props(), "router")
val props = Props(new GetLicense(endProbe.ref))
val creator = system.actorOf(
  Props( new DynamicRouteeSizer(2, props, router)),
  "DynamicRouteeSizer"
)
```

As we described in this section, you're able to dynamically change the routees of a group, but it would be preferable to avoid doing so due to the number of pitfalls.

You've learned how to use router pools and groups, but there's one type of router logic that works a little differently than the others, and that is the `ConsistentHashing` router.

9.2.3 ConsistentHashing router

The previous section showed that routers are a great and easy way to be able to scale up and even scale out. But there can be a problem with sending messages to different routees. What happens when you've implemented state in your actor, which relies on the received message? Take, for example, the Aggregator of the scatter-gather pattern from section 8.2.4. When you have a router with 10 Aggregator routees, each of which joins two related messages into one, there's a good chance that the first message will be sent to routee 1 and the second message to routee 2. When this happens, both aggregators will decide that the message can't be joined. To solve this problem, the ConsistentHashing router was introduced.

This router will send similar messages to the same routee. When the second message is received, the router will route it to the same routee as the first one. This enables the Aggregator to join the two messages. To make this work, the router must identify when two messages are similar. The ConsistentHashing router makes a hash code of the message and maps this to one of its routees. There are several steps to map a message to a routee, which are shown in figure 9.5.

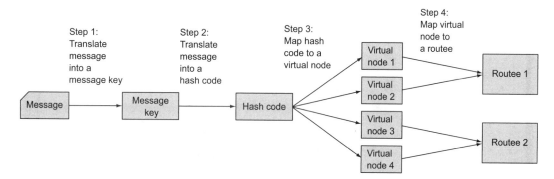

Figure 9.5 Steps the ConsistentHashing router follows to decide which routee to select

Step 1 translates a message to a message key object. Similar messages have the same key, for example, the ID of the message. It doesn't matter what type the key is; the only restriction is that this object is always the same for similar messages. This message key is different for every type of message and should be implemented somehow. The router supports three ways to translate the message into a message key:

- *A partial function is specified in the router.*
  This makes the decision specific to that router.
- *The message implements* akka.routing.ConsistentHashingRouter.Consistent-Hashable.
  This makes the decision specific for the messages used.
- *The messages can be wrapped in a* akka.routing.ConsistentHashingRouter .ConsistentHashableEnvelope.
  This makes the decision specific for the sender. The sender knows which key to use.

The last option is less preferable, because this makes the sender closely coupled to the routees. The sender needs to know that the next `ActorRef` is using a `Consistent-HashingRouter` and how to distribute the messages. The other two solutions are much more loosely coupled. Later, we'll show how to use these three different methods.

Step 2 creates a hash code from this message key. This hash code is used to select a virtual node (step 3), and the last step (4) is to select the routee that handles all the messages for that virtual node. The first thing you'll notice is the use of a virtual node. Can't we just map a hash code directly to a routee? Using virtual nodes is done to get a bigger change to equally spread all the messages over the routees. The number of virtual nodes serviced by a routee has to be configured when using a `ConsistentHashing-Router`. In our example we have two virtual nodes for each routee.

Let's take a look at an example of using a routee that will join two messages based on their IDs. We've stripped all the error recovery from this gather example.

Listing 9.12 Joining two message into one

```
trait GatherMessage {
  val id:String
  val values:Seq[String]
}

case class GatherMessageNormalImpl(id:String, values:Seq[String])
  extends GatherMessage

class SimpleGather(nextStep: ActorRef) extends Actor {
  var messages = Map[String, GatherMessage]()
  def receive = {
    case msg: GatherMessage => {
      messages.get(msg.id) match {
        case Some(previous) => {
          //join
          nextStep ! GatherMessageNormalImpl(
                      msg.id,
                      previous.values ++ msg.values)
          messages -= msg.id
        }
        case None => messages += msg.id -> msg
      }
    }
  }
}
```

The `SimpleGather` actor will join two messages with the same ID together into one message. We use a trait as a message type, to be able to use different implementations of the message, which is needed in one of the hashing examples. Let's look at the three ways to specify the message key.

SUPPLY HASHMAPPING PARTIAL FUNCTION TO ROUTER

The first way we'll examine is specifying the hash mapping of the router. When creating the router, you supply a partial function that selects the message key:

```
def hashMapping: ConsistentHashMapping = {
  case msg: GatherMessage => msg.id
}
```
Defines partial hash-mapping function

Sets mapping function
```
val router = system.actorOf(
  ConsistentHashingPool(10,
    virtualNodesFactor = 10,
    hashMapping = hashMapping
  ).props(Props(new SimpleGather(endProbe.ref))),
  name = "routerMapping"
)
```
Sets number of virtual hashing nodes per routee

This is all you need to do to use a `ConsistentHashingRouter`. You create a partial function to select a message key from the received message. When you send two messages with the same ID, the router makes sure that both messages are sent to the same routee. Let's try this:

```
router ! GatherMessageNormalImpl("1", Seq("msg1"))
router ! GatherMessageNormalImpl("1", Seq("msg2"))
endProbe.expectMsg(GatherMessageNormalImpl("1",Seq("msg1","msg2")))
```

This method can be used when the router has some specific needs to distribute this message, for example, when you have several routers in the system that are getting the same message type, but you want to use another message key. Suppose one router joins the message based on the ID, and another router counts the message with the same first value and needs the first value as the message key. When the message key is always the same for a given message, it makes more sense to implement the translation within the message.

MESSAGE HAS A HASHMAPPING

It's also possible to translate the message to a key within the message itself by extending the `ConsistentHashable` trait:

```
case class GatherMessageWithHash(id:String, values:Seq[String])
  extends GatherMessage with ConsistentHashable {

  override def consistentHashKey: Any = id
}
```

When using this message, you don't have to supply a mapping function, because the mapping function of the message is used:

```
val router = system.actorOf(
  ConsistentHashingPool(10, virtualNodesFactor = 10)
    .props(Props(new SimpleGather(endProbe.ref))),
  name = "routerMessage"
)

router ! GatherMessageWithHash("1", Seq("msg1"))
router ! GatherMessageWithHash("1", Seq("msg2"))
endProbe.expectMsg(GatherMessageNormalImpl("1",Seq("msg1","msg2")))
```

When the message key is always the same for a given message, this solution is preferable. But we mentioned that we have three ways to get the message key from a message.
So let's take a look at the last version: using the `ConsistentHashableEnvelope`.

SENDER HAS A HASHMAPPING

The last method is to supply the message key using a `ConsistentHashableEnvelope`
message.

```
val router = system.actorOf(
  ConsistentHashingPool(10, virtualNodesFactor = 10)
    .props(Props(new SimpleGather(endProbe.ref))),
  name = "routerMessage"
)

router ! ConsistentHashableEnvelope(
  message = GatherMessageNormalImpl("1", Seq("msg1")), hashKey = "1")
router ! ConsistentHashableEnvelope(
  message = GatherMessageNormalImpl("1", Seq("msg2")), hashKey = "1")
endProbe.expectMsg(GatherMessageNormalImpl("1",Seq("msg1","msg2")))
```

Instead of sending our message to the router, we send the `ConsistentHashable-
Envelope`, which contains our actual message and the `hashKey` to use as the message
key. But as we mentioned before, this solution requires that all the senders know that
a `ConsistentHashingRouter` is used and what the message key should be. One example of when this method applies is when you need all the messages from one sender to
be processed by one routee: then you can use this approach and use a `senderId` as the
`hashKey`. But this doesn't mean that each routee processes messages from one sender.
It is possible that multiple senders are processed by one routee.

We've shown three different ways to translate a message into a message key, but it is
possible to use the three solutions in one router.

In this section, we learned how to use Akka routers, which are used for performance reasons, but remember that routers are also used based on the content of a
message or state. In the next section, we describe content and state-based routing
approaches.

9.3   *Implementing the router pattern using actors*

Implementing the router pattern doesn't always require Akka routers. When the decision of the routee is based on the message or some state, it's easier to implement it in
a normal actor, because you can leverage all the benefits of actors. You do need to
address possible concurrency issues when creating a custom Akka router.

In this section we'll look at some implementations of the router pattern using normal actors. We'll start with a message-based router. In the next section, we'll use the
become/unbecome functionality to implement a state-based router. After this, we'll
discuss why it's not required for a router pattern to be implemented in a separate
actor, but that it's also possible to integrate it into the message-processing actor.

9.3.1 Content-based routing

The most common routing pattern in a system is based on the messages themselves. At the start of section 9.1, we showed an example of a message-based router. When the speed is lower than the speed limit, the driver isn't in violation, and the message need not be processed anymore, but the cleanup step has to be done. When the speed is higher than the speed limit, then it's a violation, and processing should continue to the next step, the send-message task.

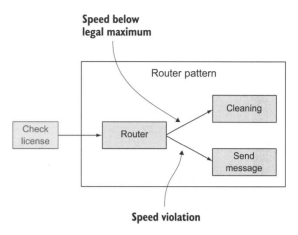

Figure 9.6   Routing based on the value of the speed

Figure 9.6 shows that, based on the content of the message, a flow is chosen. In this example we need to route based on the speed, but it can also be based on the type of the message or any other test done on the message itself. We're not showing an example, because the implementation is very functionality related, and you should be able to implement it with your current knowledge of the Akka framework. In the next section, we'll take a look at state-based routing.

9.3.2 State-based routing

This approach involves changing the routing behavior based on the state of the router. The simplest case would be a switch router that has two states: on and off. When it's in the on state, all messages are sent to the normal flow, and when it's in the off state, the messages are sent to the cleanup flow. To implement this example, we won't use the Akka router, because we want to have state in our router and the Akka router's state is not thread-safe by default. Instead, we'll use a normal actor. It's possible to implement the state as a class attribute, but because it's possible to change the behavior of an actor during its lifecycle, using the become/unbecome functionality, we can employ this as our state representation mechanism.

We'll use the become capability to change the behavior of the actor depending on its state. In our example we have two states, on and off. When the actor is in the on state, the messages should be routed to the normal flow, and when it's in the off state, the messages should go to the cleanup process. To do this we'll create two functions to handle the messages. When we want to switch to another state, we'll simply replace the receive function using the become method of the actor's context. In our example we use two messages, RouteStateOn and RouteStateOff, to change our state and therefore our behavior.

Listing 9.13 State-based router

```
case class RouteStateOn()
case class RouteStateOff()

class SwitchRouter(normalFlow: ActorRef, cleanUp: ActorRef)
  extends Actor with ActorLogging {                          Receives method
                                                             when state is on
  def on: Receive = {
    case RouteStateOn =>
      log.warning("Received on while already in on state")
    case RouteStateOff => context.become(off)                When state is on, sends
    case msg: AnyRef => {                                    message to normal flow
      normalFlow ! msg
    }
  }
  def off: Receive = {                                       Receives method
    case RouteStateOn => context.become(on)                  when state is off
    case RouteStateOff =>
      log.warning("Received off while already in off state")
    case msg: AnyRef => {
      cleanUp ! msg                                          When state is off, sends
    }                                                        message to cleanup
  }
  def receive = off                       Actor starts with state off
}
```

- Switches to state off → `case RouteStateOff => context.become(off)`
- Switches to state on → `case RouteStateOn => context.become(on)`

We start with the state `off` because this is the initial function our actor uses. When the actor receives messages, it is routed to the cleanup actor. When we send a `Route-StateOn` to our router, the `become` method is called and replaces the receive function with the `on` implementation of the receive function. All the subsequent messages are then routed to the normal flow actor.

Listing 9.14 Testing state `routerRedirect` actor

```
val normalFlowProbe = TestProbe()
val cleanupProbe = TestProbe()
val router = system.actorOf(
  Props(new SwitchRouter(
    normalFlow = normalFlowProbe.ref,
    cleanUp = cleanupProbe.ref)))

val msg = "message"
router ! msg

cleanupProbe.expectMsg(msg)
normalFlowProbe.expectNoMsg(1 second)

router ! RouteStateOn               Switches state to on

router ! msg

cleanupProbe.expectNoMsg(1 second)
normalFlowProbe.expectMsg(msg)

router ! RouteStateOff              Switches state to off
router ! msg
```

```
cleanupProbe.expectMsg(msg)
normalFlowProbe.expectNoMsg(1 second)
```

In our example, we used only the become method, but there's also an unbecome method. Calling this method causes the new receive function to be removed and the original function to be used. Let's rewrite our router using the unbecome method. (It's a semantic difference, but also a matter of following the convention provided.)

Listing 9.15 State-based router using unbecome

```
class SwitchRouter2(normalFlow: ActorRef, cleanUp: ActorRef)
  extends Actor with ActorLogging {

  def on: Receive = {
    case RouteStateOn =>
      log.warning("Received on while already in on state")
    case RouteStateOff => context.unbecome()          ◁──────┐  Using the
    case msg: AnyRef => normalFlow ! msg                      │  unbecome
  }                                                           │  method instead
  def off: Receive = {                                        │  of become off
    case RouteStateOn => context.become(on)
    case RouteStateOff =>
      log.warning("Received off while already in off state")
    case msg: AnyRef => cleanUp ! msg
  }
  def receive = {
    case msg: AnyRef => off(msg)
  }
}
```

There's one warning when using the become functionality: after a restart, the behavior of the actor is also returned to its initial state. The become and unbecome functionality can be handy and powerful when you need to change behavior during the processing of messages.

9.3.3 Router implementations

So far we've shown different routers and how you can implement each. But all these examples are implementing the clean router pattern; no processing is done in the router, it merely directs messages to the appropriate recipients. This is the correct preliminary approach when designing with these patterns, but when you're implementing the processing task and the router component, it can make sense for routing to be subsumed with processing into a single actor, as shown in figure 9.7. This is most likely to make sense when the results of processing will influence what the next step should be.

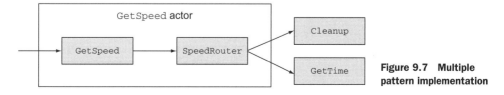

Figure 9.7 Multiple pattern implementation

In our camera example, we have a `GetSpeed` process that finds the speed. When this fails or when the speed is too low, the message has to be sent to the cleanup task; otherwise the message should be sent to the normal flow, in our case the `GetTime` task. To design this we need two patterns:

- A process task
- A router pattern

But when implementing these patterns, it's possible to implement the two components `GetSpeed` and `SpeedRouter` into one actor. The actor starts the processing task first, and depending on the result, it sends the message to either the `GetTime` or the `Cleanup` task. The decision to implement these components into one actor or two depends on the required degree of reusability. When we need the `GetSpeed` to be separate, we can't integrate both steps in one actor. But when the processing actor also has the obligation to render a decision about how the message should be further processed, it would be easier to integrate the two components. Another factor would be that the separation of normal flow and error flow is preferred for the `GetSpeed` component.

9.4 *Summary*

This chapter was all about how to route messages through different tasks. The Akka routers are an important mechanism for scaling your application, and they're very flexible, especially when using configuration. You've seen that there's different built-in logic that can be used. In this chapter you've also learned the following:

- Akka routers come in two varieties: groups and pools. Pools manage the creation and termination of the routees, and when using the group you have to manage routees yourself.
- Akka routers can easily use remote actors as routees.
- The state-based router we implemented with the become/unbecome mechanism enables us to change the behavior of the actor during its lifecycle by replacing the `receive` method. When using this approach, we have to be careful with restarts, because when the actor `restarts` the receive message is returned to the initial implementation.
- Deciding where to send the message can be based on performance, the content of the received message, or the state of the router.

We've focused on the structure of steps within the application, and how program flow can be modeled using core Akka services. In the next chapter we'll focus on how you send messages between actors, and you'll see that there are more ways to send messages than simply using the actor reference.

Message channels

$$10$$

In this chapter we'll take a closer look at the message channels that can be used to send messages from one actor to another. We'll start with the two types of channels: point-to-point and publish-subscribe. Point-to-point is the channel we've used in all our examples until now, but sometimes we need a more flexible method to send messages to receivers. In the publish-subscribe section, we'll describe a method to send messages to multiple receivers without the sender knowing which receivers need the message. The receivers are kept by the channel and can change during the operation of the application. Other names that are often used for these kinds of channels are `EventQueue` or `EventBus`. Akka has an `EventStream` that implements a publish-subscribe channel. But when this implementation isn't sufficient, Akka has a collection of traits that helps to implement a custom publish-subscribe channel.

Next we'll describe two special channels. The first is the *dead-letter channel*, which contains messages that couldn't be delivered. This is sometimes also called a *dead-message queue*. This channel can help when you're debugging why some messages aren't processed or monitoring where there are problems. In the last section, we'll describe the *guaranteed-delivery channel*. You can't create a reliable system without at least some guaranties of delivering messages. But you don't always need fully guaranteed delivery. Akka doesn't have fully guaranteed delivery, but we'll describe the level that *is* supported, which differs for sending messages to local and remote actors.

10.1 Channel types

We'll start this chapter by describing the two types of channels. The first one is the *point-to-point channel*. The name describes its characteristics: it connects one point (the sender) to another point (the receiver). Most of the time this is sufficient, but sometimes you want to send a message to a number of receivers. In this case you need multiple channels, or you use the second type of channel, the *publish-subscribe channel*. One advantage of the publish-subscribe channel is that the number of receivers can dynamically change when the application is operational. To support this kind of channel, Akka has implemented the `EventBus`.

10.1.1 Point-to-point

A channel transports the message from the sender to the receiver. The point-to-point channel sends the message to one receiver. We've already used this kind of channel in all our previous examples, so we'll just recap the important parts here to describe the differences between the two types of channels.

In the previous examples, the sender knows the next step of the process and can decide which channel to use to send its message to the next step. Sometimes there's just one channel, like in the pipes and filters examples of section 8.1. In these examples the sender has one `ActorRef` where it sends the message when the actor has finished processing. But in other cases like the `RecipientList` of section 8.2.3, the actor has multiple channels and decides which channel to use to send the message. This way the connectivity between the actors is more static in nature.

Another characteristic of the channel is that when multiple messages are sent, the order of these messages isn't changed. A point-to-point channel delivers the message to exactly one receiver, as shown in figure 10.1.

Figure 10.1   Point-to-point channel

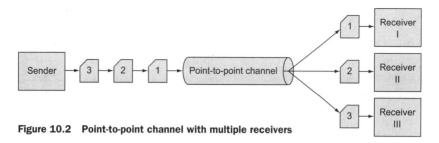

Figure 10.2 Point-to-point channel with multiple receivers

It's possible for a point-to-point channel to have multiple receivers, but the channel makes sure that only one receiver receives the message. The round-robin router in section 9.2.1 is an example of a channel having multiple receivers. The processing of the messages can be done concurrently by different receivers, but only one receiver consumes any given message. This is shown in figure 10.2.

The channel has multiple receivers, but every message is delivered to just one receiver. This kind of channel is used when the connection between sender and receiver is more static in nature. The sender knows which channel it has to use to reach the receiver.

This type of channel is the most common channel in Akka, because in Akka the `ActorRef` is the implementation of a point-to-point channel. All messages sent will be delivered to one actor, and the order of the messages sent to the `ActorRef` will not change.

10.1.2 *Publish-subscribe*

You've seen in the previous section that the point-to-point channel delivers each message to only one receiver. In these cases the sender knows where the message has to be sent. But sometimes the sender doesn't know who is interested in the message. This is the greatest difference between the point-to-point channel and the publish-subscribe channel. The channel, instead of the sender, is responsible for keeping track of the receivers who need the message. The channel can also deliver the same message to multiple receivers.

Let's assume we have a web shop application. The first step in our application is receiving the order. After this step, the system needs to take the next step in processing, which is delivering the order (for example, a book) to the customer. The receiving step sends a message to the delivery step. But to keep the inventory up to date, we also need the order message in this component. At this point the received order needs to be distributed to two parts of the system, as shown in figure 10.3.

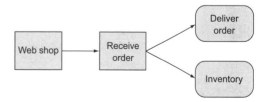

Figure 10.3 Web shop processing the order message

As a bonus, we want to send a present when a customer buys a book. We extend our system with a gift module, and again the order message is needed. Every time we add a new subsystem, we need to change the first step to send the message to more receivers. To solve this problem, we can use the publish-subscribe channel. The channel is able to send the same message to multiple receivers, without the sender knowing about the receivers. Figure 10.4 shows that the published messages are sent to the delivery and inventory subsystems.

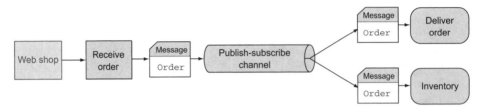

Figure 10.4   Using the publish-subscribe channel to distribute the order message

When we want to add the gift functionality, we subscribe to the channel and don't need to modify the receive-order task. Another benefit of this channel is that the number of receivers can differ during the operation and isn't static. For example, we don't want to always send a present, only on the action days. When using this channel, we're able to add the gift module to the channel only during the action period and remove the module from the channel when there is no gift action. This is shown in figure 10.5.

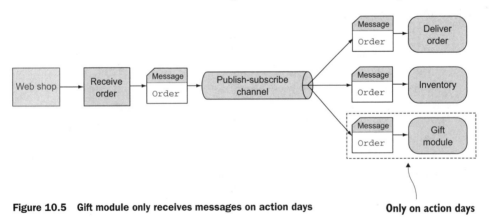

Figure 10.5   Gift module only receives messages on action days   **Only on action days**

When a receiver is interested in a message of the publisher, it subscribes itself to the channel. When the publisher sends a message through the channel, the channel makes sure that all the subscribers get the message. And when the gift module doesn't need the order messages, it unsubscribes itself from the channel. This means that the channel methods can be classified by two usages. The first usage is done at the send side: here, one must be able to publish the messages. The other usage is at the

Publish-subscribe channel

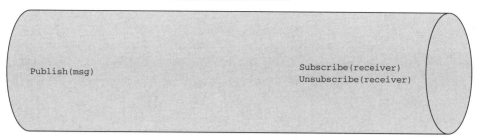

Figure 10.6 Usages of a publish-subscribe channel

receiver side: at this end, the receivers must be able to subscribe to and unsubscribe from the channel. Figure 10.6 shows the two usages.

Because the receivers can subscribe themselves to the channel, this solution is very flexible. The publisher doesn't need to know how many receivers it has. It's even possible that it may have no receivers at some point, because the number of subscribers can vary during the operation of the system.

Akka EventStream

Akka supports publish-subscribe channels. The easiest way to use a publish-subscribe channel is to use the EventStream. Every ActorSystem has one, and it's therefore available from any actor (through context.system.eventStream). The EventStream can be seen as a manager of multiple publish-subscribe channels, because the actor can subscribe to a specific message type, and when someone publishes a message of that specific type, the actor receives that message. The actor doesn't need any modifications to receive messages from the EventStream.

```
class DeliverOrder() extends Actor {

  def receive = {
    case msg: Order => ...//Process message
  }
}
```

What is unique here is how the message is sent. It isn't even necessary that the actor do the subscribing itself. It's possible to subscribe from any location in your code, as long as you have the actor reference and a reference to the EventStream to set up the subscription. Figure 10.7 shows the subscribe interface of Akka. To subscribe an actor to receive the Order messages, you need to call the subscribe method of the EventStream.

When the actor isn't interested anymore, for example when our gift action ends, the unsubscribe method can be used. In the example we unsubscribe the Gift-Module, and after this method call, the actor doesn't receive any Order messages that are published.

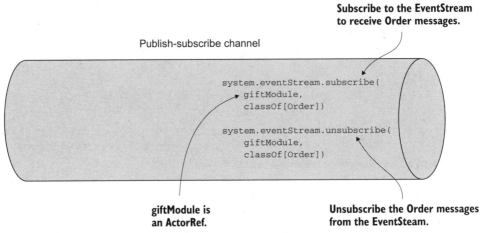

Subscribe to the EventStream
to receive Order messages.

Publish-subscribe channel

```
system.eventStream.subscribe(
    giftModule,
    classOf[Order])

system.eventStream.unsubscribe(
    giftModule,
    classOf[Order])
```

giftModule is
an ActorRef.

Unsubscribe the Order messages
from the EventSteam.

Figure 10.7 Subscribe interface of `EventStream`

This is all that has to be done when subscribing the GiftModule to receive Order messages. After calling the subscribe method, the GiftModule will receive all the Order messages that are published to the EventStream. This method can be called for different actors that need these Order messages. And when an actor needs multiple message types, the subscribe method can be called multiple times with different message types.

Publishing a message to the EventStream is also easy; just call the publish method, as shown in figure 10.8. After this call, the message msg is sent to all subscribed actors that can do the processing. This is the complete Akka implementation of the publish-subscribe channel.

In Akka it's possible to subscribe to multiple message types. For example, our Gift-Module also needs the messages when an order is canceled, because the gift shouldn't be sent then either. In this case the GiftModule has subscribed to the EventStream to receive the Order and Cancel messages. But when calling unsubscribe for the Orders, the subscription for the cancellations is still valid, and these messages are still received.

Publish-subscribe channel

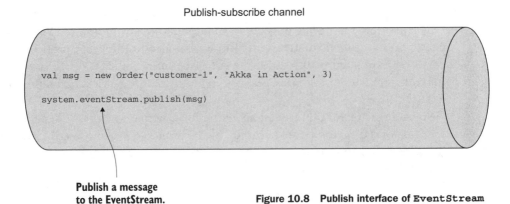

```
val msg = new Order("customer-1", "Akka in Action", 3)

system.eventStream.publish(msg)
```

Publish a message
to the EventStream.

Figure 10.8 Publish interface of `EventStream`

When stopping the `GiftModule`, we need to unsubscribe for all subscriptions. This can be done with one call:

```
system.eventStream.unsubscribe(giftModule)
```

After this call the `GiftModule` isn't subscribed to any message type anymore. The `publish`, `subscribe`, and both `unsubscribe` methods form the Akka interface of the publish-subscribe channel, which is quite simple. The following listing shows how we can test whether the Akka `EventStream` is receiving `Order` messages.

Listing 10.1 `EventStream` in action

```
val DeliverOrder = TestProbe()                          Creating Receiver actors
val giftModule = TestProbe()

system.eventStream.subscribe(
  DeliverOrder.ref,                                     Subscribes Receiver actors
  classOf[Order])                                       to receive Order messages
system.eventStream.subscribe(
  giftModule.ref,
  classOf[Order])
                                                        Publishes
val msg = new Order("me", "Akka in Action", 3)          an Order
system.eventStream.publish(msg)

DeliverOrder.expectMsg(msg)                             Message is received
giftModule.expectMsg(msg)                               by both actors

system.eventStream.unsubscribe(giftModule.ref)          Unsubscribes GiftModule

system.eventStream.publish(msg)
DeliverOrder.expectMsg(msg)                             GiftModule doesn't receive
giftModule.expectNoMsg(3 seconds)                       message anymore
```

We use the `TestProbes` as the receivers of the messages. Both receivers are subscribed to receive the `Order` messages. After publishing one message to the `EventStream`, both receivers have received the message. And after unsubscribing the `GiftModule`, only the `DeliverOrder` is receiving the messages, just as we expected.

We already mentioned the benefit of decoupling the receivers and the sender, as well as the dynamic nature of the publish-subscribe channel, but because the `Event-Stream` is available for all actors, it's also a nice solution for messages that can be sent from all over the local system and need to be collected at one or more actors. A good example is logging. Logging can be done throughout the system and needs to be collected at one point and written to a log file. Internally the `ActorLogging` is using the `EventStream` to collect the log lines from all over the system.

This `EventStream` is useful, but sometimes you'll need more control and want to write your own publish-subscribe channel. In the next subsection, we'll show how you can do that.

CUSTOM EVENTBUS

Let's assume that we only want to send a gift when someone orders more than one book. When implementing this, our `GiftModule` only needs the message when the amount is higher than 1. When using the `EventStream`, we can't do that filtering with the `EventStream`. Because the `EventStream` works on the class type of the message, we can do the filtering inside the `GiftModule`, but let's assume that this consumes resources we don't want to allow. In that case we need to create our own publish-subscribe channel, and Akka also has support to do that.

Akka has defined a generalized interface: the `EventBus`, which can be implemented to create a publish-subscribe channel. An `EventBus` is generalized so that it can be used for all implementations of a publish-subscribe channel. In the generalized form, there are three entities:

- *Event*—This is the type of all events published on that bus. In the `EventStream` the type `AnyRef` is used as the event type, which means any reference type can be used as an event.
- *Subscriber*—This is the type of subscriber allowed to register on that event bus. In the Akka `EventStream`, the subscribers are `ActorRefs`.
- *Classifier*—This defines the classifier to be used in selecting subscribers for dispatching events. In the Akka `EventStream`, the `Classifier` is the class type of the messages.

If you change the definition of these entities, it's possible to create any publish-subscribe channel. The interface has placeholders for the three entities and different publish and subscribe methods, which are also available at the `EventStream`. In the next listing, the complete interface of the `EventBus` is shown.

Listing 10.2 EventBus interface

```
package akka.event

trait EventBus {
  type Event
  type Classifier
  type Subscriber

  /**
   * Attempts to register the subscriber to the specified Classifier
   * @return true if successful and false if not (because it was
   * already subscribed to that Classifier, or otherwise)
   */
  def subscribe(subscriber: Subscriber, to: Classifier): Boolean

  /**
   * Attempts to deregister the subscriber from the specified Classifier
   * @return true if successful and false if not (because it wasn't
   * subscribed to that Classifier, or otherwise)
   */
  def unsubscribe(subscriber: Subscriber, from: Classifier): Boolean
```

```
/**
 * Attempts to deregister the subscriber from all Classifiers it may
 * be subscribed to
 */
def unsubscribe(subscriber: Subscriber): Unit

/**
 * Publishes the specified Event to this bus
 */
def publish(event: Event): Unit
}
```

The whole interface has to be implemented, and because most implementations need the same functionality, Akka also has a set of composable traits implementing the `EventBus` interface, which can be used to easily create your own implementation of the `EventBus`.

Let's implement a custom `EventBus` for our `GiftModule` to receive only the `Orders` that have multiple books. With our `EventBus` we can send and receive `Orders`; therefore, the `Event` we use in our `EventBus` will be the `Order` class. To define this in our `OrderMessageBus`, we simply set the event type defined in the `EventBus`:

```
class OrderMessageBus extends EventBus {
  type Event = Order
}
```

Another entity we need to define is the `Classifier`. In our example we want to distinguish between single-book orders and orders with multiple books. We've chosen to classify the `Order` messages on the criterion "is multiple book order" and use a Boolean as classifier. Therefore, we have to define the `Classifier` as a Boolean. This is defined as just the event:

```
class OrderMessageBus extends EventBus {
  type Event = Order
  type Classifier = Boolean
}
```

We skip the subscriber entity for now, because we'll define that a little differently. We've defined our `Classifier` and need to keep track of the subscribers for each `Classifier`, in our case tracking whether "is multiple book order" is true or false. Akka has three composable traits that can help you keep track of the subscribers. All these traits are still generic, so they can be used with any entities you have defined. This is done by introducing new abstract methods:

- *LookupClassification*—This trait uses the most basic classification. It maintains a set of subscribers for each possible classifier and extracts a classifier from each event. It extracts a classifier using the `classify` method, which should be implemented by the custom `EventBus` implementation.
- *SubchannelClassification*—This trait is used when classifiers form a hierarchy and it is desired that subscription be possible not only at the leaf nodes, but

also at the higher nodes. This trait is used in the EventStream implementation, because classes have a hierarchy and it's possible to use the superclass to subscribe to extended classes.

- *ScanningClassification*—This trait is a more complex one; it can be used when classifiers have an overlap. This means that one Event can be part of more classifiers; for example, if we give more gifts when ordering more books. When ordering more than one book, you get a book marker, but when you order more than 10, you also get a coupon for your next order. So when you order 11 copies, the order is part of the classifiers "more than 1 book" and "more than 10 books." When this order is published, the subscribers of "more than one book" need the message, but so do the subscribers of "more than 10 books." For this situation the ScanningClassification trait can be used.

In our implementation we'll use the LookupClassification. The other two classifications are similar to this one. These traits implement the subscribe and unsubscribe methods of the EventBus interface. But they also introduce new abstract methods that need to be implemented in our class. When using the LookupClassification trait, we need to implement the following:

- *classify(event: Event): Classifier*—This is used for extracting the classifier from the incoming events.
- *compareSubscribers(a: Subscriber, b: Subscriber): Int*—This method must define a sorting order for subscribers, similar to the compare method on java.lang.Comparable.
- *publish(event: Event, subscriber: Subscriber)*—This method will be invoked for each event for all subscribers that registered themselves for the events classifier.
- *mapSize: Int*—This returns the expected number of the different classifiers. This is used for the initial size of an internal data structure.

We'll use "is multiple book order" as a classifier. And this has two possible values; therefore, we'll use the value 2 for the mapSize:

```
import akka.event.{LookupClassification, EventBus}

class OrderMessageBus extends EventBus with LookupClassification {
  type Event = Order
  type Classifier = Boolean

  def mapSize = 2

  protected def classify(event: StateEventBus#Event) = {
    event.number > 1
  }
}
```

Sets mapSize to 2 → points to `def mapSize = 2`

Returns true when number is greater than 1 and otherwise false, which is used as classifier → points to `event.number > 1`

We mentioned that the LookupClassification must be able to get a classifier from our event. This is done using the classify method. In our case we just return the result of the check event.number > 1. All we need to do now is to define the subscriber; for this we use the `ActorEventBus` trait. This is probably the trait that will be used most of the time in an Akka message system, because this trait defines that the subscriber is an `ActorRef`. It also implements the `compareSubscribers` method needed by the `LookupClassification`. The only method we still need to implement before we're done is the `publish` method. The complete implementation is shown in the following listing.

Listing 10.3 Complete implementation of the `OrderMessageBus`

```
import akka.event.ActorEventBus
import akka.event.{ LookupClassification, EventBus }        ◁─── Extends our class
                                                                 with the two support
class OrderMessageBus extends EventBus    ◁─────────────────────  traits of Akka
  with LookupClassification
  with ActorEventBus {

  type Event = Order             ◁─── Defines entities
  type Classifier = Boolean                              Implements
  def mapSize = 2                                        classify
                                                         method
  protected def classify(event: OrderMessageBus#Event) = {  ◁─┘
    event.number > 1
  }                                                      Implements publish
                                                         method by sending
  protected def publish(event: OrderMessageBus#Event,    the event to the
                    subscriber: OrderMessageBus#Subscriber): Unit = {  ◁─ subscriber
    subscriber ! event
  }
}
```

We're now finished implementing our own `EventBus` that can be used to subscribe to and publish messages. In listing 10.4 you see an example of how this `EventBus` can be used.

Listing 10.4 Using the `OrderMessageBus`

```
                                            Creates OrderMessageBus
    val bus = new OrderMessageBus   ◁────┘
                                               Subscribes singleBooks
    val singleBooks = TestProbe()               to the single book
    bus.subscribe(singleBooks.ref, false)  ◁──  classifier (false)
    val multiBooks = TestProbe()
    bus.subscribe(multiBooks.ref, true)   ◁──
                                               Subscribes multiBooks
    val msg = new Order("me", "Akka in Action", 1)   to the multibook
Publishes┌─▷ bus.publish(msg)                         classifier (true)
an order │   singleBooks.expectMsg(msg)
with one │   multiBooks.expectNoMsg(3 seconds)
copy     │                                      Only singleBooks
         │   val msg2 = new Order("me", "Akka in Action", 3)  receives the message
             bus.publish(msg2)              ◁──
             singleBooks.expectNoMsg(3 seconds)    When publishing an order with
             multiBooks.expectMsg(msg2)            multiple copies, only multiBooks
                                                   receives the message
```

As you can see, our custom `EventBus` works exactly as the `EventStream`, except that we use a different classifier. Akka has several other traits that can be used. More details about these traits can be found in the Akka documentation.

As you've seen in this section, Akka has support for publish-subscribe channels. In most cases the `EventStream` will be sufficient when you need a publish-subscribe channel. But when you need more specialized channels, it's possible to create your own by implementing the `EventBus` interface. This is a generalized interface that can be implemented in any way you need. To support the implementation of an custom `EventBus`, Akka has several traits that can be used to implement a part of the `EventBus` interface.

In this section you've seen the two basic types of channels. In the next section we'll take a look at some special channels.

10.2 *Specialized channels*

In this section we'll take a look at two special channels. First we'll discuss the `Dead-Letter` channel. Only failed message are sent to this channel. Listening on this channel can help you find problems in your system.

The second channel we'll discuss is a guaranteed-delivery channel, which makes it possible to retry sending messages until they've been acknowledged.

10.2.1 *Dead letter*

The enterprise integration patterns describe a *dead-letter channel* or *dead-letter queue*. This is a channel that contain all the messages that can't be processed or delivered. This channel is also called a *dead-message queue*. This is a normal channel, but you don't normally send any messages using this channel. Only when there are problems with the message, for example, if it can't be delivered, will the message be placed on this channel. This is shown in figure 10.9.

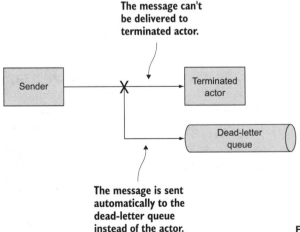

Figure 10.9   Dead-letter queue

By monitoring this channel, you know which messages aren't processed and can take corrective actions. Especially when testing your system, this queue can be helpful for figuring out why some messages aren't processed. When creating a system that isn't allowed to drop any messages, this queue can be used to re-insert the messages when the initial problems are solved.

Akka uses the `EventStream` to implement the dead-letter queue so that only the actors that are interested in the failed messages receive them. When a message is queued in a mailbox of an actor that terminates, or is sent after the termination, the message is sent to the `EventStream` of the `ActorSystem`. The message is wrapped into a `DeadLetter` object. This `Object` contains the original message, the sender of the message, and the intended receiver. This way the dead-letter queue is integrated in the `EventStream`. To get these dead-letter messages, you only need to subscribe your actor to the `EventStream` with the `DeadLetter` class as the classifier. This is the same as described in the previous section, only here we use another message type: `DeadLetter`:

```
val deadletterMonitor: ActorRef = ...      ⟵── The ... indicates some ActorRef

system.eventStream.subscribe(
  deadLetterMonitor,
  classOf[DeadLetter]
)
```

After this `subscribe`, the `deadLetterMonitor` will get all the messages that fail to be delivered. Let's look at a small example. We'll create a simple `Echo` actor that sends messages it receives back to the sender, and after starting the actor we'll send it a `PoisonPill` directly. This will result in the actor being terminated. The following listing shows that we receive the message when we subscribed to the `DeadLetter` queue.

> **Listing 10.5 Catching messages that can't be delivered**

```
    val deadLetterMonitor = TestProbe()

    system.eventStream.subscribe(              ⟵── Subscribes to DeadLetter channel
      deadLetterMonitor.ref,
      classOf[DeadLetter]
    )

    val actor = system.actorOf(Props[EchoActor], "echo")
    actor ! PoisonPill
    val msg = new Order("me", "Akka in Action", 1)       Sends message to
    actor ! msg                                    ⟵── terminated Actor

    val dead = deadLetterMonitor.expectMsgType[DeadLetter]   ⟵─┐
    dead.message must be(msg)
    dead.sender must be(testActor)             Expects a DeadLetter message in
    dead.recipient must be(actor)                  the DeadLetterMonitor
```

Terminates Echo Actor (points to `val actor = system.actorOf(...)`)

Messages sent to a terminated actor can't be processed anymore, and the `ActorRef` of this actor shouldn't be used anymore. When messages are sent to a terminated actor, these message will be sent to the `DeadLetter` queue. We can see that our message was indeed received by our `deadLetterMonitor`.

Another use of the `DeadLetter` queue is when processing fails. This is an actor-specific decision. An actor can decide that a received message couldn't be processed, and that it doesn't know what to do with it. In this situation the message can be sent to the dead-letter queue. The `ActorSystem` has a reference to the `DeadLetter` actor. When a messages needs to be sent to the dead-letter queue, you can send it to this actor:

```
system.deadLetters ! msg
```

When a message is sent to `DeadLetter`, it's wrapped in a `DeadLetter` object. But the initial receiver becomes the `DeadLetter` actor. In an autocorrecting system, information is lost when sending the message this way to the dead-letter queue. For example, the original sender is lost; the only information you get is the actor that sent the message to the queue. This can be sufficient, but when you also need to know the original sender, it's possible to send a `DeadLetter` object instead of the original message. When this message type is received, the wrapping is skipped and the message sent is put on the queue without any modification. In the next listing, we send a `DeadLetter` object and see that this message isn't modified.

Listing 10.6   Sending DeadLetter messages

```
val deadLetterMonitor = TestProbe()
val actor = system.actorOf(Props[EchoActor], "echo")      ◁──┐ Creates Actor
                                                              │ reference that
system.eventStream.subscribe(                                 │ will be used as
  deadLetterMonitor.ref,                                      │ initial recipient
  classOf[DeadLetter]
)

val msg = new Order("me", "Akka in Action", 1)
val dead = DeadLetter(msg, testActor, actor)      ◁──┐ Creates DeadLetter
system.deadLetters ! dead                             │ message and sends it
                                                      │ to DeadLetter Actor
deadLetterMonitor.expectMsg(dead)      ◁──┐
                                           │ DeadLetter message is
system.stop(actor)                         │ received in monitor
```

As shown in the example, the `DeadLetter` message is received unchanged. This makes it possible to handle all messages that aren't processed or couldn't be delivered in the same way. What to do with the messages is completely dependent on the system you create. Sometimes it isn't even important to know that messages were dropped, but when creating a highly robust system, you may want to resend the message again to the recipient like it was sent initially.

In this section we described how to catch messages that failed to be processed. In the next section, we'll describe another specialized channel: the guaranteed-delivery channel.

10.2.2 *Guaranteed delivery*

The guaranteed-delivery channel is a point-to-point channel with the guarantee that the message will be delivered to the receiver. This means that the delivery is done even when all kinds of errors occur. The channel must have various mechanisms and checks to be able to guarantee delivery; for example, the message has to be saved on disk in case the process crashes. Don't you always need the guaranteed-delivery channel when creating a system? How can you create a reliable system when it isn't guaranteed that messages are delivered? Yes, you need some guaranties, but you don't always need the maximum available guaranty.

Actually, implementations of a guaranteed-delivery channel aren't able to guarantee the delivery in all situations, for example, when a message is sent from one location and that location burns down. In that situation no possible solution can be found to send the message anywhere, because it is lost in the fire. The question you need to ask is this: Is the level of guaranty sufficient for my purpose?

When creating a system, you need to know what guarantees the channel provides and if that's sufficient for your system. Let's look at the guarantees Akka provides.

The general rule of message delivery is that messages are delivered at most once. This means that Akka promises that a message is delivered once or it's not delivered, which means that the message is lost. This doesn't look good when building a reliable system. Why doesn't Akka implement fully guaranteed delivery? The first reason is that fully guaranteed delivery poses several challenges, making it complex, and a lot of overhead is involved in sending just one message. This results in a performance penalty even when you don't need that level of guaranteed delivery.

Secondly, nobody needs *just* reliable messaging. You want to know if the request was successfully processed, which is done by receiving a business-level acknowledgement message. This isn't something Akka could deduce, because this is system dependent. The last reason why Akka doesn't implement fully guaranteed delivery is because it's always possible to add stricter guarantees on top of basic ones, when needed. The inverse is not possible: you can't make a strict system less strict without changing it at its core.

Akka can't guarantee exactly once message delivery in all cases, and in fact, no system can. But this is the basic rule for delivery of messages to local and remote actors. When we look at these two situations separately, we see that Akka isn't as bad as it sounds.

Sending local messages will not likely fail, because it's like a normal method call. This fails only when there are catastrophic VM errors, like `StackOverflowError`, `OutOfMemoryError`, or a memory access violation. In all of these cases, the actor was likely not in a position to process the message anyway. So the guarantees for sending a message to a local actor are pretty high.

Losing messages becomes an issue when you're using remote actors. With remote actors, it's a lot more likely for a message delivery failure to occur, especially when an intermediate unreliable network is involved. If someone unplugs an Ethernet cable,

or a power failure shuts down a router, messages will be lost. To solve this problem, the
`ReliableProxy` was created. This makes sending messages using remote actors almost
as reliable as sending local messages. The only consideration is that critical errors in
the JVMs of both the sender and receiver can negatively influence the reliability of this
channel.

How does `ReliableProxy` work? When `ReliableProxy` starts, it creates a tunnel
between the two `ActorSystems` on the different nodes.

As shown in figure 10.10, this tunnel has an entry, `ReliableProxy`, and an exit,
`Egress`. Egress is an actor that's started by `ReliableProxy`, and both actors implement checks and resend functionality to be able to keep track of which messages are
delivered to the remote receiver. When delivery fails, `ReliableProxy` will retransmit
messages until it succeeds. When `Egress` receives a message, it checks if it was already
received and sends it to the actual receiver. But what happens when the target actor is
terminated? When this happens it's impossible to deliver the message. This is solved
by `ReliableProxy` terminating also when the target terminates. This way the system
behaves the same way as using a direct reference. On the receiver side, the difference
between sending messages directly or using the proxy isn't visible. One restriction of
using `ReliableProxy` is that the tunnel is only one-way and for one receiver. This
means that when the receiver replies to the sender, the tunnel is *not* used. When the
reply has to be also reliable, then another tunnel has to be made between the receiver
and the sender.

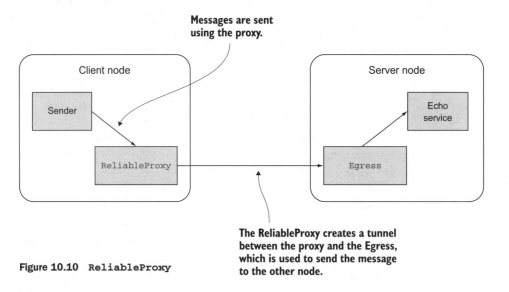

Figure 10.10   `ReliableProxy`

Now let's see this in action. Creating a reliable proxy is simple—all we need is a reference to the remote target actor:

```
import akka.contrib.pattern.ReliableProxy

val pathToEcho = "akka.tcp://actorSystem@127.0.0.1:2553/user/echo"
```

```
val proxy = system.actorOf(
         Props(new ReliableProxy(pathToEcho, 500.millis)), "proxy")
```

In the example we create a proxy using the `echo` reference. We also add a `retryAfter` value of `500` milliseconds. When a message fails, it's retried after 500 milliseconds. This is all we have to do to use `ReliableProxy`. To show the result, we create a multi-node test with two nodes, the client and server nodes. On the server node, we create an `EchoActor` as receiver, and on the client node, we run our actual test. Just as in chapter 6, we need the multi-node configuration and the `STMultiNodeSpec` for our `ReliableProxySample` test class.

Listing 10.7 Multi-node spec and multi-node configuration

```
import akka.remote.testkit.MultiNodeSpecCallbacks
import akka.remote.testkit.MultiNodeConfig
import akka.remote.testkit.MultiNodeSpec

trait STMultiNodeSpec
  extends MultiNodeSpecCallbacks
  with WordSpecLike
  with MustMatchers
  with BeforeAndAfterAll {

  override def beforeAll() = multiNodeSpecBeforeAll()

  override def afterAll() = multiNodeSpecAfterAll()
}

object ReliableProxySampleConfig extends MultiNodeConfig {
  val client = role("Client")            ◁───┐ Defines
  val server = role("Server")        ◁─── Defines server node   client node
  testTransport(on = true)       ◁───┐
}                                    │ We want to simulate transport failures

class ReliableProxySampleSpecMultiJvmNode1 extends ReliableProxySample
class ReliableProxySampleSpecMultiJvmNode2 extends ReliableProxySample
```

Because we want to demonstrate that the message is sent even when the network is down for a while, we need to turn on the `testTransport`. As we mentioned, we need to run an `EchoService` on the server node:

```
system.actorOf(
  Props(new Actor {
    def receive = {
      case msg:AnyRef => {
        sender ! msg
      }
    }
  }),
  "echo"
)
```

This service echoes every message it receives back to the sender. When this is running, we can do the actual test on the client node. Creating the full environment where we can do our test is shown next.

Listing 10.8   Setup of the environment for the `ReliableProxySample` test

```
import scala.concurrent.duration._
import concurrent.Await
import akka.contrib.pattern.ReliableProxy
import akka.remote.testconductor.Direction

class ReliableProxySample
  extends MultiNodeSpec(ReliableProxySampleConfig)
  with STMultiNodeSpec
  with ImplicitSender {

  import ReliableProxySampleConfig._

  def initialParticipants = roles.size

  "A MultiNodeSample" must {

    "wait for all nodes to enter a barrier" in {
      enterBarrier("startup")
    }

    "send to and receive from a remote node" in {
      runOn(client) {
        enterBarrier("deployed")
        val pathToEcho = node(server) / "user" / "echo"
        val echo = system.actorSelection(pathToEcho)      ◁─┐ Creates direct
        val proxy = system.actorOf(                            reference to
          Props(new ReliableProxy(pathToEcho, 500.millis)), "proxy")  ◁─ echo service

        ... Do the actual test
      }                                                    Creates
                                                           ReliableProxy
      runOn(server) {                                      tunnel
        system.actorOf(Props(new Actor {         ◁─┐ Implements
          def receive = {                              echo service
            case msg:AnyRef => {
              sender ! msg
            }
          }
        }), "echo")
        enterBarrier("deployed")
      }

      enterBarrier("finished")
    }
  }
}
```

Now that we have our complete test environment, we can implement the actual test. In listing 10.9 we show that the message that's sent while there's no communication between the nodes is only processed when we use the proxy. When using the direct actor reference, the message is lost.

Listing 10.9   Implementation of `ReliableProxySample`

```
proxy ! "message1"                              ←———————  Tests proxy under
expectMsg("message1")                                      normal conditions
Await.ready(
  testConductor.blackhole( client, server, Direction.Both),   ←——  Turns off
  1 second                                                           communication
)                                                                    between the two
                                                                     nodes
echo ! "DirectMessage"               ←——————  Sends message using both references
proxy ! "ProxyMessage"
expectNoMsg(3 seconds)
                                                              Restores
Await.ready(                                                  communication
  testConductor.passThrough( client, server, Direction.Both),   ←——
  1 second
)

expectMsg("ProxyMessage")           ←——  Message sent using the proxy is received
echo ! "DirectMessage2"             ←——
expectMsg("DirectMessage2")              Testing messages sent directly to
                                         echo actor are received when
                                         communication is restored
```

Using `ReliableProxy` gives you better guarantees for remote actors. As long as there are no critical VM errors in the JVM runtime on any nodes of the system, and the network eventually functions again, the message is delivered one time to the destination actor.

In this chapter you've seen that Akka doesn't have a guaranteed-delivery channel, but there's a level of guaranty that Akka *can* give. For local actors, the delivery is guaranteed as long as there are no critical VM errors. For remote actors, at-most-once delivery is guaranteed. But this can be improved by using `ReliableProxy` when sending a message across JVM boundaries.

These guarantees of delivery are enough for most systems, but when a system needs stronger guarantees, you can create a mechanism on top of the Akka delivery system to get those guarantees. This kind of mechanism isn't implemented by Akka because this is often system-specific and requires a performance hit that isn't necessary in most cases. There are always scenarios in which you cannot guarantee delivery or in which you need to specify guarantees on an application level.

10.3   Summary

You've seen that there are two types of messaging channels: point-to-point, which sends a message to one receiver, and publish-subscribe, which can send a message to multiple receivers. A receiver can subscribe itself to the channel, which makes receivers dynamic. At any time the number of subscribers can vary. Akka has the `Event-Stream`, which is the default implementation of a publish-subscribe channel and uses the class types of the messages as classifiers. There are several traits that you can use to make your own publish-subscribe channel when the `EventStream` is insufficient.

You've also seen that Akka has a DeadLetter channel, which uses the EventStream. This channel contains all the messages that couldn't be delivered to the requested actor, and can be used when debugging your system, to handle cases where messages are lost.

In the last section, we took a closer look at Akka's delivery guarantees, and saw that there is a difference between messages sent to local actors and remote actors. When you need stronger delivery guarantees, you can use ReliableProxy. But be careful: this is only one-way. When the receiver sends a message back to the sender, Reliable-Proxy isn't used.

In this chapter you've seen how you can send messages between actors. When you are building your application, it's possible that an actor may need state. Actors are often used to implement state machines, for instance using the become/unbecome mechanism shown in chapter 9. In the next chapter you'll see how to more formally implement finite state machines with actors. We'll also look at how state can be shared with another tool in the toolkit: agents.

Finite-state machines and agents

Previous chapters have advanced many reasons for using stateless components when implementing a system to avoid all kinds of problems, like restoring state after an error. But in most cases, there are components within a system that need state to be able to provide the required functionality. You've already seen two possible ways to keep state in an actor. The first is to use class variables, which we showed in our aggregator example (section 8.4.2). This is the simplest way. The second solution is to use the become/unbecome functionality, which we used in our state-dependent router (section 9.3.2). These two mechanisms are the more basic ways to implement state. But in some situations, these solutions are insufficient.

In this chapter we'll show you two other solutions for dealing with state. We'll start with how to design dynamic behavior, depending on the actor's state, using finite-state machine modeling. We'll create an example model that will be implemented in

233

the second section, where we'll show that Akka has support for easily implementing a finite-state machine. In the last section, we'll show how you can share state between different threads by using Akka agents. Using these agents eliminates the need to use locking mechanisms, because the state of the agents can be changed only asynchronously using events; but the state can be read synchronously, without any significant performance penalty.

11.1 Using a finite-state machine

A *finite-state machine* (FSM), also called a *state machine*, is a common language-independent modeling technique. FSMs can model a number of problems; common applications are communication protocols, language parsing, and even business application problems. What they encourage is isolation of state; you'll see our actors called on mostly to transition things from one state to another, in atomic operations. Actors receive one message at a time, so no locks will be needed. For those who haven't encountered them, we'll start with a short description. After this introduction we'll move on to an FSM example, which we'll implement with Akka in the next section.

11.1.1 Quick introduction to finite-state machines

The simplest example of a finite-state machine is a device whose operation proceeds through several states, transitioning from one to the next as certain events occur. The washing machine is usually the classic example used to explain FSMs: there's a process that requires initiation steps, and then once the machine takes over, it progresses through a sequence of specific states (filling the tub, agitation, draining, spinning). The transitions in the washing machine are all triggered by a program that wants a certain amount of time for each stage based on the user's desires (light/heavy loads, prewash, and so forth). The machine is only ever in one state at a time. The purchase order process mentioned earlier is a similar example from business: there's an established protocol for two parties to define an exchange of goods or services. With the example of the business documents, you can see that for each stage of the FSM there's a state representation (a purchase order, a quote, or a request for a quote). Modeling software this way allows you to deal with state in an atomic, isolated way, which is a core principle of the actor model.

An FSM is called a *machine* because it can only be in one of a finite number of states. Changing from one state to another is triggered by an event or condition. This state change is called a *transition*. A particular FSM is defined by a number of states and the different triggers for all the possible transitions. There are a lot of different ways to describe the FSM, but most of the time it's described with some kind of a diagram. Figure 11.1 shows a simple diagram to illustrate how we describe the FSM, because there are a number of different notations when creating an FSM diagram.

In this example we show an FSM with two states, State1 and State2. When instantiating the machine, we start in State1, transitioning from the initial state, which is shown in the diagram by the black dot. State1 has two different actions: an *entry action* and an *exit action*. (Although we won't use the exit action in this chapter, we show it so

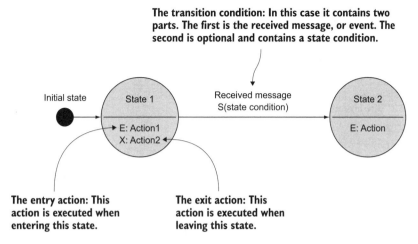

The transition condition: In this case it contains two parts. The first is the received message, or event. The second is optional and contains a state condition.

Initial state — State 1 — Received message S(state condition) — State 2

E: Action1
X: Action2

E: Action

The entry action: This action is executed when entering this state.

The exit action: This action is executed when leaving this state.

Figure 11.1   Diagram example of a finite-state machine

you'll understand how the model works.) Just as the name says, the first action is executed when the machine sets the state to State1, and the second when the machine changes from State1 to another state. In this example we have only two states, so this action is only executed when it goes to State2. In the next examples, we'll only use the entry actions, because this is a simple FSM. Exit actions can do some cleaning or restore some state, so they don't embody part of the logic of the machine. It can be seen more like a finally clause in a try-catch statement, which must always be executed when exiting the try block.

Changing state, *transition*, can only happen when the machine is triggered by an event. In the diagram this transition is shown by the arrow between State1 and State2. The arrow indicates the event and optionally a state condition (for instance, we might only transition to the spin cycle when the tank is empty). The events in an Akka FSM are the messages the actor receives. That's it for the introduction; now let's see how an FSM can help you implement a solution to a real problem.

11.1.2 Creating an FSM model

The example we'll use to show how you can use FSM support in Akka is a bookstore's inventory system. The inventory service gets requests for specific books and sends a reply. When the book is in inventory, the order system gets a reply that a book has been reserved. But it's possible that there might not be any copies of that book and that the inventory will have to ask the publisher for more books before it can service the order. These messages are shown in figure 11.2.

To keep the example simple, we have only one type of book in our inventory and we support ordering only one book at the time. When an order is received, the inventory checks if it has any copies of that book. When there are copies, the reply is created stating that the book is reserved. But when there aren't any copies of the requested book left, the processing has to wait and request more books from the publisher. The

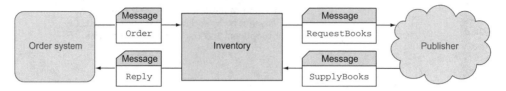

Figure 11.2   The inventory example

publisher can respond by supplying more books or with a sold out message. During the wait for more books, other orders can be received.

To describe the situation, we can use an FSM, because the inventory can be in different states and expect different messages before it can proceed to the next step. Figure 11.3 shows our problem using an FSM.

One thing the diagram doesn't depict is the fact that we can still receive Book-Requests, which will be added to the PendingRequest list while in our wait state. This is important because it represents the preservation of needed concurrency. Note that when we get back to the wait state, it's possible that there may be pending requests.

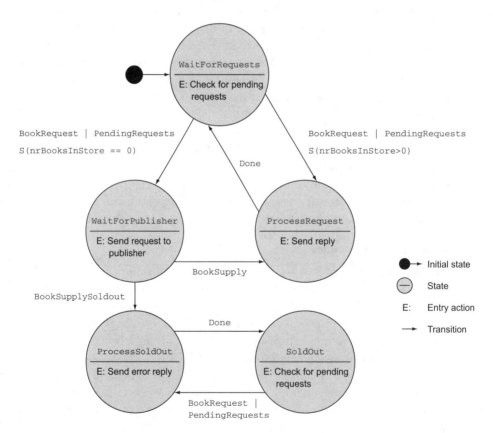

Figure 11.3   FSM of the inventory example

The entry action checks this, and if there are, triggers one or both transitions, depending on the number of books in the store. When the books are sold out, the state becomes `Process SoldOut`. This state sends an error reply to the order requester and triggers the transition to the state `SoldOut`. FSMs give you the ability to describe complex behavior in a clear, concise manner.

Now that we've described our solution using an FSM, let's see how Akka can help to implement our FSM model.

11.2 *Implementation of an FSM model*

In section 9.3.2 you saw the become/unbecome mechanism. This can help in implementing an FSM, just as we did in the state base router: you can map behaviors to states. It's possible to use the become/unbecome mechanism for small and simple FSM models. But when there are multiple transitions to one state, the entry action has to be implemented in different become/receive methods, which can be hard to maintain for more-complex FSMs. Therefore, Akka provides an `FSM` trait, which you can use when implementing an FSM model. This results in clearer and more maintainable code. In this section we'll explain how to use this `FSM` trait. We'll start by implementing the transitions of our inventory FSM, and in the next section we'll implement the entry actions to complete the implementation of the inventory FSM. At this point, we'll implement the designed FSM, but an Akka FSM also has support for using timers within the `FSM` trait, which is described next. We'll end with the termination of the Akka `FSM` trait, which enables you to do some cleanup when needed.

11.2.1 *Implementing transitions*

To start implementing an FSM model using Akka, we'll create an `Actor` with the `FSM` trait. (The `FSM` trait may only be mixed into an actor.) Akka has chosen this approach instead of extending `Actor` to make it obvious that an actor is actually created. When implementing an FSM, we need to take several steps before we have a complete FSM actor. The two biggest steps are defining the state and then the transitions. So let's get started creating our inventory FSM, by making an actor with the `FSM` trait mixed in:

```
import akka.actor.{Actor, FSM}

class Inventory() extends Actor with FSM[State, StateData] {
...
}
```

The `FSM` trait takes two type parameters:

- *State*—The super type of all state names
- *StateData*—The type of the state data that's tracked by the `FSM`

The super type is usually a sealed trait with case objects extending it, because it doesn't make sense to create extra states without creating transitions to those states. Let's start to define our states. We'll do that in the next section.

DEFINING THE STATE

The state definition process starts with a single trait (appropriately named `State`), with cases for each of the specific states our object can be in (note: this helps make the FSM code self-documenting):

```
sealed trait State
case object WaitForRequests extends State
case object ProcessRequest extends State
case object WaitForPublisher extends State
case object SoldOut extends State
case object ProcessSoldOut extends State
```

The defined states represent the states shown in figure 11.3. Next we have to create our state data:

```
case class StateData(nrBooksInStore:Int,
                     pendingRequests:Seq[BookRequest])
```

This is the data that we use when we need a state condition to decide which transition is fired, so it contains all the pending requests and the number of books in inventory. In our case we have one class, which contains the `StateData` (which is used in all states), but this isn't mandatory. It's possible to use a trait for the `StateData` as well, and create different `StateData` classes that extend the basic state trait. The first step in implementing the FSM trait is to define the initial state and the initial `StateData`. This is done using the `startWith` method:

```
class Inventory() extends Actor with FSM[State, StateData] {
  startWith(WaitForRequests, new StateData(0,Seq()))
...
}
```

Here we define that our FSM starts in the state `WaitForRequests`, and `StateData` is empty. Next we have to implement all the different state transitions. These state transitions only occur when there's an event. In the FSM trait, we define for each state which events we expect and what the next state will be. By defining the next state, we designate a transition. So we start with the events of the state `WaitForRequests`. In the next section, we'll define the actual transitions and see how we go from plan to working code.

DEFINING THE TRANSITIONS

Let's look at figure 11.4, where we have our state and the two possible transitions. You see that we can expect two possible events: the `BookRequest` or the `PendingRequests` message. Depending on the state `nrBooksInStore`, the state changes to `Process-Request` or `WaitForPublisher`, which are the transitions. We need to implement these transitions in our inventory FSM. We do that with the `when` declaration.

Listing 11.1 Defining transactions in the FSM trait

```
class Inventory() extends Actor with FSM[State, StateData] {
  startWith(WaitForRequests, new StateData(0,Seq()))

  when(WaitForRequests) {
    case Event(request:BookRequest, data:StateData) => {
      .....
    }
    case Event(PendingRequests, data:StateData) => {
      ...
    }
  }
...
}
```

Declares transitions for state **WaitForRequests**

Declares possible Event when a **BookRequest** message occurs

Declares possible Event when a **PendingRequests** message occurs

We start with the when declaration for the WaitForRequests state. This is a partial function to handle all the possible events in the specified state. In our case we can have two different events. When we're in the WaitForRequests state, a new BookRequest or a PendingRequests message can arrive. Next we have to implement the transition.

Either we'll remain in the same state or we'll transition to another one. This can be indicated by the following two methods:

```
goto(WaitForPublisher)          Declares that next state is WaitForPublisher
stay                            Declares that state doesn't change
```

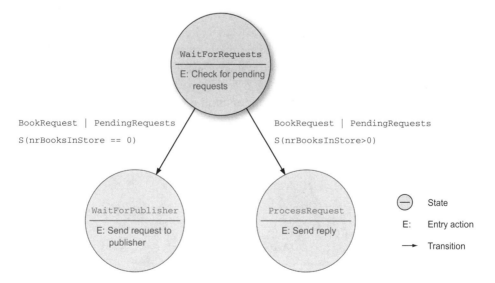

Figure 11.4 State transitions of the WaitForRequests state

Another responsibility of this transition declaration is updating the StateData. For
example, when we receive a new BookRequest event, we need to store the request in our
PendingRequests. This is done with the using declaration. When we implement the
complete transition declaration for the WaitForRequests state, we get the following.

Listing 11.2   Implementation of the WaitForRequests transactions

```
when(WaitForRequests) {
  case Event(request:BookRequest, data:StateData) => {          Creates new state
    val newStateData = data.copy(                                by appending
      pendingRequests =  data.pendingRequests :+ request)        new request
    if (newStateData.nrBooksInStore > 0) {
      goto(ProcessRequest) using newStateData                   Declares next
    } else {                                                     state and updates
      goto(WaitForPublisher) using newStateData                 StateData
    }
  }
  case Event(PendingRequests, data:StateData) => {              Uses stay when
    if (data.pendingRequests.isEmpty) {                          there aren't any
      stay                                                       pending requests
    } else if(data.nrBooksInStore > 0) {
      goto(ProcessRequest)                                      Uses goto without
    } else {                                                     updating
      goto(WaitForPublisher)                                     StateData
    }
  }
}
```

In this example we used stay without updating the StateData, but it's possible to
update the state with using too, just like the goto declaration. This is all we have to do
to declare the transitions of our first state. The next step is to implement the transitions for all our states. When we examine the possible events more closely, we see that
the event BookRequest in most states has the same effect: we generally want to just add
the request to our pending requests and do nothing else. For these events we can
declare whenUnhandled. This partial function is called when the state function doesn't
handle the event. Here we can implement the default behavior when a BookRequest is
received. The same declarations can be used as in the when declaration:

Listing 11.3   Implementing default behavior using whenUnhandled

```
whenUnhandled {
  // common code for all states
  case Event(request:BookRequest, data:StateData) => {          Only updates
    stay using data.copy(                                        StateData
      pendingRequests =  data.pendingRequests :+ request)
  }
  case Event(e, s) => {                                         Logs when event
    log.warning("received unhandled request {} in state {}/{}",  isn't handled
```

```
        e, stateName, s)
    stay
  }
}
```

In this partial function, we can also log unhanded events, which can be helpful with debugging this FSM implementation. Now we can implement the rest of the states.

Listing 11.4 Implementation of the transition of the other states

```
when(WaitForPublisher) {                              Transition declaration
  case Event(supply:BookSupply, data:StateData) => {  of the state
    goto(ProcessRequest) using data.copy(             WaitForPublisher
      nrBooksInStore = supply.nrBooks)
  }
  case Event(BookSupplySoldOut, _) => {
    goto(ProcessSoldOut)
  }
}
when(ProcessRequest) {                                Transition declaration
  case Event(Done, data:StateData) => {               of the state
    goto(WaitForRequests) using data.copy(            ProcessRequest
      nrBooksInStore = data.nrBooksInStore - 1,
      pendingRequests =  data.pendingRequests.tail)
  }
}
when(SoldOut) {                                       Transition
  case Event(request:BookRequest, data:StateData) => {  declaration
    goto(ProcessSoldOut) using new StateData(0,Seq(request))  of the state
  }                                                   SoldOut
}
when(ProcessSoldOut) {                                Transition declaration
  case Event(Done, data:StateData) => {               of the state
    goto(SoldOut) using new StateData(0,Seq())        ProcessSoldOut
  }
}
```

Now we've defined all our transitions for every possible state. This was the first step in creating an Akka FSM actor. At this moment, we have an FSM that reacts to events and changes state, but the actual functionality of the model—the entry actions—isn't implemented yet. This is covered in the next section.

11.2.2 Implementing the entry actions

The actual functionality is done by the entry and exit actions, which we'll implement now. In our FSM model, we had defined several entry actions. Just as the transitions are declared for each state, the actions are also implemented for each state. Figure 11.5 shows the initial state `WaitForRequests` again, to show the entry action we have to implement. The discreet structure of the implementation code, as you'll see, also lends itself to unit testing.

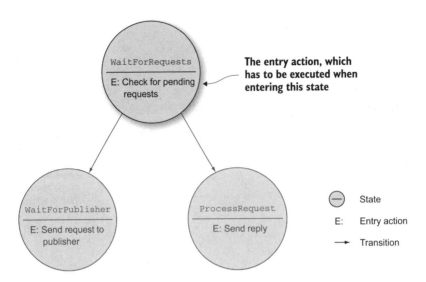

Figure 11.5   The entry action of the `WaitForRequests` state

ACTIONS ON TRANSITIONS

The entry action can be implemented in the `onTransition` declaration. It's possible to declare every possible transition because the transition callback is also a partial function and takes as input the current state and the next state:

```
onTransition {
  case WaitForRequests -> WaitForPublisher => {
    ...
  }
}
```

In this example we define the action that has to be executed when the transition occurs from `WaitForRequests` to `WaitForPublisher`. But it's also possible to use wildcards. In our example we don't care which state we're coming from, so we use the wildcard on the original state. When implementing the action, you would probably need the `StateData` because this is called when a transition occurs; both the state before and the state after the transition are available and can be used. The new state is available via the variable `nextStateData` and the old state is available via the variable `StateData`. In our example we only use the newly created state, because we have only entry actions and our state always contains the complete state. In the next listing we implement all the entry actions of our FSM.

Listing 11.5   Implementation of the entry actions

```
class Inventory(publisher:ActorRef) extends Actor
  with FSM[State, StateData] {

  startWith(WaitForRequests, new StateData(0,Seq()))
```

```
when...

onTransition {
  case _ -> WaitForRequests => {
    if (!nextStateData.pendingRequests.isEmpty) {
      // go to next state
      self ! PendingRequests
    }
  }
  case _ -> WaitForPublisher => {
    publisher ! PublisherRequest
  }
  case _ -> ProcessRequest => {
    val request = nextStateData.pendingRequests.head
    reserveId += 1
    request.target !
      new BookReply(request.context, Right(reserveId))
    self ! Done
  }
  case _ -> ProcessSoldOut => {
    nextStateData.pendingRequests.foreach(request => {
      request.target !
        new BookReply(request.context, Left("SoldOut"))
    })
    self ! Done
  }
}
}
```

Entry action to check for pending requests

Entry action to send request to publisher

Entry action to send a reply to sender and signal that processing is done

Entry action to send an error reply to all PendingRequests and signal that processing is done

If you look closely, you'll see that we don't have a declaration for the state SoldOut, and that's because that state doesn't have an entry action. Now that we've defined our complete FSM, we need to call one important method, initialize. This method is needed to initialize and start up the FSM.

Listing 11.6 Initializing the FSM

```
class Inventory(publisher:ActorRef) extends Actor
  with FSM[State, StateData] {

  startWith(WaitForRequests, new StateData(0,Seq()))

  when...

  onTransition...

  initialize
}
```

The FSM is ready; all we need is a mockup implementation for the publisher, and we can test our FSM, which is shown in the next section.

TESTING THE FSM

The following example shows the mockup implementation of the `Publisher` actor. The `Publisher` will supply a predefined number of books. When all the books are gone, the `BookSupplySoldOut` reply is sent.

Listing 11.7   An implementation of the `Publisher` actor

```
class Publisher(totalNrBooks: Int, nrBooksPerRequest: Int)
  extends Actor {

  var nrLeft = totalNrBooks
  def receive = {
    case PublisherRequest => {
      if (nrLeft == 0)
        sender() ! BookSupplySoldOut          <———— No more books left
      else {
        val supply = min(nrBooksPerRequest, nrLeft)
        nrLeft -= supply
        sender() ! new BookSupply(supply)     <———— Supply a number of books
      }
    }
  }
}
```

Now we're ready to test the FSM. We can test the FSM by sending messages and checking if we get the expected result. But while debugging this component, there's additional available information. Akka's FSM has another helpful feature: it's possible to subscribe to the state changes of the FSM. This can prove useful in programming the application functionality, but it can also be helpful when testing. It will allow you to closely check if all the expected states were encountered, and if all transitions occur at the correct time. To subscribe to the transition event, all you have to do is to send a `SubscribeTransitionCallBack` message to the FSM. In our test, we want to collect these transition events within a test probe.

Listing 11.8 Subscribing to get the transition events

First we create
Publisher actor

Notice: we pass publisher when
creating inventory actor

```
val publisher = system.actorOf(Props(new Publisher(2,2)))

val inventory = system.actorOf(Props(new Inventory(publisher)))    <———
val stateProbe = TestProbe()
inventory ! new SubscribeTransitionCallBack(stateProbe.ref)
stateProbe.expectMsg(new CurrentState(inventory, WaitForRequests))  <———
```

Probe is subscribed to
transition notifications

Probe should get a notification

When subscribing to a request, the FSM responds with a `CurrentState` message. Our FSM starts in the `WaitForRequests` just as we expected. Now that we're subscribed to the transitions, we can send a `BookRequest` and see what happens:

> **Sending this message should trigger state changes.**

```
inventory ! new BookRequest("context1", replyProbe.ref)
stateProbe.expectMsg(
  new Transition(inventory, WaitForRequests, WaitForPublisher))
stateProbe.expectMsg(
  new Transition(inventory, WaitForPublisher, ProcessRequest))
stateProbe.expectMsg(
  new Transition(inventory, ProcessRequest, WaitForRequests))
replyProbe.expectMsg(new BookReply("context1", Right(1)))
```

Inventory actor will transition through three states to handle our preliminary book request

Finally, we'll get our reply.

As you can see, the FSM goes through different states before sending a reply. First, it has to get books from the publisher. The next step is to actually process the request. Finally, the state returns into the `WaitForRequests` state. But we know that the inventory has two copies, so when we send another request, the FSM goes through different states than the first time:

```
inventory ! new BookRequest("context2", replyProbe.ref)
stateProbe.expectMsg(
  new Transition(inventory, WaitForRequests, ProcessRequest))
stateProbe.expectMsg(
  new Transition(inventory, ProcessRequest, WaitForRequests))
replyProbe.expectMsg(new BookReply("context2", Right(2)))
```

This time through, just two states, then a reply, as expected

Because there was a book available, it skipped the `WaitForPublisher` state. At this point all the books have been sold, so what happens when we send another `BookRequest`?

```
inventory ! new BookRequest("context3", replyProbe.ref)
stateProbe.expectMsg(
  new Transition(inventory, WaitForRequests, WaitForPublisher))
stateProbe.expectMsg(
  new Transition(inventory, WaitForPublisher, ProcessSoldOut))
replyProbe.expectMsg(
  new BookReply("context3", Left("SoldOut")))
stateProbe.expectMsg(
  new Transition(inventory, ProcessSoldOut, SoldOut))
```

Each test requires merely that we send the same message.

Different outcome this time: we're sold out.

Now we get the `SoldOut` message, just as we designed. This is basically the functionality of the FSM, but a lot of times FSM models use timers to generate events and trigger transitions. Akka also supports timers within its `FSM` trait.

11.2.3 *Timers within FSM*

As we mentioned earlier, an FSM can model many problems, and a lot of solutions for these problems depend on timers, such as detecting an idle connection or a failure because the reply isn't received within a specified time. To demonstrate the use of timers, we'll change our FSM a little. When it's in the state `WaitingForPublisher`, we don't wait forever for the publisher to reply. If the publisher fails to respond, we want to send the request again. Figure 11.6 shows the changed FSM.

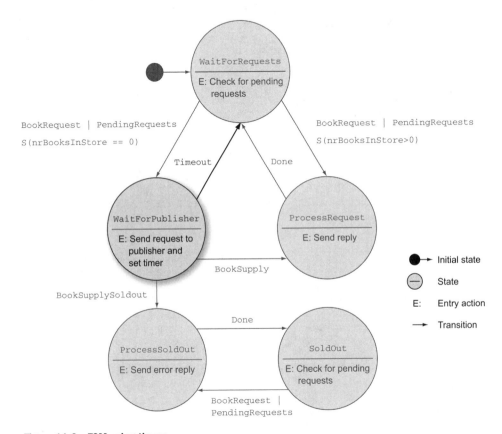

Figure 11.6   FSM using timers

The only change is that a timer is set as part of the entry action, and when this timer expires, the state changes to the `WaitForRequests` state. When this happens the `Wait-ForRequests` checks if there are `PendingRequests` (and there must be; otherwise the FSM wouldn't have been in the `WaitForPublisher` state in the first place). And because there are `PendingRequests`, the FSM goes to the `WaitForPublisher` state again, which triggers the entry action again, and a message is sent to the publisher.

    The changes we need to make here are minor. First, we have to set the timeout. This can be done by setting `stateTimeout` when declaring the state transitions of the

`WaitForPublisher` state. The second change is to define the transition when the timer expires. The changed when declaration becomes this:

```
when(WaitForPublisher, stateTimeout = 5 seconds) {        ◁─── Sets stateTimeout
  case Event(supply:BookSupply, data:StateData) => {
    goto(ProcessRequest) using data.copy(
      nrBooksInStore = supply.nrBooks)
  }
  case Event(BookSupplySoldOut, _) => {                        Defines
    goto(ProcessSoldOut)                                       timeout
  }                                                            transition
  case Event(StateTimeout,_) => goto(WaitForRequests)    ◁─┘
}
```

That is all we need to do to be able to retransmit to the publisher using a timer. This timer is canceled upon receipt of any other message while in the current state. You can rely on the fact that the `StateTimeout` message won't be processed after an intervening message. Let's see how this works by executing the following test.

Listing 11.9   Testing inventory with timers

```
val publisher = TestProbe()
val inventory = system.actorOf(
  Props(new InventoryWithTimer(publisher.ref)))
val stateProbe = TestProbe()
val replyProbe = TestProbe()

inventory ! new SubscribeTransitionCallBack(stateProbe.ref)
stateProbe.expectMsg(                                       Waits more
  new CurrentState(inventory, WaitForRequests))          than 5 seconds
                                                             for this
//start test                                                transition
inventory ! new BookRequest("context1", replyProbe.ref)
stateProbe.expectMsg(
  new Transition(inventory, WaitForRequests, WaitForPublisher))
publisher.expectMsg(PublisherRequest)
stateProbe.expectMsg(6 seconds,                        ◁─
  new Transition(inventory, WaitForPublisher, WaitForRequests))
stateProbe.expectMsg(
  new Transition(inventory, WaitForRequests, WaitForPublisher))
```

As you can see, when the publisher doesn't respond with a reply, the state changes after 5 seconds to the `WaitForRequests` state. There's another way to set the state-Timer. The timer can also be set by specifying the next state using the `forMax` method, for example, when you want to set the `stateTimer` differently, coming from another state. In the next snippet, you see an example of how you can use the `forMax` method:

```
goto(WaitForPublisher) using (newData) forMax (5 seconds)
```

This method will overrule the default timer setting specified in the `WaitFor-Publisher`when declaration. With this method it's also possible to turn off the timer by using `Duration.Inf` as the value in the `forMax` method.

Beside state timers, there's also support for sending messages using timers within FSM. The usage isn't complex, and therefore you just need a quick summary of the API. There are tree methods to deal with FSM timers. The first one is to create a timer:

```
setTimer(name: String,
         msg: Any,
         timeout: FiniteDuration,
         repeat: Boolean)
```

All the timers are referenced with their name. With this method you create a timer and define the name, the message to send when the timer expires, the interval of the timer, and if it's a repeating timer.

The next method is to cancel the timer:

```
cancelTimer(name: String)
```

This will cancel the timer immediately, and even when the timer has already fired and enqueued the message, the message won't be processed after this `cancelTimer` call.

The last method can be used to get the status of the timer at any time:

```
isTimerActive(name: String): Boolean
```

This method will return `true` when the timer is still active. This could be because the timer didn't fire yet, or because the timer has the repeat set to `true`.

11.2.4 *Termination of FSM*

Sometimes you need to do some cleanup when an actor finishes. The FSM has a specific handler for these cases: `onTermination`. This handler is also a partial function and takes a `StopEvent` as an argument:

```
StopEvent(reason: Reason, currentState: S, stateData: D)
```

There are three possible reasons this might be received.

- *Normal*—This is received when there's a normal termination.
- *Shutdown*—This is received when the FSM is stopped due to a shutdown.
- *Failure (cause: Any)*—This is received when the termination was caused by a failure.

A common termination handler would look something like this:

```
onTermination {
  case StopEvent(FSM.Normal, state, data)        => // ...
  case StopEvent(FSM.Shutdown, state, data)       => // ...
  case StopEvent(FSM.Failure(cause), state, data) => // ...
}
```

An FSM can be stopped from within the FSM. This can be done using the `stop` method, which takes the reason why the FSM is to be stopped. When the `ActorRef` is used to stop the actor, the shutdown reason is received by the termination handler.

The Akka `FSM` trait gives a complete toolkit to implement any FSM, without much extra effort. There's a clean separation between the actions of a state and the state transitions. The support of timers makes it easy to detect idle state or failures. And there's an easy translation from the FSM model to the actual implementation.

In all the examples about state in this book, the state is contained within one actor. But what can you do when you need some state among multiple actors? In the next section, we'll look at how you can do this using agents.

11.3 Implement shared state using agents

The best way to deal with state is to use that state only within one actor, but this isn't always possible. Sometimes you need to use the same state within different actors, and as we mentioned before, using shared state requires some kind of locking, and locking is hard to do correctly. For these situations, Akka has agents, which eliminate the need for locking. An agent guards the shared state and allows multiple threads to get the state, and is responsible for updating it on behalf of the various threads. Because the agent does the updating, the threads don't need to know about locking. In this section we'll describe how these agents are able to guard the state and how you can get them to share it. We'll start by addressing what agents are, and then show their basic usage. After that, we'll show extra agent functionality to track state updates.

11.3.1 Simple shared state with agents

How can the state of an agent be retrieved by using synchronous calls while updates to the state are done asynchronously? Akka accomplishes this by sending actions to the agent for each operation, where the messaging infrastructure will preclude a race condition (by assuring that only one send action at a time is running in a given `ExecutionContext`). For our example we need to share the number of copies sold for each book, so we'll create an agent that contains this value:

```
case class BookStatistics(val nameBook: String, nrSold: Int)
case class StateBookStatistics(val sequence: Long,
                    books: Map[String, BookStatistics])
```

`StateBookStatistics` is the state object, and it contains a sequence number, which can be used to check for changes and the actual book statistics. For each book a `BookStatistics` instance is created, which is put into a map using the title as the key. Figure 11.7 shows that to get the state object from the agent, we can use a simple method call.

When we need to update the number of books, we have to send the update action to the agent. In the example the first update message increases the number of books sold by one, and the second update increases the number by three. These actions can be sent from different actors or threads, but are queued like messages sent to actors.

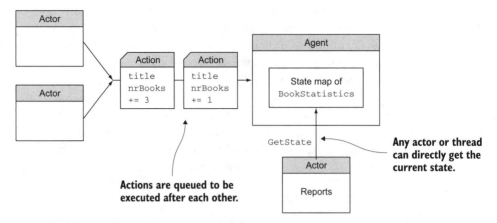

Figure 11.7 Updating and retrieving state using an agent

And just as messages sent to an actor, the actions are executed one at the time, which makes locking unnecessary.

To make this work, there's one important rule: all updates to the state must be done within the agent's execution context. This means that the state object contained by the agent must be immutable. In our example we can't update the content of the map. To be able to change it, we need to send an action to the agent to change the actual state. Let's see how we do this in the code.

We start by creating an agent. When creating an agent, we have to supply the initial state; in this case, an empty instance of StateBookStatistics:

```
import scala.concurrent.ExecutionContext.Implicits.global
import akka.agent.Agent

val stateAgent = new Agent(new StateBookStatistics(0,Map()))
```

When creating the agent, we need to provide an implicit ExecutionContext that's used by the agent. We use the global ExecutionContext defined by the import of scala.concurrent.ExecutionContext.Implicits.global. At this point the agent is guarding the state. As we mentioned earlier, the state of the agent can be simply retrieved by using synchronous calls. There are two ways to do that. The first is to make this call:

```
val currentBookStatistics = stateAgent()
```

Or you could use the second method, the get method, which does exactly the same thing:

```
val currentBookStatistics = stateAgent.get
```

Both methods return the current state of BookStatistics. So far nothing special, but updating BookStatistics can only be done by asynchronously sending actions to the agent. To update the state, we use the send method of the agent; we send the new state to the agent:

```
val newState = StateBookStatistics(1, Map(book -> bookStat ))
stateAgent send newState
```

But be careful with sending a complete, new state; this is only correct when the new state is independent of the previous state. In our case the state depends on the previous state, because other threads may have added new numbers or even other books before us. So we shouldn't use the method shown. To make sure that, when updating the state, we end up with the correct state, we invoke a function on the agent instead:

```
val book = "Akka in Action"
val nrSold = 1

stateAgent send( oldState => {
  val bookStat = oldState.books.get(book) match {
    case Some(bookState) =>
      bookState.copy(nrSold = bookState.nrSold + nrSold)
    case None =>  new BookStatistics(book, nrSold)
  }
  oldState.copy(oldState.sequence+1,
                oldState.books + (book -> bookStat))
})
```

We use the same send method, but instead of the new state, we send a function. This function is translating the old state into the new state. The function is updating the nrSold attribute with one state, and when there isn't already a BookStatistics object present for the book, a new object is created. The last step is to update the map.

Because the actions are executed one at any time, we don't need to worry that during this function the state will be changed, and therefore, we don't need a locking mechanism. You've seen how you can get the current state and how you can update the state; this is the basic functionality of an agent. But because the updates are asynchronous, it's sometimes necessary to wait for the update to be finished. This functionality is described in the next section.

11.3.2 *Waiting for the state update*

In some cases you need to update shared state and use the new state. For example, we need to know which book is selling the most, and when a book becomes popular, we want to notify the authors. To do this, we need to know when our update has been processed before we can check whether the book is the most popular. For this, agents have the alter method, which can be used for updating the state. It works exactly as the send method, only it returns a Future, which can be used to wait for the new state.

```
implicit val timeout = Timeout(1000)      ◁——— Since we'll be waiting, we need a timeout.
val future = stateAgent alter( oldState => {      ◁——┐
  val bookStat = oldState.books.get(book) match {      │  Our agent will give us
    case Some(bookState) =>                              │  a future to wait on.
```

```
      bookState.copy(nrSold = bookState.nrSold + nrSold)
    case None => new BookStatistics(book, nrSold)
  }
  oldState.copy(oldState.sequence+1,
    oldState.books + (book -> bookStat))
})
val newState = Await.result(future, 1 second)
```

> This is where we update the value.

> Our new state will be returned here when it's available.

In this example we performed the update using a function, but just as was the case with the `send` method, it's also possible to use the new state within the `alter` method. As you can see, the changed status is returned within the supplied `Future`. But this doesn't mean that this is the last update. It's possible that there are still pending changes for this state. We know that our change is processed and that the result of this change is returned, but there could be multiple changes at nearly the same time, and we want the final state, or another thread might need the final state and only knows that the process before it may have updated the state. So this thread doesn't have any reference from the `alter` method; it needs to wait. The agent provides us a `Future` for this. This future finishes when the pending state changes are all processed.

```
val future = stateAgent.future
val newState = Await.result(future, 1 second)
```

This way, we can be sure of the latest state at this moment. Keep in mind that new agents are created when using `map` or `flatMap`, leaving the original agents untouched. They're called *persistent* for this reason. An example with a map shows the creation of a new agent:

```
import scala.concurrent.ExecutionContext.Implicits.global
val agent1 = Agent(3)

val agent2 = agent1 map (_ + 1)
```

When using this notation, `agent2` is a newly created agent that contains the value 4, and `agent1` is just the same as before (it still contains the value 3).

We showed that when shared state was needed, we could use agents to manage the state. The consistency of the state is guaranteed by requiring that updates only be done in the agent's context. These updates are triggered by sending actions to the agent.

11.4   Summary

Clearly, writing applications that never hold state is an unattainable goal. In this chapter you saw several approaches to state management that Akka provides. The key take-aways are these:

- Finite-state machines, which can seem specialized and perhaps daunting, are pretty easy to implement with Akka, and the resulting code is clean and maintainable. Their implementation as a trait results in code where the actions are separated from the code that defines the transitions.

- Agents provide another means of state that's especially useful when several actors need access.
- Both techniques—FSMs and agents—allow you to employ some shared state without falling back into having to manage locks.
- Using timers with FSMs and futures with agents provides a level of orchestration in implementing state changes.

This chapter took you through examples that showed the implementation of complex, dependent interactions modifying shared state. We accomplished this while still keeping the spirit of our stateless messaging principles intact, by using mechanisms that allow us to coordinate multiple actors around a set of shared states.

System integration

In this chapter

- Exploring endpoints and how to use them
- Using Apache Camel with Akka
- Implementing an HTTP interface with Akka
- Managing consumers and producers

In this chapter we'll look at some examples of actors being used to integrate with other external systems. Today applications are increasingly complex, requiring connections to different information services and applications. It's almost impossible to create a system that doesn't either rely on information from or supply information to other systems. To be able to communicate with other systems, the two sides have to go through an agreed-upon interface. We'll start with some enterprise integration patterns (EIPs). Next, we'll describe how *akka-camel* (an Akka extension for *Apache Camel*, a project that simplifies integration over many transports) can help a system integrate with other external systems, especially in a request/response style. We'll finish with an HTTP example using *akka-http* and detail the different approaches to integration with Akka.

12.1 Message endpoints

In the preceding chapters, we showed how to build systems using various enterprise patterns. In this section we'll describe the patterns that apply when different systems need to exchange information. Consider a system that needs customer data from a customer relations application, yet you don't want to manage this data in multiple applications. The implementation of an interface between two systems isn't always easy, because the interface contains two areas: the transport layer and the data that's sent over this transport layer. Both areas have to be addressed to integrate the systems. There are also patterns to help you design the integration between multiple systems.

For example, say you're creating an order system for use in a book stockroom; our system processes orders from all kinds of customers. These customers can order the books by visiting the store. The bookstore already uses an application to sell and order books, so the new system needs to exchange data with this existing application. This can only be done if both systems agree on which messages are sent and how they're sent. Because you probably can't change the external application, you have to create a component that can send and/or receive messages from the existing application. This component is called an *endpoint*. Endpoints are part of our system, and are the glue between the external system and the rest of our system, which is shown in figure 12.1.

The endpoint has the responsibility of encapsulating the interface between the two systems in such a way that the application itself doesn't need to know how the request is received. This is done by making the transport pluggable, using a canonical data format, and standardizing on a request/response style of communication. There are a lot of different transport protocols to potentially support: HTTP, TCP, message queues, or simple files. After receiving the message, the endpoint has to translate the message into a message format that's supported by our order system. Translating the message this way means the rest of the system doesn't know that the order was received from an external system. In this example the endpoint receives a request from the external system and sends a response back. This is called a *consumer endpoint* because it consumes the request. It's also possible that our system needs some data from another system, for example, the customer details, which are kept in the customer relations application.

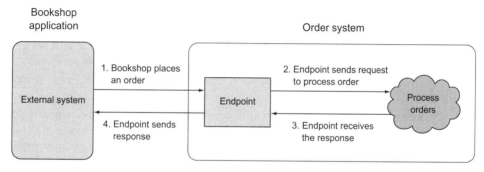

Figure 12.1 Endpoint as glue between order system and bookshop application

Order system

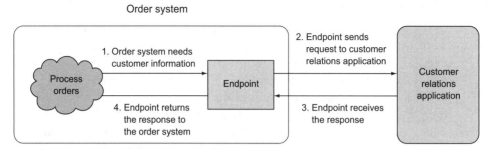

Figure 12.2   Endpoint as glue between order system and customer relation application

In figure 12.2 the order system initiates the communication between systems, and because the endpoint produces a message that's sent to the external system, this is called a *producer endpoint*. Both usages of the endpoints hide the details of the communication from the rest of the system, and when the interface between the two systems changes, only the endpoint needs to be changed. There are a few patterns in the EIP catalog that apply for such endpoints. The first pattern we'll describe is the *normalizer pattern.*

12.1.1 *Normalizer*

You've seen that our order system receives the orders from the bookshop application, but it's possible that our system could also receive orders from a web shop, or by customers sending email. You can use the normalizer pattern to make these different sources all feed into a single interface on the application side. The pattern translates the different external messages to a common, canonical message. This way all the message processing can be reused, without our system knowing that different systems are sending these messages.

We'll create three different endpoints to consume the different messages, but translate them into the same message, which is sent to the rest of the system. In figure 12.3 we have the three endpoints, which handle the details on how to get the needed information and translate it into the common message format the order system expects.

Translating the different messages into a common message is called the *normalizer pattern.* This pattern combines router and translator patterns into an endpoint. This implementation of the normalizer pattern is the most common one. But when connecting to multiple systems using different transport protocols and different messages, it's desirable to reuse the translators of the messages; this makes the pattern implementation a bit more complex. Let's assume that there's another bookshop that's connecting to this system using the same messages but using message queues to send those messages. In cases of more-complex implementations such as this, the normalizer pattern can be considered as three parts. Figure 12.4 shows the three parts. The first is the implementation of the protocol; next, a router decides which translator has to be used; and finally, the actual translation takes place.

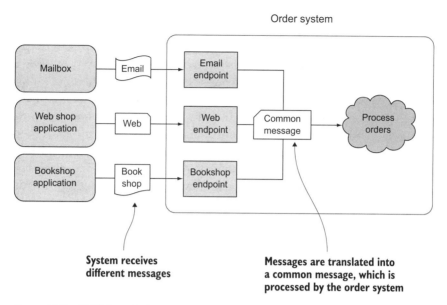

Figure 12.3 Multiple endpoint example

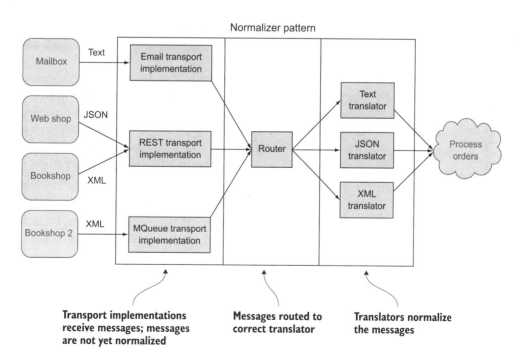

Figure 12.4 The three parts of the normalizer pattern

Being able to route the message to the correct translator requires the ability to detect the type of the incoming message. How this is done differs greatly depending on the external systems and types of messages. In our example we support three types of messages—plain-text, JSON, and XML—which can be received from any of three transport layer types—email, HTTP, and message queues. In most cases, the simplest implementation would make the most sense: the endpoint and translation (and no router) implemented as a single component. In our example it's possible to skip the router for the email and message queue protocol and go directly to the correct translator, because we receive only one type of message. This is a trade-off between flexibility and complexity; when using the router, it's possible to receive all types of messages on all protocols without any extra effort, but we have more components. Only the router needs to know how to distinguish between all the message types. Tracing the messages can be more difficult, which can make this solution more complex, and most of the time you don't need this flexibility, because only one type of system is being integrated (supporting only one message type).

12.1.2 *Canonical data model*

The normalizer pattern works well when connecting one system to another external system. But when the connectivity requirements between the systems increase, you need more and more endpoints. Let's go back to our example. We have two back office systems: the order system and the customer relations system. In the previous examples, the shops were only connected to the order system, but when they also need to communicate with the customer relations system, the implementation becomes more complex, as shown in figure 12.5.

At this point it isn't important which system is implementing the endpoints; the problem is that when it's necessary to add a new system to integrate with, we need to add more and more endpoints—one for the shop applications, and two endpoints to integrate the existing back office systems. Over time, increasing the number of systems means that the number of endpoints will spiral out of control.

To solve this problem, we can use the canonical data model. This pattern connects multiple applications using interface(s) that are independent of any specific system. Then each system we wish to integrate with will have to have incoming and outgoing messages converted to the canonical form for the given endpoint.

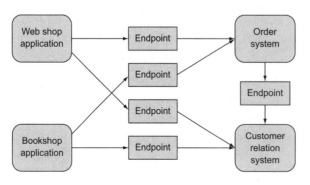

Figure 12.5 **Connectivity diagram between systems**

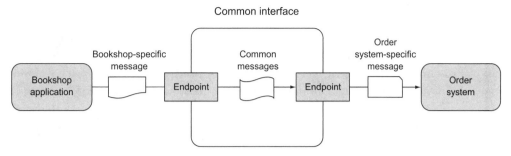

Figure 12.6　Use a common interface between systems

This way, every system has an endpoint that implements a common interface and uses common messages. Figure 12.6 shows that when the bookshop application wants to send a message to the order system, the message is first translated to the canonical format, and then it's sent using the common transport layer. The endpoint of the order system receives the common message, which translates it to an order system message. This looks like an unnecessary translation, but when applying this to a number of systems the benefit is clear; see figure 12.7

As you can see, every system or application has one endpoint. And when the web shop needs to send a message to the order system, it uses the same endpoint as when sending it to the customer relations system. When we add a new system to be integrated, we need only one endpoint instead of the four shown in figure 12.5. This reduces the number of endpoints greatly when there is a large number of integrated systems.

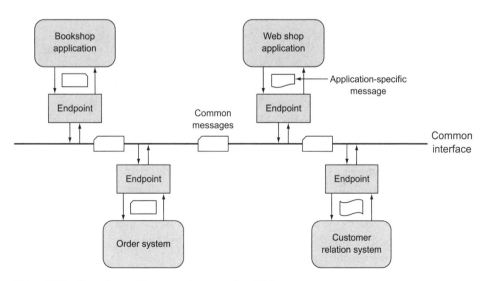

Figure 12.7　Canonical pattern used to connect multiple systems

The normalizer pattern and the canonical data model are quite helpful when you're integrating a system with other external systems or applications. The normalizer pattern is used to connect several similar clients to another system. But when the number of integrated systems increases, you need the canonical data model, which looks like the normalizer pattern, because it also uses normalized messages. The difference is that the canonical data model provides an additional level of indirection between the application's individual data formats and those used by the remote systems, whereas the normalizer is only within one application. The benefit of this additional level of indirection is that, when you add a new application to the system, only the translator into these common messages has to be created; no changes to the existing system are required.

Now that you know how you can use endpoints, the next step is to implement them. When implementing an endpoint, you need to address the transport layer and the message. Implementing the transport layer can be hard, but most of the time the implementation is application-independent. Wouldn't it be nice if someone already implemented the transport layers? In fact, this is what Apache Camel provides. Let's see how it can help you with implementing an endpoint.

12.2 *Implementing endpoints using Apache Camel*

Apache Camel's goal is to make integration easier and more accessible. Apache Camel makes it possible to implement the standard EIPs in a few lines of code. This is achieved by addressing three areas:

- Concrete implementations of the widely used EIPs
- Connectivity to a great variety of transports and APIs
- Easy-to-use domain-specific languages (DSLs) to wire EIPs and transports together

The support for a great variety of transport layers is the reason why you'd want to use Apache Camel with Akka, because this will enable you to implement different transport layers without much effort. In this section we'll explain what Apache Camel is and how to send and receive messages using the Camel `Consumer` and `Producer`.

The Akka Camel module allows you to use Apache Camel within Akka, and enables you to use all the transport protocols and APIs implemented in Apache Camel. A few examples of protocols supported are HTTP, SOAP, TCP, FTP, SMTP, and JMS. At the time of writing, approximately 80 protocols and APIs are supported.

Using akka-camel is easy. Just add `akka-camel` to the project dependencies, and you can use the Camel `Consumer` and/or `Producer` classes to create an endpoint. Using these classes will hide the implementation of the transport layer. The only functionality you have to implement is the translations between your system messages and the interface messages.

Because the transport layer implementations are completely hidden, it's possible to decide which protocol to use at runtime. This is the next great strength of using akka-camel. As long as the message structure is the same, no code changes have to be made. So when testing, you could write all the messages to the file system, because you don't have the correct external system available in the test environment, and as soon as the system is in the acceptance environment, you can change the used Camel protocol into an HTTP interface, for example, with only one configuration setting.

The akka-camel module works internally with Apache Camel classes. Important Apache Camel classes are the `CamelContext` and the `ProducerTemplate`. The `Camel-Context` represents a single Camel routing rule base, and the `ProducerTemplate` is needed when producing messages. For more details, look at the Apache Camel documentation at http://camel.apache.org. The akka-camel module hides the use of these Apache Camel classes, but sometimes you'll need them when more control of how messages are received or produced is required. The akka-camel module creates a `Camel` extension for each actor system. Because several internal actors are created, they need to be started in the correct `ActorSystem`. To get a system's `Camel` extension, you can use the `CamelExtension` object:

```
val camelExtension = CamelExtension(system)
```

When a specific Apache Camel class is needed, like the context or the `Producer-Template`, this extension can be used. You'll see some examples in the next sections. We'll start with a simple consumer example that reads files and changes them using other protocols like TCP connections and ActiveMQ. We'll end this section by creating a producer that can send messages to the created consumer. So let's begin by using akka-camel to create a consumer.

12.2.1 Implement a consumer endpoint receiving messages from an external system

The example we'll implement is an order system receiving messages from a bookshop. This order system must be able to receive messages from different book stores. Let's say the received messages are XML files in a directory. The transport layer in this case is the file system. The endpoint of the order system needs to track new files, and when there's a new file, it has to parse the XML content and create a message the system can process. Before you start implementing your endpoint consumer, you need to have your messages, shown in figure 12.8.

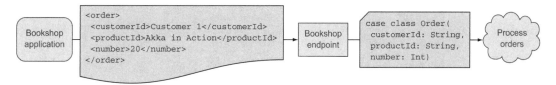

Figure 12.8   Messages received and sent by our endpoint

The first message to look at is the XML sent by the bookshop application to our endpoint indicating that customer 1 wants 20 copies of *Akka in Action*. The second message is the class definition of the message the order system can process.

IMPLEMENTING A CAMEL CONSUMER

Now that you have our messages, you can start implementing your consumer endpoint. We'll start by extending the `Actor` class with the Camel `Consumer` trait instead of the normal Akka `Actor` class:

```
class OrderConsumerXml extends akka.camel.Consumer {
  // more code to follow
}
```

The next step is to set the transport protocol; this is done by overriding the endpoint URI. This URI is used by Apache Camel to define the transport protocol and its properties. In your case you want to be able to change this URI, so you'll add the URI to your constructor. And you need to implement the `receive` method, because it's also an Akka actor. Figure 12.9 shows the implementation of the consumer.

Messages from the Camel component are received as a `CamelMessage`. A `CamelMessage` is a message from the akka-camel module, which is independent from the used protocol layer and contains a body—the actual message received—as well as a map of headers. The content of these headers can depend on the protocol used. In the examples in this section, you don't use these headers.

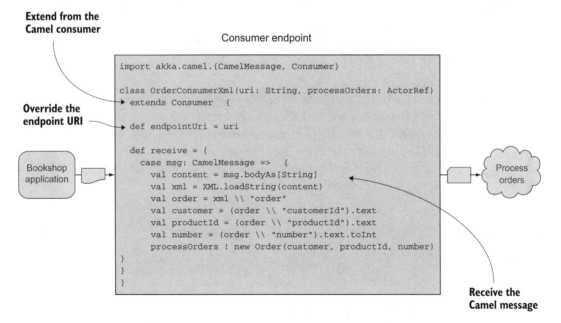

Extend from the Camel consumer

Consumer endpoint

Override the endpoint URI

```
import akka.camel.{CamelMessage, Consumer}

class OrderConsumerXml(uri: String, processOrders: ActorRef)
  extends Consumer   {

  def endpointUri = uri

  def receive = {
    case msg: CamelMessage =>   {
      val content = msg.bodyAs[String]
      val xml = XML.loadString(content)
      val order = xml \\ "order"
      val customer = (order \\ "customerId").text
      val productId = (order \\ "productId").text
      val number = (order \\ "number").text.toInt
      processOrders ! new Order(customer, productId, number)
    }
  }
}
```

Bookshop application

Process orders

Receive the Camel message

Figure 12.9   `OrderConsumerXml`, the implementation of the consumer endpoint

The body is application-dependent, so you have to implement the conversion of the data yourself. In this example you convert the body to a string and parse the XML into an Order message, and send it to the next actor that's available to process the order.

You've implemented the translation from the XML to the Order object, but how do you pick up these files? This is all done by Apache Camel. All you have to do is set the URI. Use the following URI to tell Apache Camel you want it to pick up files:

```
val camelUri = "file:messages"
```

Apache Camel defines a component for every kind of transport that it supports. The URI in the example above starts with a component name. In this case you want the file component. The second part depends on the chosen component. When using the file component, the second part is the directory where the message files are placed. You expect your files in the directory messages. All the possible components and options can be found at http://camel.apache.org/components.html.

Let's start creating the consumer so you can see how that works:

```
val probe = TestProbe()
val camelUri = "file:messages"
val consumer = system.actorOf(
  Props(new OrderConsumerXml(camelUri, probe.ref)))
```

The CamelExtension creates internal components asynchronously, and you have to wait for these components to start before you can proceed with your test. To detect that the consumer startup has finished, you need to use CamelExtension .activationFutureFor as shown in the next listing.

Listing 12.1 Making sure Camel is started

```
val camelExtention = CamelExtension(system)           ⟵┘ Gets CamelExtension for
                                                          this Akka system
val activated = camelExtention.activationFutureFor(   ⟵── Gets activation future
  consumer)(timeout = 10 seconds, executor = system.dispatcher)
Await.ready(activated, 5 seconds)            ⟵──── Waits for Camel to finish starting up
```

This extension contains the activationFutureFor method, which returns a Future. The Future triggers when the Camel route is done starting up. After that, you can proceed with our test.

Awaiting with Await.ready makes sense in the context of running tests; in more realistic code, you'd handle the result of the Future as described in chapter 5.

Listing 12.2 Test the order consumer

```
val msg = new Order("me", "Akka in Action", 10)
val xml = <order>
            <customerId>{ msg.customerId }</customerId>
            <productId>{ msg.productId }</productId>
```

```
           <number>{ msg.number }</number>
        </order>                              ←—— Creates XML content
val msgFile = new File(dir, "msg1.xml")

FileUtils.write(msgFile, xml.toString())   ←—— Writes file in message directory

probe.expectMsg(msg)                  ←—— Expects Order message to be sent by Consumer

system.stop(consumer)
```

As you can see, you receive an `Order` message when a file containing XML is placed in the message directory. Note: You're not required to provide any code dealing with checking for files and reading them in; all this functionality is provided by the Apache Camel file component.

CHANGING THE TRANSPORT LAYER OF YOUR CONSUMER

This is nice, but it's just the starting point of Camel's real benefit. Let's say that you also get these XML messages though a TCP connection. How should you implement this? Actually, you already have. To support the TCP connection, all you have to do is change the used URI and add some libraries to the runtime.

Listing 12.3   TCP test using order consumer

```
val probe = TestProbe()
val camelUri =
  "mina:tcp://localhost:8888?textline=true&sync=false"   ←—— Uses another URI
val consumer = system.actorOf(
  Props(new OrderConsumerXml(camelUri, probe.ref)))
val activated = CamelExtension(system).activationFutureFor(
  consumer)(timeout = 10 seconds, executor = system.dispatcher)
Await.ready(activated, 5 seconds)

val msg = new Order("me", "Akka in Action", 10)
val xml = <order>
            <customerId>{ msg.customerId }</customerId>
            <productId>{ msg.productId }</productId>        Due to textline option,
            <number>{ msg.number }</number>                newlines indicate end of
          </order>                                         message, so we need to
                                                           remove them
val xmlStr = xml.toString().replace("\n", "")   ←—┘
val sock = new Socket("localhost", 8888)
val ouputWriter = new PrintWriter(sock.getOutputStream, true)
ouputWriter.println(xmlStr)                 ←—┐
ouputWriter.flush()                           │
                                              │ Sends XML message using TCP
probe.expectMsg(msg)

ouputWriter.close()
system.stop(consumer)
```

In this example you use the Apache Mina component to deal with the TCP connection. The second part of the URI looks completely different, but is needed to configure the connection. You start with the protocol you need (TCP), and then you indicate on which interface and port you want to listen. After this you include two options (as parameters):

- *textline=true*—This indicates that you expect plain text over this connection, and that each message is ended with a newline.
- *sync=false*—This indicates that you don't create a response.

As you can see, without any code changes to the consumer, you can change the transport protocol. Can you change to any protocol without code changes? The answer is no; some protocols do require code changes. For example, what about a protocol that needs a confirmation? Let's see how you can do that. Let's assume that your TCP connection needs an XML response. You need to change your consumer, but it's not that hard. You just send the response to the sender and the Camel consumer will take care of the rest.

Listing 12.4 Confirm order consumer

```
class OrderConfirmConsumerXml(uri: String, next: ActorRef)
  extends Consumer {

  def endpointUri = uri

  def receive = {
    case msg: CamelMessage => {
      try {
        val content = msg.bodyAs[String]
        val xml = XML.loadString(content)
        val order = xml \ "order"
        val customer = (order \ "customerId").text
        val productId = (order \ "productId").text
        val number = (order \ "number").text.toInt
        next ! new Order(customer, productId, number)
        sender() ! "<confirm>OK</confirm>"          <--- Sends reply to
      } catch {                                            the sender
        case ex: Exception =>
          sender() ! "<confirm>%s</confirm>".format(ex.getMessage)
      }
    }
  }
}
```

That's all, and when you change the URI, you can test our new consumer. But before you do that, you also have to catch a possible exception, and didn't we say in chapter 4 that we let our actors crash if there are any problems? And that the supervisor should correct these problems? We're now implementing an endpoint that's the separation between a synchronous interface and a message-passing system, which is an asynchronous interface. On these boundaries between the synchronous and asynchronous interfaces, the rules are a little different because the synchronous interface always expects a result, even when it fails. When you try to use supervision, you're missing the sender details to correctly service the request. And you can't use the restart hook either, because the supervisor can decide to resume after an exception, which doesn't result in calling the restart hooks. Therefore, you catch the exception and are able to return the expected response. Having said this, let's test your consumer.

Listing 12.5 TCP test using order confirm consumer

```
val probe = TestProbe()
val camelUri =
  "mina:tcp://localhost:8887?textline=true"          ⟵— Removes sync parameter;
val consumer = system.actorOf(                             default is true
  Props(new OrderConfirmConsumerXml(camelUri, probe.ref)))
val activated = CamelExtension(system).activationFutureFor(
  consumer)(timeout = 10 seconds, executor = system.dispatcher)
Await.ready(activated, 5 seconds)

val msg = new Order("me", "Akka in Action", 10)
val xml = <order>
            <customerId>{ msg.customerId }</customerId>
            <productId>{ msg.productId }</productId>
            <number>{ msg.number }</number>
          </order>
val xmlStr = xml.toString().replace("\n", "")
val sock = new Socket("localhost", 8887)
val ouputWriter = new PrintWriter(sock.getOutputStream, true)
ouputWriter.println(xmlStr)
ouputWriter.flush()
val responseReader = new BufferedReader(              Receives
  new InputStreamReader(sock.getInputStream))         confirmation
val response = responseReader.readLine()         ⟵—  message
response must be("<confirm>OK</confirm>")
probe.expectMsg(msg)              ⟵— Order is still
                                     received
responseReader.close()
ouputWriter.close()
system.stop(consumer)
```

You hardly changed the consumer and were able to generate responses over TCP, which shows the benefit of Apache Camel.

USING THE CAMELCONTEXT

There's one other example we want to show. Sometimes a Camel component needs more configuration than only a URI.

For example, suppose you want to use the ActiveMQ component. To be able to use this, you need to add the component to the CamelContext and define the message queue broker. This requires the CamelContext.

Listing 12.6 Add broker configuration to CamelContext

```
val camelContext = CamelExtension(system).context       Component name
camelContext.addComponent("activemq",                   should be used in URI
  ActiveMQComponent.activeMQComponent(            ⟵—
    "vm:(broker:(tcp://localhost:8899)?persistent=false)"))
```

First you get the `CamelExtension` for the used system, and then you add the ActiveMQ component to the `CamelContext`. In this case you create a broker that listens on port 8899 (and doesn't use persistence queues).

Now you can execute the test. For this example, you use the previous example of a consumer that doesn't return a response.

Listing 12.7 Test when using ActiveMQ

```
val camelUri = "activemq:queue:xmlTest"
val consumer = system.actorOf(
  Props(new OrderConsumerXml(camelUri, probe.ref)))

val activated = CamelExtension(system).activationFutureFor(
  consumer)(timeout = 10 seconds, executor = system.dispatcher)
Await.ready(activated, 5 seconds)

val msg = new Order("me", "Akka in Action", 10)
val xml = <order>
            <customerId>{ msg.customerId }</customerId>
            <productId>{ msg.productId }</productId>
            <number>{ msg.number }</number>
          </order>
sendMQMessage(xml.toString())
probe.expectMsg(msg)

system.stop(consumer)
```

> ActiveMQ URI starting with the same name as the component when adding the ActiveMQ component

The test isn't any different from the other consumer test, other than how the message is delivered.

Because a broker is started, you also need to stop it when you're ready. This can be done using ActiveMQ's `BrokerRegistry`:

```
val brokers = BrokerRegistry.getInstance().getBrokers
brokers.foreach { case (name, broker) => broker.stop() }
```

Using the `BrokerRegistry`, you can close all the brokers. Note that `getBrokers` returns a `java.util.Map`. You use `collection.JavaConversions` to convert this map into a Scala `Map`.

As you can see, it's simple to implement a `Consumer`. And because Camel has a lot of components, this gives you the ability to support many transport protocols without any effort .

12.2.2 *Implement a producer endpoint sending messages to an external system*

In the previous section, we created an endpoint that receives messages. In this section, we'll implement the functionality to send messages using Camel. To show the producer functionality, we'll move to the other side of our example—with the consumer we were working on an endpoint at the order system, but for these examples we'll implement an endpoint in the bookshop application; see figure 12.10.

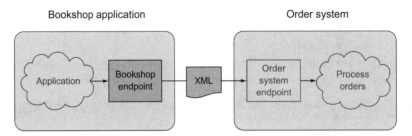

Figure 12.10   Producer endpoint sending messages

To implement a producer, akka-camel has another trait you'll extend: `Producer`. The producer is also an actor, but the receive method is already implemented. The simplest implementation is just to extend the `Producer` trait and set the URI, as shown in figure 12.11.

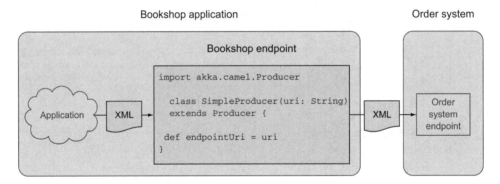

Figure 12.11   Implementation of a simple producer endpoint

This producer sends all received messages to the Camel component defined by the URI. So when you create an XML string and send it to the producer, it can be sent using a TCP connection. In this example you use your consumer from the previous section to receive the message. And because you now have two Camel actors, you can't start the test until both actors are ready. To wait for both, you use the `Future.sequence` method, which was discussed in chapter 5.

Listing 12.8   Test simple producer

```
implicit val ExecutionContext = system.dispatcher
val probe = TestProbe()
val camelUri = "mina:tcp://localhost:8885?textline=true"
val consumer = system.actorOf(
  Props(new OrderConfirmConsumerXml(camelUri, probe.ref)))

val producer = system.actorOf(
  Props(new SimpleProducer(camelUri)))          ⟵  Creates
val activatedCons = CamelExtension(system).activationFutureFor(          simple
                                                                        producer
```

```
  consumer)(timeout = 10 seconds, executor = system.dispatcher)
val activatedProd = CamelExtension(system).activationFutureFor(
  producer)(timeout = 10 seconds, executor = system.dispatcher)
val camel = Future.sequence(List(activatedCons, activatedProd))
Await.result(camel, 5 seconds)
```
⟵ **Creates Future to wait for both actors to finish starting up**

Every message will be sent to the defined URI. But most of the time you need to translate the message to another format. In your shop system, you use the `Order` object when sending messages between the system actors. To solve this you can override the `transformOutgoingMessage`. This method is called before sending the message. Here you can do the translation of your message to the expected XML.

Listing 12.9 Translate message in producer

```
class OrderProducerXml(uri: String) extends Producer {         Indicates that you
  def endpointUri = uri                                        don't expect a
  override def oneway: Boolean = true        ⟵                 response

  override protected def transformOutgoingMessage(message: Any): Any = ⟵
    message match {                                        Implementing
      case msg: Order => {                          transformOutgoingMessage
        val xml = <order>
                    <customerId>{ msg.customerId }</customerId>
                    <productId>{ msg.productId }</productId>
                    <number>{ msg.number }</number>
                  </order>
        xml.toString().replace("\n", "")  ⟵  Creates message ended
      }                                        with a newline
      case other => message
    }
}
```

In the `transformOutgoingMessage` you create an XML string and, just as in the consumer test, you need a message on a single line ended with a new line. Because your consumer doesn't send a response, you need to signal the underlying framework that it doesn't need to wait for one. Otherwise, it will be consuming resources for no reason. It's possible that you could consume all the threads, which will stop your system. So it's important to override the `oneway` attribute when there are no responses.

Now you're able to send an `Order` object to the producer endpoint, and the producer translates this into XML. But what happens when you do have responses, for example when you use the `OrderConfirmConsumerXML`? Figure 12.12 shows the default behavior of a producer that sends the received `CamelMessage`, which contains the XML response to the original sender.

But just as you need to translate your message when sending it, you need also a translation of the response. You don't want to expose the `CamelMessage` to the rest of your system. To support this you can use the `transformResponse` method. This method is used to convert the received message into a system-supported message, and the producer will send this response.

Listing 12.10   Translate responses and message in producer

```scala
class OrderConfirmProducerXml(uri: String) extends Producer {
  def endpointUri = uri
  override def oneway: Boolean = false

  override def transformOutgoingMessage(message: Any): Any =
    message match {
      case msg: Order => {
        val xml = <order>
                    <customerId>{ msg.customerId }</customerId>
                    <productId>{ msg.productId }</productId>
                    <number>{ msg.number }</number>
                  </order>
        xml.toString().replace("\n", "") + "\n"
      }
      case other => message
    }

  override def transformResponse(message: Any): Any =
    message match {
      case msg: CamelMessage => {
        try {
          val content = msg.bodyAs[String]
          val xml = XML.loadString(content)
          val res = (xml \ "confirm").text
          res
        } catch {
          case ex: Exception =>
            "TransformException: %s".format(ex.getMessage)
        }
      }
      case other => message
    }
}
```

Transforms CamelMessage into a String containing the result

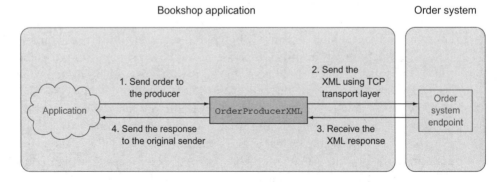

Figure 12.12   **Using responses with the Camel producer**

The `transformResponse` is called when a response is received, before it's sent to the sender of the initial request. In this example you parse the received XML and select the value of the confirm tag. Let's see how this works in a test.

Listing 12.11   Test the producer with responses

```
implicit val ExecutionContext = system.dispatcher
val probe = TestProbe()
val camelUri ="mina:tcp://localhost:9889?textline=true"
val consumer = system.actorOf(
  Props(new OrderConfirmConsumerXml(camelUri, probe.ref)))

val producer = system.actorOf(
  Props(new OrderConfirmProducerXml(camelUri)))

val activatedCons = CamelExtension(system).activationFutureFor(
  consumer)(timeout = 10 seconds, executor = system.dispatcher)
val activatedProd = CamelExtension(system).activationFutureFor(
  producer)(timeout = 10 seconds, executor = system.dispatcher)

val camel = Future.sequence(List(activatedCons, activatedProd))
Await.result(camel, 5 seconds)
val probeSend = TestProbe()
val msg = new Order("me", "Akka in Action", 10)
probeSend.send(producer, msg)
probe.expectMsg(msg)                                 Message is received
probeSend.expectMsg("OK")                            by Consumer
                                      Confirmation is received
system.stop(producer)                 by your test class
system.stop(consumer)
```

This is nice, but you don't want to send the confirmation to the original sender of the request, but to another actor. Is this possible? Yes, there's a method called `route-Response` that's responsible for sending the received response to the original sender. This can be overridden, and here you can implement the functionality to send the message to another actor. But be careful when you're also using the `transform-Response` method: you have to call it in this overridden method because the default implementation calls the `transformResponse` before sending the response message to the original sender.

As you can see, creating producers is as easy as creating consumers. Apache Camel provides a lot of functionality when creating an endpoint, and support for a lot of transport protocols. This is the greatest benefit of using the akka-camel module: to get support for a lot of protocols without additional effort.

In the next section, we'll look at two examples of consumer endpoints that contain the actual connection to the order system for creating a response.

12.3   *Implementing an HTTP interface*

In the preceding sections, you saw how Apache Camel can help you to implement endpoints that can work over many kinds of transports. A side effect of defining one way of communicating over many protocols/transports, is that it gets harder to use specific features of a particular protocol; for instance, if you want to write an HTTP interface that takes advantage of all of HTTP's features.

Next, we'll show an example of how to use Akka to build an HTTP service. Apache Camel can be used to implement a minimal HTTP interface, but when you need more functionality or specific HTTP support, Apache Camel may be too minimalist. The akka-http module provides an API to build HTTP clients and servers. The example we'll show is simple, but it addresses the issues of general integration techniques. We'll start with the example description and then show you the akka-http implementation.

12.3.1   *The HTTP example*

We'll implement our order system example again. But this time we'll also implement a mock-up of our order-processing system. We can see how the endpoint forwards the request to the system and waits for the response before returning its response. We'll do this by implementing one endpoint that uses the HTTP transport protocol. We'll use the REST architectural style for defining the API of the HTTP service. An overview of this example is shown in figure 12.13.

The example has two interfaces: one between the web shop and the endpoint, and one between the endpoint and the ProcessOrders actor. We'll start by defining the messages for both interfaces. The order system will support two functions. The first function adds a new order, and the second function gets the status of an order. The HTTP REST interface we'll implement supports a POST and a GET. With the POST we'll add a new order to our system, and with the GET we'll retrieve the status of that order. Let's start with adding an order. Figure 12.14 shows the messages and the flow.

The web shop sends a POST request to the endpoint containing the XML already used in the Camel examples in section 12.2.1. The endpoint translates it to the order message and sends it to the rest of the system (the ProcessOrders actor). When done, the response is a TrackingOrder object, which contains the order, a unique ID, and the current status. The endpoint translates this to a confirmation XML message containing the ID and status and sends it back to the web shop. In this example the new order got the id1 and the status received.

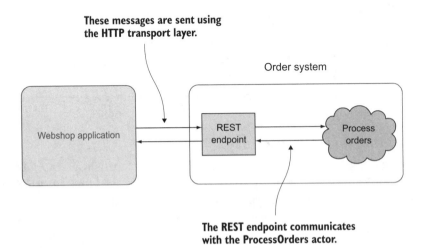

Figure 12.13   HTTP REST example overview

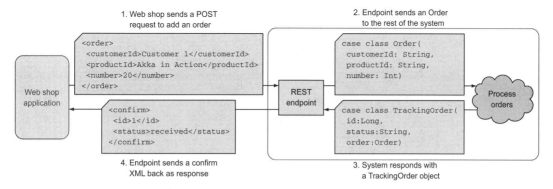

Figure 12.14   Message flow when adding an order

Figure 12.15 shows the messages when getting the status of an order already in the order system.

To get the status for the order with ID 1, the web shop will send a GET request to /orders/1. The REST endpoint translates the GET request to an OrderId. The response of the system is again a TrackingOrder message when the order is found. The endpoint translates this response into a statusResponse XML. When the order isn't found, the system will respond with a NoSuchOrder object, shown in figure 12.16.

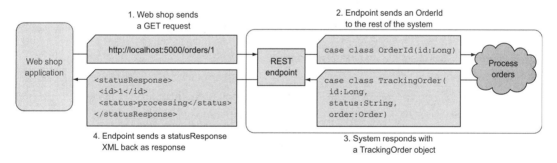

Figure 12.15   Message flow when getting the status of an order

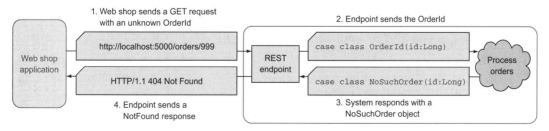

Figure 12.16   Message flow when trying to get the status of an unknown order

Process orders

**Receive a
new order**

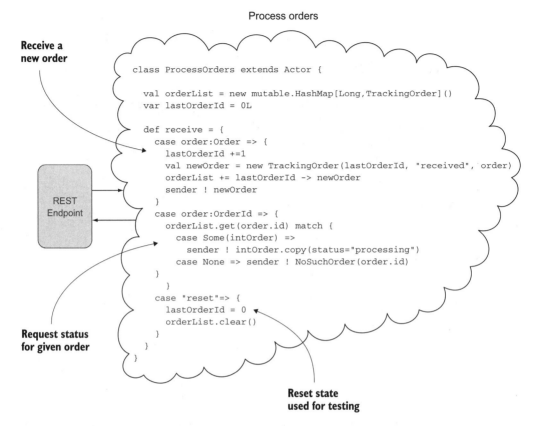

REST
Endpoint

```scala
class ProcessOrders extends Actor {

  val orderList = new mutable.HashMap[Long,TrackingOrder]()
  var lastOrderId = 0L

  def receive = {
    case order:Order => {
      lastOrderId +=1
      val newOrder = new TrackingOrder(lastOrderId, "received", order)
      orderList += lastOrderId -> newOrder
      sender ! newOrder
    }
    case order:OrderId => {
      orderList.get(order.id) match {
        case Some(intOrder) =>
          sender ! intOrder.copy(status="processing")
        case None => sender ! NoSuchOrder(order.id)
      }
    }
    case "reset"=> {
      lastOrderId = 0
      orderList.clear()
    }
  }
}
```

**Request status
for given order**

**Reset state
used for testing**

Figure 12.17   Implementation of order processing

The REST endpoint will translate the NoSuchOrder into an HTTP 404 NotFound response. Now that you've defined the messages sent through the system, you're ready to implement the order processing. Figure 12.17 shows the implementation of the interface just defined.

This is a simple representation of a complete system that implements two possible requests. We also added a reset function that can be used while testing the complete system.

Now we're ready to implement the REST endpoint using akka-http.

12.3.2 *Implementing a REST endpoint with akka-http*

To give you a feeling for how akka-http can help you in implementing a REST interface, we'll implement the same example endpoint from earlier, this time using akka-http. But keep in mind that this is only a small part of akka-http; there's much more. For instance, we'll look at examples of streaming data over HTTP in chapter 13.

We'll start by creating the HTTP routes for the REST endpoint in an `OrderService` trait. The `OrderService` trait defines an abstract method that will return an `ActorRef` to the `ProcessOrders`. It's a good practice to separate the route definitions from the usage of an actor, because this enables you to test the routes without starting the actor or by injecting a `TestProbe`, for instance. Figure 12.18 shows both the `OrderService-Api` class that will provide the necessary `ExecutionContext` and `Timeout` for using `ask` to request from the `ProcessOrder`, and the `OrderService` trait containing the routes. akka-http has its own test kit that enables you to test routes. Listing 12.12 shows how the `OrderService` will be tested.

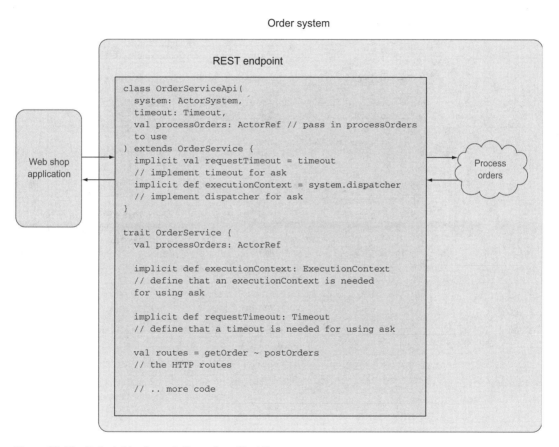

Figure 12.18   Endpoint implementation using akka-http

Listing 12.12   Testing the `OrderService`

```
package aia.integration

import scala.concurrent.duration._
import scala.xml.NodeSeq
import akka.actor.Props

import akka.http.scaladsl.marshallers.xml.ScalaXmlSupport._
import akka.http.scaladsl.model.StatusCodes
import akka.http.scaladsl.server._
import akka.http.scaladsl.testkit.ScalatestRouteTest

import org.scalatest.{ Matchers, WordSpec }

class OrderServiceTest extends WordSpec
    with Matchers
    with OrderService
    with ScalatestRouteTest {

  implicit val executionContext = system.dispatcher
  implicit val requestTimeout = akka.util.Timeout(1 second)
  val processOrders =
    system.actorOf(Props(new ProcessOrders), "orders")


  "The order service" should {
    "return NotFound if the order cannot be found" in {
      Get("/orders/1") ~> routes ~> check {
        status shouldEqual StatusCodes.NotFound
      }
    }

    "return the tracking order for an order that was posted" in {
      val xmlOrder =
      <order><customerId>customer1</customerId>
        <productId>Akka in action</productId>
        <number>10</number>
      </order>

      Post("/orders", xmlOrder) ~> routes ~> check {
        status shouldEqual StatusCodes.OK
        val xml = responseAs[NodeSeq]
        val id = (xml \ "id").text.toInt
        val orderStatus = (xml \ "status").text
        id shouldEqual 1
        orderStatus shouldEqual "received"
      }
      Get("/orders/1") ~> routes ~> check {
        status shouldEqual StatusCodes.OK
        val xml = responseAs[NodeSeq]
        val id = (xml \ "id").text.toInt
        val orderStatus = (xml \ "status").text
        id shouldEqual 1
```

Import implicits for XML support so that `responseAs[NodeSeq]` works

Mixing in the OrderService to test

Provides a DSL for testing routes

Check that a GET of an order that doesn't exist yet will result in 404 NotFound response

Check that a POST of an order followed by a GET returns the status of the order

```
        orderStatus shouldEqual "processing"
      }
    }
  }
}
```

Defining routes is done by using *directives.* You can view a directive as a rule that the received HTTP request should match. A directive has one or more of the following functions:

- Transforms the request
- Filters the request
- Completes the request

Directives are small building blocks out of which you can construct arbitrarily complex route and handling structures. The generic form is this:

```
name(arguments) { extractions => ... // inner route }
```

akka-http has a lot of predefined directives, and you can create custom directives. We use some of the most basic and common directives in this example. A Route uses directives to match an HTTP request, and extracts data from it. The route needs to complete the HTTP request with an HTTP response for every matched pattern. We'll start with defining the routes in the OrderService by composing two routes together, one route for getting the orders and one for posting the orders.

Listing 12.13 Defining the routes of the OrderService

```
val routes = getOrder ~ postOrders
```

The ~ composes routes and/or directives. You can read this as getOrder *or* post-Orders, whichever matches. Every request that doesn't conform to the postOrders or getOrder routes will get an HTTP 404 Not Found response; for example, a request with path order or using the DELETE request.

Let's zoom in to the getOrder method. The getOrder method uses a get directive to match a GET request. It then matches the "/orders/[id]" path with the path-Prefix directive, extracting the ID of the order with the IntNumberPathMatcher.

Listing 12.14 Handling GET orders/id in OrderService

```
def getOrder = get {                                        ◁────── Match on GET requests
  pathPrefix("orders" / IntNumber) { id =>
    onSuccess(processOrders.ask(OrderId(id))) {    ◁──── onSuccess passes the result of a
      case result: TrackingOrder =>                       future to an inner route; sends an
        complete(                                          OrderId to the ProcessOrders actor
          <statusResponse>                   ◁──────┐
            <id>{ result.id }</id>                  Complete the request with an
            <status>{ result.status }</status>      XML response. Translates
          </statusResponse>)                        TrackingOrder response to XML.
```

Extract id of the order

```
      case result: NoSuchOrder =>
        complete(StatusCodes.NotFound)
    }
  }
}
```

◁─── **Complete the request with a HTTP 404 NotFound response**

The `IntNumber` directive retrieves the `id` from the URL and converts it to an `Int`. When the GET request doesn't contain the `id` segment, the selection fails and an `HTTP 404 Not Found` response is sent back. When you have the ID, you can create your business object, `OrderId`, which you'll proceed to send on to your system.

Now that you have your `OrderId`, you can send the message to your system and create the response when the reply is received. This is done by using the `complete` directive.

The `complete` directive returns the response for the request. In the simplest implementation, the result is returned directly. But in our case, we need to asynchronously handle the reply from the `ProcessOrders` actor actor before we can create the response. Therefore, we use `onSuccess`, which passes the result of the future to the inner route once the future completes. The code block of the `onSuccess` method is executed when the `Future` finishes, which isn't in the current thread, so be careful what references you use. By passing a `scala.xml.NodeSeq` to the `complete` directive, akka-http marshalls the `NodeSeq` to text and sets the content type of the response automatically to `text/xml`. This is all there is to implementing the GET method.

> **MARSHALLING RESPONSES** You might have wondered how akka-http knows how to complete the HTTP response from a `scala.xml.Elem`. You need to provide a `ToEntityMarshaller` in implicit scope that can marshall the `scala.xml.Elem` to a text/html entity. This is done by importing `akka.http.scaladsl.marshallers.xml.ScalaXmlSupport._`, which contains both a `ToEntityMarshaller` and a `FromEntityUnmarshaller` for XML.

Next, we'll start to implement the POST request. This is almost the same as the GET implementation. The only difference is that you don't need the order ID from the URL, but you need the body of the post. To do this, you'll use the `entity` directive:

```
post {
  path("orders") {
    entity(as[NodeSeq]) { xml =>
      val order = toOrder(xml)
  //... more code
```

The `entity(as[NodeSeq])` directive only works if an implicit `FromEntityUnmarshaller` is in implicit scope, which is done by importing `ScalaXmlSupport._`, which contains an implicit `ToEntityMarshaller[NodeSeq]`.

The `toOrder` method, which is not shown here, converts a `scala.xml.NodeSeq` into an `Order`.

Now that you have your `Order`, you can implement the response of the POST request. The complete `postOrders` method is shown next.

Listing 12.15 Handling POST orders in `OrderService`

```
def postOrders = post {
  path("orders") {                                    ◁──────── Match POST requests
    entity(as[NodeSeq]) { xml =>                       ◁──────── Match the /orders path
      val order = toOrder(xml)                          ◁──────── Unmarshall the entity body
      onSuccess(processOrders.ask(order)) {                       as a scala.xml.NodeSeq
        case result: TrackingOrder =>
          complete(                                     ◁──────── Complete request
            <confirm>                                            with XML response
              <id>{ result.id }</id>
              <status>{ result.status }</status>
            </confirm>
          )

        case result =>                                  ◁──────────
          complete(StatusCodes.BadRequest)                       If the ProcessActor returns
      }                                                          any other message, return a
    }                                                            BadRequest status code
  }
}
```

Convert to Order →

We've now implemented the complete route. How do we proceed further? To create a real server, you need to bind the routes to an HTTP server. You can create the server when starting your application using the `Http` extension, shown here.

Listing 12.16 Starting the HTTP server

```
object OrderServiceApp extends App
    with RequestTimeout {                              ◁──────── RequestTimeout trait reads the
  val config = ConfigFactory.load()                             akka.http.server.request-timeout
  val host = config.getString("http.host")                      from configuration
  val port = config.getInt("http.port")              ◁──────────
                                                               Get the host and port
  implicit val system = ActorSystem()                          from the configuration
  implicit val ec = system.dispatcher

  val processOrders = system.actorOf(
    Props(new ProcessOrders), "process-orders"
  )                                                   ◁──────── Create the ProcessOrders actor

  val api = new OrderServiceApi(system,
    requestTimeout(config),
    processOrders).routes                             ◁──────── OrderServiceApi returns the routes

  implicit val materializer = ActorMaterializer()
  val bindingFuture: Future[ServerBinding] =
    Http().bindAndHandle(api, host, port)             ◁──── Bind the routes to the HTTP server

  val log = Logging(system.eventStream, "order-service")
  bindingFuture.map { serverBinding =>
```

Log that the service is started successfully

```
   log.info(s"Bound to ${serverBinding.localAddress} ")
 }.onFailure {
   case ex: Exception =>
     log.error(ex, "Failed to bind to {}:{}!", host, port)
     system.terminate()
 }
}
```

Log that the service has failed to bind to the host and port

You can test the `OrderServiceApp` with your favorite HTTP client by running the application in sbt.

12.4 *Summary*

System integration tends to require many of the things that Akka offers out of the box:

- Asynchronous, message-based tasks
- Easy ability to provide data conversion
- Service production/consumption

We pulled in akka-http and Camel to make integration easy, which allowed us to focus on implementing many of the typical integration patterns using just Akka, and not writing a lot of code that was tied to our chosen transports or component layers.

Akka brings a lot to the party on the system integration front. Quite often, this is the most onerous aspect of integration: dealing with the pressure of real flows going in and out, against performance constraints and reliability requirements. In addition to the topics covered here—consuming services, getting data, converting it, and producing it to other consumers—the core aspects of the actor model, concurrency, and fault tolerance represent critical contributors to making the integrated system reliable and scalable. It's easy to imagine expanding any of our pattern examples here to include some of the replaceability we saw in chapter 4, and the scaling abilities from chapters 6 and 9.

13

Streaming

In chapter 12 you learned how to integrate Akka applications with external services using requests and responses. In this chapter we'll look at integrating external services using streams of data.

A stream of data is a sequence of elements that could have no end. Conceptually, a stream is transient in that it only exists as long as there's a producer providing elements to the stream and a consumer reading elements from the stream.

One of the challenges for applications that consume streams is that you can't know beforehand how much data you'll need to handle, because more data may be produced at any time. Another challenge in streaming applications is dealing with the varying speeds of producers and consumers. If your application mediates between streaming producers and consumers, there's one problem you'll have to solve: how to buffer data without running out of memory. How can a producer know if a consumer can or can't keep up?

As you'll see in this chapter, *akka-stream* provides a way to handle unbounded streams with bounded buffers. Akka-stream is the foundational API for streaming applications in Akka. *Akka-http* (which uses akka-stream internally) provides streaming HTTP operations. Building streaming applications with Akka is quite a large topic, so this chapter will serve as an introduction to the akka-stream API and to using akka-http for streaming, from simple pipelines to more-complex graphs of stream-processing components.

The example that we'll look at in this chapter involves structured application-log processing. Many applications create some kind of log file to make debugging possible at runtime. We'll start by processing log files of any size, collecting interesting events, without loading the complete file in memory before analyzing it.

After that we'll write a log-stream processing service using akka-http. Throughout the chapter we'll build out this example.

13.1   *Basic stream processing*

Let's first look at what processing streams with akka-stream really means. Figure 13.1 shows how elements are processed one at a time in a processing node. Processing one element at a time is crucial to prevent memory overflow. As is also shown, bounded buffers can be used in some places in the processing chain.

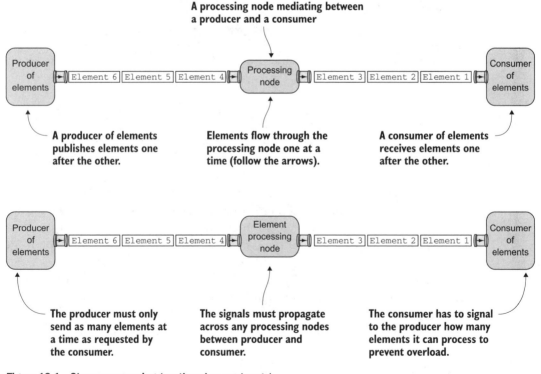

Figure 13.1   Stream processing *(continued on next page)*

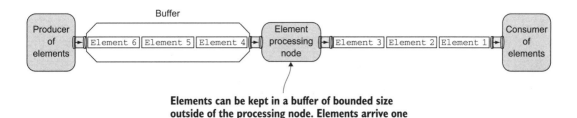

Elements can be kept in a buffer of bounded size
outside of the processing node. Elements arrive one
at a time from the perspective of the processing node.

Figure 13.1 Stream processing *(continued)*

The similarity to actors should be evident. The difference, as shown in figure 13.1, is the signaling between producers and consumers about what can be processed in bounded memory, which you'd have to build yourself when using actors. Figure 13.2 shows examples of linear processing chains that we'll need for the log-stream processor, such as filtering, transforming, and framing log events.

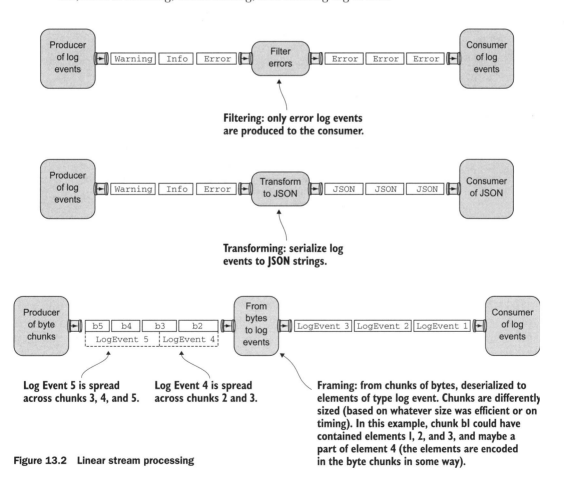

Filtering: only error log events
are produced to the consumer.

Transforming: serialize log
events to JSON strings.

Log Event 5 is spread
across chunks 3, 4, and 5.

Log Event 4 is spread
across chunks 2 and 3.

Framing: from chunks of bytes, deserialized to
elements of type log event. Chunks are differently
sized (based on whatever size was efficient or on
timing). In this example, chunk bl could have
contained elements l, 2, and 3, and maybe a
part of element 4 (the elements are encoded
in the byte chunks in some way).

Figure 13.2 Linear stream processing

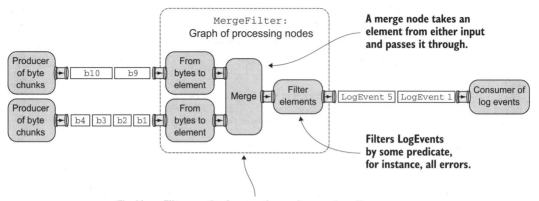

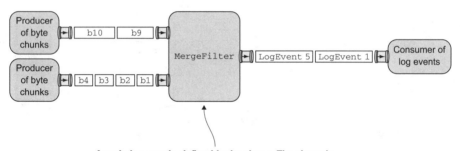

Figure 13.3   Graph processing

The log-stream processor will have to do more than just read from one producer and write to one consumer, and that's where a processing *graph* comes in. A processing graph makes it possible to build more-advanced processing logic out of existing processing nodes. For example, a graph merging two streams and filtering elements is shown in figure 13.3. Essentially, any processing node is a graph; a graph is a processing element with a number of inputs and outputs.

The final version of the log-stream processor service will receive application logs from many services on the network using HTTP and will combine different kinds of streams. It will filter, analyze, transform, and eventually send results to other services. Figure 13.4 shows a hypothetical use case of the service.

The figure shows the log-stream processor receiving log events from different parts of a Tickets application. Log events are sent to the log-stream processor immediately

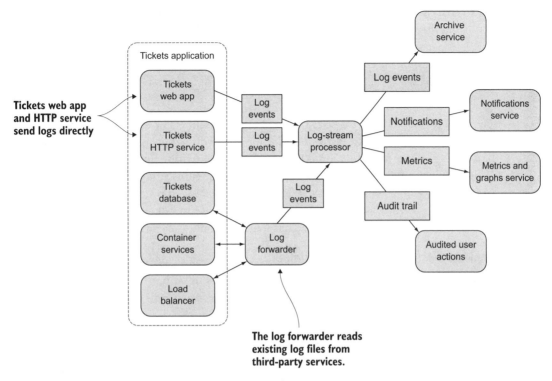

Figure 13.4 Log-stream processor use case

or after some delay. The Tickets web app and HTTP service send events through as they occur, while a log-forwarder service sends events after they've been aggregated from third-party service logs.

In the use case shown in figure 13.4, the log-stream processor sends identified log events to an archive service so that users can execute queries later. The log-stream service also identifies particular problems that occur in the application's services and uses a notification service to notify the team when human intervention is required. Some of the events are turned into metrics, which can be fed into a service that provides charts for more analysis.

Turning the log events into archived events, notifications, metrics, and an audit trail will be done in different processing flows, each requiring a separate piece of processing logic, and all feeding on the incoming log events.

This log-stream processor example will highlight a couple of goals, whose solutions will follow in the next sections of this chapter:

- *Bounded memory usage*—The log-stream processor mustn't run out of memory because the log data can't fit into memory. It should process events one by one, possibly collecting events in temporary buffers, but never trying to read all log events into memory.

- *Asynchronous, nonblocking I/O*—Resources should be used efficiently, and blocking threads should be limited as much as possible. For instance, the log-stream processor can't send data sequentially to every service and wait for all to respond in turn.
- *Varying speeds*—Producers and consumers should be able to operate at different speeds.

The final incarnation of the log-stream processor is an HTTP streaming service, but it would be great if we could start with a simpler version that just processes events from a file, writing results to a file. As you'll see, akka-stream is quite flexible. It's relatively easy to decouple the processing logic from the type of streams you read from and write to. In the next sections we'll build the log-stream processing app step by step, starting with a simple stream copy app. We'll explore the akka-stream API as we go along, and we'll discuss the choices that akka-stream has made to enable stream processing.

13.1.1 *Copying files with sources and sinks*

As a first step toward building a log-stream processing app, we'll look at a streaming copy example. Every byte that's read from a source stream will be written to a destination stream.

As always, we'll have to add dependencies to our build file, shown in the following listing.

Listing 13.1 Dependencies

```
"com.typesafe.akka" %% "akka-stream" % version,        ⟵── Stream dependency
```

Using akka-stream usually involves two steps:

1 *Define a blueprint*—A *graph* of stream-processing components. The graph defines how streams need to be processed.
2 *Execute the blueprint*—Run the graph on an `ActorSystem`. The graph is turned into actors that do all the work required to actually stream the data.

The graph (blueprint) can be shared throughout your program. After it has been created, it's immutable. The graph can be run as many times as you like, and every run is executed by a new set of actors. A running graph can return results from components within the streaming process. We'll get into the details of how all of this works later in this chapter. Don't worry if it's not completely clear right now.

We'll start with a very simple precursor to the problem of log streaming and create an app that will simply copy logs. The `StreamingCopy` app copies an input file to an output file. The blueprint in this case is a very simple *pipe*. Any data received from a stream is written to a stream. Listings 13.3 and 13.4 show the most relevant code, the former to define a blueprint and the latter to execute the blueprint.

Getting the `intputFile` and `outputFile` from command-line arguments is left out of those listings. The following listing shows the most important imports.

Listing 13.2   Imports for the StreamingCopy app

> **The scaladsl package contains the Scala DSL for working with streams; there's also a javadsl available.**

```
import akka.actor.ActorSystem
import akka.stream.{ ActorMaterializer, IOResult }
import akka.stream.scaladsl.{ FileIO, RunnableGraph, Source, Sink }    ◁──┘
import akka.util.ByteString
```

Listing 13.3   Defining a RunnableGraph to copy a stream

```
val source: Source[ByteString, Future[IOResult]] =
  FileIO.fromPath(inputFile)                          ◁──  A source to read from

val sink: Sink[ByteString, Future[IOResult]] =
  FileIO.toPath(outputFile, Set(CREATE, WRITE, APPEND))    ◁──┐ A sink to
                                                             │ write to
val runnableGraph: RunnableGraph[Future[IOResult]] =
  source.to(sink)                    ◁──┐ Connecting a source and a sink
                                         │ creates a RunnableGraph.
```

First, a `Source` and a `Sink` are defined by using `FileIO.fromPath` and `FileIO.toPath`.

`Source` and `Sink` are both stream endpoints. A `Source` has one open output, and a `Sink` has one open input. `Sources` and `Sinks` are typed; the stream element type in this case is `ByteString` for both.

The `Source` and `Sink` are connected together to form a `RunnableGraph`, shown in figure 13.5.

Blocking file I/O

We use `FileIO` in the examples because it's very easy to verify input and output in files, and the sources and sinks for file I/O are very simple.

The types of sources and sinks are relatively easy to switch, say, from file to some other medium.

Note that the `FileIO`-created sources and sinks internally use blocking file I/O. The actors created for `FileIO` sources and sinks run on a separate dispatcher, which can be set globally with `akka.stream.blocking-io-dispatcher`. It's also possible to set a custom dispatcher for graph elements through a `withAttributes` that takes an `ActorAttributes`. Section 13.1.2 shows an example setting a `supervisor-Strategy` using `ActorAttributes`.

File I/O is a situation where blocking isn't as bad as you might think. Latency to disk is far lower than streaming over a network, for instance. An async version of `FileIO` might be added in the future if it provides better performance for many concurrent file streams.

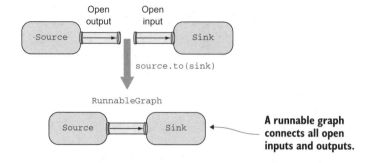

Figure 13.5   `Source`, `Sink`, and the simplest `RunnableGraph`

A runnable graph connects all open inputs and outputs.

MATERIALIZED VALUES   Sources and sinks can provide an auxiliary value when a graph is run, called a *materialized value*. In this case, it's a `Future[IOResult]` containing how many bytes were read or written. We'll discuss materialization in more detail in section 13.1.2.

The `StreamingCopy` app creates about the simplest graph we could define by using `source.to(sink)`, which creates a `RunnableGraph` that takes data from a `Source` and feeds it straight into a `Sink`.

The lines that create a source and a sink are declarative. They don't create files or open file handles, but simply capture all the information that will be needed later, once the `RunnableGraph` is run.

It's also important to note that creating the `RunnableGraph` doesn't start anything. It simply defines a blueprint for how to copy.

The following listing shows how the `RunnableGraph` is executed.

Listing 13.4   Execute a `RunnableGraph` to copy a stream

```
implicit val system = ActorSystem()
implicit val ec = system.dispatcher
implicit val materializer = ActorMaterializer()      ⟵  The materializer eventually
                                                         creates actors that execute
                                                         the graph.
runnableGraph.run().foreach { result =>              ⟵
  println(s"${result.status}, ${result.count} bytes read.")
  system.terminate()
}
                    Running the graph returns a Future[IOResult]; in this case,the
                    IOResult contains a count of bytes read from the source.
```

Running the `runnableGraph` results in the bytes being copied from source to sink— from a file to a file in this case. A graph is said to be `materialized` once it is run.

The graph is stopped in this case once all data is copied. We'll discuss the details of this in the next section.

The `FileIO` object is part of akka-stream, which provides a convenient means to create file sources and file sinks. Connecting the source and sink causes every `ByteString` read from the file source to be passed into the file sink, one at a time, once the `RunnableGraph` is materialized.

In the next section we'll look at the details of materialization and how this `RunnableGraph` is executed.

Running the examples

As usual, you can run the examples in this chapter from the sbt console. You can pass through any arguments to the `run` command that are required by the app in question.

A plugin that's very handy for running applications is sbt-revolver, which makes it possible to run an app, restart, and stop it (using `re-start` and `re-stop`), without having to exit the sbt console. It can be found here: https://github.com/spray/sbt-revolver.

The chapter-stream folder in the GitHub project also contains a `GenerateLogFile` app, which can create large test log files.

Copying a file larger than the maximum memory of the JVM (set by the `-Xmx` parameter) to verify that the app is not secretly loading the entire file into memory is an exercise you can try.

13.1.2 *Materializing runnable graphs*

The `run` method in listing 13.4 requires a `Materalizer` in `implicit` scope. An `Actor-Materializer` converts the `RunnableGraph` into actors, which execute the graph.

Let's look at what that entails in this specific example of copying files. Some of these details might change, because they're private internals of Akka, but it's very useful to trace the code and see how everything works. Figure 13.6 shows a simplified version of how the materialization of the `StreamingCopy` graph starts.

- The `ActorMaterializer` checks if the `Source` and `Sink` in the graph are properly connected, and requests the `Source` and `Sink` internals to set up resources. Internally, `fromPath` creates a `Source` from a `FileSource` (which is the internal implementation of a `SourceShape`).
- The `FileSource` is asked to create its resources and creates a `FilePublisher`, an actor that opens a `FileChannel`.
- The `toPath` method creates a `Sink` from a `FileSinkSinkModule`. The `FileSink` creates a `FileSubscriber` actor, which opens a `FileChannel`.
- The `to` method used to connect `source` and `sink` in this example internally combines the modules of source and sink together into one module.
- The `ActorMaterializer` subscribes subscribers to publishers according to how the modules are connected, in this case subscribing the `FileSubscriber` to the `FilePublisher`.
- The `FilePublisher` reads `ByteStrings` from the file until it reaches the end, closing the file once it stops.
- The `FileSubscriber` writes any `ByteStrings` it receives from the `FilePublisher` to the output file. The `FileSubscriber` closes the `FileChannel` once it stops.
- The `FilePublisher` completes the stream once it has read all the data from the file. The `FileSubscriber` receives an `OnComplete` message when this happens and closes the file that was written to.

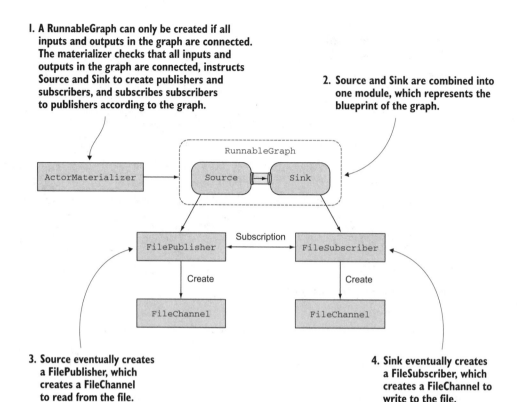

I. A RunnableGraph can only be created if all inputs and outputs in the graph are connected. The materializer checks that all inputs and outputs in the graph are connected, instructs Source and Sink to create publishers and subscribers, and subscribes subscribers to publishers according to the graph.

2. Source and Sink are combined into one module, which represents the blueprint of the graph.

3. Source eventually creates a FilePublisher, which creates a FileChannel to read from the file.

4. Sink eventually creates a FileSubscriber, which creates a FileChannel to write to the file.

Figure 13.6   Materializing the graph

A stream can be canceled using operators like `take`, `takeWhile`, and `takeWithin`, which respectively cancel the stream at a maximum number of elements processed, when a predicate function returns `true`, and when a set duration has passed. Internally these operators complete the stream in a similar way.

All actors that were created internally to execute the work are stopped at that point. Running the `RunnableGraph` again creates a new set of actors, and the whole process starts again from the beginning.

PREVENTING MEMORY OVERLOAD

If the `FilePublisher` were to read all data from the file into memory (which it doesn't), it could cause an `OutOfMemoryException`, so what does it do instead? The answer lies in how the `Publisher` and `Subscriber` interact with each other. This is shown in figure 13.7.

The `FilePublisher` can only publish up to the number of elements requested by the `FileSubscriber`.

In this case, the `FilePublisher` on the source side can only read more data from the file if the `FileSubscriber` on the sink side requests more data. This means that data is only read from the source as quickly as the sink can write the data out. In this

1. **FileSubscriber requests a finite number of elements, in this example 16, by sending a Request message.**

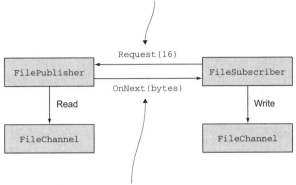

2. **FilePublisher can only publish 16 elements or fewer by sending OnNext messages.**

Figure 13.7 The Subscriber requests as much data from the Publisher as it can handle.

simple example, we only have two components in the graph; in more-complex graphs, the demand travels all the way from the end of the graph to the beginning of the graph, making sure that no publisher can ever publish faster than subscribers demand.

All the graph components in akka-stream work in a similar way. Eventually every part is translated into a Reactive Streams publisher or subscriber. It's this API that makes it possible for akka-stream to process unbounded streams of data in bounded memory and that sets the rules for how a publisher and subscriber must interact, such as never publishing more elements than are requested.

We've simplified the protocol between publisher and subscriber substantially here. What's most important is that the subscriber and publisher send each other messages about supply and demand asynchronously. They don't block each other in any way. The demand and supply are specified as a fixed number of elements. The subscriber can signal the publisher that it can only process less data, or it can signal the publisher that it could process more. The ability of the subscriber to do this is called *nonblocking back pressure*.

REACTIVE STREAMS INITIATIVE Reactive Streams is an initiative to provide a standard for asynchronous stream processing with nonblocking back pressure. There are several libraries that have implemented the Reactive Streams API, which can all integrate with each other. Akka-stream implements the Reactive Streams API and provides a higher-level API on top of it. You can read more about it at www.reactive-streams.org/.

INTERNAL BUFFERS

Akka-stream uses buffers internally to optimize throughput. Instead of requesting and publishing every single element, internally batches are requested and published.

The `FileSubscriber` can request a fixed number of elements at a time. The akka-stream library ensures that bounded memory is used when reading from and writing to files. This isn't something you have to worry about, but if you're curious, you might wonder about the maximum number of in-flight elements at any time requested by the `FileSubscriber`.

If you dive a little deeper into the code, you'll see that the `FileSubscriber` uses a `WatermarkRequestStrategy` with a high watermark set to a maximum input buffer size. The `FileSubscriber` won't request more elements than this setting.

Then there's the size of the element itself, which we haven't discussed. In this case, it's the size of a chunk read from the file, which can be set in the `fromPath` method and is 8 KB by default.

The maximum input buffer size sets the maximum number of elements, which can be set in the configuration using `akka.stream.materializer.max-input-buffer-size`. The default setting is 16, so around 128 KB of data can be in flight at maximum in this example.

The maximum input buffer can also be set through `ActorMaterializerSettings`, which can be passed to the materializer or to specific graph components, which you'll see more of throughout the chapter. `ActorMaterializerSettings` makes it possible to configure several aspects of materialization, including which dispatcher should be used for the actors executing the graph and how graph components should be supervised.

We'll look at buffering again in section 13.4.

Operator fusion

Looking ahead to the point where we'll use more nodes between sources and sinks, akka-stream uses an optimization technique called *operator fusion* to remove as many unnecessary asynchronous boundaries as possible in linear chains in the graph.

By default, as many stages in a graph as possible are run on a single actor to remove the overhead of passing the elements and the demand and supply signals across threads. The `async` method can be used to explicitly create an asynchronous boundary in a graph, so that the processing elements separated by the `async` call are guaranteed to later run on separate actors.

Operator fusion happens at materialization time. It can be turned off by setting `akka.stream.materializer.auto-fusing=off`. It's also possible to pre-fuse a graph (before it's materialized) with `Fusing.aggressive(graph)`.

COMBINING MATERIALIZED VALUES

As we mentioned before, sources and sinks can provide an auxiliary value when the graph is materialized. The file source and sink provide a `Future[IOResult]` once they complete, containing the number of bytes read and written.

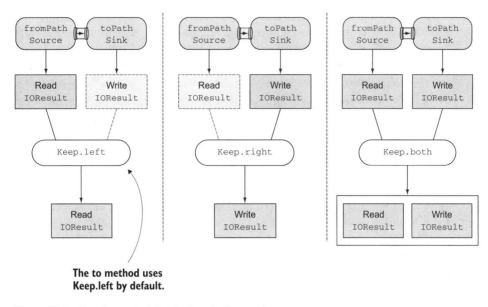

The to method uses
Keep.left by default.

Figure 13.8 Keeping materialized values in the graph

The `RunnableGraph` returns one materialized value when it's run, so how is it decided which value is passed through the graph?

The `to` method is shorthand for `toMat`, which is a method that takes an additional function argument to combine materialized values. The `Keep` object defines a couple of standard functions for this.

By default, the `to` method uses `Keep.left` to keep the materialized value on the left, which explains why the materialized value for the graph in the `StreamingCopy` example returns the `Future[IOResult]` of reading the file, as shown in figure 13.8.

You can choose to keep the left, right, none, or both values with the `toMat` method, shown next.

Listing 13.5 Keeping materialized values

```
import akka.Done
import akka.stream.scaladsl.Keep

val graphLeft: RunnableGraph[Future[IOResult]] =          Keeps the IOResult
  source.toMat(sink)(Keep.left)                           of reading the file

val graphRight: RunnableGraph[Future[IOResult]] =         Keeps the IOResult
  source.toMat(sink)(Keep.right)                          of writing the file
val graphBoth: RunnableGraph[(Future[IOResult], Future[IOResult])] =
  source.toMat(sink)(Keep.both)                           Keeps both
val graphCustom: RunnableGraph[Future[Done]] =
  source.toMat(sink) { (l, r) =>          A custom function that just
    Future.sequence(List(l,r)).map(_ => Done)    indicates the stream is done
  }
```

`Keep.left`, `Keep.right`, `Keep.both`, and `Keep.none` are simple functions that return the left, right, both, or no arguments, respectively. `Keep.left` is a good default; in a long graph the materialized value of the beginning of the graph is kept. If `Keep.right` were the default, you'd have to specify `Keep.left` in every step to keep the value of the first materialized value.

So far you've seen how a source and a sink can be combined. In the next section, we'll get back to the log events example and introduce a `Flow` component. We'll look more closely at stream operations in the context of processing and filtering events.

13.1.3 *Processing events with flows*

Now that you know the basics of defining and materializing a graph, it's time to look at an example that does more than just copy bytes. We'll start with the first version of a log processor.

The `EventFilter` app, which is a simple command-line application, takes three arguments: an input file containing the log events, an output file to write JSON-formatted events to, and the state of the events to filter on (events with that state will be written to the output file).

Let's discuss the log events format before we get into the stream operations. Log events are written as lines of text, and every element of a log event is separated from the next with a pipe character (|). The following listing shows an example of the format.

Listing 13.6   Format for log events

```
my-host-1 | web-app | ok    | 2015-08-12T12:12:00.127Z | 5 tickets sold.||
my-host-2 | web-app | ok    | 2015-08-12T12:12:01.127Z | 3 tickets sold.||
my-host-1 | web-app | ok    | 2015-08-12T12:12:02.127Z | 1 tickets sold.||
my-host-2 | web-app | error | 2015-08-12T12:12:03.127Z | exception!!||
```

A log event line for our first example consists of a host name, service name, state, time, and description field. The state can be one of the values `'ok'`, `'warning'`, `'error'`, or `'critical'`. Every line ends with a newline character (`\n`).

Every text line in the file will be parsed and turned into an `Event` case class.

Listing 13.7   The `Event` case class

```
case class Event(
  host: String,
  service: String,
  state: State,
  time: ZonedDateTime,
  description: String,
  tag: Option[String] = None,
  metric: Option[Double] = None
)
```

The `Event` case class simply has a field for every field in the log line.

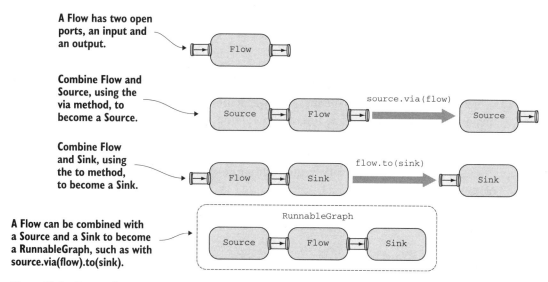

Figure 13.9 Connecting sources and sinks with flows

The *spray-json* library is used to convert an `Event` into JSON. The `EventMarshalling` trait, which is omitted here, contains JSON formats for the `Event` case class. The `EventMarshalling` trait can be found in the GitHub repository along with all the code shown in this chapter, in the chapter-stream directory.

We'll use a `Flow` between a `Source` and a `Sink`, as shown in figure 13.9.

The flow will capture all the stream-processing logic, and we'll reuse this logic later in the HTTP version of the example. Both the `Source` and a `Flow` provide methods to operate on the stream. Figure 13.10 shows the operations in the event filter flow conceptually.

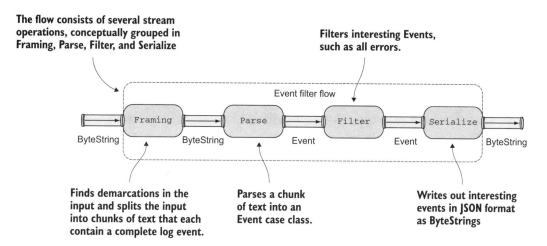

Figure 13.10 Filtering events

The first problem we face is the fact that the flow will receive any size of ByteStrings as elements from the source. We can't assume that a received ByteString contains exactly one log event line.

Akka-stream has a couple of predefined Flows for framing that can be used to identify frames of data in a stream. In this case, we can use the Framing.delimiter flow, which detects a particular ByteString as a delimiter in the stream. It buffers up to a maximum of maxLine bytes to find a frame ending with a delimiter, to make sure that corrupted input can't lead to an OutOfMemoryException.

Listing 13.8 shows the frame flow that turns arbitrarily sized ByteStrings into ByteString frames that are delimited with a newline. In our format, that indicates a complete log event line.

Listing 13.8 Framing ByteStrings

```
val frame: Flow[ByteString, String, NotUsed] =          Returns a Flow[ByteString,
  Framing.delimiter(ByteString("/n"), maxLine)   ◁─┘    String, NotUsed]
    .map(_.decodeString("UTF8"))            ◁─┐   Decodes every framed ByteString
                                                │ to a String log event line
```

The Flow has many collection-like operators, such as map and filter, that can be used to transform the elements in the stream. Listing 13.8 shows how map is used to turn every framed ByteString into a String.

We're now ready to parse the log line into an Event case class. We'll leave out the actual logic for parsing the log line (which can be found in the GitHub project as always). We'll simply map over the elements again, turning the String into an Event, as shown in listing 13.9.

> **A STREAM IS NOT A COLLECTION** You'll notice that a lot of the streaming operations sound like collection operations, such as map, filter, and collect. This might make you think that a stream is just another standard collection, which is not the case. The big difference is that the size of the stream isn't known, whereas the size is known in almost all standard collection classes like List, Set, and Map. Some methods you might have expected on a Flow, based on your experience with collection APIs, aren't available simply because you can't traverse all elements of the stream.

Listing 13.9 Parsing lines

```
val parse: Flow[String, Event, NotUsed] =
  Flow[String].map(LogStreamProcessor.parseLineEx)
    .collect { case Some(e) => e }          ◁─┐
```

Parses the string using the parseLineEx method in the LogStreamProcessor object, which returns an Option[Event], or None if an empty line is encountered

Discards empty lines and extracts the event in the Some case

The Flow[String] creates a Flow that takes String elements as input and provides String elements as output.

In this case, it's not important what the type of the materialized value will be. There's no reasonable type to choose when the Flow[String] is created. The NotUsed type is used to indicate that the materialized value isn't important and shouldn't be used. The parse flow takes Strings and outputs Events.

Next up is the filter step.

Listing 13.10   Filtering events

```
val filter: Flow[Event, Event, NotUsed] =
  Flow[Event].filter(_.state == filterState)
```

All events with a specific filterState are passed through the filter flow, and others are discarded.

The serialize flow is shown next.

Listing 13.11   Serializing events

```
val serialize: Flow[Event, ByteString, NotUsed] =
  Flow[Event].map(event => ByteString(event.toJson.compactPrint))   <─┐
```
**Serializes to JSON using
the spray-json library**

Flows can be composed using via. The next listing shows the definition of the complete event filter flow and how it's materialized.

Listing 13.12   The composed event filter flow

```
val composedFlow: Flow[ByteString, ByteString, NotUsed] =
  frame.via(parse)
    .via(filter)
    .via(serialize)

val runnableGraph: RunnableGraph[Future[IOResult]] =
  source.via(composedFlow).toMat(sink)(Keep.right)

runnableGraph.run().foreach { result =>
  println(s"Wrote ${result.count} bytes to '$outputFile'.")
  system.terminate()
}
```

We use toMat here to keep the materialized value on the right, which is the materialized value of the Sink, so we can print the total number of bytes written to the output file. The flow can, of course, also be defined all at once, as follows.

Listing 13.13   One flow for the event filter

```
val flow: Flow[ByteString, ByteString, NotUsed] =
  Framing.delimiter(ByteString("\n"), maxLine)
    .map(_.decodeString("UTF8"))
    .map(LogStreamProcessor.parseLineEx)
    .collect { case Some(e) => e }
    .filter(_.state == filterState)
    .map(event => ByteString(event.toJson.compactPrint))
```

In the next section, we'll look at what happens when errors occur, such as when there's a corrupted line in the log file.

13.1.4   *Handling errors in streams*

The `EventFilter` app was a little naive when it came to errors. The `LogStream-Processor.parseLineEx` method throws an exception when a line can't be parsed, but that's just one of the errors that could occur. You could pass in a path to a file that doesn't exist.

By default, stream processing is stopped when an exception occurs. The materialized value of the runnable graph will be a failed `Future` containing the exception. That's not very handy in this case. It would make more sense to ignore log lines that can't be parsed.

We'll look at ignoring unparsable log lines first. You can define a supervision strategy, similar to how you can define a supervision strategy for actors. The next listing shows how `Resume` can be used to drop the element causing the exception, which leads to the stream processing continuing.

Listing 13.14   Resuming the flow in `LogParseException`

```
import akka.stream.ActorAttributes
import akka.stream.Supervision

import LogStreamProcessor.LogParseException          Defines a decider, similar
                                                     to supervision in actors
val decider : Supervision.Decider = {
  case _: LogParseException => Supervision.Resume    Resumes on
  case _                    => Supervision.Stop      LogParseException
}

val parse: Flow[String, Event, NotUsed] =            Passes the supervisor
  Flow[String].map(LogStreamProcessor.parseLineEx)   through attributes
    .collect { case Some(e) => e }
    .withAttributes(ActorAttributes.supervisionStrategy(decider))
```

The supervision strategy is passed using `withAttributes`, which is available on all graph components. You can also set the supervision strategy for the complete graph using `ActorMaterializerSettings`, as follows.

Listing 13.15 Supervise graph

```
val graphDecider : Supervision.Decider = {
  case _: LogParseException => Supervision.Resume
  case _                    => Supervision.Stop
}

import akka.stream.ActorMaterializerSettings
implicit val materializer = ActorMaterializer(
  ActorMaterializerSettings(system)
    .withSupervisionStrategy(graphDecider)
)
```

Passes in supervisor strategy through ActorMaterializerSettings

Stream supervision supports `Resume`, `Stop`, and `Restart`. Some stream operations build up state, which is discarded when `Restart` is used; `Resume` doesn't discard the state.

ERRORS AS STREAM ELEMENTS Another error-handling option is to catch exceptions and use an error type that's passed through the stream just like any other element. You could, for instance, introduce an `UnparsableEvent` case class and have both `Event` and `UnparsableEvent` extend from a common `Result` sealed trait, making it possible to pattern-match on it. The complete flow would then be a `Flow[ByteString, Result, NotUsed]`. Another option is to use the `Either` type and encode errors as `left` and events as `right`, ending up with something like `Flow[ByteString, Either[Error, Result]`, `NotUsed]`. There are better alternatives to `Either` available in the community, such as Scalaz's `Disjunction`, Cats' `Xor` type, or Scalactic's `Or` type. Mapping to an `Either`-like type is left as an exercise for the reader.

Now that we've looked briefly at handling stream errors, we'll look at how we can separate the serialization protocol from the logic of filtering events. `EventFilter` is a very simple app—the main logic consists of filtering events that have a particular state. It would be great if we could reuse the parsing, filtering, and serializing steps better. Also, we started quite arbitrarily only supporting the log format as input and JSON as output. It would be great if we could also support JSON input and text log format output, for instance. In the next section, we'll look at a *bidirectional flow* to define a reusable serialization protocol that we can stack on top of the filter flow.

13.1.5 *Creating a protocol with a BidiFlow*

A `BidiFlow` is a graph component with two open inputs and two open outputs. One way to use a `BidiFlow` is to stack it on top of a flow as an adapter.

We'll use a `BidiFlow` as two flows that are used together, but it's important to note that a `BidiFlow` can be created in many more ways than just from two flows, which allows for some interesting advanced use cases.

Let's rewrite the `EventFilter` app so that it basically only deals with the `filter` method, a `Flow[Event, Event, NotUsed]`, from event to event. How the events are read from incoming bytes and how the events are written out again should be reusable as a protocol adapter. Figure 13.11 shows the structure of a `BidiFlow`.

A bidirectional flow contains two flows
that should be logically grouped together.

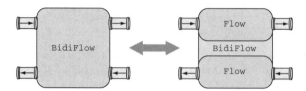

All inputs and outputs need to be
connected or the graph will not run.

Combine a BidiFlow with a Flow, using
the join method, to create a new Flow.

Figure 13.11   Bidirectional flow

The BidiFlow is stacked
on top of the filter Flow.

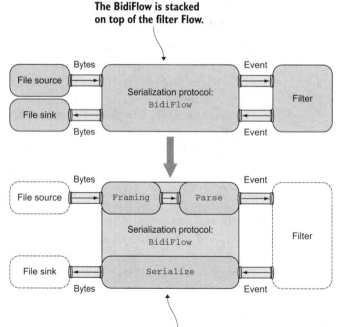

The BidiFlow internally uses two Flows:
one in from ByteString to Event, and
one out from Event to ByteString.

Figure 13.12
Serialization protocol
using a bidirectional flow

The `BidiEventFilter` app separates the serialization protocol from the logic for filtering events, as shown in figure 13.12. In this case, the "out" flow only contains a serialized flow because in this case the framing elements (newline characters) are automatically added by the serializer.

Listing 13.16 shows how a specific `BidiFlow` is created from command-line arguments. Anything other than "json" will be interpreted as the log file format.

Listing 13.16 Creating a `BidiFlow` from command-line arguments

```
val inFlow: Flow[ByteString, Event, NotUsed] =
  if(args(0).toLowerCase == "json") {
    JsonFraming.json(maxJsonObject)                                    ⟵
    .map(_.decodeString("UTF8").parseJson.convertTo[Event])
  } else {
    Framing.delimiter(ByteString("\n"), maxLine)
      .map(_.decodeString("UTF8"))
      .map(LogStreamProcessor.parseLineEx)
      .collect { case Some(event) => event }
  }
val outFlow: Flow[Event, ByteString, NotUsed] =
  if(args(1).toLowerCase == "json") {
    Flow[Event].map(event => ByteString(event.toJson.compactPrint))
  } else {
    Flow[Event].map{ event =>
      ByteString(LogStreamProcessor.logLine(event))               ⟵
    }
  }
val bidiFlow = BidiFlow.fromFlows(inFlow, outFlow)
```

> **Framing for streaming JSON; maxJsonObject is the maximum number of bytes for any JsonObject**

> **LogStreamProcessor.logLine method serializes an event to a log line**

`JsonFraming` frames incoming bytes into JSON objects. We use spray-json here to parse the bytes containing a JSON object and convert it to an `Event`. `JsonFraming` is included in the GitHub project, which is copied from Konrad Malawski's preliminary work on marshallers for streaming JSON (expected to land in an upcoming version of Akka).

`fromFlows` creates a `BidiFlow` from two flows, for deserialization and serialization. The `BidiFlow` can be joined on top of the `filter` flow with `join`, as shown in the following listing.

Listing 13.17 Joining a `BidiFlow` with a filter flow

```
val filter: Flow[Event, Event, NotUsed] =
  Flow[Event].filter(_.state == filterState)

val flow = bidiFlow.join(filter)                      ⟵
```

> **The in flow of the BidiFlow is left of the filter flow; the out flow of the BidiFlow is on the right.**

Another way to think about a `BidiFlow` is that it provides two flows that you can connect before and after an existing flow, to adapt on the input side and on the output side of the flow in question. In this case it's used to read and write in a consistent format.

In the next section, we'll build a streaming HTTP service and add more features to the log-stream processor, getting closer to a realistic application. So far we've only worked with straight pipelines of stream operations. We'll also look at broadcasting and merging streams.

13.2   Streaming HTTP

The log-stream processor will run as an HTTP service. Let's look at what that entails. Akka-http uses akka-stream, so there isn't a lot of extra glue code necessary to move from a file-based app to an HTTP service. Akka-http is a really good example of a library that embraces akka-stream. You can be sure that more will follow.

First, we'll add some more dependencies to our project.

Listing 13.18   Akka-http dependencies

```
"com.typesafe.akka" %% "akka-http-core"                      % version,
"com.typesafe.akka" %% "akka-http-experimental"              % version,
"com.typesafe.akka" %% "akka-http-spray-json-experimental" % version,
```

Akka-http dependency

Integration between akka-http and spray-json

This time we'll build a `LogsApp` that makes it possible to stream logs from and to some storage. In this case, to keep it simple, we'll write streams straight into files.

There are quite a few reactive stream-based client libraries available. Connecting the example to some other kind of (database) storage is left as an exercise for the reader.

13.2.1   Receiving a stream over HTTP

We'll allow clients of the service to stream log events data using an HTTP POST. The data will be stored in a file on the server. A POST to the URL /logs/[log_id] will create a file named [log_id] in a logs directory. For instance, /logs/1 will create the file 1 in the configured logs directory. We'll stream from that file later when the HTTP GET is implemented for /logs/[log-id]. The `LogsApp` that sets up the HTTP server is omitted here.

The HTTP route is defined in a `LogsApi` class, shown in listing 13.19. `LogsApi` has a `logsDir` that points to the directory where the logs will be stored. The `logFile` method just returns a `File` for the specific ID. The `EventMarshalling` trait is mixed in to support JSON marshalling. You'll also notice that an `ExecutionContext` and `Actor-Materializer` are in implicit scope; they'll be needed to run `Flow`s.

Listing 13.19   `LogsApi`

```
class LogsApi(
  val logsDir: Path,
  val maxLine: Int
)(
```

```
    implicit val executionContext: ExecutionContext,
    val materializer: ActorMaterializer
) extends EventMarshalling {
    def logFile(id: String) = logsDir.resolve(id)
// route logic follows..
```

We'll use the `BidiFlow` from the previous section, because it already defines the protocol from log file to JSON events. The next listing shows the `Flow` and `Sink` that will be used, as well as the `Source`, which we'll come back to when the HTTP `GET` is implemented.

Listing 13.20 Flow and Sink used in POST

```
import java.nio.file.StandardOpenOption
import java.nio.file.StandardOpenOption._

val logToJsonFlow = bidiFlow.join(Flow[Event])  ⟵──┘

def logFileSink(logId: String) =
  FileIO.toPath(logFile(logId), Set(CREATE, WRITE, APPEND))
def logFileSource(logId: String) = FileIO.fromPath(logFile(logId))
```

> The bidirectional flow is joined with a flow that passes every event through unchanged.

The events are left unchanged in this example; all log lines are converted to JSON events. Adapting the flow that's joined with the `BidiFlow` to filter events based on a query parameter is left up to the reader. `logFileSink` and `logFileSource` are convenience methods that you'll notice in examples in this section.

The HTTP `POST` is handled in the `postRoute` method, shown in listing 13.21. Because akka-http is built on top of akka-stream, receiving a stream over HTTP is rather easy. The HTTP request entity has a `dataBytes` `Source` that we can read the data from.

Completely read the entity Source before responding

It's important to completely read all data from the `dataBytesSource`. If you respond before all data is read from the source, a client that uses HTTP *persistent connections*, for example, could determine that the TCP socket is still good to use for a next request, which possibly will end up in a `Source` that's never read from again.

It's often assumed by an HTTP client that a request will be processed completely, so that it won't try to read the response before it has an indication that this has happened. Even when you're not using persistent connections, it's best to completely process the request.

This usually is a problem for blocking HTTP clients, which won't start reading the response until they write the entire request.

This doesn't mean that the request/response cycle is processed synchronously. In the examples in this section, the response is sent back asynchronously after the request has been processed.

Listing 13.21 Handling POST

```
def postRoute =
  pathPrefix("logs" / Segment) { logId =>
    pathEndOrSingleSlash {
      post {
        entity(as[HttpEntity]) { entity =>
          onComplete(
            entity
              .dataBytes
              .via(logToJsonFlow)
              .toMat(logFileSink(logId))(Keep.right)
              .run()
          ) {
            case Success(IOResult(count, Success(Done))) =>
              complete((StatusCodes.OK, LogReceipt(logId, count)))
            case Success(IOResult(count, Failure(e))) =>
              complete((
                StatusCodes.BadRequest,
                ParseError(logId, e.getMessage)
              ))
            case Failure(e) =>
              complete((
                StatusCodes.BadRequest,
                ParseError(logId, e.getMessage)
              ))
          }
        }
      }
    }
  }
```

Extracts the HttpRequest → (entity(as[HttpEntity]))

A stream of the data of this entity of type Source[ByteString, Any] ← (.dataBytes)

The protocol flow: log format in, JSON out → (.via(logToJsonFlow))

Writes the JSON to the file ← (.toMat(logFileSink(logId))(Keep.right))

Responds with a LogReceipt containing the logId and number of bytes written

Responds with a BadRequest when an error occurs

The `run` method returns a `Future[IOResult]`, so we use the `onComplete` directive, which eventually passes the result of the `Future` to the inner route, where the `Success` and `Failure` cases are handled. The response is returned with the `complete` directive.

In the next section, we'll look at how we can respond to an HTTP GET request to stream the log file in JSON format back to the client.

13.2.2 *Responding with a stream over HTTP*

Clients should be able to retrieve a stream of log events by using HTTP GET. Let's implement the route. The next listing shows the `getRoute` method.

Listing 13.22 Handling GET

```
def getRoute =
  pathPrefix("logs" / Segment) { logId =>
    pathEndOrSingleSlash {
      get {
        if(Files.exists(logFile(logId))) {
          val src = logFileSource(logId)
          complete(
```

Creates a Source[ByteString, Future[IOResult]] if the file exists

```
                    HttpEntity(ContentTypes.`application/json`, src)   ◄──┐
                )                                                          │
            } else {                                       ┌──────────────────┐
                complete(StatusCodes.NotFound)             │  Completes with an │
            }                                              │  HttpEntity, which has │
        }                                                  │  the JSON content type │
    }                                                      └──────────────────┘
}
```

BACKTICKS IN IDENTIFIERS Akka-http stays as close as possible to the HTTP specification, and this is also reflected in the naming of identifiers for HTTP headers, content types, and other elements of the HTTP specification. In Scala you can use backticks to create identifiers that contain characters that would normally not be allowed, like dashes and slashes, which are commonly found in the HTTP specification.

`HttpEntity` has an `apply` method that takes a `ContentType` and a `Source`. Streaming the data from file is as easy as passing the `Source` to this method, and completing the response with the `complete` directive. In the `POST` example, we simply assume that the data will be sent as text in the expected log format. In the `GET` example, we return the data in JSON format.

Now that we've got the simplest streaming `GET` and `POST` examples out of the way, let's look at how to use akka-http for *content negotiation*, which will make it possible for the client to `GET` and `POST` data in JSON or in log format.

13.2.3 Custom marshallers and unmarshallers for content type and negotiation

The `Accept` header allows an HTTP client to specify which format it wants to `GET`, if more than one `MediaType` is available. The HTTP client can set a `Content-Type` header to specify the format of the entity in the `POST`. We'll look at handling both these cases in this section, making it possible to interchangeably `POST` and `GET` data in JSON or log format, similar to the `BidiEventFilter` example.

Luckily, akka-http provides features for custom marshalling and unmarshalling, taking care of content negotiation, which means less work for us. Let's start with handling the `Content-Type` header in the `POST`.

HANDLING CONTENT-TYPE IN A CUSTOM UNMARSHALLER

Akka-http provides a number of predefined types for unmarshalling data from entities, byte arrays, strings, and such. It also makes it possible to create a custom `Unmarshaller`. In this example we'll only support two content types: `text/plain` to indicate the log format and `application/json` to indicate the log events in JSON format. Based on the `Content-Type`, the `entity.dataBytes` source is framed as delimited lines or as JSON, and is processed as usual.

The `Unmarshaller` trait only requires one method to be implemented.

Listing 13.23   Handling `Content-Type` in the `EventUnmarshaller`

```
import akka.http.scaladsl.unmarshalling.Unmarshaller
import akka.http.scaladsl.unmarshalling.Unmarshaller._

object EventUnmarshaller extends EventMarshalling {
  val supported = Set[ContentTypeRange](
    ContentTypes.`text/plain(UTF-8)`,
    ContentTypes.`application/json`
  )

  def create(maxLine: Int, maxJsonObject: Int) = {
    new Unmarshaller[HttpEntity, Source[Event, _]] {
      def apply(entity: HttpEntity)(implicit ec: ExecutionContext,
        materializer: Materializer): Future[Source[Event, _]] = {

        val future = entity.contentType match {
          case ContentTypes.`text/plain(UTF-8)` =>
            Future.successful(LogJson.textInFlow(maxLine))
          case ContentTypes.`application/json` =>
            Future.successful(LogJson.jsonInFlow(maxJsonObject))
          case other =>
            Future.failed(
              new UnsupportedContentTypeException(supported)
            )
        }
        future.map(flow => entity.dataBytes.via(flow))(ec)
      }
    }.forContentTypes(supported.toList:_*)
  }
}
```

- **The set of supported content type ranges**
- **apply turns an entity into a future source of events**
- **The custom Unmarshaller**
- **Pattern matches on the content type, wraps a Flow in a Future**
- **Moves the flows for the formats to a LogJson object**
- **Gets a non-exhaustive pattern-match warning**
- **Creates a new source using via on dataBytes Source**
- **Constrains the allowed content types for default akka-http behavior**

The `create` method creates an anonymous `Unmarshaller` instance. The `apply` method first creates a `Flow` to handle the incoming data, which is composed with the `dataBytesSource` using `via` to become a new `Source`.

   This `Unmarshaller` has to be put in implicit scope so that the `entity` directive can be used to extract the `Source[Event, _]`, which can be found in the `ContentNegLogsApi` class.

Listing 13.24   Using the `EventUnmarshaller` in the `POST`

```
implicit val unmarshaller = EventUnmarshaller.create(maxLine, maxJsObject)

def postRoute =
  pathPrefix("logs" / Segment) { logId =>
    pathEndOrSingleSlash {
      post {
        entity(as[Source[Event, _]]) { src =>
          onComplete(
            src.via(outFlow)
              .toMat(logFileSink(logId))(Keep.right)
              .run()
          ) {
            // Handling Future result omitted here, done the same as before.
```

- **Creates and puts the Unmarshaller in implicit scope**
- **entity(as[T]) requires the Unmarshaller in implicit scope**

Trying out `aia.stream.ContentNegLogsApp` is left as an exercise to the reader. Be sure to specify the `Content-Type`, using `httpie`, for instance. Examples are shown next.

Listing 13.25 Example POSTs with httpie, using the Content-Type header

```
http -v POST localhost:5000/logs/1 Content-Type:text/plain < test.log
http -v POST localhost:5000/logs/2 Content-Type:application/json < test.json
```

In the next section, we'll look at handling the `Accept` header for content negotiation using a custom marshaller.

CONTENT NEGOTIATION WITH A CUSTOM MARSHALLER

We'll write a custom `Marshaller` to support `text/plain` and `application/json` content types in the response. The `Accept` header can be used to specify certain media types that are acceptable for the response. Some examples are shown in the following listing using `httpie`.

Listing 13.26 Example GETs with httpie, using the Accept header

```
http -v GET localhost:5000/logs/1 'Accept:application/json'    ◁— Only accept JSON
http -v GET localhost:5000/logs/1 'Accept:text/plain'
http -v GET localhost:5000/logs/1 \
'Accept: text/html, text/plain;q=0.8, application/json;q=0.5'    ◁—
```

Only accept text (the log format)

Prefer text/html, otherwise text/plain; otherwise, JSON

The client can express that it only accepts a particular `Content-type` or that it has a specific preference. The logic that determines which `Content-Type` should be responded with is implemented in Akka. All we have to do is create a `Marshaller` that supports a set of content types.

The `LogEntityMarshaller` object creates a `ToEntityMarshaller`.

Listing 13.27 Providing marshallers for content negotiation

```
import akka.http.scaladsl.marshalling.Marshaller
import akka.http.scaladsl.marshalling.ToEntityMarshaller

object LogEntityMarshaller extends EventMarshalling {

  type LEM = ToEntityMarshaller[Source[ByteString, _]]
  def create(maxJsonObject: Int): LEM = {
    val js = ContentTypes.`application/json`
    val txt = ContentTypes.`text/plain(UTF-8)`

    val jsMarshaller = Marshaller.withFixedContentType(js) {    ◁—
      src:Source[ByteString, _] =>
      HttpEntity(js, src)
    }

    val txtMarshaller = Marshaller.withFixedContentType(txt) {    ◁—
      src:Source[ByteString, _] =>
      HttpEntity(txt, toText(src, maxJsonObject))
    }
```

Log file is stored in JSON, so streams it directly

Log file needs to be converted back to log lines

<table>
<tr><td>

oneOf creates one "super-marshaller" from the two marshallers

</td><td>

```
    Marshaller.oneOf(jsMarshaller, txtMarshaller)
  }

  def toText(src: Source[ByteString, _],
             maxJsonObject: Int): Source[ByteString, _] = {
    src.via(LogJson.jsonToLogFlow(maxJsonObject))
  }
}
```
</td></tr>
</table>

Moves the flows for the formats to a LogJson object

`Marshaller.withFixedContentType` is a convenience method that creates a `Marshaller` for a specific `Content-Type`. It takes a function, `A => B`, which is `Source[ByteString, Any] => HttpEntity` in this case. The `src` provides the bytes of the JSON log file, which is converted to an `HttpEntity`.

The `LogJson.jsonToLogFlow` method uses the same trick that we used before, joining a `BidiFlow` with a `Flow[Event]`, this time from JSON to log format.

This `Marshaller` has to be put in implicit scope so it can be used in the HTTP `GET` route.

Listing 13.28 Using the `LogEntityMarshaller` in the `GET`

```
implicit val marshaller = LogEntityMarshaller.create(maxJsObject)

def getRoute =
  pathPrefix("logs" / Segment) { logId =>
    pathEndOrSingleSlash {
      get {
        extractRequest { req =>
          if(Files.exists(logFile(logId))) {
            val src = logFileSource(logId)
            complete(Marshal(src).toResponseFor(req))
          } else {
            complete(StatusCodes.NotFound)
          }
        }
      }
    }
  }
```

Creates and puts the marshaller in implicit scope

extractRequest directive extracts request

toResponseFor uses implicit marshaller

`Marshal(src).toResponseFor(req)` takes the log file `Source` and creates a response for it based on the request (including the `Accept` header), which sets off the content negotiation using `LogEntityMarshaller`.

That concludes the examples of supporting both formats using the `Content-Type` header and content negotiation with the `Accept` header.

Both `LogsApi` and `ContentNegLogsApp` read and write events unchanged. We could filter events on their state whenever that's requested, but it would make more sense to have events split on the state (OK, warning, error, critical) and store those events in separate files, so that, for instance, all the errors could be retrieved without having to filter them every time. In the next section, we'll look at how to fan out and fan in with akka-stream. We'll split the event states into separate files on the server, but we'll also make it possible to retrieve a subselection of the states, like all states that are not OK.

JSON STREAMING SUPPORT The example here supports both a text log format and a JSON format for log events. There's an easier option for when you want to only support JSON. The EntityStreamingSupport object in the akka.http .scaladsl.common package provides a JsonEntityStreamingSupport through the EntityStreamingSupport.json, which, when put into implicit scope, makes it possible to complete an HTTP request directly with a list of events by using complete(events). It also makes it possible to get a Source[Event, NotUsed] directly from entity(asSourceOf[Event]).

13.3 *Fan in and fan out with the graph DSL*

So far we've only looked at linear processing with one input and one output. Akka-stream provides a graph DSL to describe fan-in and fan-out scenarios, which can have any number of inputs and outputs. The graph DSL is almost a kind of diagramming ASCII art—in many cases you could translate a whiteboard diagram of a graph into the DSL.

There are numerous fan-in and fan-out GraphStages that can be used to create all kinds of graphs, just like Source, Flow, and Sink. It's also possible to create your own custom GraphStage.

You can create a graph of any Shape with the graph DSL. In terms of akka-stream, a Shape defines how many inputs and outputs the graph has (these inputs and outputs are called Inlets and Outlets). In the next example, we'll create a Flow-shaped graph so it can be used in the POST route like before. Internally it will use a fan-out shape.

13.3.1 *Broadcasting to flows*

In our experience with the graph DSL, we'll split the log events along their state (one Sink for all errors, one for all warnings, and so on), so that the events don't have to be filtered every time a GET request is made for one or more of these states. Figure 13.13 shows how a BroadcastGraphStage is used to send the events to different Flows.

The graph DSL provides GraphDSL.Builder to create the nodes in the graph, and a ~> method is used to connect nodes together, much like the via method. A node in a graph is of type Graph, which could be confusing when referring to a part of the graph, so we'll use the term "node" instead in certain cases.

The following listing shows how the graph in figure 13.13 is built in code. It also shows how a flow is defined from the open inlet and outlet of the graph.

Listing 13.29 Broadcast to separate log sinks

```
import akka.stream.{ FlowShape, Graph }
import akka.stream.scaladsl.{ Broadcast, GraphDSL, RunnableGraph }

type FlowLike = Graph[FlowShape[Event, ByteString], NotUsed]

def processStates(logId: String): FlowLike = {
  val jsFlow = LogJson.jsonOutFlow
  Flow.fromGraph(
    GraphDSL.create() { implicit builder =>
```

A flow will be created from the Graph, and it will be used in the POST route.

builder is a GraphDSL.Builder

Brings the DSL methods into scope

Adds a Broadcast node to the Graph

For every other output, a filter is added in front of the JSON Flow.

Adds a Flow node to the Graph to pass through all events, unchanged in JSON format

One of the Broadcast outputs writes directly to the inlet of the js node for all events.

Creates a Flow-shaped Graph out of the inlet of the Broadcast and the outlet of the JSON Flow

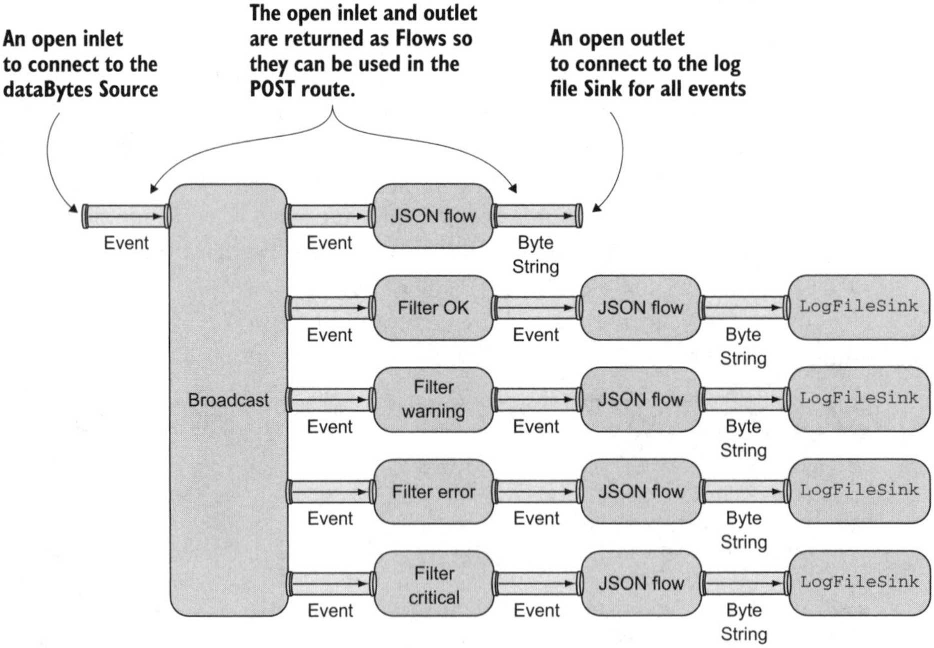

```scala
import GraphDSL.Implicits._
// all logs, ok, warning, error, critical, so 5 outputs
val bcast = builder.add(Broadcast[Event](5))
val js = builder.add(jsFlow)

val ok = Flow[Event].filter(_.state == Ok)
val warning = Flow[Event].filter(_.state == Warning)
val error = Flow[Event].filter(_.state == Error)
val critical = Flow[Event].filter(_.state == Critical)

bcast ~> js.in
bcast ~> ok       ~> jsFlow ~> logFileSink(logId, Ok)
bcast ~> warning  ~> jsFlow ~> logFileSink(logId, Warning)
bcast ~> error    ~> jsFlow ~> logFileSink(logId, Error)
bcast ~> critical ~> jsFlow ~> logFileSink(logId, Critical)

FlowShape(bcast.in, js.out)
})
}

def logFileSource(logId: String, state: State) =
  FileIO.fromPath(logStateFile(logId, state))
def logFileSink(logId: String, state: State) =
  FileIO.toPath(logStateFile(logId, state), Set(CREATE, WRITE, APPEND))
def logStateFile(logId: String, state: State) =
  logFile(s"$logId-${State.norm(state)}")
```

An open inlet to connect to the dataBytes Source

The open inlet and outlet are returned as Flows so they can be used in the POST route.

An open outlet to connect to the log file Sink for all events

Figure 13.13 Splitting events with a `BroadcastGraphStage`

> **It's Graphs and Shapes all the way down**
>
> The return type of `processStates` might not be what you expected (the `FlowLike` type alias is just there for formatting reasons). Instead of a `Flow[Event, ByteString, NotUsed]` type, a `Graph[FlowShape[Event, ByteString], NotUsed]` is used.
>
> In fact, a `Flow[-In, +Out, +Mat]` extends from a `Graph[FlowShape[In, Out], Mat]`. This shows that a `Flow` is just a `Graph` with a predefined `Shape`. If you look a little deeper into the akka-stream source code, you'll find that a `FlowShape` is a `Shape` with exactly one input and one output.
>
> All the predefined components are defined in a similar way: everything is defined as a `Graph` with a `Shape`. For instance, `Source` and `Sink` extend `Graph[SourceShape[Out], Mat]` and `Graph[SinkShape[In], Mat]`, respectively.

The `builder` argument is a `GraphDSL.Builder`, which is mutable. It's only intended to be used inside the anonymous function here to set up a graph. The `GraphDSL.Builder`'s `add` method returns a `Shape`, which describes the inlets and outlets of a `Graph`.

You should see a resemblance between the DSL code and figure 13.13. The filtered flows write to separate files, as shown by the `logFileSink(logId, state)` method calls. For example, for errors of `logId1`, a `1-errors` file is appended to.

`processStates` is used as you would expect, like any other flow.

Listing 13.30 Using `processStates` in the POST route

```
src.via(processStates(logId))
  .toMat(logFileSink(logId))(Keep.right)
  .run()
```

The GET route for returning errors for a log file is very similar to the normal GET route, except that a naming convention is used to read from a `[log-id]-error` file.

In the next section, we'll look at merging sources so you can return all logs merged together, or just the log events that weren't OK for a log file.

13.3.2 Merging flows

Let's look at the graph for merging sources. In the first example, we'll merge all the states for a log ID that aren't OK. A GET to `/logs/[log-id]/not-ok` will return all events that aren't OK. Figure 13.14 shows how a `MergeGraphStage` is used to combine three `Sources` into one.

The following listing shows how the `MergeGraphStage` is used in the graph DSL. It defines a `mergeNotOk` method that merges all the non-OK log `Sources` for a particular `logId` into one `Source`.

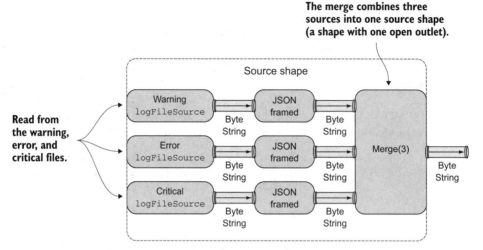

Figure 13.14   Merging non-OK states with a `MergeGraphStage`

Listing 13.31   Merge all states that are not OK

```
import akka.stream.SourceShape
import akka.stream.scaladsl.{ GraphDSL, Merge }

def mergeNotOk(logId: String): Source[ByteString, NotUsed] = {
  val warning = logFileSource(logId, Warning)
    .via(LogJson.jsonFramed(maxJsObject))
  val error = logFileSource(logId, Error)
    .via(LogJson.jsonFramed(maxJsObject))
  val critical = logFileSource(logId, Critical)
    .via(LogJson.jsonFramed(maxJsObject))

  Source.fromGraph(
    GraphDSL.create() { implicit builder =>
    import GraphDSL.Implicits._

    val warningShape = builder.add(warning)
    val errorShape = builder.add(error)
    val criticalShape = builder.add(critical)
    val merge = builder.add(Merge[ByteString](3))

    warningShape  ~> merge
    errorShape    ~> merge
    criticalShape ~> merge
    SourceShape(merge.out)
  })
}
```

A source will be
created from the
Graph, and it will be
used in the GET route.

Note that the warning, error, and critical sources are passed through a JSON framing flow first, because otherwise you could read arbitrary ByteStrings and merge
them together, resulting in garbled JSON output.

The three sources are merged with a MergeGraphStage that takes three inputs, so all inlets are taken. Merge has one outlet (merge.out). The SourceShape is created from the merge.out outlet. Source has a fromGraph convenience method that turns a Graph with a SourceShape into a Source.

The mergeNotOk method is used later in getLogNotOkRoute to create a Source to read from, as shown in the next listing.

> **THE MERGEPREFERRED GRAPHSTAGE** The MergeGraphStage randomly takes elements from any of its inputs. Akka-stream also provides a MergePreferred-GraphStage, which has one out port, one preferred input port, and zero or more secondary in ports. MergePreferred emits when one of the inputs has an element available, preferring the preferred input if multiple inputs have elements available.

Listing 13.32 Respond to GET /logs/[log-id]/not-ok

```
def getLogNotOkRoute =
  pathPrefix("logs" / Segment /"not-ok") { logId =>
    pathEndOrSingleSlash {
      get {
        extractRequest { req =>
          complete(Marshal(mergeNotOk(logId)).toResponseFor(req))
        }
      }
    }
  }
```

There's also a simplified API for merging sources, which we'll use to merge all logs. Requesting GET /logs will return all logs merged together. The next listing shows how this simplified API is used.

Listing 13.33 The mergeSources method

```
import akka.stream.scaladsl.Merge

def mergeSources[E](
  sources: Vector[Source[E, _]]          ◁─── Merges all sources
): Option[Source[E, _]] = {                    in the Vector
  if(sources.size ==0) None              ◁─── None is returned if the
  else if(sources.size == 1) Some(sources(0))   sources argument is empty.
  else {
    Some(Source.combine(                 ◁─── Combines any number of sources;
      sources(0),                              the first two arguments are of
      sources(1),                              type Source, and the third is a
      sources.drop(2) : _*                     variable length argument list
    )(Merge(_)))                         ◁─── Merge is passed in as
  }                                            the fan-in strategy.
}
```

The `Source.combine` method creates a `Source` out of a number of sources, similar to how this was done with the graph DSL. The `mergeSources` method is used to merge any number of sources of the same type. For example, the `mergeSources` method is used in the `/logs` route, shown in the following listing.

Listing 13.34 Respond to `GET /logs`

```
def getLogsRoute =                                  getFileSources, not shown here,
  pathPrefix("logs") {                             lists the files in logsDir and
    pathEndOrSingleSlash {                       converts these to Sources with
      get {                                              FileIO.fromPath.
        extractRequest { req =>
          val sources = getFileSources(logsDir).map { src =>
            src.via(LogJson.jsonFramed(maxJsObject))       Every file source needs
          }                                                to pass through the
          mergeSources(sources) match {                    JSON framing flow.
            case Some(src) =>
              complete(Marshal(src).toResponseFor(req))
            case None =>
              complete(StatusCodes.NotFound)               Merges all the file
          }                                                sources found in the
        }                                                  logsDir directory
      }
    }
  }
}
```

PREDEFINED AND CUSTOM GRAPHSTAGES   There are quite a few predefined `GraphStages` in akka-stream that aren't shown here for load balancing (`Balance`), zipping (`Zip`, `ZipWith`), and concatenating streams (`Concat`), to name a few. The graph DSL for these works much like the examples already shown. In all cases, you need to add nodes to the builder, connect the inlets and outlets of the shapes (returned by the `add` method), and return some shape from the function, which is then passed to the `Graph.create` method. It's also possible to write your own custom `GraphStage`, which is beyond the scope of this introductory chapter on akka-stream.

The `BroadcastGraphStage` shown in this section applies back pressure when any of the outputs apply back pressure, which means that you can only broadcast as fast as the slowest consumer can read. The next section will discuss how buffering can be used to allow producers and consumers to run at different speeds, and how we can mediate between producers and consumers that run at different speeds.

13.4 *Mediating between producers and consumers*

The next example we'll look at involves broadcasting events to consuming services. So far we've written the log events to disk—one file for all events for a log file, and several files for the warnings, errors, and critical errors. Switching the `Sink` to write all log events to an external service instead of disk is left as an exercise for the reader.

In this final version of the log-stream processor, events will be sent to an archival service, a notifications service, and a metrics service.

The log-stream processor will have to balance supply and demand to make sure that when one of the services applies back pressure, this won't slow down the producer of log events. In the next section, we'll discuss how buffers can be used to achieve this.

Integrating with services

In the example in this section, we expect all services to provide `Sinks`. Akka-stream has several options for integrating external services that don't provide `Sources` or `Sinks`. For example, the `mapAsync` method takes a `Future` and emits the result of the `Future` further downstream, which can come in handy when you already have a service client code that uses `Futures`.

It's also possible to integrate with other Reactive Streams implementations using `Source.fromPublisher` and `Sink.fromSubscriber`, turning any Reactive Streams `Publisher` into a `Source` and any `Subscriber` into a `Sink`.

It's also possible to integrate with `Actors` using the `ActorPublisher` and `ActorSubscriber` traits, which can be useful in specific cases.

The best and easiest option is to use an akka-stream-based library that provides `Sources`, `Sinks`, or both.

13.4.1 Using buffers

Let's look at the graph for processing events, now adapted to send data to the three service sinks. We'll zoom in to the components of the graph in this section. Figures 13.15–13.16 show the graph.

A `Broadcast` is added on every filtered flow. One output is writing to the log file `Sink` as usual, and the other output is used to send data to downstream services. (The expectation here is that the log file `Sinks` are really fast, so they aren't buffered.) A `MergePreferred` stage merges all notification summaries to a `Sink` for the notification service, preferring the critical event summaries over error and warning summaries. A critical event summary always contains one critical event. In effect, it's not rolled up but immediately sent through.

The OK events are also split off using a `Broadcast`, and they're sent to the metrics service.

The figure also shows where buffers are inserted. The buffers allow for the downstream consumers to differ in the speed at which they consume data. But when a buffer is full, a decision has to be made.

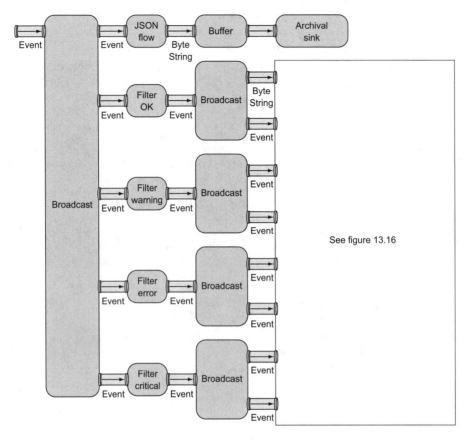

Figure 13.15   Log event processing graph

The `buffer` method on `Flow` requires two arguments: a buffer size and an `Overflow-Strategy`, which decides what should happen when the buffer is about to overflow. The `OverflowStrategy` can be set to one of `dropHead`, `dropTail`, `dropBuffer`, `drop-New`, `backpressure`, or `fail`, respectively dropping the first element in the buffer, the last element in the buffer, the entire buffer, or the newest element; or applying back pressure when the buffer is full; or failing the entire flow. Which option you choose depends on the requirements of the application and what's most important in the specific use case.

In this example, the decision has been made that, even under high load, all events must be archived, meaning that the log-stream processor flow should fail when it can't write events to the archival service sink. A producer can try again later. The buffer is set to a large size, to take the hit if the archival sink is responding slowly for a while.

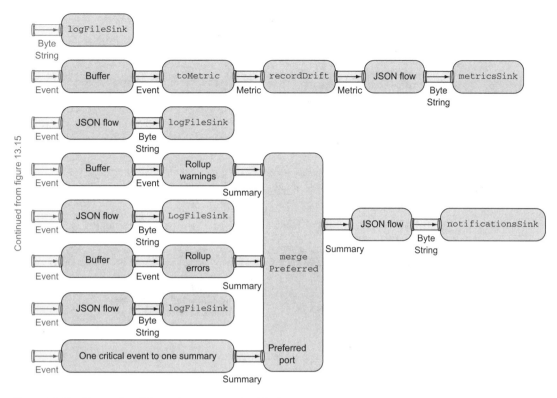

Figure 13.16   Processing OK, warning, error, and critical events

The following listing shows how the buffers are set up in the graph.

Listing 13.35   Buffers in the graph

```
val archBuf = Flow[Event]
  .buffer(archBufSize, OverflowStrategy.fail)
val warnBuf = Flow[Event]
  .buffer(warnBufSize, OverflowStrategy.dropHead)
val errBuf = Flow[Event]
  .buffer(errBufSize, OverflowStrategy.backpressure)
val metricBuf = Flow[Event]
  .buffer(errBufSize, OverflowStrategy.dropHead)
```

> **Buffer overflow in the archive flow fails the flow**

> **Oldest warnings are dropped when the buffer is about to overflow**

> **Errors buffer will back-pressure when it's full**

> **Oldest metrics are dropped when the buffer is full**

The oldest warnings can be dropped under high load if the notification service sink is slow. Error summaries must not be dropped. Critical errors aren't buffered, so the flow will back-pressure by default.

The graph is built up again with the graph DSL as follows.

Listing 13.36   Building the graph nodes

```
val bcast = builder.add(Broadcast[Event](5))
val wbcast = builder.add(Broadcast[Event](2))
val ebcast = builder.add(Broadcast[Event](2))
val cbcast = builder.add(Broadcast[Event](2))
val okcast = builder.add(Broadcast[Event](2))

val mergeNotify = builder.add(MergePreferred[Summary](2))
val archive = builder.add(jsFlow)
```

MergePreferred always has one preferred port and a number of secondary ports, in this case two. We'll look into the individual flows a little later.

First, the following listing shows how all the graph nodes are connected.

Listing 13.37   Connecting the graph nodes

```
bcast ~> archBuf   ~> archive.in        ◄─── Unfiltered events are buffered
bcast ~> ok        ~> okcast                 and connected to outgoing
bcast ~> warning   ~> wbcast                 archival service flow
bcast ~> error     ~> ebcast
bcast ~> critical  ~> cbcast

okcast ~> jsFlow ~> logFileSink(logId, Ok)
okcast ~> metricBuf ~>
   toMetric ~> recordDrift ~> metricOutFlow ~> metricsSink    Metrics flow

cbcast ~> jsFlow ~> logFileSink(logId, Critical)
cbcast ~> toNot ~> mergeNotify.preferred         ◄─── Critical errors are
                                                       preferred in the
ebcast ~> jsFlow ~> logFileSink(logId, Error)          merge, if more than
ebcast ~> errBuf ~> rollupErr ~> mergeNotify.in(0)     one input has data.    Errors flow

wbcast ~> jsFlow ~> logFileSink(logId, Warning)
wbcast ~> warnBuf ~> rollupWarn ~> mergeNotify.in(1)      Warnings flow

mergeNotify ~> notifyOutFlow ~> notificationSink

FlowShape(bcast.in, archive.out)
```

In the next section, we'll look at how we can process elements at different rates in the flows. A special kind of stream operation will be used to detach the rate of one side of a flow from the other.

13.5   *Rate-detaching parts of a graph*

The back pressure that's automatically applied by all akka-stream components sometimes needs to be *detached* from parts of the graph. There are cases where you don't want one back-pressuring node in the graph to slow down all nodes. In other cases, you'll want to be able to keep feeding data to a consumer that can operate faster than other nodes. Again, a back-pressuring node can prevent this.

The common technique for rate-detaching is to put a buffer between nodes. The buffer will delay back pressure as long as it has space.

To explain how rate-detaching works, we'll assume that the notifications service is a slow consumer. Instead of sending on every single notification when it arrives, we'll roll up notifications into a summary, essentially buffering notifications that arrive during a time window.

The metrics service is assumed to be a fast consumer, so we can do a little more processing. In this case, we'll record how much the log-stream processor is drifting behind on what the metrics service could potentially consume.

Other kinds of expanding techniques are possible, like sending calculated summaries between normal metrics events or interpolating metrics events. These are left as exercises for the reader.

13.5.1 *Slow consumer, rolling up events into summaries*

The log-stream processor will have to write `Summaries` to a notifications service that notifies operators of important events. Notification summaries are prioritized: critical events are immediately sent one by one, whereas errors and warnings are rolled up into summaries based on a time window or a maximum number of events.

To keep the interface simple, all notification messages are sent as `Summarys`, so a critical event is sent as a `Summary` containing one `Event`.

> **Listing 13.38 Summaries of one critical event**

```
val toNot = Flow[Event].map(e=> Summary(Vector(e)))
```

The warnings and errors are rolled up using `groupedWithin`, as shown in the following listing. `rollupErr` and `rollupWarn`, shown earlier in listing 13.37, use the `rollup` method defined here to turn `Events` into `Summarys`.

> **Listing 13.39 Roll up `Events` using `groupedWithin`**

```
def rollup(nr: Int, duration: FiniteDuration) =      ◁──┐  groupedWithin
  Flow[Event].groupedWithin(nr, duration)                │  returns List[Event]
    .map(events => Summary(events.toVector))

val rollupErr = rollup(nrErrors, errDuration)
val rollupWarn = rollup(nrWarnings, warnDuration)
```

> **GROUPEDWITHIN AT COMPLETION OF STREAM** It's important to note that `groupedWithin` will emit the remaining buffer as a `Summary` once the stream is completed. A log events producer in this example is expected to continually send data. If you try the `aia.stream.LogStreamProcessorApp` and send a log file to the service, you'll notice that what remains is always written to the notifications file, even if fewer events have occurred or the duration hasn't passed.

As shown in listing 13.37, the `rollupErr` and `rollupWarn` are merged into `Merge-Preferred`, preferring the critical errors that might occur.

13.5.2 *Fast consumer, expanding metrics*

The metrics service in this scenario is a fast consumer. We're still applying a buffer for when it happens to be slow, but because it might be faster than the log-stream processor, it would be interesting to know when the log-stream processor is falling behind what the metrics service could potentially consume. The following listing shows how an Event is turned into a Metric.

> **Listing 13.40 Turning an Event into a Metric**

```
val toMetric = Flow[Event].collect {
  case Event(_, service, _, time, _, Some(tag), Some(metric)) =>
    Metric(service, time, metric, tag)
}
```

The expand method makes it possible to add some information to the output when the consumer requests more than is available. Instead of applying back pressure, you can generate elements to send back to the consumer.

In this case, we'll send the same metric back, but with an additional drift field to indicate how many elements the metrics service could have consumed if the log-stream processor was fast enough.

> **Listing 13.41 Adding drift information to the Metric**

```
val recordDrift = Flow[Metric]
  .expand { metric =>
    Iterator.from(0).map(d => metric.copy(drift = d))
  }
```

The expand method takes a function argument of type Out =< Iterator[U]. The U type is inferred from the function, which is a Metric in this case. When there are no elements available from the flow, it will pull elements from this iterator. The drift field will be zero if the log-stream processor could keep up, and it will go up, repeating the Metric data to the metrics service, when the metrics service is faster.

It's important to note that the buffers we've used here can't prevent streams from failing in all scenarios. In this context, that would simply mean that a streaming HTTP request would fail. The next could possibly complete.

13.6 *Summary*

Building streaming applications with Akka is a very large topic, and we only scratched the surface here. Still, it should be evident that akka-stream provides a generic and flexible API for writing streaming applications. The ability to define a graph blueprint and execute it later is crucial for reuse.

In simple linear cases it's easy to use the combinators on Source, Flow, and Sink. The BidiFlow is an excellent component for building reusable protocols. If you've ever written streaming HTTP applications, you're likely to agree that it was remarkably easy to switch from files to akka-http in section 13.2.

The fact that akka-http is built on top of akka-stream really pays off, as you saw when we integrated content negotiation and handling content types using custom marshallers and unmarshallers.

Back pressure makes it possible to process streams in bounded memory, which is applied by default, and which can be modified with predefined methods like `buffer` and `expand`.

Akka-stream comes with a lot of useful predefined graph stages. We've only discussed a few here, and many more are expected to be added, possibly in a separate *akka-stream-contrib* library, making the need for building custom `GraphStages` (which we didn't discuss in this chapter) less necessary over time.

14

Clustering

In chapter 6 you learned how to build a distributed application with a fixed number of nodes. The approach we took, using static membership, is simple but provides no out-of-the-box support for load balancing or failover. A cluster makes it possible to dynamically grow and shrink the number of nodes used by a distributed application, and removes the fear of a single point of failure.

Many distributed applications run in environments that aren't completely under your control, like cloud computing platforms or data centers located across the world. The larger the cluster, the greater the chance of failure. Despite this, there are complete means of monitoring and controlling the lifecycle of the cluster. In the first section of this chapter, we'll look at how a node becomes a member of the cluster, how you can listen to membership events, and how you can detect that nodes have crashed in the cluster.

First we'll build a clustered app that counts the number of occurrences of each word in a piece of text. Within the context of this example, you'll learn how routers can be used to communicate with actors in the cluster, how you can build a resilient, coordinated process consisting of many actors in the cluster, and how to test a clustered actor system.

14.1 Why use clustering?

A *cluster* is a dynamic group of nodes. On each node is an actor system that listens on the network (like you saw in chapter 6). Clusters build on top of the `akka-remote` module. Clustering takes location transparency to the next level. The actor might exist locally or remotely and could reside anywhere in the cluster; your code doesn't have to concern itself with this. Figure 14.1 shows a cluster of four nodes.

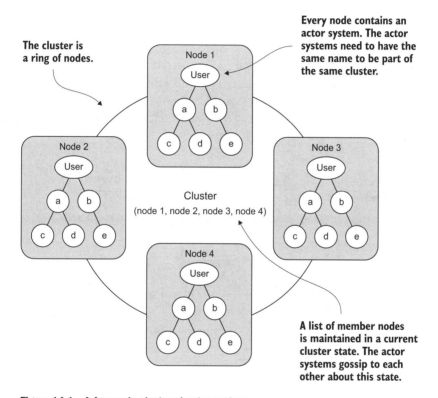

Figure 14.1   A four-node clustered actor system

The ultimate goal for the cluster module is to provide fully automated features for actor distribution, load balancing, and failover. Right now the cluster module supports the following features:

- *Cluster membership*—Fault-tolerant membership for actor systems.
- *Load balancing*—Routing messages to actors in the cluster based on a routing algorithm.

- *Node partitioning*—A node can be given a specific role in the cluster. Routers can be configured to only send messages to nodes with a specific role.
- *Partition points*—An actor system can be partitioned into actor subtrees that are located on different nodes.

We'll dive into the details of these features in this chapter and focus primarily on cluster membership and routing. Chapter 15 details mechanisms for replication of state and automatic failover.

A single-purpose data processing application is a good example of a candidate application for using clusters, for example, data processing tasks like image recognition or real-time analysis of social media. Nodes can be added or removed when more or less processing power is required. Processing jobs are supervised: if an actor fails, the job is restarted and retried on the cluster until it succeeds. We'll look at a simple example of this type of application in this chapter. Figure 14.2 shows an overview for this type of application; don't worry about the details here, because we'll introduce the terms you may not be familiar with later in this chapter.

Let's move on to writing the code to compile our clustered word count application. In the next section, we'll dig into the details of cluster membership so that the job masters and workers can find each other to work together.

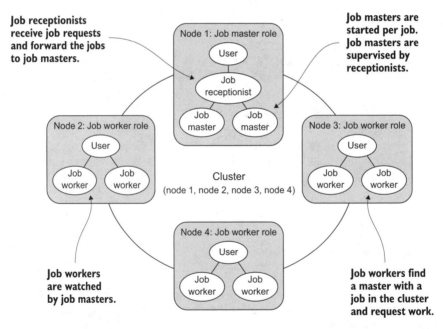

Figure 14.2   Processing jobs

14.2 Cluster membership

We will start with the creation of the cluster. The processing cluster will consist of job master and worker nodes. Figure 14.3 shows the cluster that we'll build.

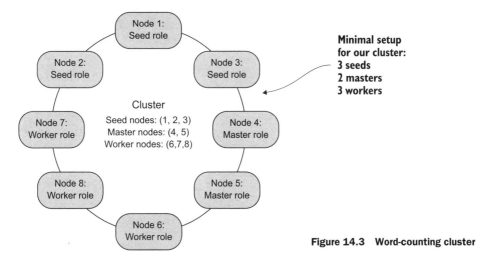

Figure 14.3   Word-counting cluster

The job master nodes control and supervise the completion of word-counting jobs. The job workers request work from a job master, process parts of the text, and return the partial results to the master. The job master reports the result once all word counting has been done. A job is repeated if any master or worker node fails during the process.

Figure 14.3 also shows another type of node that will be required in the cluster, namely, *seed nodes*. The seed nodes are essential for starting the cluster. In the next section, we'll look at how nodes become seed nodes, and how they can join and leave the cluster. We'll look at the details of how a cluster is formed and experiment with joining and leaving a simple cluster using the REPL console. You'll learn about the different states that a member node can go through and how you can subscribe to notifications of these state changes.

14.2.1 Joining the cluster

Like with any kind of group, you need a couple of "founders" to start off the process. Akka provides a seed node feature for this purpose. Seed nodes are the starting point for the cluster, and they serve as the first point of contact for other nodes. Nodes join the cluster by sending a *join* message that contains the unique address of the node that joins. The Cluster module takes care of sending this message to one of the registered seed nodes. It's not required for a node to contain any actors, so it's possible to use purely seed nodes. Figure 14.4 shows how a first seed node initializes a cluster and how other nodes join the cluster.

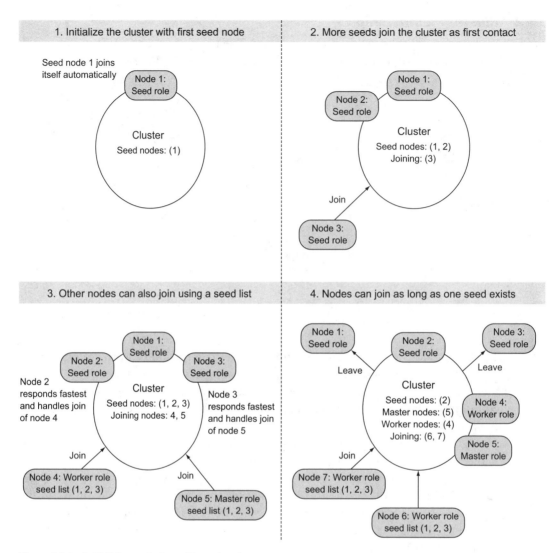

Figure 14.4   Initializing a cluster with seed nodes

Cluster doesn't (yet) support a zero-configuration discovery protocol like TCP multicast or DNS service discovery. You have to specify a list of seed nodes, or somehow know the host and port of a cluster node to join to. The first seed node in the list has a special role in initially forming the cluster. The very next seed node is dependent on the first seed node in the list. The first node in the seed list starts up and automatically joins itself and forms the cluster. The first seed node needs to be up before the next seed nodes can join the cluster. This constraint has been put in place to prevent separate clusters from forming while seed nodes are starting up.

Manually joining cluster nodes

The seed nodes feature is not required; you can create a cluster manually by starting a node that joins itself. Subsequent nodes will then have to join that node to join the cluster, by sending it a `Join` message.

This means that they'll have to know the address of the first node, so it makes more sense to use the seed functionality. There are cases where you can't know IP addresses or DNS names of servers in a network beforehand. In those cases, there are three choices that seem plausible:

- Use a list of known pure seed nodes with well-known IP addresses or DNS names, outside of the network where host name addresses can't be predetermined. These seed nodes don't run any application-specific code and purely function as a first point of contact for the rest of the cluster.
- Get your hands dirty building your own zero-configuration cluster discovery protocol that fits your network environment. This is a non-trivial task.
- Use existing service discovery/registry technology like Apache ZooKeeper, HashiCorp Consul, or CoreOs/etcd and add some "glue." Instrument every cluster node with some code to register itself with the discovery service on startup and write an adapter that gets the currently available cluster nodes from a service like this to connect to the cluster.

Mind you, a ZooKeeper solution will still require a full set of host and port combinations, so you're trading in one well-known set of addresses for another. This is also not as trivial as it sounds, since you have to keep the discovery service up to date on the availability of every cluster node, and the discovery service might depend on a different set of trade-offs than an Akka cluster, which might not be immediately apparent. Caution is advised. (Different consistency models will probably apply and your mileage may vary on experience in identifying these trade-offs.)

The seed nodes can all boot independently as long as the first seed node in the list is started at some point. A subsequent seed node will wait for the first node to come up. Other nodes join the cluster through any of the seed nodes once the first node is started and at least one other node has joined. A message is sent to all seed nodes; the first seed node to respond will get to handle the join command. The first seed node can safely leave the cluster once the cluster has two or more members. Figure 14.5 shows an overview of how a cluster of masters and workers can be formed after at least the first seed node has started:

Let's start by creating seed nodes using the REPL console, which will give more insight into how a cluster is formed.

To be clear, you wouldn't go through these steps manually once you actually deploy a clustered application. Depending on your environment, it's most likely that assigning addresses and starting the seed nodes in the cluster are part of provisioning and deployment scripts.

You can find the project for this example under the chapter-cluster directory.

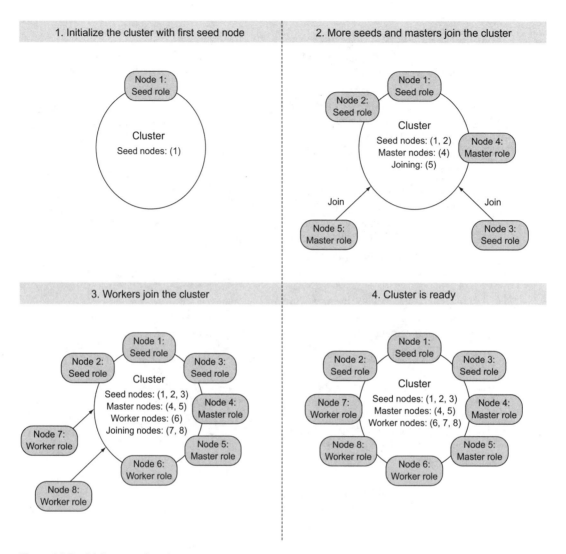

Figure 14.5 A job-processing cluster

A node first needs to be configured to use the cluster module. The `akka-cluster` dependency needs to be added to the build file as shown:

```
"com.typesafe.akka" %% "akka-cluster" % akkaVersion
```
◁ **Build file defines a val for the version of Akka**

The `akka.cluster.ClusterActorRefProvider` needs to be configured in much the same way as the `akka-remote` module needed a `akka.remote.RemoteActorRefProvider`. The `Cluster` API is provided as an Akka extension. The `ClusterActorRefProvider` initializes the `Cluster` extension when the actor system is created.

The following listing shows a minimal configuration for the seed nodes (which can be found in src/main/resources/seed.conf).

Listing 14.1 Configuring the seed nodes

```
akka {
  loglevel = INFO
  stdout-loglevel = INFO
  event-handlers = ["akka.event.Logging$DefaultLogger"]

  log-dead-letters = 0
  log-dead-letters-during-shutdown = off

  actor {
    provider = "akka.cluster.ClusterActorRefProvider" #  ⟵  Initializes cluster module
  }

  remote { #                                          ⟵  Remote configuration for this seed node
    enabled-transports = ["akka.remote.netty.tcp"]
    log-remote-lifecycle-events = off
    netty.tcp {
      hostname = "127.0.0.1"
      hostname = ${?HOST}
      port = ${PORT}
    }
  }

  cluster { #                        ⟵  Cluster configuration section
    seed-nodes = [
    "akka.tcp://words@127.0.0.1:2551",
    "akka.tcp://words@127.0.0.1:2552",
    "akka.tcp://words@127.0.0.1:2553"
    ] #                              ⟵  Seed nodes of the cluster

    roles = ["seed"] #               ⟵  Seed node is given a seed role to differentiate from workers and masters
    role {
      seed.min-nr-of-members = 1 #   ⟵  Minimum members of every role for the cluster to be deemed to be "up." In the case of seed nodes, the cluster should be up once there's at least one seed node up.
    }
  }
}
```

Keep the addresses exactly the same

Be sure to use 127.0.0.1 when you follow along; `localhost` might resolve to a different IP address depending on your setup, and Akka interprets the addresses literally. You can't depend on DNS resolution for the addresses. The value in akka.remote .netty.ctp.host is used *exactly* for the system's address; no DNS resolution is done on this. The exact value of the address is used when actor references are serialized between Akka remote nodes. So once you send a message to the remote actor referred to by such an actor reference, it will use that exact address to connect to the remote server. The main reason behind not using DNS resolution is performance. DNS resolution, if configured incorrectly, can take seconds; in a pathological case, minutes. Finding the cause for delays to be an incorrect DNS configuration is not easy and usually not immediately apparent. Not using DNS resolution simply avoids this problem, but it does mean you have to be careful with configuring the addresses.

We'll start all the nodes locally throughout these examples. If you want to test this on a network, just replace -DHOST and -DPORT with the appropriate host name and port, respectively, which sets the environment variables HOST and PORT. The seed.conf file is set up to use these environment values as overrides if they're available. Start sbt in three terminals using different ports, inside the chapter-cluster directory. sbt is started for the first seed node as shown:

```
sbt -DPORT=2551 -DHOST=127.0.0.1
```

Do the same for the other two terminals, changing the -DPORT to 2552 and 2553. Every node in the same cluster needs to have the same actor system name (words in the previous example). Switch to the first terminal, in which we'll start the first seed node.

The first node in the seed nodes must automatically start and form the cluster. Let's verify that in a REPL session. Start the console in sbt (by typing console at the sbt prompt) in the first terminal started with port 2551, and follow along with listing 14.2. Figure 14.6 shows the result.

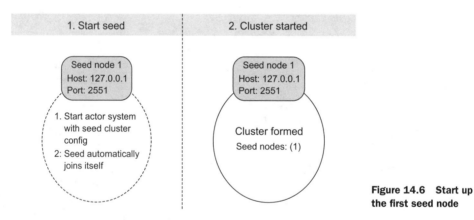

Figure 14.6 Start up the first seed node

Listing 14.2   Starting up a seed node

```
...
scala> :paste
// Entering paste mode (ctrl-D to finish)

import akka.actor._

import akka.cluster._

import com.typesafe.config._

val seedConfig = ConfigFactory.load("seed")
val seedSystem = ActorSystem("words", seedConfig)

// Exiting paste mode, now interpreting.
```

Loads configuration for the seed node, found in the file src/main/resources/seed.conf

Starts words actor system as seed node

```
[Remoting] Starting remoting                          ◄─────  Remote and cluster modules
[Remoting] listening on addresses :                           are automatically started.
[akka.tcp://words@127.0.0.1:2551]
                                                              Cluster name is same as the
...                                                           name of the actor system
[Cluster(akka://words)]                               ◄─────┘
Cluster Node [akka.tcp://words@127.0.0.1:2551]              words cluster seed node is started
- Started up successfully                              ◄─────┘
Node [akka.tcp://words@127.0.0.1:2551] is JOINING, roles [seed]
[Cluster(akka://words)] Cluster Node [akka.tcp://words@127.0.0.1:2551]
- Leader is moving node [akka.tcp://words@127.0.0.1:2551] to [Up]    ◄─────┐

                                                      words cluster seed node has
                                                      automatically joined the cluster
```

Start the console on the other two terminals and paste in the same code as in listing 14.2 to start seed nodes 2 and 3. The seeds will listen on the port that we provided as -DPORT when we started sbt. Figure 14.7 shows the result of the REPL commands for seed nodes 2 and 3.

You should see something similar to the next listing in the other two terminals, confirming that the nodes joined the cluster.

Listing 14.3 Seed node confirming joining the cluster

```
[Cluster(akka://words)] Cluster Node [akka.tcp://words@127.0.0.1:2553]
- Welcome from [akka.tcp://words@127.0.0.1:2551]      ◄─────  Output formatted for
                                                              readability; will show as
                                                              one line in the terminal
```

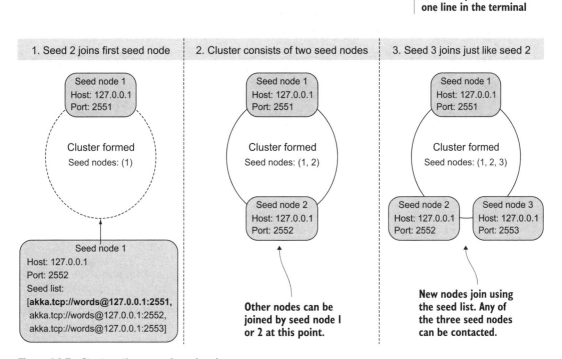

Figure 14.7 Start up the second seed node

The next listing shows the output of the first seed node. The output shows that the first seed node has determined that the two other nodes want to join.

Listing 14.4 Terminal output of seed node 1

Output abbreviated and formatted for readability.

First seed node joins itself and becomes the leader

```
[Cluster(akka://words)] Cluster Node [akka.tcp://words@127.0.0.1:2551]
            - Node [akka.tcp://words@127.0.0.1:2551] is JOINING, roles [seed])
```
Seed node 2 joins
```
- Leader is moving node [akka.tcp://words@127.0.0.1:2551] to [Up]
- Node [akka.tcp://words@127.0.0.1:2552] is JOINING, roles [seed]
- Leader is moving node [akka.tcp://words@127.0.0.1:2552] to [Up]
```
Seed node 3 joins
```
- Node [akka.tcp://words@127.0.0.1:2553] is JOINING, roles [seed]
- Leader is moving node [akka.tcp://words@127.0.0.1:2553] to [Up]
```

One of the nodes in the cluster takes on special responsibilities: to be the *leader* of the cluster. The leader decides if a member node is up or down. In this case the first seed node is the leader.

Only one node can be the leader at any point in time. Any node of the clusters can become the leader. Seed nodes 2 and 3 both request to join the cluster, which puts them in the JOINING state. The leader moves the nodes to the Up state, making them part of the cluster. All three seed nodes have now successfully joined the cluster.

14.2.2 Leaving the cluster

Let's see what happens if we let the first seed node leave the cluster. The following listing shows seed node 1 leaving the cluster.

Listing 14.5 Seed node 1 leaving the cluster

Gets address for this node
```
scala> val address = Cluster(seedSystem).selfAddress

address: akka.actor.Address = akka.tcp://words@127.0.0.1:2551

scala> Cluster(seedSystem).leave(address)
```
Lets seed node 1 leave the cluster

Marked as Leaving
```
[Cluster(akka://words)] Cluster Node [akka.tcp://words@127.0.0.1:2551]
- Marked address [akka.tcp://words@127.0.0.1:2551] as [Leaving]
[Cluster(akka://words)] Cluster Node [akka.tcp://words@127.0.0.1:2551]
```
Marked as Exiting
```
- Leader is moving node [akka.tcp://words@127.0.0.1:2551] to [Exiting]
[Cluster(akka://words)] Cluster Node [akka.tcp://words@127.0.0.1:2551]
- Shutting down...
[Cluster(akka://words)] Cluster Node [akka.tcp://words@127.0.0.1:2551]
- Successfully shut down
```

Listing 14.5 shows that seed node 1 marks itself as Leaving, and then as Exiting while it's still the leader. These state changes are communicated to all nodes in the cluster. After that, the cluster node is shut down. The actor system itself (the seedSystem) isn't shut down automatically on the node. What happens with the cluster? The leader node just shut down. Figure 14.8 shows how the first seed node leaves the cluster and how leadership is transferred.

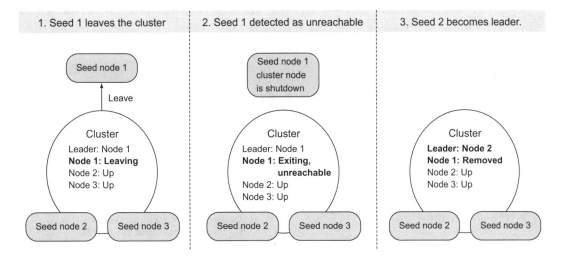

Figure 14.8 First seed node leaves the cluster

Let's look at the other terminals. One of the two remaining terminals should show output similar to this listing.

Listing 14.6 Seed node 2 becomes leader and removes seed node 1 from the cluster

```
[Cluster(akka://words)] Cluster Node [akka.tcp://words@127.0.0.1:2552]
- Marking exiting node(s) as UNREACHABLE
[Member(address = akka.tcp://words@127.0.0.1:2551, status = Exiting)].
This is expected and they will be removed.                          ◀──────┐

[Cluster(akka://words)] Cluster Node [akka.tcp://words@127.0.0.1:2552]
    ┌─▷ - Leader is removing exiting node [akka.tcp://words@127.0.0.1:2551]
```
Leader removes the exiting node   **Exiting seed node**
                                                                           has the Exiting state

Gossip protocol

You might have wondered how the seed nodes in the example knew about the fact that the first seed node was leaving, then exiting, and finally removed. Akka uses a *gossip* protocol to communicate the state of the cluster to all member nodes of the cluster.

Every node gossips to other nodes about its own state and the states that it has seen (the gossip). The protocol makes it possible for all nodes in the cluster to eventually agree about the state of every node. This agreement is called *convergence*, which occurs over time while the nodes are gossiping to each other.

A leader for the cluster can be determined after convergence. The first node, in sort order, that is Up or Leaving automatically becomes the leader. (The full remote address of the node is used to sort nodes, like akka.tcp://words@127.0.0.1:2551.)

Both remaining seed nodes detect that the first seed node has been flagged as UNREACHABLE. Both seed nodes are also aware that the first seed node has requested to leave the cluster. The second seed node automatically becomes the leader when the first seed node is in an Exiting state. The leaving node is moved from an Exiting state to a Removed state. The cluster now consists of two seed nodes.

The actor system on the first seed node can't join the cluster again by simply using Cluster(seedSystem).join(selfAddress). The actor system is removed and can only join the cluster again if it's restarted. The next listing shows how the first seed node can "rejoin."

Listing 14.7 Seed node 2 becomes leader and removes seed node 1 from the cluster

Terminates actor system

Starts new actor system with the same configuration. The actor system automatically joins the cluster.

```scala
scala> seedSystem.terminate()
scala> val seedSystem = ActorSystem("words", seedConfig)
```

An actor system can only ever join a cluster once. But a new actor system can be started with the same configuration, using the same host and port, which is what's done in listing 14.7.

Now you know how nodes can gracefully join and leave clusters. Figure 14.9 shows a state diagram of the member states that you've seen so far. The leader performs a leader action on specific member states, moving a member from Joining to Up and from Exiting to Removed.

This is not the complete picture yet. Let's look at what happens if one of the seed nodes crashes. We can simply kill the terminal that runs seed node 1 and look at the output of the other terminals. The following listing shows the output of the terminal running seed node 2 when seed node 1 has been killed abruptly.

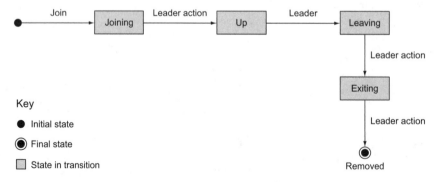

Figure 14.9 Graceful state transitions of a node joining and leaving the cluster

Seed node 1 becomes unreachable

```
Cluster Node [akka.tcp://words@127.0.0.1:2552]
- Marking node(s) as UNREACHABLE
  [Member(address = akka.tcp://words@127.0.0.1:2551, status = Up)]
```

Seed node 1 has been flagged as UNREACHABLE. The cluster uses a failure detector to detect unreachable nodes. The seed node was in an Up state when it crashed. A node can crash in any of the states you've seen before. The leader can't execute any leader actions as long as any of the nodes are unreachable, which means that no node can leave or join. The unreachable node will first have to be taken down. You can take a node down from any node in the cluster using the down method. The next listing shows how the first seed node is downed from the REPL.

```
scala> val address = Address("akka.tcp", "words", "127.0.0.1",2551)
scala> Cluster(seedSystem).down(address)
```

Seed node 1 is down.

```
[Cluster(akka://words)] Cluster Node [akka.tcp://words@127.0.0.1:2552]
- Marking unreachable node [akka.tcp://words@127.0.0.1:2551] as [Down]
- Leader is removing unreachable node [akka.tcp://words@127.0.0.1:2551]
[Remoting] Association to [akka.tcp://words@127.0.0.1:2551]
having UID [1735879100]
is irrecoverably failed. UID is now quarantined and
all messages to this UID
will be delivered to dead letters.
Remote actorsystem must be restarted to recover from this situation.
```

Seed node 1 is quarantined and removed.

The output also shows that if the seed node 1 actor system wanted to rejoin, it would have to restart. An unreachable node can also be taken down automatically. This is configured with the akka.cluster.auto-down-unreachable-after setting. The leader will automatically take unreachable nodes down after the set duration in this setting. Figure 14.10 shows all possible state transitions for a node in the cluster.

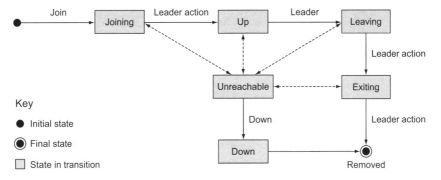

Figure 14.10   All states and transitions of a node

Failure detector

The cluster module uses an implementation of a *φ accrual failure detector* to detect unreachable nodes. The work is based on a paper by Naohiro Hayashibara, Xavier Défago, Rami Yared, and Takuya Katayama.[a] Detecting failures is a fundamental issue for fault tolerance in distributed systems.

The φ accrual failure detector calculates a value on a continuous scale (called a φ (phi) value) instead of determining a Boolean value indicating failure (if the node is reachable or not). From the referenced paper: "Roughly speaking, this value captures the degree of confidence that a corresponding monitored process has crashed. If the process actually crashes, the value is guaranteed to accrue over time and tend toward infinity, hence the name." This value is used as an indicator for suspecting that something is wrong (a suspicion level) instead of determining a hard-and-fast yes-or-no result.

The suspicion level concept makes the failure detector tunable and allows for a decoupling between application requirements and monitoring of the environment. The cluster module provides settings for the failure detector that you can tune for your specific network environment in the `akka.cluster.failure-detector` section, among which is a threshold for the φ value at which a node is deemed to be unreachable.

Nodes are very often deemed unreachable when they're in a *GC pause* state, which means that it's taking far too long to finish garbage collection, and a JVM can't do anything else until garbage collection has completed.

---

a. The φ Accrual Failure Detector, May 10 2004, www.jaist.ac.jp/~defago/files/pdf/IS_RR_2004_010.pdf

You'd definitely want to be notified if any of the nodes in a cluster fail. You can subscribe an actor to cluster events using the `subscribe` method on the `Cluster` extension. Listing 14.10 shows an actor that subscribes to cluster domain events (which can be found in src/main/scala/aia/cluster/words/ClusterDomainEventListener.scala).

Listing 14.10 Subscribing to `Cluster` domain events

```
...
import akka.cluster.{MemberStatus, Cluster}        Subscribes to the cluster domain
import akka.cluster.ClusterEvent._                     events on actor creation

class ClusterDomainEventListener extends Actor with ActorLogging {
  Cluster(context.system).subscribe(self, classOf[ClusterDomainEvent])  ◁

  def receive ={                                              ◁── Listens for cluster
    case MemberUp(member)    => log.info(s"$member UP.")          domain events
    case MemberExited(member)=> log.info(s"$member EXITED.")
    case MemberRemoved(m, previousState) =>
      if(previousState == MemberStatus.Exiting) {
```

```
        log.info(s"Member $m gracefully exited, REMOVED.")
    } else {
        log.info(s"$m downed after unreachable, REMOVED.")
    }
  case UnreachableMember(m)  => log.info(s"$m UNREACHABLE")
  case ReachableMember(m)    => log.info(s"$m REACHABLE")
  case s: CurrentClusterState => log.info(s"cluster state: $s")
}

override def postStop(): Unit = {
  Cluster(context.system).unsubscribe(self)        ◁─── Unsubscribes after
  super.postStop()                                       actor is stopped
}
}
```

The example `ClusterDomainEventListener` simply logs what has happened in the cluster.

The `Cluster` domain events tell you something about the cluster members, but in many cases it suffices to know if an actor in the cluster is still there. You can simply use `DeathWatch` using the `watch` method to watch actors in the cluster, as you'll see in the next section.

14.3 *Clustered job processing*

It's time to process some jobs with a cluster. We'll focus first on how the actors in the cluster communicate with each other to complete a task. The cluster receives a text whose words we want to count. The text is divided into parts and delivered to several worker nodes. Every worker node processes its part by counting the occurrences of every word in the text. The worker nodes process the text in parallel, which should result in faster processing. Eventually the result of the counting is sent back to the user of the cluster. The fact that we'll count the occurrences of words isn't the focus; you can process many jobs in the way we show in this section.

The example can be found in the same chapter-cluster directory as used before, for the examples on joining and leaving the cluster. Figure 14.11 shows the structure of the application.

The `JobReceptionist` and `JobMaster` actors will run on a master role node. The `JobWorkers` will run on worker role nodes. Both `JobMaster` and `JobWorker` actors are created dynamically, on demand. Whenever a `JobReceptionist` receives a `Job-Request`, it spawns a `JobMaster` for the `Job` and tells it to start work on the job. The `JobMaster` creates `JobWorkers` remotely on the worker role nodes. Figure 14.12 shows an overview of the process. We'll address each step in detail in the rest of this chapter.

Every `JobWorker` receives a `Task` message that contains a portion of the text. The `JobWorker` splits the text into words and counts the occurrence of every word, returning a `TaskResult` that contains a `Map` of word counts. The `JobMaster` receives the `Task-Results` and merges all the maps, adding up the counts for every word, which is basically the reduce step. The `WordCount` result is eventually sent back to the job receptionist.

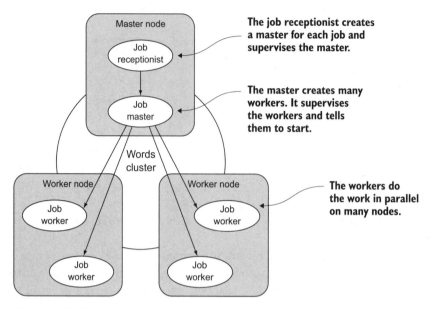

Figure 14.11   Words cluster actors

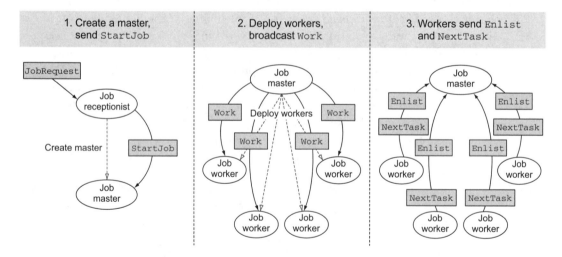

Figure 14.12   Job processing *(continued on next page)*

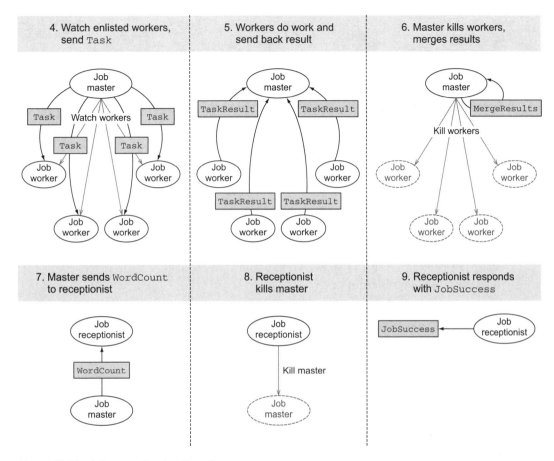

Figure 14.12   Job processing *(continued)*

In the next sections, we'll address all the steps in the overview. First, we'll start the cluster, and then we'll distribute the work that has to be done between master and workers. After that, we'll look at how we can make the job processing resilient, including restarting the job when a node crashes. Finally, we'll address how to test the cluster.

Some caveats for the example

This example is kept simple on purpose. The `JobMaster` keeps intermediate results in memory and all the data that is processed is sent between the actors.

If you have to deal with batch processing of extremely large amounts of data, you need to put effort into getting the data close to the process before processing it and stored on the same server that the process is running on, and you can't simply collect data in memory. In Hadoop-based systems, for example, this means pushing all the data onto HDFS (Hadoop Distributed File System) before processing it and writing all the results back to HDFS, as well. In our example, we'll simply send the workload

14.3.1 Starting the cluster

You can build the example in the chapter-cluster directory using sbt assembly. This
creates a words-node.jar file in the target directory. The JAR file contains three different configuration files: one for the master, one for the worker, and one for the
seed. The following listing shows how to run one seed node, one master, and two
workers locally on different ports.

Listing 14.11   Running nodes

```
java -DPORT=2551 \
     -Dconfig.resource=/seed.conf \
     -jar target/words-node.jar
java -DPORT=2554 \
     -Dconfig.resource=/master.conf \
     -jar target/words-node.jar
java -DPORT=2555 \
     -Dconfig.resource=/worker.conf \
     -jar target/words-node.jar
java -DPORT=2556 \
     -Dconfig.resource=/worker.conf \
     -jar target/words-node.jar
```

The listing only starts one seed node, which is fine for now. (The master.conf and
worker.conf files define a list of local seed nodes running on 127.0.0.1 and ports 2551,
2552, and 2553; since 2551 is the first seed node, this will work fine.) The seed node
list can also be configured using a system property, if you'd like to run the seed nodes
on other hosts and ports.

> **OVERRIDING THE SEED NODE LIST FROM THE COMMAND LINE** You can override
> the seed node list with -Dakka.cluster.seed-nodes.[n]=[seednode] where
> *[n]* needs to be replaced with the position in the seed list starting with 0 and
> *[seednode]* with the seed node value.

The master can't do anything without the workers, so it would make sense to have the
JobReceptionist on the master start up only when the cluster has some set minimum
number of worker nodes running. You can specify the minimum number of members

with a certain role in the cluster configuration. The next listing shows part of the master .conf file for this purpose.

Listing 14.12 Configure minimum number of worker nodes for `MemberUp` event

```
role {
  worker.min-nr-of-members = 2
}
```

The configuration of the master node specifies that there should be at least two worker nodes in the cluster. The `Cluster` module provides a `registerOnMemberUp` method to register a function that's executed when the member node is up—in this case, the master node, which takes the minimum number of worker nodes into account. The function is called when the master node has successfully joined the cluster and when there are two or more worker nodes running in the cluster. The following listing shows the `Main` class that's used to start all types of nodes in the words cluster.

Listing 14.13 Configuring minimum number of worker nodes for `MemberUp` event

```
object Main extends App {
  val config = ConfigFactory.load()
  val system = ActorSystem("words", config)

  println(s"Starting node with roles: ${Cluster(system).selfRoles}")

  val roles = system.settings
                    .config
                    .getStringList("akka.cluster.roles")
  if(roles.contains("master")) {
    Cluster(system).registerOnMemberUp {
      val receptionist = system.actorOf(Props[JobReceptionist],
                                    "receptionist")
      println("Master node is ready.")
    }
  }
}
```

Only start JobReceptionist if this node has a master role

JobReceptionist is only created when cluster is up with at least two worker role nodes present

Registers code block to be executed when the member is up

The worker node doesn't need to start any actors; the `JobWorkers` will be started on demand, as you'll see in the next section. We'll use a router to deploy and communicate with the `JobWorkers`.

14.3.2 *Work distribution using routers*

The `JobMaster` needs to first create the `JobWorkers` and then broadcast the `Work` message to them. Using routers in the cluster is exactly the same as using routers locally. We just need to change how we create the routers. We'll use a router with a `Broadcast-PoolRouterConfig` to communicate with the `JobWorkers`. A `Pool` is a `RouterConfig` that creates actors, whereas a `Group` is a `RouterConfig` that's used to route to already-existing actors, as explained in chapter 9. In this case we want to dynamically create the `JobWorker`s and kill them after the job is done, so a `Pool` is the best option. The Job-Master actor uses a separate trait to create the router. The separate trait will come in handy during testing, as you'll see later. The trait is shown in the next listing, which creates the worker router (which can be found in src/main/scala/aia/cluster/words /JobMaster.scala).

Listing 14.14   Creating a clustered `BroadcastPool` router

```
trait CreateWorkerRouter { this: Actor =>        ◁——— Needs to mixin with an actor
  def createWorkerRouter: ActorRef = {
    context.actorOf(
      ClusterRouterPool(BroadcastPool(10),       ◁——— ClusterRouterPool takes a Pool
        ClusterRouterPoolSettings(
          totalInstances = 1000,    ◁——— Total maximum number of workers in cluster
          maxInstancesPerNode = 20,
          allowLocalRoutees = false,
          useRole = None
        )
      ).props(Props[JobWorker]),     ◁┐ Creates JobWorkers
      name = "worker-router")           with standard Props
  }
}
```

Max number of workers per node ⟶ `maxInstancesPerNode = 20,`

Nodes with this role will be routed to. ⟶ `useRole = None`

Do not create local routees. We only want Workers on the other nodes. ⟶ `allowLocalRoutees = false,`

ROUTER CONFIGURATION   In this case the `JobMaster` is created dynamically for every job, so it needs to create a new router every time, which is why it's done in code. It's also possible to configure router deployment using the configuration, as described in chapter 9. You can specify a cluster section in the deployment configuration to enable the router for clustering and set the `ClusterRouter` pool or group settings, like `use-role` and `allow-local-routees`.

The `CreateWorkerRouter` trait only does one thing: create the router to the workers. Creating the clustered router is very similar to creating a normal router. All you need to do is pass in a `ClusterRouterPool` that can use any of the existing pools—Broadcast-Pool, `RoundRobinPool`, and `ConsistentHashingPool` and the like. ClusterRouter-PoolSettings controls how instances of the `JobWorker`s are created. `JobWorker`s will be added to joining worker nodes as long as the `totalInstances` haven't been reached yet. In the configuration in listing 14.14, 50 nodes can join the cluster before the router stops deploying new `JobWorker`s. When the `JobMaster` is created, it creates the router, as shown in the next listing, and uses it to send out messages to the workers, also shown in figure 14.13.

Listing 14.15   Using the router to broadcast `Work` messages

```
class JobMaster extends Actor
                with ActorLogging
                with CreateWorkerRouter {    ◁┐ Mixes in CreateWorkerRouter trait
  // inside the body of the JobMaster actor..
  val router = createWorkerRouter    ◁——— Creates router
```

```
def receive = idle

def idle: Receive = {
  case StartJob(jobName, text) =>
    textParts = text.grouped(10).toVector
    val cancel = system.scheduler.schedule(0 millis,
                                            1000 millis,        Schedules a
                                            router,             message to
                                            Work(jobName, self))  router
    become(working(jobName, sender(), cancel))
}
// more code
```

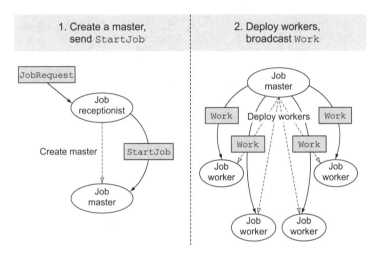

Figure 14.13 Deploying JobWorkers and broadcasting Work messages

The code snippet in listing 14.15 also shows something else. The JobMaster actor is a state machine and uses become to go from one state to the next. It starts in the idle state until the job receptionist sends it a StartJob message. Once the JobMaster receives this message, it splits up the text into parts of 10 lines and schedules the Work messages without delay to the workers. It then transitions to the Working state to start handling responses from the workers. The Work message is scheduled in case other worker nodes join the cluster after the job has been started. State machines make a distributed coordinated task more comprehensible. In fact, both the JobMaster and JobWorker actors are state machines.

There's also a ClusterRouterGroup, which has ClusterRouterGroupSettings similar to how the ClusterRouterPool is set up. The actors that are being routed to need to be running before a group router can send messages to them. The words cluster can have many master role nodes. Every master role node starts up with a JobReceptionist actor. In the case where you want to send messages to every JobReceptionist, you could use a ClusterRouterGroup, for instance, sending a message to the Job-Receptionists to cancel all currently running jobs in the cluster. Listing 14.16

shows how you can create a router that looks up JobReceptionists on master role nodes in the cluster (an example can be found in src/main/scala/aia/cluster/words /ReceptionistRouterLookup.scala).

Listing 14.16   Sending messages to all JobReceptionists in the cluster

```
val receptionistRouter = context.actorOf(
    ClusterRouterGroup(                          ←——— ClusterRouterGroup
      BroadcastGroup(Nil),                 ←—┐ Number of instances is overridden
      ClusterRouterGroupSettings(            | by cluster group settings
        totalInstances = 100,
        routeesPaths = List("/user/receptionist"),   ←—┐ Path for looking up
        allowLocalRoutees = true,                        | (top-level)
        useRole = Some("master")    ←—┐                  | receptionist actor
      )                               | Routes to master
    ).props(),                        | nodes only
    name = "receptionist-router")
```

Now you've seen how the JobMaster distributes the Work message to the JobWorkers. In the next section, we'll look at how the JobWorkers request more work from the JobMaster until the work is done, and how the cluster recovers from failure during job processing.

14.3.3   *Resilient jobs*

The JobWorker receives the Work message and sends a message back to the JobMaster that it wants to enlist itself for work. It also immediately sends the NextTask message to ask for the first task to process. Figure 14.14 shows the flow of messages. Listing 14.17 shows how the JobWorker transitions from the idle state to the enlisted state.

The JobWorker indicates to the JobMaster that it wants to take part in the job by sending an Enlist message. The Enlist message contains the JobWorker's ActorRef so that the JobMaster can use it later. The JobMaster watches all the Job-Workers that enlist, in case one or more of them crashes, and stops all the JobWorkers once the job is finished.

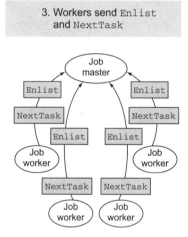

Figure 14.14   JobWorker enlists itself and requests NextTask

Listing 14.17   JobWorker transitions from idle to enlisted state

```
def receive = idle                          ←——— Starts as idle

def idle: Receive = {                       ┌—— Receives the Work message
  case Work(jobName, master) =>       ←—┘
    become(enlisted(jobName, master))       ←——— Becomes enlisted

    log.info(s"Enlisted, will start working for job '${jobName}'.")
```

```
  master ! Enlist(self)                   ⟵————  Sends Enlist message to master
  master ! NextTask                       ⟵┐

  watch(master)                            Sends NextTask
  setReceiveTimeout(30 seconds)            to master

def enlisted(jobName:String, master:ActorRef): Receive = {
  case ReceiveTimeout =>
    master ! NextTask
  case Terminated(master) =>
    setReceiveTimeout(Duration.Undefined)
    log.error(s"Master terminated for ${jobName}, stopping self.")
    stop(self)
  ...
}
```

The JobWorker switches to the Enlisted state and expects to receive a Task message from the master to process. The JobWorker watches the JobMaster and sets a ReceiveTimeout. If the JobWorker receives no messages within the ReceiveTimeout, it will ask the JobMaster again for a NextTask, as shown in the enlisted Receive function. The JobWorker stops itself if the JobMaster dies. As you can see, there's nothing special about the watch and Terminated messages; DeathWatch works just like in nonclustered actor systems. The JobMaster is in the working state in the meantime, shown in figure 14.15 and the next listing.

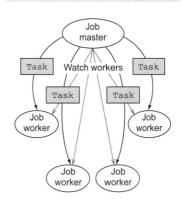

Figure 14.15 **JobMaster** sends **Tasks** to **JobWorkers** and watches them

Listing 14.18 JobMaster enlists worker and sends Tasks to JobWorkers

```
// inside the JobMaster..                            Uses StoppingStrategy

import SupervisorStrategy._
override def supervisorStrategy: SupervisorStrategy = stoppingStrategy  ⟵

def working(jobName:String,
            receptionist:ActorRef,                   Watches worker that
            cancellable:Cancellable): Receive = {    enlisted and keeps track
                                                     of workers in a list
  case Enlist(worker) =>                        ⟵┘
    watch(worker)
    workers  = workers + worker                 Receives NextTask request
                                                 from worker and sends
  case NextTask =>                        ⟵┘    back a Task message
    if(textParts.isEmpty) {
      sender() ! WorkLoadDepleted
    } else {
      sender() ! Task(textParts.head, self)
      workGiven = workGiven + 1
```

```
      textParts = textParts.tail
    }
  case ReceiveTimeout =>
    if(workers.isEmpty) {
      log.info(s"No workers responded in time. Cancelling $jobName.")
      stop(self)
    } else setReceiveTimeout(Duration.Undefined)

  case Terminated(worker) =>
    log.info(s"Worker $worker got terminated. Cancelling $jobName.")
    stop(self)
```

> **JobMaster stops if no workers have enlisted within a ReceiveTimeout**

> **JobMaster stops if any of the JobWorkers fail**

```
//more code to follow..
```

The listing shows that the `JobMaster` registers and watches the workers that want to take part in the work. The `JobMaster` sends back a `WorkLoad-Depleted` to the `JobWorker` if there's no more work to be done.

The `JobMaster` also uses a `ReceiveTimeout` (which is set when the job is started) just in case no `JobWorkers` ever report to enlist. The `JobMaster` stops itself if the `ReceiveTimeout` occurs. It also stops itself if any `JobWorker` is stopped. The `Job-Master` is the supervisor of all the `JobWorkers` it deployed (the router automatically escalates problems). Using a `StoppingStrategy` makes sure that a failing `JobWorker` is automatically stopped, which triggers the `Terminated` message that the `JobMaster` is watching out for.

The `JobWorker` receives a `Task`, processes the

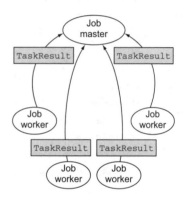

Figure 14.16 `JobWorker` processes `Task` and sends back `TaskResult`

`Task`, sends back a `TaskResult`, and asks for the `NextTask`. Figure 14.16 and the following listing show the enlisted state of the `JobWorker`.

Listing 14.19   `JobWorker` processes `Task` and sends back `TaskResult`

```
def enlisted(jobName:String, master:ActorRef): Receive = {
  case ReceiveTimeout =>
    master ! NextTask

  case Task(textPart, master) =>
    val countMap = processTask(textPart)
    processed = processed + 1
    master ! TaskResult(countMap)
    master ! NextTask

  case WorkLoadDepleted =>
    log.info(s"Work load ${jobName} is depleted, retiring...")
    setReceiveTimeout(Duration.Undefined)
    become(retired(jobName))
```

> ⟵ **Processes task**

> ⟵ **Sends result to JobMaster**

> ⟵ **Asks for next task**

> ⟵ **Switches off ReceiveTimeout and retires; job is done**

```
    case Terminated(master) =>
      setReceiveTimeout(Duration.Undefined)
      log.error(s"Master terminated for ${jobName}, stopping self.")
      stop(self)
}

  def retired(jobName: String): Receive = {          ⟵── Retired state
    case Terminated(master) =>
      log.error(s"Master terminated for ${jobName}, stopping self.")
      stop(self)
    case _ => log.error("I'm retired.")
  }  // definition of processTask follows in the code...
```

There are some benefits to requesting the work from the `JobWorker` as is done in this example. The main one is that the workload is automatically balanced between the `JobWorkers` because the `JobWorkers` request the work. A `JobWorker` that has more resources available to do work simply requests tasks more often than a `JobWorker` that's under a higher load. If the `JobMaster` were instead forced to send tasks to all `JobWorkers` in round-robin fashion, it would be possible that one or more of the `Job-Workers` could be overloaded while others sit idle.

ADAPTIVELOADBALANCINGPOOL AND ADAPTIVELOADBALANCINGGROUP There's an alternative to requesting work from the worker nodes. The `AdaptiveLoad-BalancingPool` and `AdaptiveLoadBalancingGroup` routers use the cluster metrics to decide which node is best suited to receive messages. The metrics can be configured to use *JMX* or *Hyperic Sigar*.[1]

The `JobMaster` receives `TaskResult` messages in the working state and merges the results when there's a task result for every task that was sent out. Figure 14.17 and the following listing show how the `JobMaster` transitions to the finishing state when all work is done to merge the intermediate results, sending back the `WordCount`.

Listing 14.20 JobMaster stores and merges intermediate results, completes the Job

```
def working(jobName:String,
            receptionist:ActorRef,
            cancellable:Cancellable): Receive = {

    ...

    case TaskResult(countMap) =>
      intermediateResult = intermediateResult :+ countMap      ⟵──┐  Stores intermediate
      workReceived = workReceived + 1                              │  results coming from
                                                                   │  JobWorkers
      if(textParts.isEmpty && workGiven == workReceived) {
        cancellable.cancel()                          ⟵──┐  Remember scheduled
        become(finishing(jobName, receptionist, workers))  │  task that sends out
        setReceiveTimeout(Duration.Undefined)              │  Work messages? It's
                                                           │  now time to cancel it.
```

Transitions to finishing state (annotation pointing to the `become(finishing...)` lines)

----

[1] Read more about Hyperic Sigar here: http://sigar.hyperic.com/

```
        self ! MergeResults
      }
    }
    ...
    def finishing(jobName: String,
                  receptionist: ActorRef,
                  workers: Set[ActorRef]): Receive = {
      case MergeResults =>
        val mergedMap = merge()
        workers.foreach(stop(_))
        receptionist ! WordCount(jobName, mergedMap)

      case Terminated(worker) =>
        log.info(s"Job $jobName is finishing, stopping.")
    }
    ...
```

Sends MergeResults to self so that results are merged in the finishing state

Receiving MergeResults message the JobMaster sent to itself

Merging all results

Kills all workers; job is done

Sends final result to JobReceptionist

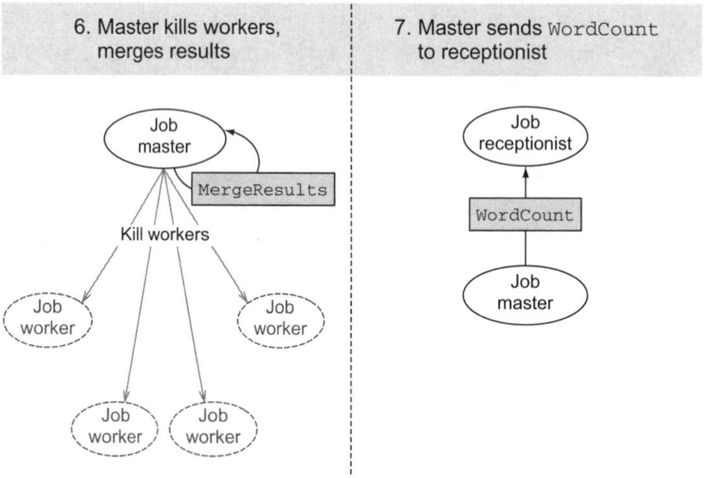

Figure 14.17 `JobWorker` processes tasks and sends back `TaskResult`

The `JobReceptionist` finally receives the `WordCount` and kills the `JobMaster`, which completes the process. The `JobWorker` crashes when it encounters a text with the word FAIL in it to simulate failures by throwing an exception. The `JobReceptionist` watches the `JobMasters` it creates. It also uses a `StoppingStrategy` in case the `JobMaster` crashes. Let's look at the supervision hierarchy for this actor system and how `Death-Watch` is used to detect failure in figure 14.18.

We use `ReceiveTimeout` to detect that the actors aren't receiving messages in time so that we can take action. The `JobReceptionist` keeps track of the jobs it has sent out. When it receives a `Terminated` message, it checks if the job has been completed. If not, it sends itself the original `JobRequest`, which results in the process starting over again. The `JobReceptionist` simulates the resolution of the failure simulated with the FAIL text by removing the text from the job after a number of retries, as shown next.

Listing 14.21 `JobReceptionist` retries `JobRequest` on `JobMaster` failure

```
case Terminated(jobMaster) =>
  jobs.find(_.jobMaster == jobMaster).foreach { failedJob =>
    log.error(s"$jobMaster terminated before finishing job.")

    val name = failedJob.name
    log.error(s"Job ${name} failed.")
    val nrOfRetries = retries.getOrElse(name, 0)

    if(maxRetries > nrOfRetries) {
      if(nrOfRetries == maxRetries -1) {
        // Simulating that the Job worker
        // will work just before max retries
        val text = failedJob.text.filterNot(_.contains("FAIL"))
        self.tell(JobRequest(name, text), failedJob.respondTo)
      } else self.tell(JobRequest(name, failedJob.text),
                       failedJob.respondTo)

      updateRetries
    }
  }
}
```

Sends
JobRequest
without
simulated
failure ⟵

⟵ **Sends JobRequest again**

We'll use this simulation of failures in the next section where we'll test the words cluster.

The receptionist creates a new job master when it notices that a master has died (up to x retries).

The job master stops itself when it notices that a job worker has died.

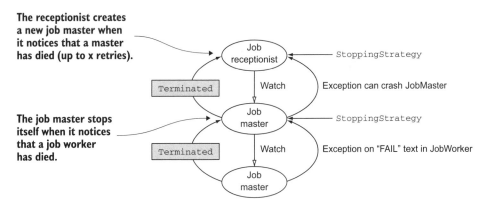

Figure 14.18 Supervision hierarchy for the words actor system

14.3.4 *Testing the cluster*

You can use the `sbt-multi-jvm` plugin and the `multi-node-testkit` module just like the `akka-remote` module. It's also still convenient to test the actors locally, which is easily done if we isolate the creation of actors and routers into traits. Listing 14.22 shows how test versions of the `Receptionist` and the `JobMaster` are created for the

test (which can be found in src/test/scala/aia/cluster/words/LocalWordsSpec.scala).
Traits are used to override the creation of the worker routers and job masters.

Listing 14.22   `JobReceptionist` retries `JobRequest` on `JobMaster` failure

**This trait requires that the "mixee" define a
context, which is the JobMaster class in our case.**

```
trait CreateLocalWorkerRouter extends CreateWorkerRouter {
    def context: ActorContext

    override def createWorkerRouter: ActorRef = {
      context.actorOf(BroadcastPool(5).props(Props[JobWorker]),
                      "worker-router")                  ◁── Creates nonclustered router
    }
}

class TestJobMaster extends JobMaster
                    with CreateLocalWorkerRouter        ◁─┘
                                                           Creates test version
                                                           of JobMaster,
                                                           overriding how the
                                                           router is created

class TestReceptionist extends JobReceptionist          ◁─┐ Creates test version
                       with CreateMaster {                 │ of JobMaster
    override def createMaster(name: String): ActorRef = {
        context.actorOf(Props[TestJobMaster], name)     ◁─┘
    }
}
```

**Creates test version of JobReceptionist,
overriding how the JobMaster is created**

The local test is shown in listing 14.23. As you can see, the test is business as usual:
JobRequests are sent to the JobReceptionist. The response is verified using expect-
Msg (the ImplicitSender automatically makes the testActor the sender of all mes-
sages, as described in chapter 3).

Listing 14.23   Local words test

```
class LocalWordsSpec extends TestKit(ActorSystem("test"))
                     with WordSpec
                     with MustMatchers
                     with StopSystemAfterAll
                     with ImplicitSender {                   Creates test
                                                             version of
  val receptionist = system.actorOf(Props[TestReceptionist], ◁─ JobReceptionist
                              JobReceptionist.name)
  val words = List("this is a test ",
                   "this is a test",
                   "this is",
                   "this")

  "The words system" must {
    "count the occurrence of words in a text" in {
      receptionist ! JobRequest("test2", words)
      expectMsg(JobSuccess("test2", Map("this" -> 4,
                                        "is"   -> 3,
                                        "a"    -> 2,
                                        "test" -> 2)))
```

```
          expectNoMsg
      }
      ...
      "continue to process a job with intermittent failures" in {
          val wordsWithFail = List("this", "is", "a", "test", "FAIL!")
          receptionist ! JobRequest("test4", wordsWithFail)
          expectMsg(JobSuccess("test4", Map("this" -> 1,
                                            "is"   -> 1,
                                            "a"    -> 1,
                                            "test" -> 1)))
          expectNoMsg
      }
    }
  }
}
```

Failure is simulated by a job worker throwing an exception on finding the word FAIL in text

The multi-node test doesn't modify the creation of the actors and the router. To test the cluster, we first have to create a `MultiNodeConfig`, as shown in the next listing, which can be found in src/multi-jvm/scala/aia/cluster/words/WordsClusterSpecConfig .scala.

Listing 14.24 The `MultiNode` configuration

```
import akka.remote.testkit.MultiNodeConfig
import com.typesafe.config.ConfigFactory

object WordsClusterSpecConfig extends MultiNodeConfig {
  val seed = role("seed")
  val master = role("master")
  val worker1 = role("worker-1")
  val worker2 = role("worker-2")

  commonConfig(ConfigFactory.parseString("""
    akka.actor.provider="akka.cluster.ClusterActorRefProvider"
                                  """))
}
```

Defines roles in the test

Provides a test configuration. ClusterActorRefProvider makes sure cluster is initialized. You can add more common configuration here for all nodes in the test.

The `MultiNodeConfig` is used in the `MultiNodeSpec`, as you might recall from chapter 6. The `WordsClusterSpecConfig` is used in the `WordsClusterSpec`, which is shown next (which can be found in src/multi-jvm/scala/aia/cluster/words/WordsCluster-Spec.scala).

Listing 14.25 Words cluster spec

```
class WordsClusterSpecMultiJvmNode1 extends WordsClusterSpec
class WordsClusterSpecMultiJvmNode2 extends WordsClusterSpec
class WordsClusterSpecMultiJvmNode3 extends WordsClusterSpec
class WordsClusterSpecMultiJvmNode4 extends WordsClusterSpec

class WordsClusterSpec extends MultiNodeSpec(WordsClusterSpecConfig)
with STMultiNodeSpec with ImplicitSender {

  import WordsClusterSpecConfig._

  def initialParticipants = roles.size
```

One class extending WordsClusterSpec for every node in the test

```
                val seedAddress = node(seed).address
                val masterAddress = node(master).address
                val worker1Address = node(worker1).address
                val worker2Address = node(worker2).address

                muteDeadLetters(classOf[Any])(system)
                "A Words cluster" must {

                  "form the cluster" in within(10 seconds) {

                    Cluster(system).subscribe(testActor, classOf[MemberUp])
                    expectMsgClass(classOf[CurrentClusterState])

                    Cluster(system).join(seedAddress)

                    receiveN(4).map { case MemberUp(m) => m.address }.toSet must be(
                    Set(seedAddress, masterAddress, worker1Address, worker2Address))

                    Cluster(system).unsubscribe(testActor)

                    enterBarrier("cluster-up")
                  }
                  "execute a words job" in within(10 seconds) {
                    runOn(master) {
                      val receptionist = system.actorOf(Props[JobReceptionist],
                                                        "receptionist")
                      val text = List("some", "some very long text", "some long text")
                      receptionist ! JobRequest("job-1", text)
                      expectMsg(JobSuccess("job-1", Map("some" -> 3,
                                                        "very" -> 1,
                                                        "long" -> 2,
                                                        "text" -> 2)))
                    }
                    enterBarrier("job-done")
                  }
                  ...
                }
              }
```

Annotations:
- **Gets address for every node**
- **Subscribes testActor so it's possible to expect the cluster member events**
- **Joins seed node. The config is not using a seed list, so we manually start the seed role node.**
- **Verifies that all nodes have joined**
- **Runs a job on master and verifies results. Other nodes only call enterBarrier.**

The actual test is almost exactly the same as the local version, as you can see. The clustered version only makes sure that the cluster is up before the test is run on the master. The test that recovers from failure isn't shown here, but is exactly the same as the test in listing 14.25 with a "FAIL" text added to the text to trigger the failure, just like in the local version.

> **Cluster client**
>
> The test sends the `JobRequest` from the master node. You might wonder how you can talk to a cluster from the outside; for instance, in this case how you can send a `JobRequest` to one of the nodes in the cluster from outside the cluster?
>
> The `akka-contrib` module contains a couple of cluster patterns; one of them is the `ClusterClient`. A `ClusterClient` is an actor initialized with a list of initial contacts (for instance, the seed nodes) that forwards messages to actors in the cluster using `ClusterRecipient` actors on every node.

That concludes our discussion of how actors can be tested in a cluster. We've just shown a few test cases here; in real life you'd obviously test far more scenarios. Testing locally has the benefit of testing the logic of how the actors communicate, whereas the `multi-node-testkit` can help you find issues in cluster startup or other cluster-specific issues. We hope we've demonstrated that testing a clustered actor system isn't very different from testing local actors, and doesn't necessarily have to be hard. Multi-node tests are great for high-level integration tests where you can verify sequentially how a cluster initializes or what happens if a node crashes.

14.4 Summary

Dynamically growing and shrinking a simple application ended up being rather simple with the `Cluster` extension. Joining and leaving the cluster is easily done, and you can test the functionality in a REPL console, a tool that allows you to experiment and verify how things work. If you've followed along with the REPL sessions, it should've been immediately apparent how solid this extension is; crashes in the cluster are properly detected and death watch works just as you'd expect.

Clustering has been a notoriously painful chasm to cross, usually requiring a lot of admin and programming changes. In this chapter you saw that Akka makes it much easier, and doesn't require rewriting code. In the process, you also learned

- How easy it is to form a cluster
- The node lifecycle state machine
- How to put it all together into a working app
- How to test the cluster logic

The example wasn't about counting words, but about Akka's generic way of processing jobs in parallel in a cluster. We made use of clustered routers and some simple messages for actors to work together and deal with failure.

Finally, we were able to test everything, another big advantage you quickly get used to when using Akka. Being able to unit test a cluster is a unique feature, and makes it possible to find problems in your application before you get to large-scale production deployment. The words cluster actors used some temporary state about the job, spread among the various actors. We could reproduce the input from the `JobRequest` that was stored at the `JobReceptionist` when a failure occurred in the masters or the workers. One situation this solution can't recover from is when the `JobReceptionist` crashes, because the `JobRequest` data will be lost, making it impossible to resend it to a master. In the next chapter, we'll look at how you can even restore state for actors from a persistent store using the akka-persistence module.

Actor persistence

The in-memory state of an actor is lost when an actor is stopped or restarted, or when the actor system crashes or shuts down. This chapter is all about how to make this state *durable* using the akka-persistence module.

It's quite common to use a database API for creating, retrieving, updating, and deleting records (also known as *CRUD* operations). Database records are often used to represent the *current state* of a system. The database acts as a container for shared mutable state in this case.

It should come as no surprise that Akka persistence prefers a more immutable approach. The design technique on which Akka persistence is based is called *event sourcing* and is covered in the first section of this chapter. In short, you'll learn how to capture state changes as a *sequence of immutable events* in a database *journal*.

Next we'll look at the `PersistentActor`. A persistent actor makes it easy for an actor to record its state as events and to recover from the events after a crash or restart.

The Akka cluster and persistence modules can be used together to build clustered applications that can continue to operate even if nodes in the cluster crash or get replaced. We'll look at two cluster extensions, *cluster singleton* and *cluster sharding*, which can both be used to run persistent actors in an Akka cluster, for different reasons.

But first let's start with event sourcing, the design technique that underpins Akka persistence. In the case that you're already familiar with event sourcing, you can skip the next section and go straight to section 15.1.3, "Event sourcing for actors."

Why would an actor need to recover its state?

Just to step back for a moment, it doesn't make sense to make every actor persistent just because you can. So when is it really necessary to keep actor state around?

This has a lot to do with how you design your system, what you're modelling with actors, and how other systems interact with the actors.

An actor that has a lifetime that's longer than one message (or request/response) and that accumulates valuable information over time often requires persistent state. This kind of actor has an identity—some identification that can be used to reach it later. An example of this is a shopping basket actor; a user goes back and forth between searching for products and a shopping basket to add and remove products. You wouldn't want to incorrectly show an empty basket after the actor has crashed and restarted.

Another case is where many systems send messages to an actor that models a state machine to orchestrate messages between systems. The actor can keep track of which messages it has received and can build up some context around the communication between the systems. An example of this is a system that takes orders from a website and coordinates the process of claiming stocks, delivery of orders, and any required accounting by integrating with several existing services. If the actor restarts, you'll need to continue in the right state so that the connected systems can pick up where they left off for the order in question.

These are just some examples of where you'd need to persist the actor state.

There's no need to persist state if an actor can do all its work simply by processing the messages it receives. An example of this is an actor that's created from stateless HTTP requests, containing all the information that the actor needs. A client will need to retry the HTTP request if the actor fails in that case.

15.1 Recovering state with event sourcing

Event sourcing is a technique that's been in use for a long time. We'll use a simple example to show the difference between event sourcing and working with records in CRUD style, which we expect you to be familiar with. In this case we'll take the example of a calculator that only needs to remember the last result it calculated.

15.1.1 *Updating records in place*

Updating records in place is commonplace when using a SQL database for OLTP (online transaction processing). Figure 15.1 shows how SQL insert and update statements can be used to keep track of the calculation result shown in the calculator.

	SQL statement	Results table

1. Start with one record:
```
insert into results
values (1, 0)
```

id	Result
1	0

2. Add 1:
```
update results
set result = result + 1
where id = 1
```

id	Result
1	1

3. Multiply by 3:
```
update results
set result = result * 3
where id = 1
```

id	Result
1	3

4. Divide by 4:
```
update results
set result = result / 4
where id = 1
```

id	Result
1	0.75

Figure 15.1   Storing state with updates

The calculator inserts one row on startup; the statement for finding out if the record already exists is omitted. Every calculation is executed in the database, using update statements on one row in the table. (You can assume that every update will be executed in its own transaction.)

Figure 15.1 shows that the calculator displays 0.75 as the result. The application queries the result when it's restarted, shown in figure 15.2.

SQL statement   Query result

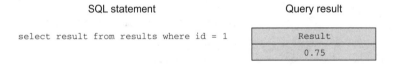

```
select result from results where id = 1
```

Result
0.75

Figure 15.2   Calculator selects last known state from database

This is all pretty straightforward; the record only stores the most recently calculated result. There's no way to know how the user got to 0.75 or what the intermediate results were *after* the calculation completed. (We're ignoring the fact that it's theoretically possible to observe some intermediate results in a SQL query that runs concurrently with the updates in a low isolation level.)

If you wanted to know all calculations that the user performed, you would have to store this in a separate table.

Every calculation is done inside a SQL statement. Every calculation depends on the previous result that's stored in the record in the database table.

15.1.2 *Persisting state without updates*

The event-sourced approach is up next. Instead of storing the last result in one record, we'll capture every successful operation in a *journal* as an *event*. An event needs to capture exactly what has happened; in this case we'll store the name of the operation and its argument. Again simple SQL statements are used as an example; the journal is represented as a simple database table. Figure 15.3 shows the statements that are used to keep track of all calculations.

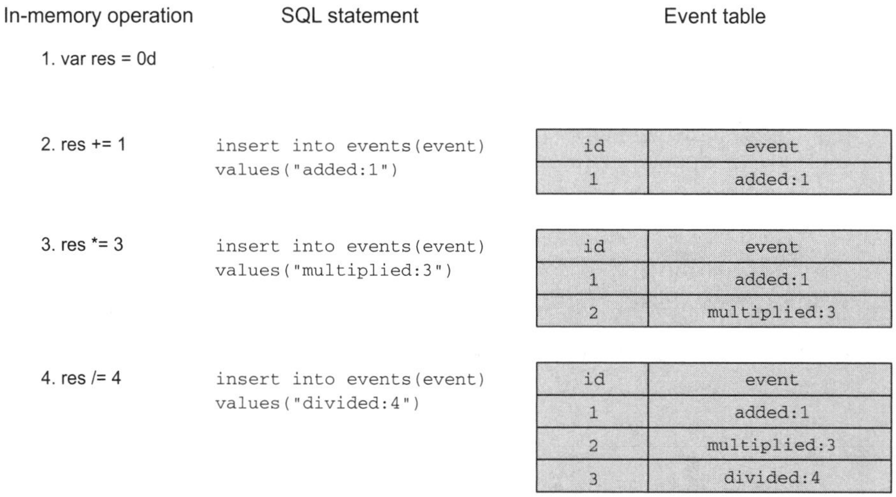

In-memory operation	SQL statement	Event table

1. var res = 0d

2. res += 1
```
insert into events(event)
values("added:1")
```

id	event
1	added:1

3. res *= 3
```
insert into events(event)
values("multiplied:3")
```

id	event
1	added:1
2	multiplied:3

4. res /= 4
```
insert into events(event)
values("divided:4")
```

id	event
1	added:1
2	multiplied:3
3	divided:4

Figure 15.3 Storing all successful operations as events

The calculations are done in-memory; an event is stored after a successful operation. The ID column uses a database sequence and is automatically incremented with every insert. (And you can assume that every insert is executed in its own transaction or that some autocommit feature is used.)

The events describe the successful operations that were executed on the initial state, which starts off as zero. A simple variable is used to keep track of the last result. Every event is crudely serialized as a string, the name of the event and the argument separated by a colon.

Now let's look at how the calculator restores the last known state from the events. The calculator starts at the initial value of 0 and applies every operation in exactly the same order. The calculator app reads and deserializes the events, interprets each event, and executes the same operations to get to the result of 0.75, shown in figure 15.4.

As you can see, event sourcing is a simple concept. In the next section, we'll go a little deeper into how event sourcing can be used to make actors durable.

1. Select * from events order by id ASC

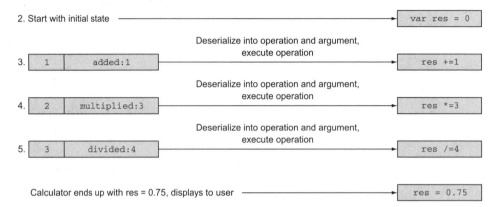

Figure 15.4   **Calculator recalculates last known state from initial value and events**

> ## Which one is "simpler"?
>
> The CRUD-style solution would fit just fine for this simple calculator application. It requires less storage space, and the recovery of the last result is simpler. The calculator app example is simply used to highlight the difference between the two approaches.
>
> Shared mutable state is still our enemy. Pushing it to the database doesn't make the problem go away. The interactions with the database become increasingly complex when CRUD operations are allowed without constraints. The combination of actors and the persistence module provides a simple way to implement event sourcing without having to do too much work yourself, as you'll see in this chapter.

15.1.3   *Event sourcing for actors*

One of the biggest benefits of event sourcing is that writing to and reading from the database are separated into two distinct phases. Reading from the journal only happens when recovering the state of a persistent actor. Once the actor has recovered its state, it's business as usual: the actor can simply process messages and keep state in memory, as long as it makes sure to persist events.

A journal has a simple interface. Leaving out some details, it only needs to support appending serialized events and reading deserialized events from a position in the journal. The events in the journal are effectively immutable; the events can't be changed after they've been written. Once again immutability wins over mutability when it comes to the complexity of concurrent access.

Akka persistence defines a journal interface that makes it possible for anyone to write a *journal plugin*. There's even a TCK (technology compatibility kit) to test compatibility with Akka persistence. Events can be stored in a SQL database, a NoSQL database, an embedded database, or a file-based system, as long as the journal plugin can append events in order and make it possible to read them again in the same order. You can find quite a few journal plugins already available from the Akka community page at http://akka.io/community/.

Event sourcing also has some drawbacks. An obvious drawback is the increase in required storage space. All events from day one need to be recovered after a crash, and every change in state has to be executed to finally get to the last known state, which could potentially take a lot of time at the start of an application.

Creating *snapshots* of the actor state, which we'll look at in section 15.2.3, can reduce the required storage space and speed up recovery of current state. In short this means that it's possible to skip many events and only process snapshots, possibly even only the last known snapshot, after which events can be recovered again.

If the actor state doesn't fit in memory, we obviously have another problem. *Sharding*, which is the distribution of state across servers, makes it possible to scale out the required space for in-memory state. The *cluster sharding* module, which is discussed in section 15.3.2, provides a sharding strategy for actors.

It's safe to say that event sourcing requires some form of serialization of events. Serialization can be done automatically in some cases; in other cases, you'll need to write some specific code. Imagine that you change an event in your application (rename a field, for instance, or add a required field)—how will you be able to deserialize both the old and the new versions of this event from the journal? Versioning serialized data can be a tricky problem; we'll discuss a few options in section 15.2.4.

Event sourcing really only provides a way to recover state from events; it's not a solution for ad hoc queries. A well-known approach for ad hoc queries is to replicate events to a system that's optimized for analysis.

In the next section, we'll start building the calculator to get the basics out of the way. After that we'll look at a more involved example of an online shopping service.

15.2 Persistent actors

First we'll need to add the dependency to our build file.

Listing 15.1 akka-persistence dependency

```
parallelExecution in Test := false

fork := true

libraryDependencies ++= {
  val akkaVersion      = "2.4.9"
```

Disables parallel tests, since we'll use a shared file-based journal for testing

Forking tests, in case the native LevelDB database is used

```
Seq(
  "com.typesafe.akka" %%  "akka-actor"        % akkaVersion,
  "com.typesafe.akka" %%  "akka-persistence" % akkaVersion,
      // other dependencies for the rest of this chapter
  )
}
```

Dependency on akka-persistence

Akka persistence comes bundled with two LevelDB (https://github.com/google /leveldb) journal plugins (which should be used for testing purposes only), a local plugin, and a shared plugin. The local plugin can only be used by one actor system; the shared plugin can be used by many actor systems, which comes in handy when testing persistence in a cluster.

The plugins use a native LevelDB library (https://github.com/fusesource/leveldbjni) or a Java port of the LevelDB project (https://github.com/dain/leveldb). Listings 15.2 and 15.3 show how to configure the plugins to use the Java port instead of the native library.

> **Listing 15.2   Configuring the Java library for the local LevelDB journal plugin**

```
akka.persistence.journal.leveldb.native = off
```

> **Listing 15.3   Configuring the Java library for the shared LevelDB journal plugin**

```
akka.persistence.journal.leveldb-shared.store.native = off
```

Forking tests are required for using the native library; otherwise you'll get a linking error.

Now that we have a minimal build file, we can start building the calculator in the next section.

15.2.1 *Persistent actor*

A *persistent actor* works in two modes: it recovers from events or it processes commands. *Commands* are messages that are sent to the actor to execute some logic; *events* provide evidence that the actor has executed the logic correctly. The first thing to do is define the commands and events for the calculator actor. The following listing shows the commands that the calculator can handle and the events that occur when the calculator validates the commands.

> **Listing 15.4   Calculator commands and events**

```
sealed trait Command
case object Clear extends Command
case class Add(value: Double) extends Command
case class Subtract(value: Double) extends Command
case class Divide(value: Double) extends Command
case class Multiply(value: Double) extends Command
case object PrintResult extends Command
case object GetResult extends Command
```

All commands extend Command trait. Console output is simplified to show most relevant messages.

```
sealed trait Event                                          ◁─────  All events extend
case object Reset extends Event                                     Event trait
case class Added(value: Double) extends Event
case class Subtracted(value: Double) extends Event
case class Divided(value: Double) extends Event
case class Multiplied(value: Double) extends Event
```

Commands and events are separated by extending from distinct sealed traits, `Command` for commands and `Event` for events. (A *sealed* trait allows the Scala compiler to check whether a pattern match on case classes extending the trait is complete.) Akka persistence provides a `PersistentActor` trait that extends the `Actor` trait. Every persistent actor requires a `persistentId`, which is used to uniquely identify the events in the journal for that actor. (Without it there would be no way to separate one actor's events from another.) The ID is automatically passed to the journal when a persistent actor persists an event. In the calculator example, there's only one calculator; listing 15.5 shows that the calculator uses a fixed `persistenceId`—my-calculator—which is defined in `Calculator.name`. The state of the calculator is kept in a `CalculationResult` case class, which is shown in listing 15.8.

Listing 15.5   Extend persistent actor and define `persistenceId`

```
class Calculator extends PersistentActor with ActorLogging {
  import Calculator._

  def persistenceId = Calculator.name

  var state = CalculationResult()
  // more code to follow ..
```

A persistent actor requires two receive definitions—`receiveCommand` and `receiveRecover`—instead of the one `receive` definition that you've seen so far. `receiveCommand` is used to handle messages after the actor has recovered, and `receiveRecover` is used to receive past events and snapshots while the actor is recovering.

The `receiveCommand` definition in listing 15.6 shows how the `persist` method is used to persist the command immediately as an event, except in the case of division, where the argument is first validated to prevent a divide-by-zero error.

Listing 15.6   `receive` for handling messages after recovery

```
val receiveCommand: Receive = {
  case Add(value)      => persist(Added(value))(updateState)
  case Subtract(value) => persist(Subtracted(value))(updateState)
  case Divide(value)   => if(value != 0) persist(Divided(value))(updateState)
  case Multiply(value) => persist(Multiplied(value))(updateState)
  case PrintResult     => println(s"the result is: ${state.result}")
  case GetResult       => sender() ! state.result
  case Clear           => persist(Reset)(updateState)
}
```

`updateState` does the required calculation and updates the calculation result (called state in the code, which is the `CalculationResult`). The `updateState` function shown in listing 15.7 is passed to the persist method, which takes two argument lists: the first for the event to persist, and the second for a function to handle the persisted event, which is called after the event has been successfully persisted in the journal.

The function to handle the persisted event is called asynchronously, but akka-persistence makes sure that the next command isn't handled before this function is completed, so it's safe to refer to sender() from this function, quite unlike normal asynchronous calls from within actors. This does come at some performance overhead, since messages will have to be stashed. If your application doesn't require this guarantee, then you can use persistAsync, which doesn't stash incoming commands.

Listing 15.7   Updating the internal state

```
val updateState: Event => Unit = {
  case Reset                => state = state.reset
  case Added(value)         => state = state.add(value)
  case Subtracted(value)    => state = state.subtract(value)
  case Divided(value)       => state = state.divide(value)
  case Multiplied(value)    => state = state.multiply(value)
}
```

CalculationResult supports the operations that the calculator requires and returns a new immutable value at every operation, shown in listing 15.8. The updateState function calls one of the methods of CalculationResult and assigns it to the state variable.

Listing 15.8   Perform calculation and return next state

```
case class CalculationResult(result: Double = 0) {
  def reset = copy(result = 0)
  def add(value: Double) = copy(result = this.result + value)
  def subtract(value: Double) = copy(result = this.result - value)
  def divide(value: Double) = copy(result = this.result / value)
  def multiply(value: Double) = copy(result = this.result * value)
}
```

To summarize the write side of this calculator actor: Every correct calculation command becomes an event that gets stored in the journal. The state is set to the new calculation result after the associated event is stored.

Let's look at receiveRecover for the calculator in listing 15.9, which will be called with all the events that have occurred when the actor (re-)starts. It will have to execute exactly the same logic that was used when the commands were processed correctly, so we'll use the same updateState function here.

Listing 15.9   `receive` for recovery

This message is sent once recovery has completed.

```
val receiveRecover: Receive = {
  case event: Event     => updateState(event)
  case RecoveryCompleted => log.info("Calculator recovery completed")
}
```

Every calculator event that has ever been appended to the journal using the same `persistenceId` is passed to the same `updateState` function to have the exact same effect as before, updating the calculation result.

`receiveRecover` is used when the actor is started or restarted. New commands that are received while the actor recovers are handled in order once the actor has finished recovering.

Here are some takeaways from this simple code example that we'll use in our next examples:

- Commands are immediately converted into events or validated first in the case of division.
- Commands turn into events if the commands are valid and if they affect the state of the actor. Events cause state updates in the actor after recovery and during recovery; the logic is exactly the same.
- Writing the logic in an `updateState` function is recommended to avoid code duplication in the `receiveCommand` and `receiveRecover` definitions.
- The `CalculationResult` contains the calculator logic in an immutable way (by providing a copy of the result at every operation). This makes the `updateState` function really simple to implement and to read.

In the next section, we'll write a test for this simple example.

15.2.2 Testing

Next let's see how we can test the calculator. The unit test in listing 15.10 shows that we can test this actor as usual, provided we use a base class for testing with Akka persistence and include a trait for cleaning up the journal. This is necessary since the LevelDB journal writes to the same directory for all tests, by default in a journal directory inside the current working directory. Sadly there's no Akka persistence test kit that does this setup for you automatically, or provides other persistence-related test features, but for now some simple helpers will do the trick. Since we turned off parallel tests earlier, every test can use the journal in isolation.

Listing 15.10   Unit test for the calculator

```
package aia.persistence.calculator

import akka.actor._
import akka.testkit._
import org.scalatest._

class CalculatorSpec extends PersistenceSpec(ActorSystem("test"))
    with PersistenceCleanup {

  "The Calculator" should {
    "recover last known result after crash" in {
      val calc = system.actorOf(Calculator.props, Calculator.name)
      calc ! Calculator.Add(1d)
      calc ! Calculator.GetResult
      expectMsg(1d)
```

```
      calc ! Calculator.Subtract(0.5d)
      calc ! Calculator.GetResult
      expectMsg(0.5d)

      killActors(calc)

      val calcResurrected = system.actorOf(Calculator.props, Calculator.name)
      calcResurrected ! Calculator.GetResult
      expectMsg(0.5d)

      calcResurrected ! Calculator.Add(1d)
      calcResurrected ! Calculator.GetResult
      expectMsg(1.5d)
    }
  }
}
```

The unit test contains a simple example to verify that the calculator correctly recovers from a crash. The calculator responds with the result of the calculation when it receives a GetResult message. The PersistenceSpec defines killActors, which watches, stops, and awaits termination of all actors passed to it. The calculator is killed, after which a new calculator is created and continues where it left off.

The following listing shows the PersistenceSpec class and the Persistence-Cleanup trait.

Listing 15.11 Base class for persistence specs

```
import java.io.File
import com.typesafe.config._

import scala.util._

import akka.actor._
import akka.persistence._
import org.scalatest._

import org.apache.commons.io.FileUtils

abstract class PersistenceSpec(system: ActorSystem) extends TestKit(system)
  with ImplicitSender
  with WordSpecLike
  with Matchers
  with BeforeAndAfterAll
  with PersistenceCleanup {

  def this(name: String, config: Config) = this(ActorSystem(name, config))
  override protected def beforeAll() = deleteStorageLocations()

  override protected def afterAll() = {
    deleteStorageLocations()
    TestKit.shutdownActorSystem(system)
  }

  def killActors(actors: ActorRef*) = {
    actors.foreach { actor =>
      watch(actor)
      system.stop(actor)
```

```
        expectTerminated(actor)
      }
    }
  }
}

trait PersistenceCleanup {
  def system: ActorSystem

  val storageLocations = List(
    "akka.persistence.journal.leveldb.dir",
    "akka.persistence.journal.leveldb-shared.store.dir",
    "akka.persistence.snapshot-store.local.dir").map { s =>
    new File(system.settings.config.getString(s))
  }

  def deleteStorageLocations(): Unit = {
    storageLocations.foreach(dir => Try(FileUtils.deleteDirectory(dir)))
  }
}
```

The `PersistenceCleanup` trait defines a `deleteStorageLocations` method that removes directories created by the LevelDB journal (as well as the default snapshot journal, which we'll talk about a little more in section 15.2.3). It gets the configured directories from the Akka configuration. The `PersistenceSpec` deletes any leftover directories before the unit test starts, deletes the directories after all specifications, and shuts down the actor system used during the test.

`CalculatorSpec` creates an actor system with default configuration for the test, but it's also possible to pass in a custom configuration to the test, using the auxiliary constructor of `PersistenceSpec`, which takes a system name and a config object. `PersistenceCleanup` uses `org.apache.commons.io.FileUtils` to delete the directories; the dependency for the `commons-io` library can be found in the sbt build file.

The `PersistenceSpec` will be used for unit tests in the upcoming sections. In the next section we'll look at using snapshots to speed up recovery.

15.2.3 *Snapshots*

As mentioned before, snapshots can be used to speed up the recovery of an actor. Snapshots are stored in a separate `SnapshotStore`. The default snapshot store stores files on disk in a directory configured by akka.persistence.snapshot-store.local.dir.

To show how snapshots work, we'll use an example of a shopping basket actor. In the next sections, we'll go through the persistence aspects of an online shopping service, focused on handling shopping baskets. The following listing shows the commands and events for a `Basket` actor.

Listing 15.12 Basket commands and events

Basket commands are
shopper commands; Shopper
actor will be shown later

```
sealed trait Command extends Shopper.Command       ◁───────
```

```
case class Add(item: Item, shopperId: Long) extends Command
case class RemoveItem(productId: String, shopperId: Long) extends Command
case class UpdateItem(productId: String,
                      number: Int,
                      shopperId: Long) extends Command
case class Clear(shopperId: Long) extends Command
case class Replace(items: Items, shopperId: Long) extends Command
case class GetItems(shopperId: Long) extends Command

case class CountRecoveredEvents(shopperId: Long) extends Command
case class RecoveredEventsCount(count: Long)

sealed trait Event extends Serializable
case class Added(item: Item) extends Event
case class ItemRemoved(productId: String) extends Event
case class ItemUpdated(productId: String, number: Int) extends Event
case class Replaced(items: Items) extends Event
case class Cleared(clearedItems: Items) extends Event

case class Snapshot(items: Items)
```

Basket is cleared once it's paid for ⊳ (annotation pointing to `case class Clear(shopperId: Long) extends Command`)

Event indicating that basket has been cleared ◁ (annotation pointing to `case class Cleared(clearedItems: Items) extends Event`)

A basket contains items, and as you would expect, you can add, remove, and update items in a basket and clear the basket once it's paid for. Every shopper in the online service has a basket, adds items to the basket, and eventually pays for the items in the basket. The `Basket` actor contains `Items` to represent its state.

Listing 15.13 `Items`

```
case class Items(list: List[Item]) {
  // more code for working with the item..
```

Listing 15.14 `Item`

```
case class Item(productId: String, number: Int, unitPrice: BigDecimal) {
  // more code for working with the item..
```

The details of items are left out; methods to add, remove, and clear items return a new immutable copy, similar to the approach taken with the `CalculationResult`. The basket is cleared once the shopper has paid. It makes sense to make a snapshot once the basket is cleared; there's no need to know about the previous items in the basket if all you want to do is show the current shopping basket as quickly as possible after a restart.

For now we'll only look at the relevant code for snapshots; in later sections we'll look at how the `Basket` actor is created as part of the complete service. We'll start with the `updateState` and `receiveCommand` methods.

```
private val updateState: (Event => Unit) = {
  case Added(item)              => items = items.add(item)
  case ItemRemoved(id)          => items = items.removeItem(id)
  case ItemUpdated(id, number)  => items = items.updateItem(id, number)
  case Replaced(newItems)       => items = newItems
  case Cleared(clearedItems)    => items = items.clear
}
```

```
def receiveCommand = {
  case Add(item, _) =>
    persist(Added(item))(updateState)

  case RemoveItem(id, _) =>
    if(items.containsProduct(id)) {
      persist(ItemRemoved(id)){ removed =>
        updateState(removed)
        sender() ! Some(removed)
      }
    } else {
      sender() ! None
    }

  case UpdateItem(id, number, _) =>
    if(items.containsProduct(id)) {
      persist(ItemUpdated(id, number)){ updated =>
        updateState(updated)
        sender() ! Some(updated)
      }
    } else {
      sender() ! None
    }

  case Replace(items, _) =>
    persist(Replaced(items))(updateState)

  case Clear(_) =>
    persist(Cleared(items)){ e =>
      updateState(e)
      //basket is cleared after payment.
      saveSnapshot(Basket.Snapshot(items))     // Saves snapshot when basket is cleared
    }

  case GetItems(_) =>
    sender() ! items
  case CountRecoveredEvents(_) =>
    sender() ! RecoveredEventsCount(nrEventsRecovered)     // Snapshot successfully saved
  case SaveSnapshotSuccess(metadata) =>
    log.info(s"Snapshot saved with metadata $metadata")
  case SaveSnapshotFailure(metadata, reason) =>
    log.error(s"Failed to save snapshot: $metadata, $reason.")
}
```

Snapshot couldn't be saved

The `Items` in the basket are saved as a snapshot using the `saveSnapshot` method. `SaveSnapshotSuccess` or `SaveSnapshotFailure` is eventually returned to indicate if the snapshot could be saved. In this example it's purely an optimization to save the snapshot, so we don't take any action when the snapshot couldn't be saved. The following listing shows the `receiveRecover` for the `Basket` actor.

Listing 15.17 Basket `receiveRecover`

```
def receiveRecover = {
  case event: Event =>
    nrEventsRecovered = nrEventsRecovered + 1
    updateState(event)
  case SnapshotOffer(_, snapshot: Basket.Snapshot) =>        ◁─┐  Snapshot
    log.info(s"Recovering baskets from snapshot: $snapshot for $persistenceId      is offered
      ")                                                            during
    items = snapshot.items                                         recovery
}
```

`receiveRecover` uses the `updateState` as expected, but it also handles a `Snapshot-Offer` message. By default the last saved snapshot is passed to the actor before any events that follow the snapshot. Any events that occurred before the snapshot aren't passed to `receiveRecover`. In this case this means that all events for baskets that have been paid for don't have to be processed during recovery.

> **RECOVERY CUSTOMIZATION** By default only the latest snapshot taken is offered during recovery, which is the most common case. There's a way to customize from which snapshot a persistent actor should recover; you can override the `recovery` method. The `Recovery` value returned from this method selects a snapshot to start recovering from by `sequenceNr` and/or `timestamp`, and optionally a `sequenceNr` until which to recover or a max number of messages to recover.

The `CountRecoveredEvents` command is added to test if the events are really skipped during recovery. Listing 15.17 shows that `nrEventsRecovered` is incremented with every event; the `Basket` actor returns the number of recovered events when it receives a `CountRecoveredEvents`, shown in listing 15.16. The `BasketSnapshotSpec` in listing 15.18 shows a unit test to validate that events are skipped after snapshots are made (once baskets are cleared).

Listing 15.18 `BasketSnapshotSpec`

```
package aia.persistence

import scala.concurrent.duration._

import akka.actor._
import akka.testkit._
import org.scalatest._

class BasketSpec extends PersistenceSpec(ActorSystem("test"))
    with PersistenceCleanup {
```

```
val shopperId = 2L
val macbookPro = Item("Apple Macbook Pro", 1, BigDecimal(2499.99))
val macPro = Item("Apple Mac Pro", 1, BigDecimal(10499.99))
val displays = Item("4K Display", 3, BigDecimal(2499.99))
val appleMouse = Item("Apple Mouse", 1, BigDecimal(99.99))
val appleKeyboard = Item("Apple Keyboard", 1, BigDecimal(79.99))
val dWave = Item("D-Wave One", 1, BigDecimal(14999999.99))

"The basket" should {
  "skip basket events that occured before Cleared during recovery" in {
    val basket = system.actorOf(Basket.props, Basket.name(shopperId))
    basket ! Basket.Add(macbookPro, shopperId)
    basket ! Basket.Add(displays, shopperId)
    basket ! Basket.GetItems(shopperId)
    expectMsg(Items(macbookPro, displays))

    basket ! Basket.Clear(shopperId)                        ◁──────┐

    basket ! Basket.Add(macPro, shopperId)                         │  Clearing
    basket ! Basket.RemoveItem(macPro.productId, shopperId)        │  basket causes
    expectMsg(Some(Basket.ItemRemoved(macPro.productId)))          │  a snapshot

    basket ! Basket.Clear(shopperId)                        ◁──────┘
    basket ! Basket.Add(dWave, shopperId)
    basket ! Basket.Add(displays, shopperId)

    basket ! Basket.GetItems(shopperId)
    expectMsg(Items(dWave, displays))

    killActors(basket)

    val basketResurrected = system.actorOf(Basket.props,
      Basket.name(shopperId))
    basketResurrected ! Basket.GetItems(shopperId)
    expectMsg(Items(dWave, displays))

    basketResurrected ! Basket.CountRecoveredEvents(shopperId)
    expectMsg(Basket.RecoveredEventsCount(2))         ◁──┐
                                                         │  Assert that only events
    killActors(basketResurrected)                        │  after last snapshot are
  }                                                      │  processed during recovery
}
}
```

Counting the number of snapshots that are offered is left as an exercise to the reader. This is a simple example of snapshots: the snapshot that we save is always empty, which we use as a marker in the journal to prevent having to process all previous basket interactions.

As you've seen, a persistent actor can recover itself from snapshots and events stored in a journal. There might be cases where you'd like to read events from the journal outside of the recovery process of a persistent actor. In the next section, we'll look at how events can be read directly from a journal.

15.2.4 *Persistence query*

Persistence query is an experimental module for querying a journal, out of band from the recovery of persistent actors. We'll take only a brief look at the module in this section, since it's experimental and not essentially required for recovering actor state, the focus of this chapter. It's important to note that this is not a tool for ad hoc query like SQL. The best use case for persistent query is to continuously read events out of band from the persistent actors and update these events in another database in a shape more suitable for querying.

If you have very limited querying requirements, persistence query might suffice for your use case directly. Persistence query supports getting all events, getting events for a particular persistenceId, and getting events by a specific tag (which requires an event adapter to explicitly tag events into the journal, not described here).

That might sound limited, but these features are enough to read all or a subset of events and write them to your database of choice for querying. Persistence query provides an API to read from an akka-stream Source of events.

In this section we'll focus on how you can access a Source of events; updating a database for querying is left as an exercise for the reader. Let's first add the dependency for it.

Listing 15.19   Add persistence-query dependency

```
libraryDependencies ++= {
val akkaVersion       = "2.4.9"
Seq(
  // other dependencies omitted ..
  "com.typesafe.akka" %% "akka-persistence-query-experimental" % akkaVersion,
  // other dependencies omitted ..
)
```

A LevelDB read journal is bundled in this dependency, which we'll use in this section. It's expected that most community journal plugins will support a read journal. The following listing shows how to get access to the LevelDB ReadJournal.

Listing 15.20   Get the ReadJournal

```
implicit val mat = ActorMaterializer()(system)
val queries =
  PersistenceQuery(system).readJournalFor[LeveldbReadJournal](
    LeveldbReadJournal.Identifier
  )
```

You need to provide an implicit ActorMaterializer, which is common when using akka-stream. The readJournalFor method on the PersistenceQuery extension returns a specific read journal, in this case a LeveldbReadJournal.

The LeveldbReadJournal supports all types of queries, which can be found in the All-PersistenceIdsQuery, CurrentPersistenceIdsQuery, EventsByPersistenceIdQuery,

`CurrentEventsByPersistenceIdQuery`, `EventsByTagQuery`, and `CurrentEventsByTag-Query` traits. Other journal plugins might decide to implement all, some, or none of these traits.

There are basically two types of queries: methods starting with `current` return a `Source` that completes the stream once all currently stored events have been provided through the `Source`, and methods that don't start with `current` won't complete the stream, and will continuously provide "live" events as they arrive. (The stream can of course complete with a failure when the journal can't be read; you'll have to handle total stream failure yourself.)

The next listing shows how you can read the current basket events that are stored in the LevelDB journal for a specific basket.

Listing 15.21 Get current basket events

```
val src: Source[EventEnvelope, NotUsed] =
    queries.currentEventsByPersistenceId(
        Basket.name(shopperId), 0L, Long.MaxValue)

val events: Source[Basket.Event, NotUsed] =
    src.map(_.event.asInstanceOf[Basket.Event])

val res: Future[Seq[Basket.Event]] = events.runWith(Sink.seq)
```

Gets a source to the current events for a specific basket, from the beginning, until the last event stored.

Since we're only writing Basket.Event type events to the journal, it's safe to cast the events here.

You could run a source with a Sink.seq to get all the events for testing purposes. You would probably await the future to compare it with a list of known events.

The `persistenceId` in the `Basket` actor is set to the same value as what is returned by `Basket.name`, which is why this example works. The `currentEventsByPersistenceId` method takes two arguments, a `fromSequenceNr` and a `toSequenceNr`; using 0 and `Long.MaxValue`, respectively, returns all events in the journal for the `persistenceId`. The following listing shows how you can read a live stream of basket events that are stored in the LevelDB journal for a specific basket.

Listing 15.22 Get a live stream of basket events

```
val src: Source[EventEnvelope, NotUsed] =
    queries.eventsByPersistenceId(
        Basket.name(shopperId), 0L, Long.MaxValue)

val dbRows: Source[DbRow, NotUsed] =
    src.map(eventEnvelope => toDbRow(eventEnvelope))
    events.runWith(reactiveDatabaseSink)
```

Gets a source to all events for a specific basket, which doesn't end.

You could translate the events into "database rows," which could be written to some database sink; details are omitted here.

The `Source` returned by `eventsByPersistenceId` will never complete; it will continue to provide events when they occur. Translating events to some database representation and writing them to a database sink, shown in the previous listing, should be read more as "incomplete pseudo code" than real code; this is left as an exercise for the reader. You would have to keep track of the sequence number that you stored previously in case some error occurs or if this logic is restarted for any reason. A good option for keeping track of sequence numbers is to write these out into the target database. (The EventEnvelope has a sequenceNr field.) At restart, you can then take the maximum sequence number in the target database and continue from there.

In the next section, we'll look at how events and snapshots are serialized.

15.2.5 *Serialization*

Serialization is configured through Akka's serialization infrastructure. Java serialization is used by default. This is fine for testing purposes, but shouldn't be used in production; in most cases you need a more efficient serializer.

Using anything but the default takes some work, which is the topic of this section.

Writing a custom serializer is the best choice if you want full control over how events and snapshots are serialized, which is what we'll do in this section.

> **Seriously, write a custom serializer?**
>
> Writing a custom serializer is a bit of work. If you find that the default serializer isn't fast enough for your use case, or if you need to execute custom logic to automatically migrate from previously serialized data, then writing a custom serializer is a good choice.
>
> Aren't there any other options, you might ask? The akka-remote module contains a serializer for the Google Protocol Buffers format (https://github.com/google/protobuf), but this serializer only works with protobuf-generated classes, which works best if you start out with protobuf definitions. Classes are then generated from the protobuf definitions, which are then used directly as events.
>
> Another option is to use a third-party akka-serialization library. A library called akka-kryo-serialization (https://github.com/romix/akka-kryo-serialization) is an example of a serialization library that claims to support serialization of most Scala classes automatically, using the *kryo* format. The library still needs some configuration though, and doesn't support version migration.
>
> *Stamina* (https://github.com/scalapenos/stamina) is an akka-serialization toolkit specifically built for akka-persistence. It has an optional module for JSON serialization using spray-json. Stamina provides a DSL for versioning and automigrating serialized data (also called *upcasting*), which makes it possible to upgrade your service without having to stop the service and convert the entire journal before starting the service again.

Before we look into the actual code of the custom serializers, let's have a look at how to configure them. The code in the next listing shows how you can configure a custom serializer for all Basket.Event classes and the Basket snapshot class: Basket.Snapshot.

Listing 15.23 Serialization configuration

```
akka {
  actor {                                          Registers custom serializers
    serializers {
      basket = "aia.persistence.BasketEventSerializer"
      basketSnapshot = "aia.persistence.BasketSnapshotSerializer"
    }
    serialization-bindings {                        Binds classes that
      "aia.persistence.Basket$Event" = basket       need custom
      "aia.persistence.Basket$Snapshot" = basketSnapshot    serialization to a
    }                                               specific serializer
  }
}
```

Any class that's not bound will automatically use the default serializer. Class names need to be fully qualified. In this case `Event` and `Snapshot` are part of the `Basket` companion object. The Scala compiler creates a Java class for the object with a dollar sign added to the end, which explains the strange, fully qualified class names (FQCNs) of `Basket.Event` and `Basket.Snapshot`.

Any serializer needs to create a byte array representation of the event or snapshot in question. A serializer needs to be able to reconstruct the correct event or snapshot from that same byte array later on. The next listing shows the trait that we need to implement in a custom serializer.

Listing 15.24 Akka `Serializer` trait

```
trait Serializer {
  /**
   * Completely unique value to identify this
   * implementation of Serializer,
   * used to optimize network traffic
   * Values from 0 to 16 is reserved for Akka internal usage
   */
  def identifier: Int

  /**
   * Serializes the given object into an Array of Byte
   */
  def toBinary(o: AnyRef): Array[Byte]

  /**
   * Returns whether this serializer needs a manifest
   * in the fromBinary method
   */
  def includeManifest: Boolean

  /**
   * Produces an object from an array of bytes,
   * with an optional type-hint;
   * the class should be loaded using ActorSystem.dynamicAccess.
   */
  def fromBinary(bytes: Array[Byte], manifest: Option[Class[_]]): AnyRef
}
```

In general, any serializer will need to write a discriminator into the serialized bytes to be able to read them back again later. This can be a serialized class name, or simply a numerical ID to identify a type. Using Java serialization, Akka can automatically write a class manifest into the serialized bytes, if includeManifest is set to true in the custom serializer.

The custom serializers for the basket event and snapshot will use the spray-json library to read and write in JSON format (we have to pick something, after all). The full list of JSON formats is defined in a JsonFormats object, which is omitted from the listings here. Let's first look at the BasketEventSerializer, which is used to serialize Basket.Events.

Listing 15.25   Custom `Basket` event serializer

```
import scala.util.Try
import akka.serialization._                         JsonFormats (omitted here)
import spray.json._                                  contains spray-json formats for
                                                     basket events and snapshots.
class BasketEventSerializer extends Serializer {  ◄
  import JsonFormats._
                                                     Registers custom serializers
  val includeManifest: Boolean = false          ◄
  val identifier = 123678213

  def toBinary(obj: AnyRef): Array[Byte] = {
    obj match {                                      Only serializes basket events
      case e: Basket.Event =>                    ◄
        BasketEventFormat.write(e).compactPrint.getBytes
      case msg =>
        throw new Exception(s"Cannot serialize $msg with ${this.getClass}")
    }
  }
                                                     Converts byte array to
  def fromBinary(bytes: Array[Byte],                 a spray-json AST
              clazz: Option[Class[_]]): AnyRef = {    (abstract syntax tree)
    val jsonAst = new String(bytes).parseJson    ◄
    BasketEventFormat.read(jsonAst)              ◄   Converts json to Basket.Event
  }                                                  using a BasketEventFormat
}
```

Every serializer needs unique ID (→ val identifier = 123678213)

The BasketEventFormat in JsonFormats writes a JSON array for every event. The first element is a discriminator to indicate which event is stored in the second element of the array. This same discriminator is used to determine which event format to use to deserialize the event. BasketEventFormat is shown next.

Listing 15.26   `BasketEventFormat`

```
implicit object BasketEventFormat
    extends RootJsonFormat[Basket.Event] {
  import Basket._
  val addedId   = JsNumber(1)
  val removedId = JsNumber(2)
  val updatedId = JsNumber(3)
```

```scala
val replacedId = JsNumber(4)
val clearedId = JsNumber(5)

def write(event: Event) = {
  event match {
    case e: Added =>
      JsArray(addedId, addedEventFormat.write(e))
    case e: ItemRemoved =>
      JsArray(removedId, removedEventFormat.write(e))
    case e: ItemUpdated =>
      JsArray(updatedId, updatedEventFormat.write(e))
    case e: Replaced =>
      JsArray(replacedId, replacedEventFormat.write(e))
    case e: Cleared =>
      JsArray(clearedId, clearedEventFormat.write(e))
  }
}
def read(json: JsValue): Basket.Event = {
  json match {
    case JsArray(Vector(`addedId`,jsEvent)) =>
      addedEventFormat.read(jsEvent)
    case JsArray(Vector(`removedId`,jsEvent)) =>
      removedEventFormat.read(jsEvent)
    case JsArray(Vector(`updatedId`,jsEvent)) =>
      updatedEventFormat.read(jsEvent)
    case JsArray(Vector(`replacedId`,jsEvent)) =>
      replacedEventFormat.read(jsEvent)
    case JsArray(Vector(`clearedId`,jsEvent)) =>
      clearedEventFormat.read(jsEvent)
    case j =>
      deserializationError("Expected basket event, but got " + j)
  }
}
}
```

The `BasketSnapshotSerializer` is shown in listing 15.27. It uses the implicitly defined format defined in `JsonFormats` for converting between JSON and `Basket-Snapshot`s.

A custom serializer like this can also be used to automatically migrate old versions of serialized data. One solution would be to write a discriminator value into the bytes, similar to the one that determines the event type, which is then used to select a custom piece of logic to read all older versions of serialized data into the most current version. (The Stamina library does something along these lines and provides a nice DSL to define version migrations.)

Listing 15.27 Custom `Basket` snapshot serializer

```scala
class BasketSnapshotSerializer extends Serializer {
  import JsonFormats._

  val includeManifest: Boolean = false
  val identifier = 1242134234
```

```
def toBinary(obj: AnyRef): Array[Byte] = {
  obj match {
    case snap: Basket.Snapshot => snap.toJson.compactPrint.getBytes
    case msg => throw new Exception(s"Cannot serialize $msg")
  }
}

def fromBinary(bytes: Array[Byte],
               clazz: Option[Class[_]]): AnyRef = {
  val jsonStr = new String(bytes)
  jsonStr.parseJson.convertTo[Basket.Snapshot]
}
}
```

Event adapters

akka-persistence doesn't just serialize the events and snapshots directly into byte arrays into the `Journal` or `SnapshotStore`. The serialized objects are wrapped into an internal protobuf format, which is required for internal bookkeeping. This means that you can't simply query the backend database of a journal plugin for some JSON structure when your custom serializer serializes events to JSON, like in the example you've just seen.

An `EventAdapter` simplifies this. It sits between the journal and the event that's read or written, making it possible to write arbitrary transformations between the two. This makes it possible to decouple the event from the persisted data model.

The `EventAdapter` will have to *fit* on the `Journal` plugin. An `EventAdapter` could convert events to JSON objects, but for this to work, the `Journal` has to also handle JSON objects differently than any event object that would normally get serialized to bytes and wrapped into the internal structure.

The custom serializers shown here simply serve as examples. Serialization is a hard problem to solve generically for all cases. The custom solution described here isn't ideal, but at least provides an idea of the issues that you can encounter. Integrating one of the community's serializer plugins is left as an exercise to the reader. In the next section, we'll look at persisting actors in a cluster.

15.3   *Clustered persistence*

So far we've looked at recovering actor state in a local actor system. In this section we'll build the online shopping service out further. First, we'll look at the local actor system solution in a little more detail.

Then, we'll change the application so it can run on a cluster as a *cluster singleton*. A cluster singleton allows you to run exactly one instance of an actor (and its children) on a node (with the same role) in an Akka cluster.

The cluster singleton automatically starts all shopping baskets on another node when the current singleton node has crashed, so the shopping baskets need to be

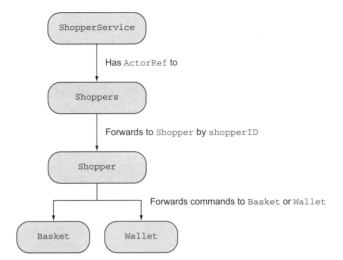

Figure 15.5 Overview of the shopping service

persisted somewhere else, preferably in a distributed database like Apache Cassandra. This will improve the fault tolerance of the shopping service, but it doesn't solve the fact that we possibly need to keep more baskets in memory than can fit on one node in the cluster.

For this we'll look at *cluster sharding*, which makes it possible to divide shopping baskets across the cluster according to a sharding strategy.

But before we get to those details, let's look at the overall structure of the online shopping service. Figure 15.5 shows an overview of the shopping service.

The project on GitHub contains an HTTP service for shopping baskets (the ShopperService). The ShopperService takes an ActorRef to a Shoppers actor. This actor creates or finds a Shopper actor for every unique shopperId. If no Shopper exists yet for the unique ID, then one will be created; if the Shopper already exists, it will be returned. The shopper forwards any request to a specific Shopper actor based on a command. A shopper command always contains the shopperId. Both Basket and Wallet commands are also Shopper commands.

You could imagine that a cookie is automatically generated when a user visits the online store for the first time. The same cookie is used when the user returns to the online store. The cookie contains a unique ID to track the shopper, which is called a shopperId in the example. (Cookies are left out of the example HTTP service.) The shopperId in the example is a simple Long value; you would probably use a random universally unique identifier (UUID) in a real application. The following listing shows a piece of the ShoppersRoutes trait that defines the HTTP routes of the service.

Listing 15.28 ShoppersRoutes

```
trait ShoppersRoutes extends
    ShopperMarshalling {
  def routes =
```

```
      deleteItem ~
      updateItem ~
      getBasket ~
      updateBasket ~
      deleteBasket ~
      pay

  def shoppers: ActorRef

  implicit def timeout: Timeout
  implicit def executionContext: ExecutionContext

  def pay = {
    post {
      pathPrefix("shopper" / ShopperIdSegment / "pay") { shopperId =>
        shoppers ! Shopper.PayBasket(shopperId)
        complete(OK)
      }
    }
  }
}
```

The `LocalShoppers` actor is shown next.

Listing 15.29   LocalShoppers actor

```
package aia.persistence

import akka.actor._

object LocalShoppers {
  def props = Props(new LocalShoppers)
  def name = "local-shoppers"
}

class LocalShoppers extends Actor
    with ShopperLookup {
  def receive = forwardToShopper
}

trait ShopperLookup {
  implicit def context: ActorContext

  def forwardToShopper: Actor.Receive = {
    case cmd: Shopper.Command =>
      context.child(Shopper.name(cmd.shopperId))
        .fold(createAndForward(cmd, cmd.shopperId))(forwardCommand(cmd))
  }

  def forwardCommand(cmd: Shopper.Command)(shopper: ActorRef) =
    shopper forward cmd

  def createAndForward(cmd: Shopper.Command, shopperId: Long) = {
    createShopper(shopperId) forward cmd
  }

  def createShopper(shopperId: Long) =
    context.actorOf(Shopper.props(shopperId),
      Shopper.name(shopperId))
}
```

Looking up a `Shopper` actor has been factored out into a `ShopperLookup`, since we can reuse it in a slightly modified manner for both the cluster singleton and cluster sharding extensions.

The `Shopper` actor is shown next.

Listing 15.30 Shopper actor

```
import akka.actor._

object Shopper {
  def props(shopperId: Long) = Props(new Shopper)
  def name(shopperId: Long) = shopperId.toString

  trait Command {
    def shopperId: Long
  }

  case class PayBasket(shopperId: Long) extends Command
  // for simplicity every shopper got 40k to spend.
  val cash = 40000
}

class Shopper extends Actor {
  import Shopper._

  def shopperId = self.path.name.toLong

  val basket = context.actorOf(Basket.props,
    Basket.name(shopperId))

  val wallet = context.actorOf(Wallet.props(shopperId, cash),
    Wallet.name(shopperId))

  def receive = {
    case cmd: Basket.Command => basket forward cmd
    case cmd: Wallet.Command => wallet forward cmd

    case PayBasket(shopperId) => basket ! Basket.GetItems(shopperId)
    case Items(list) => wallet ! Wallet.Pay(list, shopperId)
    case Wallet.Paid(_, shopperId) => basket ! Basket.Clear(shopperId)
  }
}
```

> Every Shopper command has a shopperId.

The `Shopper` creates a `Basket` actor and a `Wallet` actor, and forwards commands to these actors. Paying for a basket is orchestrated by the `Shopper` actor. It first sends `GetItems` to the `Basket`; once it receives the `Items`, it sends a `Pay` message to the `Wallet`, which responds with a `Paid` message. The `Shopper` then sends a `Clear` message to the basket to complete the flow. In the next section, we'll look at the changes we have to make for running the `Shoppers` actor as a cluster singleton.

15.3.1 *Cluster singleton*

The next topic we'll look at is the cluster singleton extension. We'll run the `Shoppers` actor as a singleton in the cluster, meaning there will always be only one `Shoppers` actor in the cluster.

The cluster singleton extension is part of the cluster-tools module; the cluster sharding extension is part of the cluster-sharding module; so dependencies need to be added to the project.

Listing 15.31 Cluster singleton and sharding dependencies

```
libraryDependencies ++= {
  val akkaVersion       = "2.4.9"
  Seq(
    // other dependencies omitted ..
    "com.typesafe.akka" %% "akka-cluster-tools"    % akkaVersion,
    "com.typesafe.akka" %% "akka-cluster-sharding" % akkaVersion,
    // other dependencies omitted ..
  )
```

The cluster singleton extension requires a correct cluster configuration, which can be found in the application.conf file in src/main/resources, discussed in chapter 13. Figure 15.6 shows the changes that we'll make.

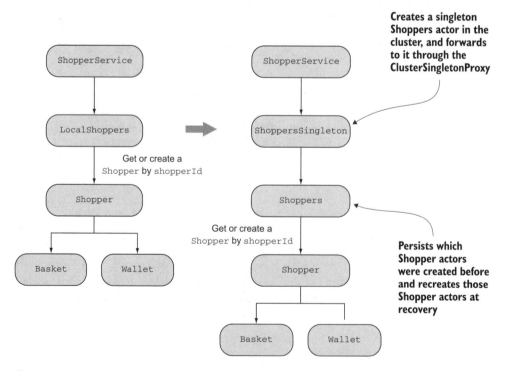

Figure 15.6 From local to cluster singleton

A ShoppersSingleton actor reference will be passed to the ShoppingService instead of the LocalShoppers actor reference. The ShoppersSingleton actor is shown next.

Listing 15.32 ShoppersSingleton

```
import akka.actor._
import akka.cluster.singleton.ClusterSingletonManager
import akka.cluster.singleton.ClusterSingletonManagerSettings
import akka.cluster.singleton.ClusterSingletonProxy
import akka.cluster.singleton.ClusterSingletonProxySettings
import akka.persistence._

object ShoppersSingleton {
  def props = Props(new ShoppersSingleton)
  def name = "shoppers-singleton"
}

class ShoppersSingleton extends Actor {

  val singletonManager = context.system.actorOf(
    ClusterSingletonManager.props(
      Shoppers.props,
      PoisonPill,
      ClusterSingletonManagerSettings(context.system)
        .withRole(None)
        .withSingletonName(Shoppers.name)
    )
  )

  val shoppers = context.system.actorOf(
    ClusterSingletonProxy.props(
      singletonManager.path.child(Shoppers.name)
        .toStringWithoutAddress,
      ClusterSingletonProxySettings(context.system)
        .withRole(None)
        .withSingletonName("shoppers-proxy")
    )
  )

  def receive = {
    case command: Shopper.Command => shoppers forward command
  }
}
```

The ShoppersSingleton actor functions as a reference to the actual singleton in the cluster. Every node in the cluster will start up a ShoppersSingleton actor. Only one of the nodes will actually run the Shoppers actor as a singleton.

The ShoppersSingleton creates a reference to the ClusterSingletonManager. The singleton manager ensures that there's only one Shoppers actor at any point in time in the cluster. All we need to do is pass it the Props and name of the singleton actor that we want to use (via singletonProps and singletonName). The Shoppers-Singleton also creates a proxy to the Shoppers singleton actor, which it forwards messages to. This proxy always points to the current singleton in the cluster.

The Shoppers actor is the actual singleton. It's a PersistentActor, and it stores which shoppers have successfully been created as events. The Shoppers actor can recover these events and re-create the Shopper actors after a crash, which makes it possible for the cluster singleton to move to another node.

It's important to note that the cluster singleton focuses on preventing more than one active singleton in the cluster at any time. When a cluster singleton crashes, there's a period of time in which the next cluster singleton hasn't been started yet, which means that you could potentially lose messages during that time.

Both baskets and wallets are also persistent actors, so they automatically re-create themselves from events as well when they're re-created by the Shopper.

The Shoppers actor is shown next.

Listing 15.33 Shoppers actor

```
object Shoppers {
  def props = Props(new Shoppers)
  def name = "shoppers"

  sealed trait Event
  case class ShopperCreated(shopperId: Long)
}

class Shoppers extends PersistentActor
    with ShopperLookup {
  import Shoppers._

  def persistenceId = "shoppers"

  def receiveCommand = forwardToShopper

  override def createAndForward(cmd: Shopper.Command, shopperId: Long) = {
    val shopper = createShopper(shopperId)
    persistAsync(ShopperCreated(shopperId)) { _ =>
      forwardCommand(cmd)(shopper)
    }
  }

  def receiveRecover = {
    case ShopperCreated(shopperId) =>
      context.child(Shopper.name(shopperId))
        .getOrElse(createShopper(shopperId))
  }
}
```

The createAndForward method is overridden to also persist a ShopperCreated event. We can safely use persistAsync here; there's no need to re-create the shoppers in exactly the same order. You can try the cluster singleton by executing sbt run and selecting the aia.persistence.SingletonMain as the main class to start. In a real scenario, you'd have a load balancer in front of all the nodes. The REST service on any node can communicate with the cluster singleton through the cluster proxy in the ShoppersSingleton actor. You do need to choose a different journal implementation for testing this.

If you only want to run it locally, you can use the shared LevelDB journal, which is only meant for testing purposes, since it only stores data locally.

One option for production use is the `akka-persistence-cassandra` journal plugin (https://github.com/krasserm/akka-persistence-cassandra/) for *Apache Cassandra*.

Apache Cassandra is a highly scalable and available database that replicates data between cluster nodes. Storing actor state in Apache Cassandra means that the application can survive failing nodes both in the database cluster as well as in the Akka cluster.

As you can see, we didn't have to change much to go from a local shopper service to a service that can tolerate node failures in a cluster. In the next section, we'll look at the changes that we have to make to shard actors across the cluster.

15.3.2 *Cluster sharding*

Next up is cluster sharding. We'll shard shoppers based on their `shopperId`. Cluster sharding divides actors to nodes in shards. Every `shopperId` only falls within one shard. The `ClusterSharding` module takes care of allocating and rebalancing actors into the shards across the cluster. Figure 15.7 shows the changes that we'll make.

The `ClusterSharding` extension has a `shardRegion` method that returns an actor reference to a `ShardRegion` actor. The `ShardRegion` actor is used to forward commands to the sharded actor, in this case a slightly modified version of the `Shopper`

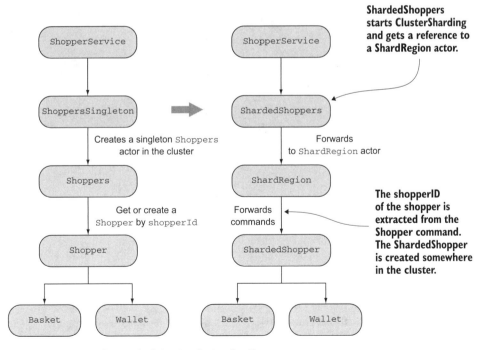

Figure 15.7 From cluster singleton to cluster sharding

actor called `ShardedShopper`. The following listing shows the sharded version of the `Shoppers` actor, `ShardedShoppers`.

Listing 15.34　`ShardedShoppers`

```
package aia.persistence.sharded

import aia.persistence._
import akka.actor._
import akka.cluster.sharding.{ClusterSharding, ClusterShardingSettings}

object ShardedShoppers {
  def props= Props(new ShardedShoppers)
  def name = "sharded-shoppers"
}

class ShardedShoppers extends Actor {

  ClusterSharding(context.system).start(
    ShardedShopper.shardName,
    ShardedShopper.props,
    ClusterShardingSettings(context.system),
    ShardedShopper.extractEntityId,
    ShardedShopper.extractShardId
  )

  def shardedShopper = {
    ClusterSharding(context.system).shardRegion(ShardedShopper.shardName)
  }

  def receive = {
    case cmd: Shopper.Command =>
      shardedShopper forward cmd
  }
}
```

The `ShardedShoppers` actor starts the `ClusterSharding` extension. It provides all the required details to start a `ShardedShopper` in a shard somewhere in the cluster. The `typeName` is the name of the type of actor that will be sharded. A sharded actor is also called an *entry*, which explains the name `entryProps`. The `ClusterSharding` extension provides an actor reference to the `ShardRegion` actor for the shard, which forwards messages to the sharded actors, in this case the `ShardedShopper` actor.

Every node on the cluster runs a `ShardRegion`; a `ShardingCoordinator` (which runs as a cluster singleton) determines which `ShardRegion` will own the shard behind the scenes, shown in figure 15.8.

A `ShardRegion` manages a number of `Shards`, which are basically groupings of sharded actors. A `Shard` actor eventually creates the sharded actor from the props provided to the `ClusterSharding.start` method. You don't have to worry about the fact that the `Shard` actor sits between your sharded actor and the `ShardRegion` actor.

Listing 15.35 shows the sharded version of the `Shoppers` actor, `ShardedShopper`.

Every Shard can have many sharded child actors, in this example, many ShardedShoppers.

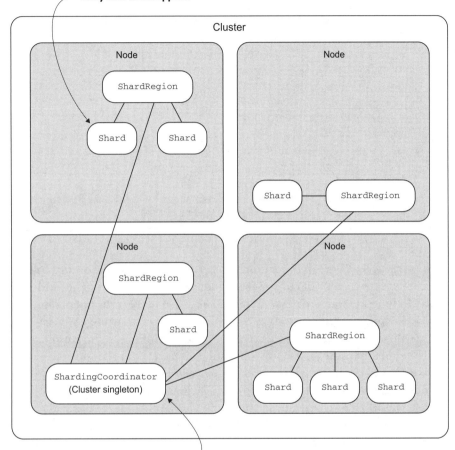

The ShardingCoordinator decides which ShardRegion contains which Shards.

Figure 15.8   Shards in the cluster

Listing 15.35   ShardedShopper

```
package aia.persistence.sharded

import aia.persistence._
import akka.actor._
import akka.cluster.sharding.ShardRegion
import akka.cluster.sharding.ShardRegion.Passivate

object ShardedShopper {
  def props = Props(new ShardedShopper)
  def name(shopperId: Long) = shopperId.toString
```

```
    case object StopShopping

    val shardName: String = "shoppers"

    val extractEntityId: ShardRegion.ExtractEntityId = {
      case cmd: Shopper.Command => (cmd.shopperId.toString, cmd)
    }

    val extractShardId: ShardRegion.ExtractShardId = {
      case cmd: Shopper.Command => (cmd.shopperId % 12).toString
    }
  }

class ShardedShopper extends Shopper {
    import ShardedShopper._

    context.setReceiveTimeout(Settings(context.system).passivateTimeout)

    override def unhandled(msg: Any) = msg match {
      case ReceiveTimeout =>
        context.parent ! Passivate(stopMessage = ShardedShopper.StopShopping)
      case StopShopping => context.stop(self)
    }
  }
```

The `ShardedShopper`'s companion object defines two important functions: the `ExtractEntityID` function to extract an identifier out of a command, and an `Extract-ShardId` function that creates a unique *shard ID* from every shopper command. In this case we simply use the `shopperId` as the identifier for sharding. We can be sure that there will be no duplicate `ShardedShopper` actors running in the cluster.

Note that the `ShardedShoppers` in listing 15.34 doesn't start any `ShardedShoppers`, unlike the singleton version of the `Shoppers` actor. The `ClusterSharding` module will automatically start a `ShardedShopper` once it tries to forward a command. It will extract the ID and `shardId` from the command and create a `ShardedShopper` appropriately, using the `entryProps` that has been passed in earlier. The same `Sharded-Shopper` will be used for subsequent commands.

The `ShardedShopper` actor simply extends the `Shopper` actor and only defines what should happen if it doesn't receive commands for a long time. A sharded shopper can be passivated when it's not used for a while to control memory usage.

The `ShardedShopper` asks the `Shard` actor to be passivated if it receives no commands. The `Shard` in turn sends the `ShardedShopper` the `stopMessage` that's requested inside the `Passivate` message so it can stop itself. This works in a way similar to a `PoisonPill`: all enqueued messages in the `ShardRegion` are handled first before the `ShardedShopper` is stopped.

You can try the cluster sharding solution by executing `sbt run` and selecting `aia.persistence.sharded.ShardedMain` as the main class to start. Just like in chapter 14, you should change the port at which the application runs. Configuring the journal for Apache Cassandra (or something similar) is left as an exercise for the reader. Looking back, we started out with a shoppers app that could only run on one node. It took very few code changes to make the shoppers application work in a cluster as a cluster singleton. Taking the next step, sharding shoppers across the cluster, also didn't require a lot of code changes, which once again shows how Akka benefits from a message-driven approach.

One of the reasons why we didn't have to change much from local to singleton to sharding is because the commands for the shopper already contained the `shopperId`, which was required for the sharding.

15.4 Summary

- Event sourcing proved to be a simple and fitting strategy for persisting actor state. Persistent actors turn valid commands into events that are persisted in a journal; these events are ready to be used for recovery when they crash. Persistent actors are relatively easy to test (provided that a small amount of base functionality is used to delete the journal).

- It doesn't make a lot of sense to persist all events in a journal on the same node where the actors are running, because you could easily lose all data if that one server crashes. Using a journal plugin that's backed by a replicated database increases chances for survival.

- Keeping all actors on one node isn't a very good idea either, since that would mean that your application is immediately unavailable the moment that node crashes.

- A cluster singleton can be used to hop from a crashed node onto one that still works. We've shown how little work is required to change our local `Shoppers` actor into a cluster singleton.

- Cluster sharding takes availability one level further, allowing the required memory space to grow beyond one singleton node. Sharded actors are created on demand and can be passivated when idle. This makes it possible to elastically use the available nodes in the cluster. And again, it didn't take a lot of work to get to a cluster sharded version of the shopping service.

Performance tips

We've pretty much run the gamut of Akka's actor functionality thus far in the book. We started with structuring your applications to use actors, how to deal with state and errors, and how to connect with external systems and deal with persistence. You've also seen how you can scale out using clusters. We've used the Akka actors like a black box: you send messages to the ActorRef, and your receive method implementation is called with the message. The fact that you don't need to know the internals of Akka is one of its biggest strengths. But there are times when you need more control over the performance metrics of an actor system. In this chapter we'll show how you can customize and configure Akka to improve the overall performance.

Performance tuning is hard to do, and it's different for every application. This is because the performance requirements vary, and all the components in a system will affect each other in different ways. The general approach is to find out which part is slow, and why. Based on the answer to those questions, find a solution. In this chapter we'll focus on improving performance by configuring the threading backend that actors run on.

Here's how the chapter progresses:

- First, a quick introduction to performance tuning and important performance metrics.
- Measuring the actors in a system by creating our own custom mailbox and an actor trait. Both implementations create statistical messages that enable us to find problem areas.
- The next step is to solve the problem area. We'll start by describing the different options to improve one actor.
- But sometimes you just need to use resources more efficiently. In the last sections, we'll focus on the use of threads. We'll start with a discussion of how to detect that we have threading problems; after that, we'll look at different solutions by changing the dispatcher configuration, which is used by the actors. Next we'll describe how an actor can be configured to process many messages at a time on the same thread. Changing this configuration enables you to make a trade-off between fairness and increased performance.
- Finally, we'll show how you can create your own dispatcher type for dynamically creating multiple thread pools.

16.1 Performance analysis

To address performance problems, you need to understand how problems arise and how different parts interact with each other. When you understand the mechanism, you can determine what you need to measure to analyze your system, find performance problems, and solve them. In this section you'll gain insight into how performance is affected, by determining which metrics are playing a key part in the system's overall performance.

We'll start by identifying the performance problem area of a system, followed by describing the most important performance metrics and terms.

16.1.1 System performance

Experience teaches that even though it's difficult to see which of the many interacting parts of a system are limiting performance, it's often only a small part affecting the system's total performance. The *Pareto principle* (better known as the *80–20 rule*) applies here: 80% of performance improvements can be made by addressing only 20% of the system. This is good and bad news. The good news is that it's possible to make minor changes to the system to improve performance. The bad news is that only changes to

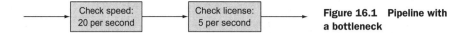

Figure 16.1   Pipeline with a bottleneck

that 20% will have any effect on the performance of the system. These parts that are limiting the performance of the whole system are called *bottlenecks*.

Let's look at a simple example from chapter 8 where we created a pipes and filters pattern. We used two filters in a traffic camera example, which created the pipeline shown in figure 16.1.

When we look at this system, we can easily detect our bottleneck. The step "check license" can only service 5 images per second, while the first step can service 20 per second. Here we see that one step dictates the performance of the whole chain; therefore, the bottleneck of this system is the check-license step.

When our simple system needs to process two images per second, there isn't a performance problem at all, because the system can easily process that amount and even has spare capacity. There will always be some part of the system that can be said to constrain performance, but it's only a bottleneck if the amount the system is constrained exceeds an operational constraint on the business side.

So basically we keep on solving bottlenecks until we achieve our performance requirements. But there's a catch. Solving the first bottleneck gives us the biggest improvement. Solving the next bottleneck will result in a lesser improvement (the concept of diminishing returns).

This is because the system will become more balanced with each change and reaches the limit of using all your resources. In figure 16.2 you see the performance reaching the limit when bottlenecks are removed. When you need a performance higher than this limit, you have to increase your resources, for example, by scaling out.

This, again, is one of the reasons why efforts should focus on requirements. One of the most common conclusions of metrics studies is that programmers tend to spend time optimizing things that have little effect on overall system performance (given the users' experience). Akka helps address this by keeping the model closer to the requirements; we're talking here about things that translate directly into the usage realm—licenses, speeders, and so on.

Thus far, we've been talking about performance in general, but there are two types of performance problems:

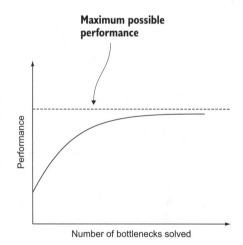

Figure 16.2   Performance effect of solving bottlenecks

- *The throughput is too low*—The number of requests that can be served is too low, such as the capacity of the check-license step in our example.
- *The latency is too long*—Each request takes too long to be processed; for example, the rendering of a requested web page takes too long.

When having one of these problems, most people call it a performance problem. But the solutions to the problems can require vastly different amounts of time. Throughput problems are usually solved by scaling, but latency problems generally require design changes in your application. Solving performance problems of actors will be the focus of section 16.3, where we'll show you how to improve performance by addressing bottlenecks. But first you need to learn a bit more about performance factors and parameters. You've just seen two of these: throughput and latency. We'll cover these in more detail, and look also at other parameters. You'll then have a good understanding of what can affect performance, before we address improving it in section 16.3.

Again, these are a function of the fact that our system is composed of actors and messages, not classes and functions, so we're adapting what you already know about performance to the Akka realm.

16.1.2 *Performance parameters*

Invariably, in the question of investigating the performance characteristics of a computer system, a lot of terms will make an appearance. We'll start with a quick explanation of the most important ones. Then we'll look at a single actor including the mailbox, as shown in figure 16.3. This figure shows the three most important performance metrics: arrival rate, throughput, and service time.

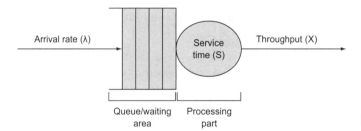

Arrival rate (λ)

Service time (S)

Throughput (X)

Queue/waiting area

Processing part

Figure 16.3 An actor node

Let's start with the *arrival rate*. This is the number of jobs or messages arriving during a period. For example, if eight messages were to arrive during our observation period of 2 seconds, the arrival rate would be four per second.

The next metric appeared in the previous section: the processing rate of the messages. This is called the *throughput* of the actor. The throughput is the number of completions during a period. Most will recognise this term, if not from prior performance tuning, then because network performance is measured in how many packets were successfully processed. As figure 16.4 shows, when a system is balanced, as it is at the top of the figure, it's able to service all the jobs that arrive without making anyone

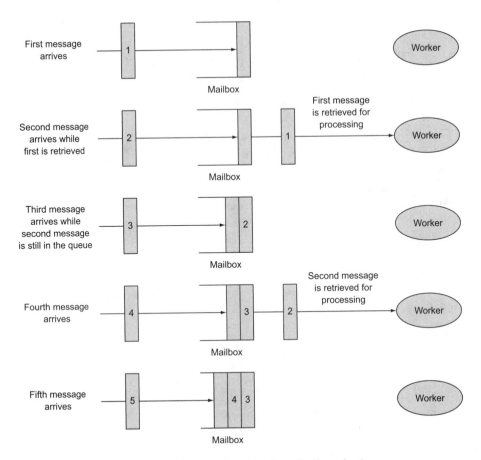

Figure 16.4 **Unbalanced node. Arrival rate is greater than the throughput.**

wait. This means that the arrival rate is equal to the throughput (or at least doesn't exceed it). When the service isn't balanced, moving down in the figure, waiting invariably creeps in because the workers are all busy. In this way, message-oriented systems are really no different than thread pools (as you'll see later).

In this case the node can't keep up with the arrival of the messages, and the messages accumulate in the mailbox. This is a classic performance problem. It's important to realize, though, that we don't want to eliminate waiting; if the system never has any work waiting, we'll end up with workers that are doing nothing. Optimal performance is right in the middle—each time a task is completed, there's another one to do, but the wait time is vanishingly small.

The last parameter shown in figure 16.3 is the *service time*. The service time of a node is the time needed to process a single job. Sometimes the *service rate* is mentioned within these models. This is the average number of jobs serviced during a time period and is represented by μ. The relation between the service time (S) and service rate is this:

$$\mu = 1/S$$

The service time is closely related to the latency, because the latency is the time between the exit and the entry. The difference between the service time and the latency is the waiting time of a message in the mailbox. When the messages don't need to wait in the mailbox for other messages to be completed, the service time is the latency.

The last performance term that's often used within performance analysis is the *utilization*. This is the percentage of the time the node is busy processing messages. When the utilization of a process is 50%, the process is processing jobs 50% of the time and is idle 50% of the time. The utilization gives an impression of how much more the system can process, when pushed to the maximum. And when the utilization is equal to 100%, then the system is unbalanced or saturated. Why? Because if the demand grows at all, wait times will ensue immediately.

These are the most important terms pertaining to performance. If you paid attention, you noticed that the queue size is an important metric indicating that there's a problem. When the queue size grows, it means that the actor is saturated and holding the entire system back.

Now that you know what the different performance metrics mean and their relations to each other, we can start dealing with our performance problems. The first step is to find the actors that have performance issues. In the next section, we'll provide possible solutions to measure an actor system to find the bottlenecks.

16.2 Performance measurement of actors

Before you can improve the performance of the system, you need to know how it's behaving. As you saw in section 16.1.1, you should only change the problem areas, so you need to know where the problem areas are. To do this, you need to measure your system. You've learned that growing queue sizes and utilization are important indicators of actors with performance problems. How can you get that information from your application? In this section we'll show you an example of how to build your own means for measuring performance.

Looking at the metrics queue sizes and utilization, you see that you can divide the data into two components. The queue sizes have to be retrieved from the mailbox, and the utilization needs the statistics of the processing unit. In figure 16.5 we show the interesting times when a messages is sent to an actor and is processed.

When you translate this to your Akka actors, you need the following data (from the Akka mailbox):

- When a message is received and added to the mailbox
- When it was sent to be processed, removed from the mailbox, and handed over to the processing unit
- When the message was done processing and left the processing unit

When you have these times for each message, you can get all the performance metrics you need to analyze your system. For example, the latency is the difference between the arrival time and the leaving time. In this section we'll create an example that retrieves this information. We'll start by making our own custom mailbox that retrieves

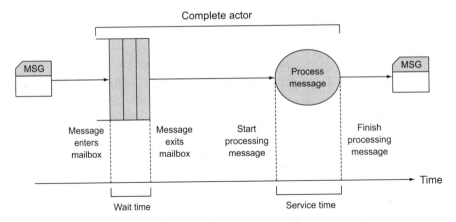

Figure 16.5   Important timestamps when processing a message

the data needed to trace the message in the mailbox. In the second part, we'll create a trait to get the statistics of the `receive` method. Both examples will send statistics to the Akka `EventStream`. Depending on our needs, we could just log these messages or do some processing first. We don't describe in the book how to collect these statistics messages, but with the knowledge you have now, it isn't hard to implement by yourself.

> **MICRO BENCHMARKING**   A common problem with finding performance problems is how to add code measurements that won't affect the performance you're trying to measure.
>
> Just like adding `println` statements to your code for debugging, measuring timestamps with `System.currentTimeMillis` is a simple way to get a rough indicator to the problem in many cases. In other cases it falls short entirely.
>
> Use a micro benchmarking tool like JMH (http://openjdk.java.net/projects /code-tools/jmh/) when more fine-grained performance testing is required.

16.2.1   Collect mailbox data

From the mailbox, we want to know the maximum queue size and the average waiting time. To get this information, we need to know when a message arrives in the queue and when it leaves. First, we'll create our own mailbox. In this mailbox, we'll collect data and send it using the `EventStream` to one actor that processes the data into the performance statistics we need for detecting bottlenecks.

To create a custom queue and use it, we need two parts. The first is a message queue that will be used as the mailbox, and the second is a factory class that creates a mailbox when necessary. Figure 16.6 shows the class diagram of our mailbox implementation.

The Akka dispatcher is using a factory class (`MailboxType`) to create new mailboxes. By switching the `MailboxType`, we're able to create different mailboxes. When we want to create our own mailbox, we'll need to implement a `MessageQueue` and a `MailboxType`. We'll start with mailbox creation.

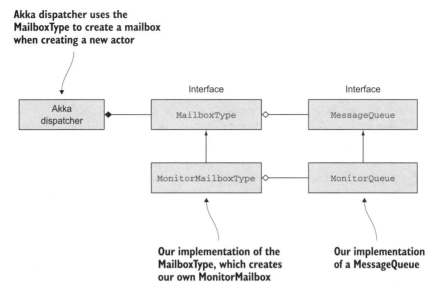

Figure 16.6   Custom mailbox class diagram

CREATING A CUSTOM MAILBOX

To create a custom mailbox, we need to implement the `MessageQueue` trait.

- *def enqueue(receiver: ActorRef, handle: Envelope)*—This method is called when trying to add an `Envelope`. The `Envelope` contains the sender and the actual message.
- *def dequeue(): Envelope*—This method is called to get the next message.
- *def numberOfMessages: Int*—This returns the current number of messages held in this queue.
- *def hasMessages: Boolean*—This indicates whether this queue is non-empty.
- *def cleanUp(owner: ActorRef, deadLetters: MessageQueue)*—This method is called when the mailbox is disposed of. Normally it's expected to transfer all remaining messages into the dead-letter queue.

We'll implement a custom `MonitorQueue` which will be created by a `MonitorMailbox-Type`. But first we'll define the case class containing the trace data needed to calculate the statistics, called `MailboxStatistics`. We'll also define a class used to contain the trace data while collecting the data, `MonitorEnvelope`, while the message is waiting in the mailbox, as shown in the next listing.

Listing 16.1   Data containers used to store mailbox statistics

```
case class MonitorEnvelope(queueSize: Int,
                           receiver: String,
                           entryTime: Long,           Message to send
                           handle: Envelope)          the trace data
```

```
case class MailboxStatistics(queueSize: Int,
                             receiver: String,
                             sender: String,
                             entryTime: Long,
                             exitTime: Long)
```

Envelope to collect the trace data

The class `MailboxStatistics` contains the receiver, which is the actor that we're monitoring. `entryTime` and `exitTime` contain the time the message arrived or left the mailbox. Actually we don't need the `queueSize`, because we can calculate it from the statistics, but it's easier to add the current stack size too.

In the `MonitorEnvelope`, the handle is the original `Envelope` received from the Akka framework. Now we can create the `MonitorQueue`.

The constructor of the `MonitorQueue` will take a `system` parameter so we can get to the `eventStream` later, which is shown in listing 16.2. We also need to define the semantics that this queue will support. Since we want to use this mailbox for all actors in the system, we're adding the `UnboundedMessageQueueSemantics` and the `LoggerMessageQueueSemantics`. The latter is necessary since actors used internally in Akka for logging requires these semantics.

Listing 16.2   Extending from the `MessageQueue` trait and mixing in semantics

Later on we'll use system.eventStream to publish statistics

Semantics required for standard actors to function on this mailbox

Semantics required for Akka logging to function on this mailbox

```
class MonitorQueue(val system: ActorSystem)
    extends MessageQueue
    with UnboundedMessageQueueSemantics
    with LoggerMessageQueueSemantics {
  private final val queue = new ConcurrentLinkedQueue[MonitorEnvelope]()
```

The type of queue that is used internally

SELECTING A MAILBOX WITH SPECIFIC MESSAGE QUEUE SEMANTICS   The semantics traits are simple marker traits (they do not define any methods). In this use case we don't need to define our own semantics, though it can be convenient in certain cases, since an actor can require a specific semantics by using a `RequiresMessageQueue`; for instance, the `DefaultLogger` requires `LoggerMessageQueueSemantics` by mixing in a `RequiresMessageQueue[LoggerMessageQueueSemantics]` trait. You can link a mailbox to semantics using the `akka.actor.mailbox.requirements` configuration setting.

Next we'll implement the `enqueue` method, which creates a `MonitorEnvelope` and adds it to the queue.

Listing 16.3   Implementing the `enqueue` method of the `MessageQueue` trait

```
def enqueue(receiver: ActorRef, handle: Envelope): Unit = {
  val env = MonitorEnvelope(queueSize = queue.size() + 1,
    receiver = receiver.toString(),
```

```
      entryTime = System.currentTimeMillis(),
      handle = handle)
  queue add env
}
```

The `queueSize` is the current size plus one, because this new message isn't added to the queue yet. Then we set about implementing the `dequeue` method. `dequeue` checks if the polled message is a `MailboxStatistics` instance, in which case it skips it, since we want to use the `MonitorQueue` for all mailboxes, and if we don't exclude these messages, this will recursively create `MailboxStatistics` messages when it's used by our statistics collector.

The next listing shows the implementation of the `dequeue` method.

Listing 16.4 Implementing the `dequeue` method of the `MessageQueue` trait

```
def dequeue(): Envelope = {
  val monitor = queue.poll()
  if (monitor != null) {
    monitor.handle.message match {
      case stat: MailboxStatistics => //skip message      ◁──  Skips MailboxStatistics
                                                                to avoid recursive
                                                                sending of message
      case _ => {                                          ◁──  Sends MailboxStatistics
        val stat = MailboxStatistics(                           to event stream
          queueSize = monitor.queueSize,
          receiver = monitor.receiver,
          sender = monitor.handle.sender.toString(),
          entryTime = monitor.entryTime,
          exitTime = System.currentTimeMillis())
        system.eventStream.publish(stat)
      }
    }
    monitor.handle      ◁──  Returns original envelope
  } else {                   to Akka system
    null                ◁──  Returns null when there are
  }                          no envelopes waiting
}
```

When we're processing a normal message, we create a `MailboxStatistics` and publish it to the `EventStream`. When we don't have any messages, we need to return `null` to indicate that there aren't any messages. At this point we've implemented our functionality, and all that's left is to implement the other supporting methods defined in the `MessageQueue` trait.

Listing 16.5 Finish the implementation of the `MessageQueue` trait

```
def numberOfMessages = queue.size      ◁──  Returns number of envelopes in queue
def hasMessages = !queue.isEmpty       ◁──  Implements hasMessages

def cleanUp(owner: ActorRef, deadLetters: MessageQueue): Unit = {   ◁──┐
  if (hasMessages) {                                                    │
    var envelope = dequeue                           On cleanup, sends all waiting
    while (envelope ne null) {                       messages to dead-letter queue
```

```
        deadLetters.enqueue(owner, envelope)
        envelope = dequeue
    }
  }
}
```

We use the `dequeue` method so the statistics are created too.

Our mailbox trait is ready to be used in the factory class, described in the next section.

IMPLEMENTING MAILBOXTYPE

The factory class, which creates the actual mailbox, implements the `MailboxType` trait. This trait has only one method, but we also need a specific constructor, so this should also be considered as part of the interface of the `MailboxType`. Then the interface becomes this:

- *def this(settings: ActorSystem.Settings, config: Config)*—This is the constructor used by Akka to create the MailboxType.

- *def create(owner: Option[ActorRef], system: Option[ActorSystem]): MessageQueue*—This method is used to create a new mailbox.

When we want to use our custom mailbox, we need to implement this interface. Our fully implemented `MailboxType` is shown next.

Listing 16.6   Implementation of the `MailboxType` using our custom mailbox

```
class MonitorMailboxType(settings: ActorSystem.Settings, config: Config)
    extends akka.dispatch.MailboxType
    with ProducesMessageQueue[MonitorQueue]{        ◁──┤ Implements constructor
                                                        expected by Akka
  final override def create(owner: Option[ActorRef],
                      system: Option[ActorSystem]): MessageQueue = {
    system match {
      case Some(sys) =>                              ──┐ Creates the MonitorQueue,
        new MonitorQueue(sys)                        ◁─┘ passes in the system
      case _ =>
        throw new IllegalArgumentException("requires a system")   ◁──┐
    }
  }                                                    When we don't have an
}                                                      ActorSystem, we can't create
                                                       and use our MessageQueue.
```

When we don't get an `ActorSystem`, we throw an exception because we need the `ActorSystem` to be able to operate. Now we're done implementing the new custom mailbox. All that's left is to configure the Akka framework that it will use as its mailbox.

CONFIGURATION OF MAILBOXES

When we want to use another mailbox, we can configure this in the application.conf file. There are multiple ways to use the mailbox. The type of the mailbox is bound to the dispatcher used, so we can create a new dispatcher type and use our mailbox. This is done by setting the `mailbox-type` in the application.conf configuration file, and we use the dispatcher when creating a new actor. One way is shown in the following snippet:

```
my-dispatcher {
  mailbox-type = aia.performance.monitor.MonitorMailboxType      ⟵┐ Sets mailbox type of
}                                                                  │ dispatcher in
val a = system.actorOf(                                            │ application.conf file
  Props[MyActor].withDispatcher("my-dispatcher")      ⟵┐ Creates an actor using our
)                                                       │ dispatcher configuration
```

We mentioned before that there are other ways to get Akka to use our mailbox. The mailbox is still bound to the chosen dispatcher, but we can also overrule which mailbox the default dispatcher should use, with the result that we don't have to change the creation of our actors. To change the mailbox used by the default dispatcher, we can add the following lines in the configuration file:

```
akka {
  actor {
    default-mailbox {
      mailbox-type = "aia.performance.monitor.MonitorMailboxType"
    }
  }
}
```

This way, we use our custom mailbox for every actor. Let's see if everything is working as designed.

To test the mailbox, we need an actor that we can monitor. Let's create a simple one. It does a delay before receiving a message, to simulate the processing of the message. This delay simulates the service time of our performance model.

```
class ProcessTestActor(serviceTime:Duration) extends Actor {
  def receive = {
    case _ => {
      Thread.sleep(serviceTime.toMillis)
    }
  }
}
```

Now that we have an actor to monitor, let's send some messages to this actor.

Listing 16.7 Test the custom mailbox

```
                  val statProbe = TestProbe()
                  system.eventStream.subscribe(
                    statProbe.ref,
                    classOf[MailboxStatistics])
                  val testActor = system.actorOf(Props(       ⟵─┐ Creates actor
Sends three │       new ProcessTestActor(1.second)), "monitorActor2")  normally
messages    └⟶  statProbe.send(testActor, "message")
                  statProbe.send(testActor, "message2")
```

```
statProbe.send(testActor, "message3")
val stat = statProbe.expectMsgType[MailboxStatistics]

stat.queueSize must be(1)
val stat2 = statProbe.expectMsgType[MailboxStatistics]

stat2.queueSize must (be(2) or be(1))
val stat3 = statProbe.expectMsgType[MailboxStatistics]

stat3.queueSize must (be(3) or be(2))                    <-
```

Last message should have a queue size of 3 or 2, depending on whether first message has already been removed from queue

As you can see, we get a MailboxStatistics for each message sent on the Event-Stream. At this point, we have completed the code to be able to trace the mailbox of our actors. We've created our own custom mailbox to put the tracing data of the mailbox on the EventStream, and learned that we need a factory class and the mailbox type to be able to use the mailbox. In the configuration we can define which factory class has to be used when creating a mailbox for a new actor. Now that we can trace the mailbox, let's turn our attention to the processing of messages.

16.2.2 Collecting processing data

The data we need for tracing performance can be retrieved by overriding the actor's receive method. This example requires the receive method of an actor to be changed for monitoring it, which is more intrusive than the mailbox example, because we have the ability to add the functionality without changing the original code. To be able to use the next example, we need to add the trait with every actor we want to trace. Again we start by defining the statistics message:

```
case class ActorStatistics( receiver: String,
                            sender: String,
                            entryTime: Long,
                            exitTime: Long)
```

The receiver is the actor we monitor, and our statistics contain the entry and exit times. We also add the sender, which can give more information on the messages processed, but we're not using this in these examples. Now that we have our Actor-Statistics, we can implement the functionality by creating the trait that overrides the receive method.

Listing 16.8 Tracing actor `receive` method

```
trait MonitorActor extends Actor {

  abstract override def receive = {
    case m: Any => {
      val start = System.currentTimeMillis()
      super.receive(m)                        <--- Calls receive method of actor
      val end = System.currentTimeMillis()

      val stat = ActorStatistics(             <--- Creates and sends statistics
        self.toString(),
        sender.toString(),
```

```
        start,
        end)
      context.system.eventStream.publish(stat)
    }
  }
}
```

We use the abstract override to get in between the actor and the Akka framework. This way we can capture the start and end time of processing the message. When the processing is done, we create the `ActorStatistics` and publish it to the event stream.

To do this, we can simply mixin the trait when creating the actor:

```
val testActor = system.actorOf(Props(
                new ProcessTestActor(1.second) with MonitorActor)
                ,"monitorActor")
```

When we send a message to the `ProcessTestActor`, we expect an `ActorStatistics` message on the `EventStream`.

Listing 16.9   Testing the `MonitorActor` trait

```
val statProbe = TestProbe()
system.eventStream.subscribe(
  statProbe.ref,
  classOf[ActorStatistics])

val testActor = system.actorOf(Props(          ◁─┐ Creates actor with
  new ProcessTestActor(1.second) with MonitorActor)   MonitorActor trait
  ,"monitorActor")

statProbe.send(testActor,"message")

val stat = statProbe.expectMsgType[ActorStatistics]   ◁─┐ Result must be close
stat.exitTime -                                          to specified service
    stat.entryTime must be (1000L plusOrMinus 10)        time of 1 second
```

And just as expected, the processing time (exit time minus entry time) is close to the set service time of our test actor.

At this point we're also able to trace the processing of the messages. We now have a trait that creates the tracing data and distributes that data using the `EventStream`. Now we can start to analyze the data and find our actors with performance issues. When we've identified our bottlenecks, we're ready to solve them. In the next sections, we'll look at different ways to address those bottlenecks.

16.3   *Improving performance by addressing bottlenecks*

To improve the system's performance, you only have to improve the performance of the bottlenecks. There are a variety of solutions, but some have more impact on throughput, and others more directly impact latency. Depending on your requirements and implementation, you can choose the solution best suited to your needs. When the bottleneck is a resource shared between actors, you need to direct the

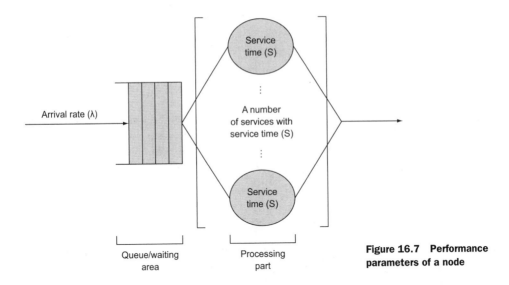

Figure 16.7 Performance parameters of a node

resource to the tasks most critical for your system and away from tasks that aren't that critical and can wait. This tuning is always a trade-off. But when the bottleneck isn't a resource problem, you can make changes to your system to improve performance.

When you look at a queueing node in figure 16.7, you see that it contains two parts: the queue and the processing unit. You'll also note the two performance parameters we just explored in section 16.1.2: arrival rate and the service time. We added a third parameter to add more instances of an actor: the *number of services*. This is actually a scaling-up action. To improve the performance of an actor, you can change three parameters:

- *Number of services*—Increasing the number of services increases the possible throughput of the node.
- *Arrival rate*—Reducing the number of messages to be processed makes it easier to keep up with the arrival rate.
- *Service time*—Making processing faster improves latency and makes it possible to process more messages, which also improves the throughput.

When you want to improve performance, you have to change one or more of these parameters. The most common change is to increase the number of services. This will work when throughput is a problem, and the process isn't limited by the CPU. When the task uses a lot of CPU, it's possible that adding more services could increase the service times. The services compete for CPU power, which can decrease the total performance.

Another approach is reducing the number of tasks that need to be processed. This approach is often forgotten, but reducing the arrival rate can be an easy fix that can result in a dramatic improvement. Most of the time, this fix requires changing the design of the system. But this doesn't have to be a hard thing to do. In section 8.1.2 on the pipes and filters pattern, you saw that simply changing the order of two steps can make an impressive improvement in performance.

The last approach is to reduce service time. This will increase throughput and decrease response time, and will always improve performance. This is also the hardest to achieve, because the functionality has to be the same, and most of the time it's hard to remove steps to reduce service time. One thing worth checking is if the actor is using blocking calls. This will increase service time, and the fix is often easy: rewrite your actor to use nonblocking calls by making it event-driven. Another option to reduce service time is to parallelize the processing. Break up the task and divide it over multiple actors, and make sure that tasks are processed in parallel by using, for example, the scatter-gather pattern, explained in chapter 8.

But there are also other changes that can improve performance, for example, when server resources like CPU, memory, or disk usage are the problem. If utilization of these resources is 80% or more, they're probably holding your system back. This can be because you use more resources than you have available, which can be solved by buying bigger and faster platforms, or you can scale out. This approach would also require a design change, but with Akka scaling out doesn't need to be a big problem, as we've shown in chapter 13 using clusters.

But resource problems don't always mean that you need more. Sometimes you need to use what you have more sensibly. For example, threads can cause issues when you use too many or too few. This can be solved by configuring the Akka framework differently and using available threads more effectively. In the next section, you'll learn how to tune Akka's thread pools by assigning one thread to each task, which eliminates the repeated context-switch of the thread.

16.4 Configure dispatcher

In chapter 1 we mentioned that the dispatcher of an actor is responsible for assigning threads to the actor when there's a message waiting in the mailbox. Until now you didn't need to know about the details of the dispatcher (although we changed the behavior earlier in chapter 9 with the routers). Most of the time, the dispatcher instance is shared between multiple actors. It's possible to change the configuration of the default dispatcher or create a new dispatcher with a different configuration. In this section we'll start by figuring out how to recognize a thread pool problem. Next, we'll create a new dispatcher for a group of actors. And after that we'll show how you can change the thread pool size and how to use a dynamically sized thread pool by using another executor.

16.4.1 Recognizing thread pool problems

In chapter 9 you saw that you can change the behavior of actors by using the `BalancingDispatcher`. But there are more configuration changes we can make to the default dispatcher that will affect performance. Let's start with a simple example. Figure 16.8 shows a receiver actor and 100 workers.

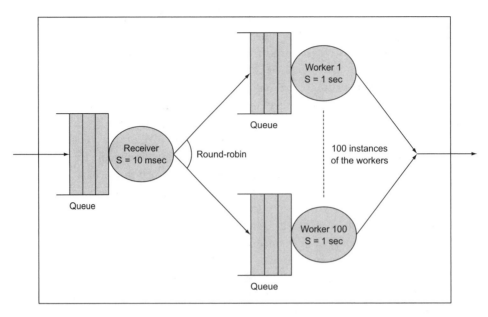

Figure 16.8   Example system with a receiver and 100 workers

The receiver has a service time of 10 ms, and there are 100 workers with a service time of 1 second. The maximum throughput of the system is 100/s. When we implement this example in Akka, we get some unexpected results. We use an arrival rate of 66 messages/s, which is below the 80% threshold we discussed. The system shouldn't have any problems keeping up. But when we monitor it, we see that the queue size of the receiver is increasing over time (as column 2 of table 16.1 shows).

Table 16.1   Monitor metrics of the test example

Period number	Receiver: Max mailbox size	Receiver: Utilization	Worker 1: Max mailbox size	Worker 1: Utilization
1	70	5%	1	6%
2	179	8%	1	6%
3	285	8%	1	10%
4	385	7%	1	6%

According to these numbers, the receiver can't process the messages before the next message arrives, which is strange because the service time is 10 ms, and the time between the messages is 15 ms. What's happening? You learned from our discussion of performance metrics that when an actor is the bottleneck, the queue size increases and the utilization approaches 100%. But in our example, you see the queue size is growing but the utilization is still low at 6%. This means that the actor is waiting for something else. The problem is the number of threads available for the actors to process. By default, the number of threads available is three times the number of available processors within your server, with a minimum of 8 and a maximum of 64 threads. In this example we have a two-core processor, so there are 8 threads available (minimum number of threads). During the time that 8 workers are busy processing messages, the receiver has to wait until one worker has finished before it can process the waiting messages.

How can we improve this performance? The actor's dispatcher is responsible to give the actor a thread when there are messages. To improve this situation, we need to change the configuration of the dispatcher used by the actors.

16.4.2 *Using multiple instances of dispatchers*

The behavior of the dispatcher can be changed by changing its configuration or dispatcher type. Akka has four built-in types, as shown in table 16.2.

Table 16.2   Available built-in dispatchers

Type	Description	Use case
Dispatcher	This is the default dispatcher, which binds its actors to a thread pool. The executor can be configured, but uses the `fork-join-executor` as default. This means that it has a fixed thread pool size.	Most of the time, you'll use this dispatcher. In almost all our previous examples, we used this dispatcher.
PinnedDispatcher	This dispatcher binds an actor to a single and unique thread. This means that the thread isn't shared between actors.	This dispatcher can be used when an actor has a high utilization and has a high priority to process messages, so it always needs a thread and can't wait to get a new thread. But you'll see that usually better solutions are available.
BalancingDispatcher	This dispatcher redistributes the messages from busy actors to idle actors.	We used this dispatcher in the router load-balancing example in section 9.1.1.
CallingThreadDispatcher	This dispatcher uses the current thread to process the messages of an actor. This is only used for testing.	Every time you use `TestActorRef` to create an actor in your unit test, this dispatcher is used.

When we look at our receiver actor with 100 workers, we could use the `Pinned-Dispatcher` for our receiver. This way it doesn't share the thread with the workers. And when we do, it solves the problem of the receiver being the bottleneck. Most of the time a `PinnedDispatcher` isn't a solid solution. We used thread pools in the first place to reduce the number of threads and use them more efficiently. In our example the thread will be idle 33% of the time if we use a `PinnedDispatcher`. But the idea of not letting the receiver compete with the workers is a possible solution. To achieve this, we give the workers their own thread pool by using a new instance of the dispatcher. This way we get two dispatchers, each with its own thread pool.

We'll start by defining the dispatcher in our configuration, and using this dispatcher for our workers.

Listing 16.10   Defining and using a new dispatcher configuration

```
application.conf:
worker-dispatcher {}                              ← Defines new dispatcher
                                                    in application.conf       Uses worker
Code:                                                                         dispatcher for
val end = TestProbe()                                                         the workers
val workers = system.actorOf(
  Props( new ProcessRequest(1 second, end.ref) with MonitorActor)
      .withDispatcher("worker-dispatcher")
      .withRouter(RoundRobinRouter(nrOfInstances = nrWorkers))   ←
  ,"Workers")
```

When we do the same test as before, we get the results shown in table 16.3.

Table 16.3   Monitoring metrics of the test example using a different thread pool for the workers

Period number	Receiver: Max mailbox size	Receiver: Utilization	Worker 1: Max mailbox size	Worker 1: Utilization
1	2	15%	1	6%
2	1	66%	2	0%
3	1	66%	5	33%
4	1	66%	7	0%

We see that the receiver is now performing as expected and is able to keep up with the arriving messages, because the maximum queue size is 1. This means that the previous message was removed from the queue before the next one arrived. And when we look at the utilization, we see that it is 66%, exactly what we expect: every second we process 66 messages that take 10 ms each.

But now the workers can't keep up with the arriving messages, as indicated by column 5. Actually, we see that there are periods when the worker isn't processing *any* message during the measurement period (utilization is 0%). By using another thread pool, we only moved the problem from the receiver to the workers. This happens a lot when tuning a system. Tuning is usually a trade-off. Giving one task more resources means that other tasks get less. The trick is to direct the resources to the most critical tasks for your system, away from tasks that are less critical and can wait. Does this mean we can't do anything to improve this situation? Do we have to live with this result?

16.4.3 *Changing thread pool size statically*

In our example we see that the workers can't keep up with the arrival of messages, which is caused because we have too few threads, so why don't we increase the number of threads? We can, but the result greatly depends on how much CPU the workers need to process a message.

Increasing the number of threads will have an adverse effect on the total performance when the processing is heavily dependent on CPU power, because one CPU core can only execute one thread at any given moment. When it has to service multiple threads, it has to switch context between multiple threads. This context switch also takes CPU time, which reduces the time used to service the threads. When the ratio of number of threads to available CPU cores becomes too large, the performance will only decrease. Figure 16.9 shows the relationship between the performance and number of threads for a given number of CPU cores.

The first part of the graph (up to the first dotted vertical line) is almost linear, until the number of threads is equal to the number of available cores. When the number of threads increases even more, the performance still increases, but at a slower rate until it reaches the optimum. After that, the performance decreases when the number of threads increases. This graph assumes that all the available threads need CPU power. So there's always an optimum number of threads. How can you know if you can increase the number of threads? Usually the utilization of the processors can give you an indication. When this is 80% or higher, increasing the number of threads will probably not help to increase the performance.

But when the CPU utilization is low, you can increase the number of threads. In this case the processing of messages is mainly waiting. The first thing you should do is check whether you can avoid the waiting. In this example it looks like freezing your actor and not using nonblocking calls, for example, using the `ask` pattern, would help. When you can't solve the waiting problem, it's possible to increase the number of threads. In our example we're not using any CPU power, so let's see in our next configuration example if increasing the thread number works.

The number of used threads can be configured with three configuration parameters in the dispatcher configuration:

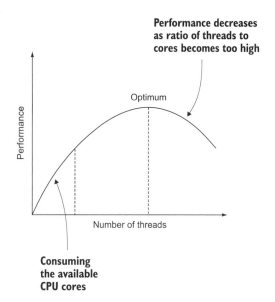

Figure 16.9   Performance versus number of threads

Min number of threads

Max number of threads

Factor used to calculate number of threads from available processors

```
worker-dispatcher {
    fork-join-executor {
        parallelism-min = 8
        parallelism-factor = 3.0
        parallelism-max = 64
    }
}
```

The number of threads used is the number of available processors multiplied by the parallelism-factor, but with a minimum of parallelism-min and a maximum of parallelism-max. For example, when we have an eight-core CPU, we get 24 threads (8 × 3). But when we have only two cores available, we get 8 threads, although the number would be 6 (2 × 3), because we've set a minimum of 8.

We want to use 100 threads independent of the number of cores available; therefore, we set the minimum and maximum to 100:

```
worker-dispatcher {
    fork-join-executor {
        parallelism-min = 100
        parallelism-max = 100
    }
}
```

Finally, when we run the example, we can process all the received messages in time. Table 16.4 shows that with the change, the workers also have a utilization of 66% and a queue size of 1.

Table 16.4 Monitoring metrics of the test example using 100 threads for the workers

Period number	Receiver: Max mailbox size	Receiver: Utilization	Worker 1: Max mailbox size	Worker 1: Utilization
1	2	36	2	34
2	1	66	1	66
3	1	66	1	66
4	1	66	1	66
5	1	66	1	66

In this case we could increase the performance of our system by increasing the number of threads. In this example we used a new dispatcher for only the workers. This is better than changing the default dispatcher and increasing the number of threads, because normally this is just a small part of the complete system, and when we increase the number of threads, it's possible that 100 other actors will run simultaneously. And it's possible that the performance will drop drastically because these actors depend on CPU power, and the ratio between active threads and CPU cores is out of balance. When using a separate dispatcher, only the workers run simultaneously in large numbers, and the other actors use the default available threads.

In this section you've seen how you could increase the number of threads, but there are situations when you want to change the thread size dynamically, for example, if the worker load changes drastically during operation time. This is also possible with Akka, but we need to change the executor used by the dispatcher.

16.4.4 Using a dynamic thread pool size

In the previous section, we had a static number of workers. We could increase the number of threads, because we knew how many workers we had. But when the number of workers depends on the system's work load, you don't know how many threads you need. For example, suppose we have a web server, and for each user request a worker actor is created. The number workers depends on the number of concurrent users on the web server. We could handle this by using a fixed number of threads, which works perfectly most of the time. The important question is this: what size do we use for the thread pool? When it's too small, we get a performance penalty, because requests are waiting for each other to get a thread, like the first example of the previous section, shown in table 16.1. But when we make the thread pool too big, we're wasting resources. This is again a trade-off between resources and performance. But when the number of workers is normally low or stable but sometimes increases drastically, a dynamic thread pool can improve performance without wasting resources. The dynamic thread pool increases in size when the number of workers increases, but decreases when the threads are idle too long. This will clean up the unused threads, which otherwise would waste resources.

To use a dynamic thread pool, we need to change the executor used by the dispatcher. This is done by setting the executor configuration item of the dispatcher configuration. There are three possible values for this configuration item, as shown in table 16.5.

Table 16.5 Configuring executors

Executor	Description	Use case
`fork-join-executor`	This is the default executor and uses the fork join executor.	This executor performs better than the thread pool executor under high workloads.
`thread-pool-executor`	This is the other standard supported executor and uses the thread-pool executor.	This executor is used when you need a dynamic thread pool, because a dynamic thread pool isn't supported by the `fork-join-executor`.

Table 16.5 Configuring executors *(continued)*

Executor	Description	Use case
Fully qualified class name (FQCN)	You can create your own `ExecutorServiceConfigurator`, which returns a factory that will create a Java `ExecutorService`, which will be used as executor.	When neither built-in executor suffices, you can use your own executor.

When you need a dynamic thread pool, you need to use the `thread-pool-executor`, and this executor also has to be configured. The default configuration is shown in the next code listing.

Listing 16.11 Configuring a dispatcher using the `thread-pool-executor`

```
my-dispatcher {
  type = "Dispatcher"
  executor = "thread-pool-executor"            ◁── Uses thread pool executor

  thread-pool-executor {
    core-pool-size-min = 8            Sets minimal thread pool size.
    core-pool-size-factor = 3.0       This works just like the fork-join
    core-pool-size-max = 64           parallelism configuration.

    max-pool-size-min = 8
    max-pool-size-factor  = 3.0
    max-pool-size-max = 64            Sets maximum thread pool size.

    task-queue-size = -1                         ◁──┐ Sets size of waiting
                                                     thread requests before
    # Specifies which type of task queue will be used,  the thread pool size is
    # can be "array" or "linked" (default)            increased. -1 means
    task-queue-type = "linked"                        unbounded and results
                                                      in never increasing the
    # Keep alive time for threads                     thread pool.
    keep-alive-time = 60s                ◁──┐ Time a thread can
                                             be idle before it's
    # Allow core threads to time out         cleaned up
    allow-core-timeout = on
  }
}
```

The minimum and maximum thread pool sizes are calculated, as can be seen in the `fork-join-executor` in section 16.4.1. When you want to use a dynamic thread pool, you need to set the `task-queue-size`. This will define how quickly the pool size will grow when there are more thread requests than threads. By default it's set to -1, indicating that the queue is unbounded and the pool size will never increase. The last configuration item we want to address is the `keep-alive-time`. This is the idle time before a thread will be cleaned up, and it determines how quickly the pool size will decrease.

In our example we set the `core-pool-size` close to or just below the normal number of threads we need, and set the `max-pool-size` to a size where the system is still able to perform, or to the maximum supported number of concurrent users.

You've seen in this section how you can influence the thread pool used by the dispatcher that assigns threads to an actor. But there's another mechanism that's used to release the thread and give it back to the thread pool. By not returning the thread when an actor has more messages to process, you eliminate waiting for a new thread and the overhead of assigning a thread. In busy applications this can improve the overall performance of the system.

16.5 Changing thread releasing

In previous sections you saw how you can increase the number of threads, and that there's an optimum number, which is related to the number of CPU cores. When there are too many threads, the context switching will degrade performance. A similar problem can arise when different actors have a lot of messages to process. For each message an actor has to process, it needs a thread. When there are a lot of messages waiting for different actors, the threads have to be switched between the actors. This switching can also have a negative influence on performance.

Akka has a mechanism that influences the switching of threads between actors. The trick is not to switch a thread after each message when there are messages still in the mailbox waiting to be processed. A dispatcher has a configuration parameter, throughput, and this parameter is set to the maximum number of messages an actor may process before it has to release the thread back to the pool:

```
my-dispatcher {
  fork-join-executor {
    parallelism-min = 4
    parallelism-max = 4
  }
  throughput = 5
}
```

The default is set to 5. This way the number of thread switches is reduced, and overall performance is improved.

To show the effect of the throughput parameter, we'll use a dispatcher with four threads and 40 workers with a service time close to zero. At the start, we'll give each worker 40,000 messages, and we'll measure how much time it takes to process all the messages. We'll do this for several values of throughput. The results are shown in figure 16.10.

As you can see, increasing the throughput parameter will improve performance because messages are processed faster.[1]

In these examples we have better performance when we set the parameter high, so why is the default 5 and not 20? This is because increasing throughput also has negative effects. Let's suppose we have an actor with 20 messages in its mailbox, but the

---

[1] The Akka "Let it crash" blog has a nice post on how to process 5 million messages per second by changing the throughput parameter: http://letitcrash.com/post/20397701710/50-million-messages-per-second-on-a-single-machine.

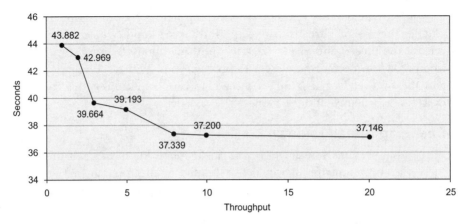

Figure 16.10   Performance versus the `throughput` parameter

service time is high, for example, 2 seconds. When the `throughput` parameter is set to 20, the actor will claim the thread for 40 seconds before releasing the thread. Therefore, other actors wait a long time before they can process their messages. In this case the benefit of the `throughput` parameter is less when the service time is greater, because the time it takes to switch threads is far less than the service time, which can be negligible. The result is that actors with a high service time can take the threads for a long time. For this there's another parameter, `throughput-deadline-time`, which defines how long an actor can keep a thread even when there are still messages and the maximum `throughput` hasn't been reached yet:

```
my-dispatcher {
  throughput = 20
  throughput-deadline-time = 200ms
}
```

By default, this parameter is set to `0ms`, meaning that there isn't a deadline. This parameter can be used when you have a mix of short and long service times. An actor with a short service time processes the maximum number of messages after obtaining a thread, while an actor with a long service time will only process one message or multiple messages until it reaches 200 ms each time it obtains a thread.

16.5.1 *Limitations on thread release settings*

Why can't we use these settings as our default? There are two reasons. The first one is fairness. Because the thread isn't released after the first message, the messages of other actors need to wait longer to be processed. For the system as a whole, this can be beneficial, but for individual messages, it can be a disadvantage. With batch-like systems, it doesn't matter when messages are processed, but when you're waiting for a message, for instance, one that's used to create a web page, you don't want to wait longer than your neighbor. In these cases you want to set the `throughput` lower, even when it means that the total performance will decrease.

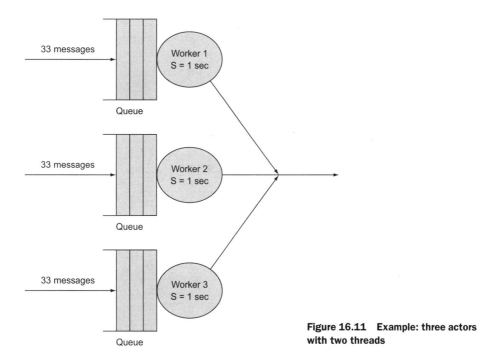

Figure 16.11   Example: three actors with two threads

Another problem with a high value for the `throughput` parameter is that the process of balancing the work over many threads can negatively impact performance. Let's take a look at another example, shown in figure 16.11. Here we have three actors and only two threads. The service time of the actors is 1 second. We send 99 messages to the actors (33 each).

This system should be able to process all the messages in close to 50 seconds (99 × 1 second / 2 threads). But when we change the throughput, we see an unexpected result in figure 16.12.

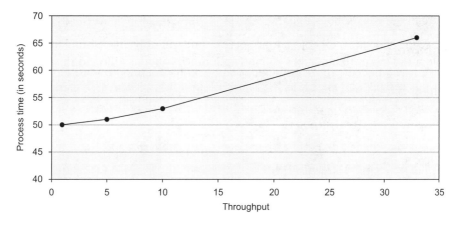

Figure 16.12   Effect of the `throughput` parameter

To explain this, we have to look at the time the actors spend processing. Let's take the most extreme value: 33. When we start the test, we see in figure 16.13 that the first two actors are processing all their messages. Because throughput is set to 33, they're able to clean their mailboxes completely. When they're done, only the third actor has to process its messages. This means that during the second part, one thread is idle and causes the processing time of the second part to double.

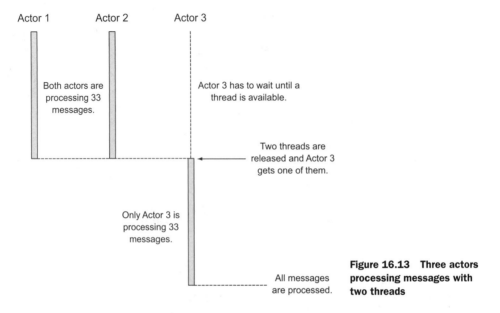

Figure 16.13   Three actors processing messages with two threads

Changing the release configuration can help to improve the performance, but whether you need to increase or decrease the throughput configuration is completely dependent on the arrival rate and the function of the system. Choosing the wrong setting could well decrease performance.

In the previous sections, you've seen that you can improve the performance by increasing threads, but sometimes this isn't enough, and you need more dispatchers.

16.6 *Summary*

You've seen that the threading mechanism can have a big influence on system performance. When there are too few threads, actors wait for each other to finish. Too many threads, and the CPU is wasting precious time switching threads, many of which are doing nothing. You learned

- How you can detect actors waiting for available threads
- How to create multiple thread pools
- How you can change the number of threads (statically or dynamically)
- Configuring actors' thread releasing

We've discussed in earlier chapters that in a distributed system, the communication between nodes can be optimized to increase overall system performance. In this chapter we showed that many of the same techniques can be applied in local applications to achieve the same goals.

Looking ahead

17

In previous chapters we've hinted at several upcoming Akka features. Akka is a fast-moving project; at the time of writing, a couple of important features are under development that are worth mentioning and keeping track of.

This chapter will discuss two important features to look out for in the near future that are currently being developed. Every section will have a short preview of what the module enables or how it will change the way you currently use Akka features.

The actor model that's described in this book uses untyped messages, as noted in chapter 1. Scala has a rich type system, and many developers are drawn to Scala because of type safety, which is why some argue against actors in their current form, especially if they're used as components to build applications. We'll look at the akka-typed module that will make it possible to write type-safe actors.

Another module to look out for is *Akka distributed data*. This module makes it possible to distribute state in-memory in an akka cluster using *conflict-free replicated data types (CRDTs)*. We'll briefly discuss the module and what we expect you could use it for.

17.1   *akka-typed module*

The akka-typed module will provide a typed Actor API. It can be difficult to understand at times why a simple change in (untyped) actor code suddenly breaks the application in runtime. Listing 17.1 shows an example that compiles but that will never work. It shows the `Basket` actor from chapter 14, and some code asking for the items in the basket.

Listing 17.1   Basket actor example

```
object Basket {
   // .. other messages ..
   case class GetItems(shopperId: Long)
   // .. other messages ..
}
class Basket extends PersistentActor {
  def receiveCommand = {
    // .. other commands ..
    case GetItems(shopperId) =>
    // .. other commands ..
  }
}
//.. somewhere else, asking the Basket Actor ..
val futureResult = basketActor.ask(GetItems).mapTo(Items)
```

> **Returns a failed Future; reason is an AskTimeoutException**

The code to ask the `Basket` for its items and the `Basket` code itself are shown together for a reason. It's now easy to see why this will never work, but that's not always the case when code is spread around many files. In case you haven't noticed what the problem is here, we send a `GetItems` to the `Basket` instead of a `GetItems(shopperId)`. The code compiles because `ask` takes `Any`, and `GetItems` extends `Any`. Opening up a REPL makes it crystal clear.

Listing 17.2   Checking the type in the REPL

```
chapter-looking-ahead > console
[info] Starting scala interpreter...
[info]
Welcome to Scala version 2.11.8 ... (output truncated)
Type in expressions to have them evaluated.
Type :help for more information.

scala> GetItems
res0: aia.next.Basket.GetItems.type = GetItems

scala> GetItems(1L)
res1: aia.next.Basket.GetItems = GetItems(1)
```

> **GetItems is type of GetItems case class, not an instance of it**

As you can see, we've erroneously tried to send the *type* of the `GetItems` case class to the `Basket` actor. This is one of those small mistakes you can make that can take a long time to find, ending in a facepalm. This kind of problem can occur frequently during maintenance of an existing application: someone adds or removes a field from a message and forgets to change the receive method of an actor. In other cases a simple typo can cause this. The compiler should have helped us more here, but it can't because of how the current `ActorRef` works; you can send it literally any message.

akka-typed provides a DSL to build actors that is quite different than you've seen so far. Messages are checked during compile time to prevent the issue that you've just seen. The next listing shows how getting items from a `TypedBasket` actor would look like in a unit test.

Listing 17.3 Getting items with akka-typed

```
"return the items in a typesafe way" in {
  import akka.typed._
  import akka.typed.ScalaDSL._
  import akka.typed.AskPattern._
  import scala.concurrent.Future
  import scala.concurrent.duration._
  import scala.concurrent.Await

  implicit val timeout = akka.util.Timeout(1 second)

  val macbookPro =
    TypedBasket.Item("Apple Macbook Pro", 1, BigDecimal(2499.99))
  val displays =
    TypedBasket.Item("4K Display", 3, BigDecimal(2499.99))

  val sys: ActorSystem[TypedBasket.Command] =
    ActorSystem("typed-basket", Props(TypedBasket.basketBehavior))

  sys ! TypedBasket.Add(macbookPro, shopperId)
  sys ! TypedBasket.Add(displays, shopperId)

  val items: Future[TypedBasket.Items] =
    sys ? (TypedBasket.GetItems(shopperId, _))

  val res = Await.result(items, 10 seconds)
  res should equal(TypedBasket.Items(Vector(macbookPro, displays)))
  //sys ? Basket.GetItems          ◁─┐
  sys.terminate()                     │   This now does not compile.
}
```

The big change here is that `ActorSystem` and `ActorRef` now take a type argument that describes the messages that they can receive. This makes it possible for the compiler to check the message types.

Listing 17.4 shows a part of the `TypedBasket` actor, where only getting items has been implemented. (The `Basket` actor is a `PersistentActor` in the original example in chapter 14, which is ignored for now; we expect that it will be possible at some point to build persistent actors with akka-typed in the future.)

Listing 17.4 TypedBasket

```scala
package aia.next

import akka.typed._
import akka.typed.ScalaDSL._
import akka.typed.AskPattern._
import scala.concurrent.Future
import scala.concurrent.duration._
import scala.concurrent.Await

object TypedBasket {
  sealed trait Command {
    def shopperId: Long
  }

  final case class GetItems(shopperId: Long,
                            replyTo: ActorRef[Items]) extends Command
  final case class Add(item: Item, shopperId: Long) extends Command

  // a simplified version of Items and Item
  case class Items(list: Vector[Item]= Vector.empty[Item])
  case class Item(productId: String, number: Int, unitPrice: BigDecimal)

  val basketBehavior =
  ContextAware[Command] { ctx =>
    var items = Items()

    Static {
      case GetItems(productId, replyTo) =>
       replyTo ! items
      case Add(item, productId) =>
        items = Items(items.list :+ item)
      //case GetItems =>                    <───┐
    }                                           │  **This now does not compile.**
  }
}
```

The Akka team found out during their research that a big part of the problem lies in the sender() method. It's one of the things that makes it impossible to simply turn the current actor API into a typed one: every message could be sent by any sender, making it impossible to type it on the receiving side.

akka-typed doesn't have a sender() method, which means that if you want to send a message back to the calling actor, you'll have to send its actor reference along in the message. Putting the sender in the message has benefits in untyped actors too: you always know who sent the message, so you don't need to keep this state anywhere else.

akka-typed saves us from having to define a sender() method to keep this state, sidestepping the issue altogether.

Defining the actor looks a lot different from what you have gotten used to; actors are now defined in terms of typed *behaviors*. Every message is passed to an immutable behavior. The behavior of an actor can change over time by switching between behaviors, or the behavior can stay the same.

In this case the behavior is defined as a `Static` behavior, which means that the `TypedBasket` actor won't change its behavior. This behavior is wrapped in a `Context-Aware` that takes an `ActorContext[T] => Behavior[T]` function, which will be used as the behavior of the actor. This basically allows us to get to the context, but also to define the `items` actor state.

There are a lot more changes in akka-typed compared to the current actor module. `preStart`, `preRestart`, and other methods, for example, are replaced by special signal messages.

The akka-typed API looks promising, but is highly likely to change since it hasn't been pushed to its limits yet by anyone, and right now it shouldn't be used in production. The benefits of types are huge, so we expect the module to become very important in upcoming versions of Akka.

17.2 *Akka Distributed Data*

Another module to look out for is Akka Distributed Data, which provides replicated in-memory data structures in an Akka cluster. The data structures are so-called *conflict-free replicated data types (CRDTs)*, which are eventually consistent. It doesn't matter in which order you execute operations on the data type or if you repeat operations: the result is eventually correct.

CRDTs always have a `merge` function that can take many data entries living on different nodes and merge these automatically into one consistent view of the data, without any coordination between the nodes. The types of data structures that you can use are limited: they have to be CRDTs. Akka Distributed Data provides a couple of data structures out of the box, but it's also possible to build your own data structure, as long as it implements a `merge` function according to the rules of CRDTs (it needs to be associative, commutative, and idempotent).

Akka Distributed Data provides a `Replicator` actor that replicates a data structure throughout the Akka cluster. Data structures are stored under a user-defined key, and it's also possible to subscribe to the key to receive updates on the data structure.

The shopping basket example in this book is a good example of where Akka Distributed Data could be used. The items could be modeled as a CRDT set, called an `ORset`. Every basket would eventually show up in the correct state on every node in the cluster. There's a CRDT data structure for collaborative editing of documents, another example of where Akka Distributed Data could be a good solution. Combining Akka Distributed Data with Akka persistence could make it possible to recover the in-memory state from a journal after a crash.

17.3 *Summary*

We've touched on two important updates that could have a big impact in future Akka releases. This is obviously not a complete list of up-and-coming features, and time will tell how successful every module will prove to be.

akka-typed provides more type safety, which means more errors will be found at compile time, making it easier to build and (more importantly) maintain actor-based applications, which we expect to be very convenient to use.

Although this is definitely a good first step, a lot more research has to be done in how modern type theory can be applied to safely check communication protocols, not to mention how this will be implemented in Scala in akka-typed.

Akka Distributed Data will require you to think about your problem domain in terms of CRDTs; if it is possible to express the problem in these kinds of data types, there is a potentially high benefit to be gained.

It's incredible to see how many different problems benefit from the message-driven approach of Akka actors; it's hard to predict what will come next.

index

U

UnboundedMessageQueue-
　Semantics 396
unfiltered events 318
universally unique identifier.
　See UUID
unmarshalling 305
UnparsableEvent class 299
Unreachable state 334
unsubscribe method 217–218
Up state 332
upcasting 372
updateState function 362, 366
upper-bound attribute 196
user guardian 85
user space 82

use-role setting 342
using declarations 240
utilization 393
UUID (universally unique
　identifier) 377

V

varying speeds 286
via method 309
VirtualMachineError 105

W

warning source 312
warning value 294

WatermarkRequestStrategy
　292
web dyno 46
whenUnhandled declarations
　240
withAttributes 287, 298
withinTimeRange
　argument 90
worker.conf file 340

X

-Xmx parameter 289